Sexual Violence against Jewish Women during the Holocaust

HBI SERIES ON JEWISH WOMEN

Shulamit Reinharz, *General Editor*
Sylvia Barack Fishman, *Associate Editor*

The HBI Series on Jewish Women, created by the Hadassah-Brandeis Institute, publishes a wide range of books by and about Jewish women in diverse contexts and time periods. Of interest to scholars and the educated public, the HBI Series on Jewish Women fills major gaps in Jewish Studies and in Women and Gender Studies as well as their intersection.

The HBI Series on Jewish Women is supported by a generous gift from Dr. Laura S. Schor.

For the complete list of books that are available in this series, please see www.upne.com

Sonja M. Hedgepeth and Rochelle G. Saidel, editors, *Sexual Violence against Jewish Women during the Holocaust*

Carol K. Ingall, editor, *The Women Who Reconstructed American Jewish Education: 1910–1965*

Gaby Brimmer and Elena Poniatowska, *Gaby Brimmer*

Harriet Hartman and Moshe Hartman, *Gender and American Jews: Patterns in Work, Education, and Family in Contemporary Life*

Dvora E. Weisberg, *Levirate Marriage and the Family in Ancient Judaism*

Ellen M. Umansky and Dianne Ashton, editors, *Four Centuries of Jewish Women's Spirituality: A Sourcebook*

Carole S. Kessner, *Marie Syrkin: Values Beyond the Self*

Ruth Kark, Margalit Shilo, and Galit Hasan-Rokem, editors, *Jewish Women in Pre-State Israel: Life History, Politics, and Culture*

Tova Hartman, *Feminism Encounters Traditional Judaism: Resistance and Accommodation*

Anne Lapidus Lerner, *Eternally Eve: Images of Eve in the Hebrew Bible, Midrash, and Modern Jewish Poetry*

Margalit Shilo, *Princess or Prisoner? Jewish Women in Jerusalem, 1840–1914*

Marcia Falk, translator, *The Song of Songs: Love Lyrics from the Bible*

Sylvia Barack Fishman, *Double or Nothing? Jewish Families and Mixed Marriage*

Avraham Grossman, *Pious and Rebellious: Jewish Women in Medieval Europe*

Iris Parush, *Reading Jewish Women: Marginality and Modernization in Nineteenth-Century Eastern European Jewish Society*

Shulamit Reinharz and Mark A. Raider, editors, *American Jewish Women and the Zionist Enterprise*

Tamar Ross, *Expanding the Palace of Torah: Orthodoxy and Feminism*

Farideh Goldin, *Wedding Song: Memoirs of an Iranian Jewish Woman*

Elizabeth Wyner Mark, editor, *The Covenant of Circumcision: New Perspectives on an Ancient Jewish Rite*

Rochelle L. Millen, *Women, Birth, and Death in Jewish Law and Practice*

Kalpana Misra and Melanie S. Rich, editors, *Jewish Feminism in Israel: Some Contemporary Perspectives*

Judith R. Baskin, *Midrashic Women: Formations of the Feminine in Rabbinic Literature*

ChaeRan Y. Freeze, *Jewish Marriage and Divorce in Imperial Russia*

Mark A. Raider and Miriam B. Raider-Roth, editors, *The Plough Woman: Records of the Pioneer Women of Palestine*

Pamela S. Nadell and Jonathan D. Sarna, editors, *Women and American Judaism: Historical Perspectives*

Ludmila Shtern, *Leaving Leningrad: The True Adventures of a Soviet Émigré*

Sexual Violence

AGAINST JEWISH WOMEN DURING THE HOLOCAUST

Edited by
Sonja M. Hedgepeth and
Rochelle G. Saidel

Brandeis University Press
Waltham, Massachusetts

BRANDEIS UNIVERSITY PRESS
© 2010 Sonja M. Hedgepeth and Rochelle G. Saidel
Manufactured in the United States of America
Designed by Katherine B. Kimball
Typeset in Quadraat by Integrated Publishing Solutions

For permission to reproduce any of the material in this book, contact
Brandeis University Press, 415 South Street, Waltham MA 02453,
or visit http://www.brandeis.edu/library/bup.html

This book was published with the generous support of the Lucius N. Littauer Foundation.

Published in cooperation with Remember the Women Institute.

Library of Congress Cataloging-in-Publication Data

Sexual violence against Jewish women during the Holocaust / edited by Sonja M.
Hedgepeth and Rochelle G. Saidel.
    p.   cm. — (HBI series on Jewish women)
    Includes bibliographical references and index.
    ISBN 978-1-58465-903-7 (cloth : alk. paper) — ISBN 978-1-58465-905-1 (pbk. :
alk. paper) —ISBN 978-1-58465-904-4 (electronic)
    1. Jewish women in the Holocaust.   2. Jewish women—Violence against—
Europe—History—20th century.   3. World War, 1939–1945—Atrocities—Europe.   4. Eugenics—Germany—History—20th century.   5. Holocaust, Jewish
(1939–1945), in literature.   6. Holocaust, Jewish (1939–1945), in motion
pictures.   I. Hedgepeth, Sonja M. (Sonja Maria), 1952–   II. Saidel, Rochelle G.
    D804.47.S49 2010
    940.53918082—dc22   2010035052

This book is dedicated to the victims
of sexual violence during the Holocaust—
those who were silenced, those who have spoken out,
and those who have chosen to remain silent.

Contents

Foreword by Shulamit Reinharz   ix

Acknowledgments   xi

Introduction   SONJA M. HEDGEPETH AND ROCHELLE G. SAIDEL   1

I. Aspects of Sexual Abuse   11

1. Death and the Maidens: "Prostitution," Rape, and Sexual Slavery during World War II   NOMI LEVENKRON   13

2. Sexualized Violence against Women during Nazi "Racial" Persecution   BRIGITTE HALBMAYR   29

3. Sexual Exploitation of Women in Nazi Concentration Camp Brothels   ROBERT SOMMER   45

4. Schillinger and the Dancer: Representing Agency and Sexual Violence in Holocaust Testimonies   KIRSTY CHATWOOD   61

II. Rape of Jewish Women   75

5. "Only Pretty Women Were Raped": The Effect of Sexual Violence on Gender Identities in the Concentration Camps
MONIKA J. FLASCHKA   77

6. The Tragic Fate of Ukrainian Jewish Women under Nazi Occupation, 1941–1944   ANATOLY PODOLSKY   94

7. The Rape of Jewish Women during the Holocaust
HELENE J. SINNREICH   108

8. Rape and Sexual Abuse in Hiding   ZOË WAXMAN   124

Contents

III. Assaults on Motherhood   137

9. Reproduction under the Swastika: The Other Side of the
Glorification of Motherhood   HELGA AMESBERGER   139

10. Forced Sterilization and Abortion as Sexual Abuse
ELLEN BEN-SEFER   156

IV. Sexual Violence in Literature and Cinema   175

11. Sexual Abuse in Holocaust Literature: Memoir and Fiction
S. LILLIAN KREMER   177

12. "Stoning the Messenger": Yehiel Dinur's *House of Dolls*
and *Piepel*   MIRYAM SIVAN   200

13. Nava Semel's *And the Rat Laughed*: A Tale of Sexual Violation
SONJA M. HEDGEPETH AND ROCHELLE G. SAIDEL   217

14. "Public Property": Sexual Abuse of Women and Girls in
Cinematic Memory   YVONNE KOZLOVSKY-GOLAN   234

V. The Violated Self   253

15. Sexual Abuse of Jewish Women during and after the
Holocaust: A Psychological Perspective   EVA FOGELMAN   255

16. The Shame Is Always There   ESTHER DROR AND RUTH LINN   275

Contributors   293
Index   297

Foreword

SHULAMIT REINHARZ

It is now sixty-five years since the end of World War II and the Holocaust. Ever since the liberation of the death camps and the attempt to resume some semblance of normalcy post-Holocaust, scholars and survivors have been trying to document and even explain the countless facets of this inhuman period. As time passes and publications accumulate, scholars have been able to ask increasingly specific questions. One of these questions, only recently broached, concerns the nature of women's experience, in all its multiple dimensions, during the Holocaust. The original reluctance of the public, and researchers as well, to study women's experience rested in the mistaken notion that an underlying question was "who suffered more, women or men?" But that is not why certain scholars wanted to examine women's experience. Instead, they were motivated by the same intention as those who studied the specifics of different national communities (for example, Dutch, German or Polish Jews), or those who focus on the camps versus the experience of people in hiding, or any other specificity.

Even now, sixty-five years later we are learning that we suffer from stereotypes about the Holocaust, stereotypes such as the notion that all the killing took place on the way to or in the camps. In actuality, if the focus is on the Jews of Eastern Europe (rather than the Western countries), Jews were killed close to where they lived and buried in mass graves. The focus on Jewish women's experience enables us to understand the whole phenomenon with much more sophistication and precision. This new focus also uncovers new features of the Holocaust, such as the role of couriers (who were almost always women) and the relation between those in hiding (frequently women) and those hiding them (frequently men). Thus, this book, although terribly painful to read, belongs squarely in the Hadassah-Brandeis Institute Series on Jewish Women, whose mission is to develop fresh ways of thinking about Jews and gender. This book asks—what happened to the women during the Holocaust? Was there anything different in their experience because they were women? The shocking answer is a resounding "yes." Women were raped (by soldiers of the

Third Reich even though sexual intercourse between Jews and Aryans was strictly forbidden); women were sterilized (by physicians of the Third Reich); women were assigned to brothels for soldiers and other prisoners; special experiments were performed on women; and women frequently had the special burden of saving their children in addition to themselves. This book—the first of its kind—addresses many of these topics. As the first interdisciplinary anthology on women and sexual abuse during the Holocaust, this volume paves the way for other researchers to delve deeper, to address additional questions.

As a child of Holocaust survivors myself, I have read extensively in the literature about the topic, both literary and scholarly. I have talked to numerous survivors, and I am conducting a study of my own. Prior to reading this collection of essays, I had not noticed the issue of "rape." But since reading the collection, I find the phenomenon mentioned repeatedly in testimonies and written works. It's as if the issue was always there, but I didn't see it because no one had pointed it out and labeled it as such. I also did not notice sexual abuse because it was always part of a larger story such as deportation, camp life, and murder. I expect that after reading this volume, others will react as I did. The awareness will haunt them—they will see what was hidden but always there before their very eyes.

I wish this were a book we did not have to publish; I wish that these horrors had not occurred. But they clearly did, as each author points out in detail. And it is now our responsibility to come to grips with what this revelation means. Rape is almost always a component of war and terror. The Holocaust was no exception. Women who regrettably underwent this experience can, perhaps, take some comfort in knowing that their misfortune is finally being recognized. Sonja Hedgepeth and Rochelle Saidel are to be congratulated for beginning the exploration of this untold, horrific chapter in the history of men and women, and of Jews and antisemites. It is a story of sexual and religious oppression and their intersection. It is a story that, after sixty-five years, is finally being told.

Acknowledgments

Sexual abuse of women during the Holocaust is not an easy subject to deal with, and we are grateful to the authors of the chapters in this book, as well as to the institutions, friends, and family who supported us in various ways as we struggled with it. All of the chapter authors have demonstrated unwavering commitment to this subject matter, and without their expert contributions, this book would not exist. Israeli author Nava Semel, feminist artist Judy Chicago, and Judy Cohen, a Holocaust survivor living in Toronto, also granted us interviews that provided insights for our work. The Van Leer Institute in Jerusalem gave us permission to reprint part of an article from their Hebrew journal, *Theory and Criticism*. We are also appreciative that the University of Southern California Shoah Foundation Institute for Visual History and Education, through Crispin Brooks, the Fortunoff Video Archive for Holocaust Testimonies at Yale University Library, through Joanne Rudof, and other archives gave our authors permission to use their testimonies.

Both Yad Vashem in Jerusalem and the United States Holocaust Memorial Museum in Washington, D.C., served as important sources for bibliographic material. The Ghetto Fighters' House in Israel provided us with the artwork for the cover. Our chapters came to us not only in English, but also in Hebrew, German, and Russian. We appreciate the help with translation that we received from Sonia Grober, Guilherme Ary Plonski, Barbara Schmutzler, and Elena Yurchenko. Daniel Wolk provided technical help that kept our computers going despite all odds. Along the way, the friends who offered valuable suggestions and sometimes a needed hug included Toby Back, Hanna Batista, Moshe Borger, Batya Brutin, Aviva Cantor, Karin Doerr, Scott Fraser, Allen Hibbard, Janet Higgins, Elizabeth Howitt, Aviva Klopper, Danby Meital, Nancy Ordway, Michael Rice, Jeff F. Segall, Rachel Lulov Segall, Sarina Shamir, and Morris Wyszogrod. Our husbands, Guilherme Ary Plonski and Josef Vishengrad, encouraged us and lived with us through some dark moments as we grappled with the subject matter.

We found it difficult to work on a book about sexual violation and the Holocaust, and we recognize that personal fear of rape is understood and shared by many women. This is not only true for those who were violated during the

Holocaust or as victims of war but also for the woman who makes her way across a dark parking lot to her car or considers whether she should cut through an unlit alley. Although the book's focus is on sexual violence against Jewish women, we include information about girls and non-Jewish women, as well as about Jewish and non-Jewish men and boys. If we have brought to the surface memories that cause pain to survivors or their families, we sincerely apologize.

The book was written under the auspices of Remember the Women Institute, and the project was generously funded by the Five Millers Family Foundation and the S and J Foundation, through Eva Fogelman and Gertrude Stein. We thank Shulamit Reinharz and Sylvia Barack Fishman, editors for the Hadassah-Brandeis Institute Series on Jewish Women, Brandeis University Press, and Phyllis Deutsch, editor-in-chief at University Press of New England, for believing in us and especially for understanding the need to publish this volume. We are also grateful to production editor Elizabeth Ann Brash, the other staff members at the press who worked on this book, and to our supportive and insightful peer reviewers, Joanna Michlic and John K. Roth. We also thank our superb copy editor, Bronwyn Becker, for her careful and caring reading of the manuscript; and Gloria Steinem and Deborah E. Lipstadt for recognizing the significance of this book.

In a sense, this book began at Brandeis University in 1996, the year that we met each other at a National Endowment for the Humanities summer seminar, "Cultural Responses to the Holocaust in the United States and Abroad," led by Alan Mintz. Since then, we have often worked together as friends and colleagues on issues related to women and the Holocaust. Because our friendship and subsequent teamwork began at Brandeis University, we are especially gratified that Brandeis University Press/University Press of New England is publishing this groundbreaking volume in the Hadassah-Brandeis Institute Series on Jewish Women.

Sonja M. Hedgepeth and Rochelle G. Saidel
Jerusalem, 2010

Introduction

SONJA M. HEDGEPETH AND ROCHELLE G. SAIDEL

This is the first English-language book to address the sexual violation of Jewish women during the Holocaust, a virtually unexplored subject. John K. Roth has suggested that the study of "events that are utterly particular but charged with intensity" can lead to understanding wider historical perspectives.[1] In this spirit of scholarly inquiry, this volume, by broadening and deepening the comprehension of Jewish women's experiences of rape and other forms of sexual violence during the Holocaust, will enrich understanding and provoke continued study of this subject.

The archives of the United States Holocaust Memorial Museum and Yad Vashem include eyewitness accounts that speak to the fact of rape and sexual abuse during the Holocaust. Their Web sites acknowledge the sexual violation of Jewish women.[2] The catalogue for a temporary exhibit at Yad Vashem includes information about a survivor who testified in postwar Germany about a Nazi who had raped her in Kowel, Poland.[3] The recently accessible archives of the International Tracing Service in Bad Arolsen, Germany, hold Nazi documentation about forced prostitution and other atrocities that corroborates claims about the punitive use of women's bodies during World War II.[4] Sexual violence began to be mentioned in some memoirs, documentary films, literature, and reports right after the Holocaust. In addition, more than five hundred testimonies housed in the University of Southern California Shoah Foundation Institute for Visual History and Education mention rape.[5] These references include rape by Germans and their Nazi collaborators, as well as by other Jews, in ghettos and in hiding; by Germans and collaborators, and by Jewish and non-Jewish prisoners, in camps; and by liberators. In addition to rape, there is another index term for "coerced sexual activities," which brings the number of citations of sexual violence (including rape) to more than a thousand.

As suggested by these sources, a majority of evidence is found in survivors' testimonies, of one kind or another, rather than in statistical data. By its very nature, and throughout history, sexual violation has not been accompanied by official documentation. During wartime, when laws governing civil societies fall by the wayside, such documentation is especially rare.

Although the Nazis kept meticulous records, there is virtually no official Nazi documentation of rape and sexual abuse of Jewish women. (Accounts were kept for authorized brothels, but they did not knowingly "employ" Jewish sex slaves.) There is no such thing as a "rape certificate"; in fact, rape victims were often murdered. Even when survivors disclose sexual violation in their memoirs, such allusions are often covert and offered without detail, echoing their modesty or shame. Because of the supposed lack of reliable "hard evidence," it has been too easy for some Holocaust historians to discount and discredit allegations of rape and other forms of sexual violence against Jewish women.[6]

Nevertheless, there is a solid core of testimonies and memoirs by victims and witnesses that serves as evidence. In the absence of official documents, we must accept that a large number of testimonies by victims and witnesses do constitute documentation and proof, however subjective or personal they may be. We must treat them seriously as historical documentation, buttressed by women's experiences not only during the Holocaust but also in war. Rape has always been part of the violence of enemy combatants; this was no less true for Jewish women during the Holocaust. Our aim in this volume is to demonstrate the reality of this claim through careful examination of the sources that do exist. The authors included here comprise an interdisciplinary group of scholars with a wide range of methodologies. They examine testimonies, documents, memoirs, literature, and film. All take seriously the mission of building on earlier studies of women and the Holocaust. Together, they bring a new level of inquiry to this topic.

Although there has been an impressive proliferation of Holocaust memorials and museums since the late 1970s, sexual abuse has hardly been acknowledged as a theme, much less a central topic, worthy of investigation. For example, in the Auschwitz memorial in Poland, guides are trained to discuss mass genocide, but block 24a, the official camp brothel, is not mentioned. Nor has Yad Vashem (the official Israeli Holocaust memorial established in 1953) dealt openly with sexual abuse.[7] There is little about women's experiences as women in the new permanent exhibit, and a temporary exhibit about women, "Spots of Light: To Be a Woman in the Holocaust," which opened in 2007, mentioned but did not emphasize the question of sexual abuse.[8] As Andrea Dworkin wrote: "If the forced prostitution of Jewish women had been documented and understood, why the erasure from the contemporary collective knowledge—and all the museums and monuments? In fact, every act of prostitution in the camps—Jewish, German, Russian, Polish, etc.—was rape; why isn't a raped woman the symbol of the Holocaust—and why isn't rape part of all the exhibits in all the museums and all the memorials?"[9]

When in the 1980s some feminist Holocaust scholars began to suggest that women suffered differently (but not more or less severely) than men during the Holocaust, most mainstream scholars either ignored or criticized their research.[10] Holocaust scholars in the United States and Israel generally kept gender and sexual abuse questions out of the discourse. The first public event that addressed women, gender, and the Holocaust took place in March 1983, when Esther Katz and Joan Ringelheim organized the groundbreaking "Conference on Women Surviving the Holocaust" at Stern College in New York. "The 1983 conference is the wellspring that shaped the field and established the parameters, almost presciently," according to Elizabeth Baer and Myrna Goldenberg; "it uncovered the seeds of resentment evoked by a gendered study, for such an approach inevitably invites comparison and then judgment."[11] The conference raised ire among some of its participants; Rochelle Saidel observed that some Holocaust survivors became enraged when an audience member asked about sexual experiences in concentration camps.

Yet Ringelheim pressed on, writing in 1990 of the need "to reveal the ignored and complex relationship between anti-Semitism (as a form of racism against Jews) and sexism prior to and during the Holocaust." She added: "While it appears that anti-Semitism contains a monolithic view of Jews, in fact it looks at and treats Jews who are male and female differently. Our ignorance of these differences creates blind spots in the memories and reconstructions of the Holocaust."[12] Sadly, most Holocaust historians never gave Ringelheim's work serious consideration.

In 1993 Carol Rittner and John K. Roth co-edited the anthology *Different Voices: Women and the Holocaust*, which strove to answer two questions: Where were the women during the Holocaust; and how do the particularities of women's experiences in that event compare and contrast with those of men? Rittner and Roth believed that "[a] lot of significant detail has gone unmentioned if not unnoticed" and sought to expose some of "the particularities of women's experiences and reflections [that] have been submerged and ignored."[13] Two years later at the Hebrew University of Jerusalem, Dalia Ofer, an Israeli professor of history and Holocaust studies, and Lenore Weitzman, an American sociology professor, organized a seminar on women and the Holocaust, with the papers later published as *Women in the Holocaust*.[14] Ofer and Weitzman began the introduction to their 1998 book by asking: "Why women? Should a book on the Holocaust—which targeted all Jews for annihilation irrespective of their sex or age or any other social characteristic—focus on women?"[15] They took up the topic of the resistance to research on gender in Holocaust studies, which helped to trigger Gabriel Schoenfeld's vituperative 1998 response in *Commentary*.[16] Five years later, Baer and Goldenberg still felt the need to offer an explanation for focusing on women in their work *Experience and Expression: Women, Nazis, and the Holocaust*. To bolster their case, they quoted Yehuda Bauer of Yad Vashem, a highly respected Holocaust historian, who wrote: "And if all human experience has a gender-related agenda, as women's studies tells us, the Holocaust can be no exception."[17]

Despite resistance, these and other Holocaust scholars have succeeded in the past decade in bringing gender into discussions of the Holocaust. In 1999, the then twenty-nine-year-old Annual Scholars' Conference on the Holocaust and the Churches presented "Women's Holocaust History: Books in Print," its first plenary session on women and the Holocaust.[18] The existence of a core set of books documenting research undertaken on women and the Holocaust made such a session possible.[19] Since 1999, several other books have been published,[20] and workshops, plenaries, and panels about women and the Holocaust have taken place at the Scholars' Conference, Lessons and Legacies conferences, the educators' conferences at Yad Vashem, and the Association of Holocaust Organizations conferences. Since 2001, a conference devoted to women and the Holocaust has taken place biennially at Beit Berl College, Beit Terezin, and Beit Lohamei Haghettaot in Israel. A biennial conference on the Holocaust held at the Jagiellonian University in Kraków, Poland, chose women (but not sexual violence) as its theme in 2005. At all of these events, some individual papers addressed sexual abuse; none, however, featured discussions of sexual violence against women, a topic seemingly even more untouchable and likely to cause rancor than the (less controversial and more generic) discussions of women and the Holocaust.

A conference in 2007 about forced prostitution and war in the twentieth and the beginning of the twenty-first century, held at the Ravensbrück concentration camp memorial in Germany, offered scholarly work pertinent to women and the Holocaust. However, the first conference sessions completely devoted to the topic of the sexual violation of women during the Holocaust were organized by the editors of this volume, first at Middle Tennessee State University in 2007, then in Jerusalem at the 15th World Congress of Jewish Studies in 2009. In 2010, we believe we no longer have to justify scholarly interest in this subject.

By focusing on the sexual abuse of women, this volume goes beyond previous studies of women's experiences during the Holocaust. As with most

innovative work, we know this book will have its critics and may be controversial. Nonetheless, we believe that what John K. Roth wrote regarding the
study of women during the Holocaust in general also applies to the more specific investigation of the sexual violation of women: "Far from reducing the
Holocaust to an example of sexism, let alone making the Holocaust prone to
some alleged hijacking by gender studies, an emphasis on what happened to
women during the Holocaust reveals what otherwise would remain hidden: a
fuller picture of the unprecedented and unrelenting killing that was the Final
Solution."[21]

This volume's sixteen essays written by historians, social scientists, psychol-
ogists, literary critics, a film scholar, a human rights attorney, and a professor
of nursing offer that "fuller picture." Contributors come from Austria, Canada, Germany, Great Britain, Israel, Ukraine, and the United States—diverse
nations that approach Holocaust history differently. Grappling with the complexities of a difficult subject, members of this interdisciplinary and international group sometimes use the same sources but interpret them differently.
One author's historical approach substantiates another's literary analysis; a
psychological study may reinforce a film analysis. In this way, the essays rever-
berate, providing a pioneering overview of this topic, and will generate new
discussions about women and the Holocaust.

Readers will see the terms "sexual abuse," "sexual violation," "sexual violence," and "sexualized violence" used throughout the volume. Although es-
sayists sometimes use different terms to signify the specific abuse under scru-
tiny, in all cases these terms denote forced sexual contact. Part 1, "Aspects of
Sexual Abuse," explores the different types of sexual violation to which Jewish
women were subjected. In "Death and the Maidens: 'Prostitution,' Rape, and
Sexual Slavery during World War II," Nomi Levenkron outlines the scope of
crimes that range from sexual humiliation to sexual slavery, from bartering sex
for food to rape. Brigitte Halbmayr, in her essay, "Sexualized Violence against
Women during Nazi 'Racial' Persecution," suggests a new conceptual framework for more accurately describing women's experiences to include indirect
expressions of assault, such as imposed public nakedness or humiliating
methods of physical examination. Robert Sommer's chapter, "Sexual Exploitation of Women in Nazi Concentration Camp Brothels," uses Nazi documentation to analyze official Nazi-run brothels for privileged prisoners and the SS.
In "Schillinger and the Dancer: Representing Agency and Sexual Violence in
Holocaust Testimonies," Kirsty Chatwood explores the term "agency" and its
relationship to sexual abuse in Holocaust testimonies. Sometimes a woman
tried to use sexuality to outwit her tormentors and save her life.

Part 2, "Rape of Jewish Women," focuses specifically on rape as a form of aggression.[22] In "'Only Pretty Women Were Raped:' The Effect of Sexual Violence on Gender Identities in the Concentration Camps," Monika J. Flaschka uses survivor testimonies to analyze the effect of rape on women's images of themselves. She found a pattern of survivor statements that make the case that attractive women were more often targeted. Anatoly Podolsky draws on hitherto unexamined Ukrainian and Russian data for his richly conceived "The Tragic Fate of Ukrainian Jewish Women under Nazi Occupation, 1941–1944." His access to newly opened archives in the former Soviet Union enables him to provide material generally unavailable to English-language readers. Helene J. Sinnreich gives a more generalized overview in "The Rape of Jewish Women during the Holocaust," even naming some Nazi perpetrators as well as a Jewish leader who committed rape in the Lodz ghetto. In "Rape and Sexual Abuse in Hiding," Zoë Waxman focuses on the subject of rape in hiding and points to the difficulties women have had in describing this ordeal. Her essay demonstrates that sometimes so-called righteous people who hid Jews from Nazis took advantage of the situation and sexually assaulted those they were supposed to be protecting. Each of the essays in this section draws attention to the additional connotations that the term "rape"—forced unlawful sexual intercourse against a person's will —signifies in the context of the Holocaust. If a woman allowed herself to be sexually violated by her so-called protector in order to stay alive, she still experienced a form of rape.

As part 3, "Assaults on Motherhood," shows, forced sterilization and forced abortion also constituted sexual abuse of women. In "Reproduction under the Swastika: The Other Side of the Glorification of Motherhood," Helga Amesberger documents how Nazi control of persecuted women's sexuality impacted pregnancy and motherhood. In "Forced Sterilization and Abortion as Sexual Abuse," Ellen Ben-Sefer argues that in Nazi Germany, forced sterilization was directed at those deemed unworthy to procreate. The procedure, originally part of the eugenics movement ("racial hygiene"), was later incorporated into "medical" experiments and used as an instrument of annihilation in the camps.

Literature and cinema make important contributions to our understanding of women's fate during the Holocaust, lending the women voices and faces that we can recognize. In the introduction to her book on Holocaust fiction, Sara R. Horowitz wrote that her study "presumes fiction as a serious vehicle for thinking about the Holocaust."[23] Like Horowitz and others, we believe that an examination of literary and film depictions of the Holocaust can be of great use. In fact, Holocaust literature and films may help to ensure the preservation of memory about historical events and even spark curiosity about the past; these media are the means by which most young people first learn about the Holocaust. According to Daniel R. Schwarz, "As the historical period of the Shoah recedes, imaginative literature will help keep those events alive. Do we not know more about the War of the Roses and the history of Britain from Shakespeare than from Holinshed's chronicles?"[24]

Part 4, "Sexual Violence in Literature and Cinema," examines how sexual abuse of women during the Holocaust has been addressed in literature and film, especially in the United States and Israel. In "Sexual Abuse in Holocaust Literature: Memoir and Fiction," S. Lillian Kremer suggests a reciprocal relationship between the two genres, demonstrating how survivors' first-hand knowledge of sexual assault found in memoirs is reworked in novels and a screenplay. Miryam Sivan analyzes the controversy that continues to surround Holocaust novels by an underappreciated Israeli author in "'Stoning the Messenger': Yehiel Dinur's *House of Dolls* and *Piepel*." In "Nava Semel's *And the Rat Laughed*: A Tale of Sexual Violence," Sonja M. Hedgepeth and Rochelle G. Saidel discuss Semel's Holocaust novel based on the memories of hidden children who were molested by their supposed protectors. In "'Public Property': Sexual Abuse of Women and Girls in Cinematic Memory," Yvonne Kozlovsky-Golan shows how women's experience of sexual abuse in documentaries and feature films is often obfuscated by the camera lens or director's point of view.

The volume closes with part 5, "The Violated Self," offering two essays with psychological perspectives drawn from Holocaust testimonies and interviews. These add an important dimension to understanding the trauma of sexual abuse, as survivors may choose to reveal, distort, or leave hidden parts of their experience in order to develop strategies for living normal lives. Eva Fogelman provides an analysis of three different accounts of sexual abuse in "Sexual Abuse of Jewish Women during and after the Holocaust: A Psychological Perspective." In "The Shame Is Always There," Esther Dror and Ruth Linn present cases of Israeli survivors. These final essays also reveal some of the scholarly and emotional challenges of working directly with survivors and survivor testimony.

While we were preparing this book, we spoke with Judy Weiszenberg Cohen of Toronto, who has developed an important resource for scholars and students of women and the Holocaust. Originally from Debrecen, Hungary, and herself a survivor of Auschwitz, Cohen has created and maintains the Web site Women and the Holocaust: A Cyberspace of Their Own.[25] Cohen shared with us her insights about sexual violence against women, reiterating from her own experience some of the truths that this book brings to light.[26] She told us there was "indescribable, hopeless hunger" in Auschwitz, and that the "fear of rape" was omnipresent. She said that when women had sexual relations in exchange for food or shelter, or to save their children, these sexual relations, though seemingly consensual, were nonetheless rape "in a moral and ethical sense."

Cohen provided testimony that rape and other sexual violence perpetrated against Jewish women during the Holocaust caused traumas that were slow or impossible to heal. She spoke forcefully of the humiliation of the survivors: "The taboo in those days was so strong," she said. "Women, of course, [wouldn't] talk about it. I know someone who was working very closely with the aged Holocaust survivors before they died at the Baycrest Centre for Geriatric Care in Toronto. I can tell you she was like the 'mother confessor.' [The survivors] would tell her before they died, 'I was raped.' These were grandmothers and great-grandmothers. They added, 'but please don't tell my family.'"

To explain this long-term shame, Cohen said, "I think that the way we were conditioned, it was always the women's fault. You did something, you were provocative . . . there were certain things that happened that after the war were shameful to admit." Cohen is a strong advocate for this volume; she believes that it will "complete the picture" by showing how Jewish women experienced "all the regular horrors of being abused from A to Z," a range that, for women, often included sexual violence.

With humility and compassion, we present this book as a challenge to claims that Jewish women were not raped or sexually violated during the Holocaust. This collection of essays expands our understanding of women's experiences by including in Holocaust history the sexual abuses they endured. We acknowledge that this book is only a beginning, intended to encourage dialogue and studies by other scholars.

Notes

1. John K. Roth, "Equality, Neutrality, Particularity," in Elizabeth R. Baer and Myrna Goldenberg, *Experience and Expression: Women, the Nazis, and the Holocaust* (Detroit: Wayne State University Press, 2003), 14.

2. For references to rape on the Web site of the United States Holocaust Museum, see, for example, http://www.ushmm.org/wlc/article.php?lang=en&ModuleId=10005176 and http://www.ushmm.org/wlc/media_oi.php?lang=en&ModuleId=10005176&MediaId=1118; for Yad Vashem, see, for example, http://www1.yadvashem.org/exhibitions/women-eng/womanhood.html (accessed December 17, 2009).

3. Nina Rusman testified in Germany in 1964 at a trial against Manthay, a commander of the German gendarmerie, that he had raped her, she had become pregnant, and she was later unable to conceive because of a forced abortion. See Yehudit Inbar,

ed., *Spots of Light: To Be a Woman in the Holocaust* (catalogue) (Jerusalem: Yad Vashem, 2007), 77–78.

4. For example, see chapter 3 by Robert Sommer in this volume.

5. Chapter 5 by Monika J. Flashka, chapter 7 by Helene Sinnreich, and chapter 15 by Eva Fogelman in this volume use testimonies from this archive. No other known oral history project specifically asked survivors to talk about rape.

6. Nazi laws against *Rassenschande* (sexual relations between "Aryans" and "non-Aryans") have prompted some historians to conclude that Jewish women were not raped, faulty reasoning that does not account for the persistence of rape in countries that have laws against it. Nazi guards could rape with impunity: if accused of *Rassenschande*, they could simply deny their actions.

7. For decades, the history museum has exhibited a photograph of women stripped naked and about to be shot by the Nazis and their collaborators in Latvia. This display of nudity was criticized by ultra-Orthodox Jews in 1995. Ten years later, when Yad Vashem installed a new permanent exhibit in an updated museum, there were again demands by ultra-Orthodox critics for removal of this photograph, which does not show violation beyond forced nakedness.

8. Inbar, *Spots of Light*, 67.

9. Andrea Dworkin, *Scapegoat: The Jews, Israel, and Women's Liberation* (New York: The Free Press, 2000), 315.

10. For a historiography of gendered approaches to the Holocaust, see Elizabeth R. Baer and Myrna Goldenberg, *Experience and Expression: Women, the Nazis, and the Holocaust* (Detroit: Wayne State University Press, 2003), xvii—xxvii.

11. Ibid., xviii.

12. Joan Ringelheim, "Thoughts about Women and the Holocaust," in *Thinking the Unthinkable: Meanings of the Holocaust*, ed. Roger S. Gottleib (New York: Paulist Press, 1990), 145.

13. Carol Ann Rittner and John K. Roth, eds., *Different Voices: Women and the Holocaust* (St. Paul, MN: Paragon House, 1993), xi.

14. Dalia Ofer and Lenore Weitzman, eds., *Women in the Holocaust* (New Haven: Yale University Press, 1998).

15. Ibid., 1.

16. See Gabriel Schoenfeld, "Auschwitz and the Professors," *Commentary* 105/6 (June 1998): 42–45; see also the response, "Controversy: Holocaust Studies: Gabriel Schoenfeld and Critics," *Commentary* 106/2 (August 1998): 14–25. Schoenfeld accused researchers on women, gender, and the Holocaust of having "counseled, nudged, prodded, and rebuked survivors until they believed that gender issues were important in concentration camps," adding that we will "sever Jewish women, in their own minds, from their families as well as from the larger community."

17. Yehuda Bauer, *Rethinking the Holocaust* (New Haven: Yale University Press, 2001), 167, quoted in Baer and Goldenberg, *Experience and Expression*, xxvii.

18. Myrna Goldenberg and Rochelle G. Saidel co-chaired this session. Goldenberg has continued to be at the forefront of efforts to put issues regarding women, including sexual abuse, into Holocaust studies discourse. With Elizabeth Baer, she co-edited

Experience and Expression: Women, the Nazis, and the Holocaust. Saidel, co-editor of this volume, wrote *The Jewish Women of Ravensbrück Concentration Camp* (Madison: University of Wisconsin Press, 2004).

19. Books on women and the Holocaust published from 1998 to 1999 included Judith Tydor Baumel, *Double Jeopardy: Gender and the Holocaust* (London: Vallentine Mitchell, 1998); Brana Gurewitsch, ed., *Mothers, Sisters, Resisters: Oral Histories of Women Who Survived the Holocaust* (Tuscaloosa: University of Alabama Press, 1998); Marion A. Kaplan, *Between Dignity and Despair: Jewish Life in Nazi Germany* (New York: Oxford University Press, 1998); Dalia Ofer and Lenore Weitzman, eds., *Women in the Holocaust* (New Haven: Yale University Press, 1998); Roger A. Ritvo and Diane M. Plotkin, *Sisters in Sorrow: Voices of Care in the Holocaust* (College Station: Texas A & M University Press, 1998); S. Lillian Kremer, *Women's Holocaust Writing: Memory and Imagination* (Lincoln: University of Nebraska Press, 1999); Esther Fuchs, ed., *Women and the Holocaust* (Blue Ridge Summit, PA: University Press of America, 1999).

20. These include Baer and Goldenberg, *Experience and Expression*; Marcia Sachs Littell, ed., *Women in the Holocaust: Responses, Insights and Perspectives* (Merion Station, PA: Merion Westfield Press, 2001); Nechama Tec, *Resilience and Courage: Women, Men, and the Holocaust* (New Haven: Yale University Press, 2003); Saidel, *Jewish Women of Ravensbrück*; Esther Hertzog, ed., *Life, Death and Sacrifice: Women and Family in the Holocaust* (Jerusalem: Gefen, 2008). Holocaust memoirs by women have been available since shortly after World War II and have continued to proliferate. Various authors in this volume refer to them, especially S. Lillian Kremer, chapter 11.

21. Roth, "Equality, Neutrality, Particularity," in Baer and Goldenberg, *Experience and Expression*, 11–12.

22. According to Susan M. Shaw and Janet Lee, "Resisting Violence Against Women," in *Women's Voices, Feminist Visions: Classic and Contemporary Readings*, ed. Susan M. Shaw and Janet Lee (New York: McGraw-Hill, 2006), 562: "Although rape can be broadly defined as sex without consent, it is understood as a crime of aggression because the focus is on hurting and dominating. More specifically, it is the penetration of any bodily orifice by a penis or object without consent."

23. Sara R. Horowitz, *Voicing the Void: Muteness and Memory in Holocaust Fiction* (Albany: State University of New York Press, 1997), 1.

24. Daniel R. Schwarz, *Imagining the Holocaust* (New York: St. Martin's Griffin, 1999), 6.

25. See http://www.theverylongview.com/WATH/.

26. All quotes and comments are from an interview with Judy Weiszenberg Cohen by Sonja Hedgepeth, Toronto, May 22, 2009.

ASPECTS OF
Sexual Abuse

1

Death and the Maidens

"Prostitution," Rape, and Sexual Slavery during World War II

NOMI LEVENKRON

Armies have always marched over the bodies of countless women—women they raped, prostituted, inseminated, and enslaved. Sexual assault also occurs in peacetime, but in times of war, this phenomenon multiplies and the number of victims grows significantly. Although one might expect these assaults on women to be accompanied afterward by granting social legitimacy to the victims, redress of this kind is not always forthcoming. At times society itself makes the rehabilitation process much more difficult for the victims by ostracizing and stigmatizing them as loose or immoral. In this situation, the victim is frequently denied the right to tell her story in full. The society in which she grew up will tend to examine her actions through a magnifying glass, trying to identify the ways in which her own actions contributed to the sexual assault on her, and then refuse to help her rebuild her life.

The story of the sexual assaults on Jewish women in the course of the Holocaust and World War II is a story that has been largely repressed and silenced. Like other subjects touching on female sexuality (such as trafficking Jewish Eastern European women to South America in the late nineteenth and early twentieth centuries[1]), silencing has been deemed preferable to opposing the taboo against talking about the subject, and banishment preferable to inclusion.

In most countries, peacetime rape is considered a crime against the woman herself or against the man to whom she "belongs," and in war, sexual assault by combatants is routine. In war, when a man's life "isn't worth a tinker's damn," a woman's life and her autonomy over her body are worth even less. Until just a few years ago, rape was considered an insignificant byproduct of armed conflicts—traditional soldiers' wages. The victors raped the women of the vanquished and considered their actions as an inseparable part of the war. Rape in wartime is not an act of sexualized violence committed by a solitary soldier against a solitary woman in a defeated country. Wartime rape has much wider social and cultural implications for the woman and the social group to which she belongs.[2] The soldier invades the woman's body just as he invades her country; he crushes her body as well as her right to autonomy and control over her life.

The twentieth century brought about a change in the status of rape, recognizing it as a tool of genocide. Even when racial laws expressly prohibited soldiers from engaging in sexual relations with the conquered population, these laws were not always followed. At times the prohibition resulted in its opposite. The enemy's women became more desirable prey but also more invisible as human beings, and their ultimate insignificance engendered complete indifference to their suffering.[3] German soldiers raped Belgian women when they invaded that country during World War I; the Turks raped Armenian women during the Armenian genocide in 1915; the Japanese assaulted Chinese women during the Rape of Nanking in 1937–1938 and established brothels for their soldiers where women of "lower races," such as Korean women, were kept[4]; the Russians celebrated the defeat of Germany in 1944–1945 with the mass rape of millions of women—German, Polish, Russian, and Jewish; Americans raped Vietnamese women in the 1960s and established brothels holding Vietnamese refugees near their military bases; Pakistani soldiers raped Bengali women in 1971; during the Rwandan genocide in the 1990s, Hutus raped Tutsi women; and in the same decade's blood-soaked Yugoslavian episode, Muslim women were raped again and again and again in special camps set up for this very purpose. In some cases, women were released from the camps alive only after becoming pregnant and passing the stage when they could still abort the fetus. At the time of this writing, armed militias in Darfur and the Democratic Republic of Congo, staging repeated attacks, are raping thousands of women.[5]

This chapter discusses the ostracism of Jewish women who experienced sexual assault during the Holocaust and World War II, and the social mechanisms that allowed such ostracism to take place. I examine the types of sexual assault Jewish women were exposed to in the course of the war, including rape, sexual slavery, sex in exchange for some commodity, and sexual humiliation. The information used is largely based on memoirs written by survivors, which I find fascinating not only because of what they say but possibly even more so because of what they do not say. I also examine the use of social ostracism against women who transgressed the social code of modesty, even when they did so against their will in the setting of wartime rape. The chapter makes the case that a violated woman's own community, as well as the enemy, inflicts real damage on her.

Sexual Molestation of Jewish Women during World War II

I have chosen the term "sexual molestation" because the range of terms used to describe the abuse of women during the course of war is wide and includes a long list of acts, chief of which are rape and sexual slavery, but which also include sexual harassment, sex for food, and other practices. According to the definition of the Israeli Laws of Punishment, "rape is a forced sexual act against a woman without her consent."[6] All the acts described in this chapter could fall under this definition of rape. However, social attitudes of both per-petrators and victims were different during World War II, and I want to trace the attitudes that prevailed then. While my focus is on the war itself, I also ad-dress the years preceding it (1933–1939) and the weeks that followed the end of the war (May–June 1945), to the extent needed to illustrate the issues.

Although a vast literature has documented nearly all aspects of the Holo-caust, for many years the debate on the gender issue was absent from the gen-eral research. In Israel, gender research on the Holocaust began only in the last decade.[7] Even now, insufficient attention has been given to the issues of sexual exploitation of Jewish women. The Nazis saw them both as sexual ob-jects and as a biological danger, as it is women's wombs that bear future generations. What Jewish women endured in this period as a result of such thinking justifies a separate discussion on the topic of gender issues. None-theless, a great deal of criticism has been directed at the exploration of gender issues during the Holocaust for fear that it would trivialize the Shoah, over-shadowing it by a feminist agenda.[8]

Another prevalent fear has been that this kind of research would diminish understanding of the magnitude of the suffering during the Holocaust in gen-eral, and that of daily life in particular, under the Nazi regime.[9] Even those researchers who have dealt with the issue of gender in connection with the Holocaust have usually preferred to address other questions related to gender and femininity rather than sexuality as such.

The debate on the Holocaust within the context of sexuality has raised a storm of protest. There are those who view it as eroticizing destruction, which needs to be denounced at every level. Writer and Holocaust survivor Ruth Bondy describes how she felt when she first heard about the discussion of the theme of sexual molestation during the Holocaust:

Everything in me is outraged at the mention of this concept. It was [done] for hunger. They did not do this for the sake of the small amount of food they would get for themselves but for their husbands and their children . . . The theme of sexuality during the Holocaust has been blown out of all proportion dating from the time of Ka-Tzetnik. This subject attracts far more attention than that of the slaughter but is inconsequential compared with all that happened. If two million Jewish women were murdered during the Holocaust, sexual molestation was the lot of a few but violence was the lot of the many. They faced cruel choices connected to annihilation, which is soul searing, whereas the coupling of sex and destruction makes for more striking headlines.[10]

The exact number of women who experienced sexual molestation during the Holocaust cannot be determined, and there is no point in attempting to assess it. Some women were murdered afterward, most preferred silence, and the rapists by and large did not leave documents testifying to their actions.[11] Even in times of peace, recording acts of sexual molestation is difficult, and much more so in times of war. In her poem "Starvation Camp Near Jaslo," the Polish poet Wisława Szymborska wrote, "History rounds off skeletons to zero," and this is also true as far as the victims of sexual molestation are concerned.[12] It is far easier to count the number of skeletons than the number of those raped: skeletons are far more tangible and visible, but the living women who were raped hide, for they fear the stigma that is likely to cling to them if they reveal what was done to them. Few and sparse are the lines dedicated in historical documentation to sexual molestation in times of war, though they do exist, for example in Emmanuel Ringelblum's archive, rare underground newspapers, and in various chronicles.[13]

Survivors' feelings of shame and their sense of guilt that they survived, especially if they survived through the use of their sexuality, created a veil of silence on the topic that lasted for many years before being breached—especially when the topic was the use of the body in exchange for a portion of food. Some of the women felt that it was not fitting to mention sexual assault in their memoirs because doing so would constitute a desecration of the dead. For others the memory was too difficult to bear, and they found it embarrassing to talk or write about. Yet others thought that the rape of a solitary woman in the face of the destruction of a whole nation was not of particular importance.[14] Even after the end of the war, social norms did not change to such a degree that it became possible for women to tell their stories. A woman who provided sexual favors for food was defined one-dimensionally as a prostitute rather than as a person who struggled for survival.

However, research on this topic is of paramount importance if we are to learn the patterns that typify sexual assault of women in times of genocide— patterns that repeat themselves in different ways, as can be seen in the kinds of genocide perpetrated after the Holocaust. Therefore, dealing with this subject constitutes a moral obligation toward the women who experienced this kind of abuse. There can be no doubt that the sensitive nature of the topic demands of us that it be treated with caution, but this is insufficient reason to avoid addressing the issue. On the contrary, continuing to ignore the topic can only provide legitimacy for the perpetrators and will perpetuate the process stigmatizing victims in society.

Openness about discussing the Holocaust is today at its peak. Similarly, the taboo on sexuality has now begun to lose its grip in some fields. It seems that the time has come to examine this topic, which was shoved aside for so many years. I suggest an artificial division into four categories concerning sexual assault: rape, sexual slavery, bartering sex in exchange for some commodity, and sexual humiliation. This division is far from definitive, especially when we are analyzing events that took place more then sixty years ago.

Rape

On March 6, 1940, Emmanuel Ringelblum wrote the following in his diary: "At 2 Talumatzky Street, three officers [Germans in uniform] raped a woman. Shouting was heard throughout the courtyard. The Gestapo is interested in cases of racial defilement, but people are afraid to report the incident."[15] Jewish women were sometimes forced to have sexual relations with Jewish men for the enjoyment of the soldiers who looked on. At the beginning of September 1940, Ringelblum wrote the following, again in his diary: "In S[osnowiec], a soldier went into Jewish homes and forced the men to have sexual relations with women in his presence. Shortly after this he was arrested."[16] In September 1941, the Yiddish paper *Proletarisher Gedank*—one of the underground newspapers of the Warsaw ghetto that reported the deportation of the Jews of Nowy Dwor and Plonsk into the fortress in Pomiechowek—stated the following: "To shed light on the degree of Hitleristic degeneration it is sufficient to give a few frightening examples: the hangmen forced the Jew P. R. to choose four girls and to rape them before their eyes; when burying the dead they ordered the grave diggers to sing, etc."[17]

Jewish women were also sexually assaulted by the Germans' collaborators— for example, the Ukrainians. In the underground newspaper *Junge Stimme*, the following appeared in October 1941: "In Lvov, with the help of the Ukrainians, terrible pogroms were enacted. Women were raped in the middle of the streets. The murderers dragged Jewish women out of their apartments and cut off their breasts in the middle of the street. It is estimated that the number of victims reached a few thousand."[18] Mussia Dajches describes the attitude of Ukrainian collaborators toward the Jewish women: "The best and most loyal helpers of the Germans were the Ukrainians. When they began to seal the carriages packed with people and goods ([at this time] we still took possessions with us), they forced their way in, violent and drunk like Lot, and started raping the women. Jewish women, young and healthy, who had been selected and designated for forced labor."[19]

In addition to these assaults, Jewish women were sometimes forced to carry out the sexual demands of German women who served in the camps in different capacities,[20] and they were raped or molested by camp guards when body searches for valuables were carried out. Writing of Auschwitz, Raya Kagan reported that "the first deportations of women from Slovakia had 'gynecological examinations' that were officially described as a search for valuables that women were prone to hide. Hitler's hangmen examined all young women and raped them."[21] And even more devastating, Jewish women were occasionally victims of rape by Jewish men in the ghettos and camps.[22]

The end of the war did not bring about the end of sexual violence. When the Russians conquered Germany, waves of rape and looting swept the county, and for some Jewish women, the liberation began with rape by the liberators. Anthony Beevor describes the case of a Jewish woman named Ellen Getz, who fled the prison where she had been held after a heavy bombardment and hid in a basement.[23] The Russians found her there and began to rape her. When some of the Germans tried to explain to them that this was a woman who had been hounded by the Nazis, the Russian soldiers simply replied, "A woman is a woman." According to the testimony of one of the Russian soldiers, the common explanation was, "We set you free, so why not?"[24] Many of those raped became pregnant or contracted venereal diseases. A wave of suicides swept Germany during this period. The pages of A Woman in Berlin, written by an anonymous diarist who detailed her situation and that of other women during the days following the fall of Berlin, are filled with descriptions of the rape of German women by Russian soldiers.[25]

It has been argued that Jews who served as officers in the Red Army tried their best to protect Jewish women, but there is also evidence to the contrary. According to the testimony of Naama Yukovski: "Some of us girls from the Jewish group went to the captain of the Red Army, who was also a Jew, to complain about the Russian soldiers who went wild and raped them. He looked at us and said, 'Really? Why do you need gentiles, why not come to my bed?' In those days I slept under my bed out of fear."[26]

Sexual Slavery

In the course of World War II, Jewish women were forced to serve as sex slaves either privately or in a loosely organized manner. Sometimes they were defined as prostitutes and used as forced sex workers for soldiers and guards. Sometimes they were kept in private homes. Most were victims of repeated acts of rape, sometimes over long periods of time. Some were given their lives in exchange, but only as long as they could be used as sex slaves. Then they were sent to their death.

The Reich took care of the perceived sexual needs of its soldiers in the field, and the laws of racial purity did not always prevent the official use of Jewish women for this purpose (especially since some Jewish women passed as Aryans). It is also impossible to disprove the claim that repeated demands were made of the Jewish community to provide for the sexual demands of German soldiers by establishing brothels in the ghettos. In his diary, Ringelblum wrote that in Czestochowa the Germans compelled the community to create brothels, and in Bialeh Podolsk they obligated the community to pay the prostituted women for every visit by a German client.[27] Ringelblum also noted that he had heard that the Nazis demanded that the Judenrat (Jewish council) in the Warsaw ghetto establish a brothel for the soldiers and that Adam Czerniaków, head of the Judenrat, refused the request. "When he was threatened with his life, he replied that as an engineer he knows well how to mix the components of the poison," Ringelblum wrote.[28]

Official brothels were also created in Auschwitz, Buchenwald, Mauthausen, Dora-Mittelbau, and Dachau. Many of the women sent to the brothels were non-Jewish prisoners from the women's camp in Ravensbrück.[29] The "clients" were prisoners with special privileges, and their visits were either a reward given to the most efficient workers or an incentive to induce more efficient work. According to some accounts, some Jewish women may have been held in some of these places,[30] but we do not know of any institutionalized brothels in concentration camps in which large groups of Jewish women served privileged prisoners or German soldiers.[31]

On the other hand, we do know of cases of private sexual slavery perpetrated by German officers. In parts of Galicia in Poland and elsewhere, Jewish women were kept as sex slaves, and sometimes the most beautiful women from deportations to the camps were chosen to work in the homes of camp officers. Most were murdered later, and some were pregnant when they were sent to their deaths.[32]

Bartering Sex: "Here we do not love, here we screw"[33]

Among the various forms of sexual abuse the most highly stigmatized was that of "sex for food." Wars in general, and World War II in particular, re-created timeworn arrangements between women and men, between conquered and conqueror: sex for food, sex for hiding places, sex for survival. The prevalent view was that an element of choice existed in any arrangement of sex as an exchange. Therefore, women who were suspected of being guilty suffered from being treated with contempt and disgrace, scorn in which even survivors were at times complicit, criticizing the women harshly and self-righteously.

When one encounters such cases in memoirs, they generally relate to other women who were with the writer in the camp, who emphasizes that she herself did not engage in these acts. And yet, is it possible to define this kind of arrangement of sex for food in the time of the Holocaust as prostitution? There is no doubt that the answer is no. In times of war and especially genocide, when this arrangement was the only means by which a women could save her life or that of her family, one cannot consider the act prostitution, whether made by choice or through force. It was but one of the ways to survive, open to people who found themselves in impossible situations. When a woman is found in a situation of "choiceless choices,"[34] there is only the appearance of choice.

One striking example of sexual relations in such circumstances appears in Ringelblum's diary. He documents the actions of the Jewish police, who arrested people in order to send them to death camps and released them only in exchange for money or sex: "There were cases in which these police, in addition to money, also demanded an insidious payment in kind—the women's bodies . . . for this purpose they had a special room in the hospital."[35] Is it possible to point an accusing finger at a woman who under such circumstances entered that hospital room with a policeman? Is it possible to view this as a case of prostitution? The answer is no. Nonetheless, the very fact that the term prostitution became entrenched in this context in military and social discourse indicates how slight the willingness was to forgive women who had committed this social transgression.

The practice of sex for food took place between Jewish men who had managed to keep some of their possessions in the ghetto and Jewish women, between German soldiers and Jewish women, and between concentration camp inmates with special privileges and Jewish women. In simple terms, relations like these ensued between men who were powerful and women who were powerless. Some of these interactions began with rape but in time became a kind of arrangement between the sides in which a woman supplied sex for food and other commodities. As Raya Kagan explained quite simply as early as 1947: "The root cause of it all was hunger, the cruel hunger that occurs with particular viciousness in winter, that drove women into the arms of the men."[36]

A case like this is described in the testimony of Bella Rosenblum:

> I believe that if Germans were not restricted by their laws of racial purity, the fate of many Jewish women would have been much worse. In our camp we saw how one of the German engineers took two Jewish girls into his room. Whenever he had the inclination, he took one of them for himself exclusively. Every one of these girls had a family in the camp. They at least tried to sweeten the bitter pill by requesting, or sometimes by threatening suicide, clemency for their families. The German could not always refuse. So it worked out that under the circumstances families did not oppose the actions that were forcibly taken against the girls of the family. One cannot judge a person in these circumstances. I only tell about this special circumstance and unique situation in which people found themselves trapped. And these were not the only two girls. As I mentioned earlier, there were also special relations between Germans and Jewish women. I myself didn't, so I do not know the details.[37]

Even Jewish women who managed to escape from the camps and find a hiding place did not always find safety.[38] They were attacked by the people who sheltered them and exploited their absolute dependency. In this context, Debórah Dwork points out that "perhaps under the circumstances of domination and dependency it was inevitable that violence be expressed through sexuality."[39] Sometimes women were attacked by other Jews hiding with them. Paula Weinstein describes in her testimony "an unpleasant incident" that happened to her when she hid in a Christian household with a Jewish couple. She was left alone in the house with the Jewish man:

> During the day, when the others went out to work, we both remained in the house, Zygmunt and I. We became friends. We spoke. When the man saw it was all right, he began to touch me, to stroke me. I was so young, I did not understand what was going on. Each time he began to touch me more aggressively all over. He became horrible, threatening. Once, when he nearly raped me, I threatened that I would tell on him, that I would call out. He stopped at that moment, but on the following day he continued.[40]

The fate of women who lived in the forests with partisans was similar: they were forced to enter into a kind of marriage arrangement with a partisan. Whoever did not find a so-called husband was doomed to a life of danger and deprivation. One of the women who was saved in this way described her situation by saying: "I do not agree that women were selling themselves, but it was not real love either. To be sure, men rather than women, would select a partner. But if a women did not like a man, no one forced her."[41]

Humiliation with Sexual Undertones

In the course of their general daily humiliations, women were at times sexually humiliated even in the absence of sexual intercourse. They were forced to strip in front of soldiers, to stand naked for many hours, even days, in an endless parade, to wait naked in line for their turn to be disinfected. They were whipped naked and made to dance naked. When the Jews of Zyrardow, Poland, were driven into the ghetto in February 1941, Jewish women were humiliated in the street, an event described in the underground newspaper Bulletin: "From two in the afternoon until two at night they kept the women in Spokovina Street, they threatened them with shaving off their hair and extorted money from them. For long hours they stood naked and were objects of shame and disgrace. As for their clothes, these were 'well cared for.'"[42]

Jewish women were also exposed to various verbal insults by the jailers in the camps, insults that often bore sexual connotations. Sometimes body searches were carried out, ostensibly to find valuables but in fact for the purpose of humiliating them. Body searches were carried out on both living and dead women.

On Shame, Sexuality, and Ostracism

Very few men have ever been called on to account by courts of law for their wartime actions, and most perpetrators have yet to be tried for genocide, in general, or rape, in particular. The International Military Court in Nuremberg was established in 1945 for the purpose of trying war criminals active in the course of the war. In those trials, the crime of rape did not merit its own independent reference, but rather was treated as ancillary to other crimes. The Tokyo court that tried Japanese war criminals did not include rape among crimes against humanity, although it was determined that rape by soldiers was a transgression of the rules of engagement. The real breakthrough with regard to wartime rape occurred only when war criminals from Rwanda and Yugoslavia were brought to trial. The special courts established to try the perpetrators for the crimes committed in these countries included the crime of rape in their charter, and several of the accused were convicted of this crime in addition to others.

It is not too much to say that the silence of the justice system has assisted rapists to elude punishment and to legitimize their actions. By contrast, women have almost always been forced by their societies to render an accounting for actions taken in wartime—both the actions they themselves were compelled to take and the actions of others they were forced to accept. In the nationalistic militaristic discourse, the topic of feminine sexuality, and particularly its violation, holds a special place. Perhaps more than any other wartime trauma, rape is perceived as the scene of the violent encounter between the personal trauma and the collective trauma. It is turned from being a painful personal trauma into a mortal blow to national pride, a trauma that women are asked to prevent at any cost. Over time, in different cultures and religions, women were told explicitly and implicitly to put an end to their lives if the danger of being raped by the enemy was hovering over them. Sexual contact with enemy soldiers was seen as breaking collective boundaries, a dangerous, immoral contact, worthy of condemnation.

Throughout history, national martyrology has often been enlisted in the collective cause. The threat experienced by the patriarchal-national entity, created by the concern that collective boundaries would be breached through sexuality, was translated into the most effective of all social weapons: shame. The message transmitted to women was simple: a glorious death or a life of disgrace. In wars, sexuality and shame became inextricably linked and created a nefarious dilemma of fatal inclusion or unbearable ostracism. Women who followed social conventions and took their own lives rather than be "dishonored" earned the status of veritable holiness. By contrast, women who had sexual congress with the enemy, whether of their own free will or against their wishes, were stamped with shame and shunned by the community.

Even in cases of rape, women who had sexual contact with the enemy were often considered the real enemy. They were "the enemy within," the enemy whose betrayal hurt much more than an attack from outside the country's borders. The sentence for such an enemy could only be disgrace. At times, this disgrace was given legal expression, but it primarily had a social effect: women who breached the code of conduct in wartime had disgrace heaped on them by their communities. As a result of the emphasis on national honor, the term "choice" became loaded with double meaning. On one hand, the women had their choice of sexual partner *taken away* from them, and it was made clear to them that if their sexuality was dishonored by the enemy they would be better off dead. On the other hand, the choice was *forced on* them, and even women who were raped were seen as having chosen their fate and, therefore, deserving of scorn.

This phenomenon was particularly striking in societies where modesty was women's principal or even their only admission ticket into the collective. Here even women who were raped were defined as whores. Sexuality defined the boundaries of the collective and therefore held within it the danger of this boundary being breached. In wartime, a woman's sexuality became the essence of her being.

Because of the interplay between sexuality and disgrace in wartime, the fact that the rapist-soldiers eventually left did not always relieve the suffering of the raped women, who were forced to cope with severe emotional traumas, unwanted pregnancies, and venereal diseases. Above all, they suffered from the hostility of their own communities that viewed them as "loose," "whores by choice," and "immoral." The "comfort women," who were victims of sexual abuse by Japanese soldiers during World War II, were often forced to leave their villages as a result of the opprobrium directed at them. Bengali women raped by Pakistani soldiers were ostracized by their villages, and women in the Democratic Republic of Congo are now routinely raped and rejected, while those in Darfur have to build their own huts and live by themselves.

The diarist from Berlin quoted earlier was abandoned by her partner after she told him Russian soldiers had raped her at the end of World War II. After documenting the rapes and assaults that occurred around her, the beginning of the national reckoning, her own attempts to survive—the rapes she experienced, the hunger, the attempts to gain "protection" from a senior Russian officer so that, as she defines it, she would be raped by only one as opposed to many—she reveals a final assault: "You've all turned into a bunch of shameless bitches," her former partner tells her, "every one of you in the building. Don't you realize? . . . It's horrible being around you. You've lost all sense of measure."[43] Two days later, he leaves home saying he is going to look for food, and he never comes back.

Conclusions

The anonymous German woman's partner treated her exactly like the Jewish community treated Jewish women after the war, when it became known that they had had sexual relations with the enemy. Without any regard to the question of the circumstances of these relations, shunning and ostracism became the lot of these women. That is one reason that so many have kept silent. Sexual assaults are not unique to wartime, but in wars they multiply and harm a larger number of victims. Therefore, the question is not only how to act in wartime to prevent sexual attacks on women by enemy soldiers. Another important question is how to act after the war to minimize, to the extent possible, the additional damage inflicted on these women by their own communities.

Notes

Parts of this chapter first appeared in Hebrew in an article published in the journal *Theory and Criticism* 32 (Spring 2008): 15–44. Used with permission of the Van Leer Institute. Translation by Sonia Grober and Susann Codish.

1. See Edward Bristow, *Prostitution and Prejudice: The Jewish Fight Against the White Slave Trade* (New York: Schocken Books, 1983) for more information on this topic.

2. Susan Brownmiller, *Against Our Will: Men, Women and Rape* (Harmondsworth, Middlesex: Penguin Books, 1975), 52.

3. Andrea Dworkin, "The Unremembered: Searching for Women at the Holocaust Memorial Museum," *Ms.* 40 (November–December 1994): 52.

4. Although called "brothels" by the soldiers, these places were experienced by the women as the scene of their rape. By using the term brothels, I am in no way implying acceptance of the term; rather, it is being used as a description from the vantage point of the conquering army.

5. Rape in the Democratic Republic of Congo was the subject of Lynn Nottage's powerful off-Broadway play *Ruined*, which exposes the horrors of the Congolese war and the bravery of the women subjected to its brutality. The play premiered in Chicago in November 2008 and opened in February 2009 in New York City. It won the Pulitzer Prize for drama in 2009. "Ruined" is a euphemism for "raped," and the term encompasses mutilation of genitalia, psychological ruin, and rejection by society.

6. Section 345 of the Penal Code (1977). For more information about rape according to Israeli law, see Frances Raday, "The Concept of Gender Equality in a Jewish State," in *Women in Law*, ed. Shimon Shetreet (New York: Kluwer Law International, 1998), 56–57.

7. In the last decade there have been four international conferences in Israel on this topic. In 2006 a volume of articles based on one of the conferences was published in Hebrew, entitled *Women and Family in the Holocaust*, ed. Esther Hertzog (Netanya: Otzar Hamishpat, 2006). An English version of the book followed: *Life, Death and Sacrifice: Women and Family in the Holocaust*, ed. Esther Hertzog (Jerusalem/New York: Gefen, 2008). In 2007 Yad Vashem in Jerusalem presented an exhibition curated by Yehudit Inbar and titled "Spots of Light: To Be a Woman in the Holocaust." The exhibition dealt with love, motherhood, femininity, friendship, fighting, faith, food, and creativity, but sexuality was virtually absent. See http://www1.yadvashem.org/exhibitions/women-heb/splash .html (accessed June 8, 2009).

8. For discussion on this topic, see Joan Ringelheim, "The Split between Gender and the Holocaust," in *Women in the Holocaust*, ed. Dalia Ofer and Lenore J. Weitzman (New Haven: Yale University Press, 1998), 340–350 and, in the same volume, Lenore J. Weitzman and Dalia Ofer, "Introduction: The Role of Gender in the Holocaust," 1–18.

9. Elizabeth D. Heineman, "Sexuality and Nazism: The Doubly Unspeakable?" *Journal of the History of Sexuality* 11 (January–April 2002): 22–66.

10. Ruth Bondy, a survivor of the Holocaust, is a journalist, writer, and translator, and one of the founders of Beit Terezin. The material quoted here is taken from a lecture she gave at the conference "Women and the Holocaust: Gender Issues in Holocaust Research," September 5–7, 2005, Beit Berl, Beit Terezin, and Beit Lohamei Hagettaot, Israel. For a discussion about Ka-Tzetnik, see chapter 12 by Miryam Sivan in this volume.

11. However, certain types of sexual molestation were documented with precision. See, for example, Julia Roos, "Backlash against Prostitutes' Rights: Origins and Dynamics of Nazi Prostitution Policies," *Journal of the History of Sexuality* 11(January/April 2002): 67–94.

12. Wisława Szymborska, "Starvation Camp at Jaslo," in *Miracle Fair: Selected Poems of Wisława Szymborska* (New York: W. W. Norton, 2001), 38.

13. Ringelblum documented the history of the Warsaw ghetto in an archive called "Oneg Shabbat" from the time the ghetto was created until it was liquidated in 1943. He and his assistants researched and reported on actual events and informed the Jews in the ghetto about the significance of the threat they were facing.

14. Ringelheim, "The Split between Gender and the Holocaust," 349.

15. Emmanuel Ringelblum, *Yoman ve-Reshimot Mitkufat ha-Milhama* [Diary and notes from the Warsaw ghetto: September 1939–December 1942] (Jerusalem: Yad Vashem and Lohamei Hagettaot, the Ghetto Fighters' House, 1992), 84. In English, see Emmanuel Ringelblum, *Notes from the Warsaw Ghetto* (New York: McGraw-Hill, 1958).

16. Ringelblum, *Yoman ve-Reshimot Mitkufat ha-Milhama*, 113.

17. Daniel Blatman, ed., *Ghetto Varshaw—Sipur Etoni* [Warsaw ghetto—A journalist's story] (Jerusalem: Yad Vashem, 2002), 106.

18. Ukrainians were active partners in the murder of the Jews of Lvov and in the rape of Jewish women there. The Germans entered Lvov on June 30, 1941. From the time of their entry until July 3, they perpetrated extreme forms of violence against the Jewish population, assisted by groups of Nationalistic Ukrainians. Quoted in Blatman, *Ghetto Varshaw*, 378.

19. Mussia Dajches, "Avdut Betzel ha-Aima" [Slavery in the shadow of fear], in *Lachmat Nashim: Sipur shel Mahane K'fia Nazi* [Women's war: The story of a Nazi forced labor camp], ed. Nathan Livneh (Israel: Igud Yotzeh Vilna Vehasviva b'Yisrael, Organization of Former Residents of Vilna and Vicinity in Israel, 1979), 9.

20. For example, Irma Grese was an SS supervisor in Auschwitz who carried out sexual assaults on women and often murdered them after the act. A number of the supervisors and those who had prisoner jobs in the camps were criminals who had previously served jail sentences for prostitution and other offenses.

21. Raya Kagan, *Nashim be-Lishkat Gehinom* [Hell's office women] (Kibbutz Hameuchad: Sifriyat Po'alim, 1947), 51.

22. One documented case of a Jewish man accused of rape in a ghetto is that of a man named Ordinanz, who was put on trial in the Lodz ghetto. See *The Chronicle of the Lodz Ghetto, 1941–1944*, ed. Lucjan Dobroszycki (New Haven: Yale University Press, 1984), 384, entry for September 24, 1943.

23. Anthony Beevor's *Berlin: The Downfall, 1945* (London: Penguin, 2003) includes numerous references to rape in Berlin: 274, 295, 300, 312–314, 326–327, 345–346, 409–412, 414, 418.

24. See Felicja Karay, *Pagazim v'Heruzim: Mahane Nashim Hasag-Leipzig* [Shells and beads: Hasag-Leipzig camp for women] (Tel Aviv: Moreshet, 1997), 244. Published in English as *Hasag-Leipzig Slave Labour Camp for Women* (London: Vallentine Mitchell, 2002).

25. Anonymous, *A Woman in Berlin* (New York: Metropolitan Books, 2005).

26. Naama Yukovski, in *Dafei Idut* [Pages of testimony], vol. 2, ed. and interviewer, Zvika Dror (Tel Aviv: Lohamei Hagettaot and Hakibutz Hameuchad,1984), 1296.

27. Ringelblum, *Yoman ve-Reshimot Mitkufat ha-Milhama*, 141.

28. Ibid., 215.

29. Rochelle G. Saidel, *The Jewish Women of Ravensbrück Concentration Camp* (Madison: University of Wisconsin Press, 2004), 214. For more details about brothels, see chapter 3 by Sommer in this volume.

30. Julia Roos, "Backlash against Prostitutes' Rights," 67–94.

31. For more information on organized brothels, see chapter 3 by Robert Sommer in this volume.

32. Felicja Karay, "Women in the Forced Labor Camp," in *Women in the Holocaust*, ed. Ofer and Weitzman, 291.

33. This sentence is taken from Fania Fénelon with Marcelle Routier, *Playing for Time*, trans. Judith Landry (New York: Athenaeum, 1977), 117.

34. This phrase was coined by Lawrence Langer in his *Versions of Survival: The Holocaust and the Human Spirit* (Albany: State University of New York Press, 1982), 74.

35. Ringelblum, *Yoman ve-Reshimot Mitkufat ha-Milhama*, 432.

36. Kagan, *Nashim be-Lishkat Gehinom*, 136.

37. Bella Rosenblum, in *Dafei Idut*, vol. 3, 1618; see also, Karay, *Pagazim v'Heruzim*, 129.

38. It was easier for women to go underground than it was for men. In Poland, for instance, girls studied in Polish schools, absorbed the local culture, and spoke the language, which helped them find a hiding place. Furthermore, they could not be physically identified as Jewish, unlike men. Yet they were not free from other dangers, including exposure. Joan Ringelheim wrote cynically that if we took Anne Frank's diary as the exclusive model for life in hiding, we might think that the only danger in store for those in hiding was discovery by the Germans. Ringelheim, "The Split between Gender and the Holocaust," 345.

39. Dwork Debórah, *Children with a Star: Jewish Youth in Nazi Europe* (New Haven: Yale University Press, 1991), 32.

40. Paula Weinstein, in *Dafei Idut*, 1023.

41. Nechama Tec, "Women Among the Forest Partisans," in *Women in the Holocaust*, ed. Ofer and Weitzman, 229.

42. Blatman, *Ghetto Varshaw*, 208.

43. Anonymous, *Woman in Berlin*, 259.

2

Sexualized Violence against Women during Nazi "Racial" Persecution

BRIGITTE HALBMAYR

A Framework for Sexualized Violence

With Resolution 1820 of June 19, 2008, the United Nations Security Council for the first time denounced violence committed against women and girls in wars. While "violence" is not clearly defined, it is evident that the resolution is aimed mainly at sexual violence and makes "its condemnation in the strongest terms of all sexual and other forms of violence committed against civilians in armed conflict, in particular women and children."[1] This chapter deals specifically with sexualized violence against women during Nazi persecution, but first the discussion requires a definition of my terminology and a framework regarding other sexualized violence. The specific nature of sexualized violence during National Socialism was unique, but it was also part of the historical continuity of violence against women in areas of conflict and war.

Sexual Violence—Sexualized Violence

I use the term "sexualized violence" instead of "sexual violence." Violent sex is supposedly also sex, as Insa Eschebach and Regina Mühlhäuser state: "A rapist gets pleasure, he enjoys his sexual predominance, he enjoys the conquest of a physical and emotional body without the consent of the other. And those who are made helpless in such a situation are not only confronted by the aggression of the attacker, but also by his sexual power."[2] Although this statement may be correct, usage of the term sexualized violence in the context of the concentration camps seems to me to be more accurate for several reasons.[3] The issue is not about the sexuality of the perpetrators, but rather that violence is committed via sexuality. The term sexualized violence makes it clear that male violence against females is not about sexuality but is a show of power on the part of the perpetrator and includes many forms of violence with sexual connotations, including humiliation, intimidation, and destruction. My point of departure is the definition by peace researcher Johan Galtung, who sees violence as a given "when people are influenced in a way that their actual corporeal and spiritual fulfillment is less than their potential fulfillment."[4] From this we can derive that violent acts can be understood as sexualized if they are directed at the most intimate part of a person and, as such, against that person's physical, emotional, and spiritual integrity. It must be stressed that the goal of all forms of sexualized violence is the demonstration of power and dominance through the humiliation and degradation of the other.

This definition of the term covers direct physical expressions of violence that are bodily attacks, an unauthorized crossing of body boundaries. They range from flagrant sexual advances to rape. In Nazi concentration camps, sexualized violence also included forced sex labor, sex for survival, forced sterilization, forced abortion, and other "medical" procedures.[5] This definition of sexualized violence also allows for the inclusion of indirect, often emotional expressions of violence, such as imposed public nakedness and accompanying feelings of shame, infringement on intimate space, deplorable hygienic conditions, leering stares, suggestive insults, and humiliating methods of physical examination, all part of the constant impending danger of becoming the victim of sexual assault by the SS or camp guards.

Violence against Women: Universal and Timeless

"The offspring of the woman who sings were born of rape and horror . . ." With these words Wajdi Mouawad, the Lebanese-Canadian author of the play *Incendies* (Scorched), reveals the secret that had compelled twins, at their mother's behest, to return to the place of their conception and birth. There they learn that their brother and father, one and the same person, had raped their mother while she was incarcerated in the prison that he headed.[6] Singing was her survival strategy. Although the playwright set this story about violence and self-imposed silence in Lebanon, it is not bound by location or time. In just the last twenty years, the news of terror and sexualized violence waged against civilian populations has reached us from all corners of the world, including Bosnia, Rwanda, Darfur, Congo, and Iraq.

Much has been done to uncover, report, and document acts of sexualized violence, which are timeless and universal. Likewise, political condemnations have been made and counter-measures have been taken. However, these facts do not release us from an obligation to closely analyze sexualized violence and identify the many forms that it can take. First of all, the features of various forms of violence having sexual connotations must be differentiated. Rape is certainly one of the most serious forms of violent assault, and it is important to study it theoretically as well as empirically. While doing so, we need to take into account not only extreme cases, but also other kinds of abuse. If we focus only on the extreme, we may miss other sexualized violence to which even larger numbers of women have been subjected. Another point of inquiry is the historical-political context of the sexualized violence. For example, sexualized violence had a different connotation in the genocides in Rwanda and the former Yugoslavia than it did under the Nazi regime. Unlike the cases in Rwanda and former Yugoslavia, where rape was used as a strategy of war, sexualized violence was not an inherent part of the genocidal process during the Holocaust. Instead, it was part of the continuum of violence that resulted from genocide. Rape was not an instrument of genocide, but was the byproduct of intentional annihilation.[7]

One also has to make a distinction regarding the various states of violence in particular places. As Miranda Alison stresses, in wars, women "of the enemy" become the target of sexual violence because of their central significance for the construction and preservation of the ethnic-national group.[8] The mass rape and forced pregnancies of the women of the enemy—such as the 1990s cases of Bosnian Muslim women in former Yugoslavia or the Tutsi women in Rwanda—demonstrate the extent to which the female body is seen as the "symbolic representation of the national body."[9]

Another key aspect of an analysis of sexualized violence is explaining the different motives of the perpetrators. Because the female body is perceived as terrain on which not only gender but also ethnicity is negotiated and sanctioned, assigning meaning to motive is complex. To what extent can violence against women, whether in civilian life or in war, be explained by using the usual approach of looking at male aggression and dominance? To what degree beyond this must one seek representations, meanings, and fantasies, that is, ideological notions? Here I am not looking for individual motives of violent men, but for the norms and values in sociopolitical structures that influence the actions of the individual. How can a structural approach that takes into account intersecting forms of discrimination explain the different manifestations of sexualized violence?

In the end, the various residual effects on a sexually assaulted individual must also be analyzed. Apart from injury to personal integrity and lingering emotional and physical damage, society's response to these traumas can add to or mitigate victims' suffering. Social taboos that prevent victims from talking cause them further harm and hinder them from processing the suffering they had to endure. As Regina Mühlhäuser aptly summarized, sexual violence is "not to be understood as always being the same crime. It is instead about a variety of actions carried out by the perpetrator for different reasons, having a number of results for the victims."[10]

The root cause for sexualized violence is widely seen as located in the beginnings of misogyny, that is, in sexism. In general, sexualized violence is often seen as a manifestation of power and a claim to ownership (accompanied by a supposed right to oppress) of men over women, rooted in the centuries-old tradition of patriarchal societies. Thus sexualized violence is supposedly an expression of a hatred of women, a way to discipline women and assign them their social standing. At the same time, the male perpetrator seeks to prove his superior status through sexualized violence—to the victim, to his environs, but also to himself.

Read this way, sexualized violence is exclusively a sign of male dominance and aggression, which one can trace back to gender-based inequality, discrimination, and misogyny. In addition, violence against women described this way, as a universal male tendency, presupposes that "all men want to keep all women in a state of fear."[11] However, this does not explain why some men rape and others don't, or why conditions vary to such a great extent in disparate societies and at different times. It does not make clear why women are targeted to different degrees under the same circumstance, as I will show in my discussion of sexualized violence in the concentration camps. Nor does it clarify why rape and other sexual forms of violence are not equally used as weapons of war in every armed conflict, as Miranda Alison has pointed out.[12] Therefore, additional ideological aspects must be considered.

Forms of Sexualized Violence in Nazi Concentration Camps

In Nazi concentration camps there were specific prevailing conditions for sexual violence against women.[13] The SS had complete power over prisoners, and extreme exploitation, abuse, and dehumanization, often leading to annihilation, characterized daily life. Wolfgang Sofsky speaks of the concentration camp as the place of "absolute power."[14] Sexualized violence took place not only in the form of breaking rules but often in their implementation.

Racism as the Guiding Principle of National Socialism

Extreme racism dominated National Socialist ideology. This racism was particularly aimed at two groups of people, Jews and so-called Gypsies (Roma and Sinti). Anti-Semitism and anti-Gypsy sentiment were driving forces for Nazi illusions of power and controlled all spheres of society and politics.[15] Strict distinctions were drawn between *Herrenrasse* (master race) and *Untermenschen* (inferior race), between "Aryans" and other "lower races," between being worthy or unworthy of life. The extermination of "non-Aryans" and those classified as *gemeinschaftsfremd* (alien to the communal body) because of social or physical features was an aspect of the creation of a "racially pure master humankind," transformed by means of Nazi population and sexual politics.

Even in the concentration camps the classification of people into "racial" groups was a deciding factor in who survived and who experienced torture. Jewish women were often housed in their own barracks, which were the worst, and they were in the lowest position in the hierarchy of prisoners. Their status usually barred them from functioning in administrative jobs or easier work commandos, and allowed them fewer opportunities to "organize" or trade desirable items. It also made them more vulnerable to sexualized violence. In some extermination camps where Jewish prisoners of both genders were housed in close proximity to each other, there was heightened danger of sexualized violence committed not only by SS men or guards but also by male inmates.

Bearing these structural differences in mind, I would like to pursue the following question: To what degree were Jewish women affected differently than non-Jewish women by sexualized violence during persecution? In other words, to what extent did persecution due to so-called race make a difference and influence Jewish women's likelihood of experiencing sexualized violence?

Sexualized Misogynous Violence

Women prisoners were affected more or less in the same ways by numerous forms of sexualized violence in concentration camps. Forced nudity was part of the entry processing and therefore an unavoidable experience of sexualized violence. No matter how short the descriptions or how sketchy the memories about arrival, almost every woman telling her story in an interview mentions that she had to take off all of her clothes. In these stories, the presence of male

SS guards or inmates is dominant and perceived as embarrassing or shocking. Physical examinations were especially demeaning when they were conducted by men, as the following account about the lice check upon arrival illustrates: "What was humiliating was that we had to undergo an examination for lice. They told us to stand on a stool, but they were *male* deportees who had to look and see if we had lice, even in hidden places" (emphasis in the original).[16] Here, in a special way, one sees the critical importance of gender differences between female victims and male perpetrators in the context of Nazi persecution and imprisonment in concentration camps.[17] Again and again, reports mention verbal humiliation and vulgar insults as well as beatings and intimate touching.

Women experienced not only the embarrassment of forced nakedness during the arrival process but they also—for example, in Ravensbrück women's concentration camp—received beatings on their buttocks. Furthermore, nakedness while standing *Appell* (roll call) was an added punishment, especially in the winter, as well as an additional humiliation during selections. Two Jewish sisters, Sarah and Esther, remember that they had to run around the block naked during a selection in Auschwitz-Birkenau to prove that they were still able to perform physical labor.[18] Relieving oneself in the latrines in front of the eyes of the SS men or in the presence of male prisoners was another especially mortifying episode that has been recounted over and over. In the words of Zipora Nir, another Jewish survivor: "One of the most terrible things there was the toilet, there were such holes that we sat on, and across from us, with their backs sat men, yes. That is really a great humiliation."[19]

Loss of the ability to menstruate, which almost all women experienced, also caused humiliation. At first many of them worried and were afraid they would be infertile as a result. That is why I consider the inability to menstruate as a form of sexualized violence. The most likely explanation for widespread amenorrhea is the catastrophic living conditions in the concentration camps (lack of nutrition, hard labor, extreme physical duress), which reduced bodily functions to those merely needed to survive. However, the women were also relieved not to have monthly menses, given the lack of hygienic conditions in the camps. In cases where women still had their periods soon after arrival, lack of material for sanitary napkins brought them yet more embarrassment. As one survivor explained the situation: "[In the beginning] very many women still had their period, and you didn't even have any opportunity at all. Blood ran down the women's legs, they could not help themselves and so on, one did not even have the chance to wash oneself with cold water every day."[20] And another said: "When I got it for the first time outdoors and I went to the *Blockälteste* [senior block inmate], because I needed something, and she said to me: 'Hold your hand underneath.' So you can imagine how we really stank."[21]

Other forms of sexualized violence derived from the humiliating conditions and "daily life" in concentration camps. Conditions of extreme overcrowding, food shortage, lack of hygiene, and exploitation of female labor led to situations in which personal boundaries were continuously crossed and the women were subjected to shameless voyeurism. Their honor was wounded and their personal pride negated through verbal degradation. For example, Slava Primozic tells about the humiliating order forbidding the women to go to the toilet: "When one went to work, outdoors, to cut branches, one was not allowed to leave in order to relieve oneself, everyone did this standing up, and, always the dogs, and with all the guards, all while standing."[22]

Forced sexual acts were closely linked to the fight for survival and accentuated hierarchy within the concentration camp system. Through a relationship with an SS man or a prisoner of higher rank within the hierarchical system, a woman prisoner could significantly increase her chances for survival. She might, for example, gain greater access to better food, clothing, and items for taking care of herself, as well as the possibility of an easier work commando. However, she also put herself in greater danger, especially in relationships with SS men, which had to remain secret. Thus sex for survival must be seen as sexual coercion, even if it seems that there was a willing exchange of sex for all kinds of wares.

Again and again, survivor testimonies mention rape of women. While rape is often recounted as having occurred to someone else, in some cases women testify about the violent act committed against themselves.[23] The permanent danger that one could become the victim of forcible sexual assaults becomes apparent. If an SS man took a liking to a woman prisoner, there was hardly any way for her to resist or to get away. For this reason, women tried to remain inconspicuous or made themselves look older.[24]

The danger of rape also came from fellow male prisoners. Regina Anna Langsam Lewkowicz, a Jewish survivor, testified about her arrival at Mauthausen:

[W]e stand there in absolute darkness and you don't know what is happening. And then you see vague *figures* [emphasis in original] in dark capes and they come toward a section of us, to our women, and something moves. But what is moving there, that you don't know . . . At that time I was fifteen. You had never been given the facts of life. And what those unclear motions under the capes there in the distance were, you didn't have a clue. You didn't understand it until later. Hey, you didn't make a sound. They, the women, were simply attacked, had to shut their mouths, and, and, and had to endure what was happening, everything under such a black cape. In the dark, black corridor.[25]

Jewish survivor Irena Liebman described the following arrival scene at Mauthausen, which illustrates how difficult it is to differentiate between these two kinds of violence:

Then we sat there on something like ground. We waited. They wanted to show us where we were supposed to go, et cetera. Then suddenly one of the criminal Germans came and he had two tins of sardines. And he went to one woman and he had intercourse with her, one of those thin scarecrows . . . He gave [her] the two [tins], she stood up and he did his thing. And it was the first time I saw that, you understand what that means?[26]

The perpetrators, even members of the SS, were committing the crime of *Rassenschande* (race defilement) with this kind of violence against Jewish women. The Jewish women's categorization as part of an "inferior race" may have protected them somewhat, but certainly did not guarantee immunity from sexualized assault. It is far more likely that SS men especially made these most vulnerable women feel their all-pervading power. When the perpetrators of sexualized violence against Jewish women were Jewish fellow prisoners, the abuse affected the women's feelings even more painfully.[27]

"Racial" Aspects of Sexualized Violence

Shaving of body hair illustrates to what extent differently categorized groups of women prisoners were subjected to different forms of sexualized violence. Hair was supposedly shaved off primarily for hygienic reasons, such as fighting the spread of head lice. However, for certain groups of women this shaving, regardless of actual lice infestation, was also meant to humiliate. Some Jewish women, as well as Russian, Polish, and German women incarcerated for *Rassenschande*, were shaved many times during their time in a camp.[28] The shearing of hair was a means of punishment and symbolic stigmatization, and the intention was racist violence.

Jewish survivor Marta Kos said that shaving off her hair left "the deepest impression of all of the time spent in the concentration camp."[29] Newly arrived prisoners not only had the hair on their heads shorn but also that of their armpits and pubic area—an embarrassing procedure that was often carried out in the presence of SS men or, sometimes, male prisoners. As a consequence of the shaved heads, women did not recognize close relatives or good friends. Along with their terror, they felt lost and abandoned. Zipora Nir remembered:

> Afterward they shaved us and that is one of my traumas, that—that was very hard for me. It is really interesting that when I read memoirs of other women, it was an awful shock for most of them. We did not get a—tattoo, that is, we did not get a number. Those were such large transports that presumably they were not able to do it. But that they shaved us was a kind of humiliation that haunts me even to this day. For example, that I have long hair, and I really should have gone to a hairdresser a long time ago. It isn't important whether it is long or short, but bald? When I see that young people do that for fun, it is hard for me, really hard. . . . That was one of the greatest degradations. But that—that they shaved us from head to toe, all that—that, that, that is a terrible humiliation. I don't know. For me it was very difficult. There were women who laughed afterward, because they no longer recognized the other person. And we looked so strange.[30]

Libusé Nachtmanová, a Czech survivor, described how SS men came into the shower rooms. Normally a naked woman would cover her breasts or pubic area with her hands. The shorn women covered their heads with their hands. "They were more ashamed of the loss of their hair than their nudity," she said.[31] For women hair is a symbol of femininity. Shaving heads was regarded as a violation of the body's integrity and a negation of individual and gender-specific identity.

Forced sterilization in the name of pseudo-scientific experiments, a more permanent and severe form of violence, was carried out on thousands of women.[32] At the behest of Heinrich Himmler, by 1941 the SS was looking for a medical means of sterilization that would make the victim unknowingly infertile "in the shortest amount of time in the easiest way possible, [applicable to] unlimited masses of people."[33] There is evidence of forced sterilization by means of radiation, injections, and operations. As the victims were mostly Roma and Sinti, as well as Jewish women (including children as young as eight years old), these forced sterilizations are considered as a racist measure.[34] Anja Lundholm reported thousands of daily sterilizations in Auschwitz.[35] The operations took place without anesthesia, and many did not survive the unimaginable agony.

In addition to the sterilizations, forced abortions were performed first and foremost because of the Nazis' racist ideology.[36] While abortion was forbidden to "Aryan" women as future mothers of the "master race," the propagation of those regarded as inferior was prevented as much as possible—both inside and outside the concentration camps.[37] Abortions were not rare in concentration camps, and as with forced sterilization, the victims were primarily (although not exclusively) Jewish and Gypsy (Roma and Sinti) women. Other women classified as "asocial" (a broader category that included Gypsies) were also deemed unworthy of procreation. Women in the asocial category included prostitutes, lesbians, and indigents. In addition, forced abortions were performed on women who became pregnant while "employed" as forced sex workers in the prisoner brothels.

A decrease in the number of abortions, as occurred beginning in 1943 in the Ravensbrück concentration camp, merely points to the fact that it was a priority to exploit the labor force. Abortions endangered the life of the pregnant women and thus negated their value as human labor. Furthermore, if the women came to term, the SS knew how to get rid of the newborn babies by murdering them or letting them starve to death.[38] Forced abortions were carried out with the intention of Vernichtung durch Arbeit (extermination through work), total exploitation of the capacity to do work followed by annihilation. In the extermination camps this situation was even more horrifying because Jewish pregnant women were taken immediately to the gas chamber.

In ten concentration camps, forced sex labor in brothels for privileged male prisoners presented another emotionally and physically difficult form of sexualized violence. In discussions about daily life in the concentration camps, mentioning this form of violence has been taboo for decades, and this topic has only been explored since the early 1990s.[39]

The selection of women for forced sex labor also followed "racial" criteria, as only Reichsdeutsche (citizens of Germany proper) were to be chosen to serve as slave laborers in the brothels. These regulations were not always followed, and Roma and Sinti women, Polish women, and Ukrainian women, as well as political prisoners and "criminals," were sent to official brothels. However, there is no evidence that Jewish women were ever knowingly used for regulated forced sex labor in official concentration camp brothels. Mostly, those selected to serve as prostitutes were in the "asocial" category, including women who had been arrested for prostitution on the outside. There were also regulations for male brothel visitors: in the beginning only Reichsdeutsche were permitted, but later men of other nations (never Russians, Jews, Sinti, or Roma) were allowed this privilege.

The examples of sexualized racist violence given here clearly show how the Nazi definitions of "race" caused women belonging to different groups to be treated differently. For example, Jewish women were generally not subjected to the particular sexualized violence of institutionalized prostitution in camp brothels, because of their affiliation with a "racially" defined group.

Consequences of Sexualized Violence in Concentration Camps

The sexualized violence that women experienced left them with lifelong physical and emotional wounds that they mostly had to address on their own.[40] Today psychological counseling is regularly employed as a component for coping with catastrophes, but none was available for Holocaust survivors coming out of the camps. Victims of sexualized violence often found themselves ostracized by society—a common consequence of the taboos surrounding their violent experiences—and confirmed in the shame that they carried within them. The many examples include women who did not dare to return home because they were ashamed of their relationship with a Polish forced laborer, for which they had been put into a camp; former forced sex workers in prisoner brothels who held silence about their violent experiences until their deaths; women who could not bear children as a result of sexualized violence during incarceration in a concentration camp; Jewish women who as concentration camp survivors arrived in Israel or pre-Israel Palestine and were falsely condemned as having been prostitutes of the SS. Sometimes survivor medical reports failed to acknowledge a connection between imprisonment in a concentration camp and later health problems (such as kidney disease, loss of teeth, extreme nervousness, tumors on the uterus, or miscarriages).

How then were these women supposed to be able to give an account of the violence they had experienced? Similarly, Soviet survivors did not dare to talk about their imprisonment in concentration camps. If they did so, they ran the risk of being accused of having collaborated with the enemy. Here I raise the question of whether we have begun too late to research the sexualized violence of women under Nazi persecution. Unfortunately, earlier researchers did not take notice or were not fully aware of the sexualized violence women had experienced in concentration camps. In addition, the social and political demands made by postwar societies, which sought to quickly forget both the war and related concentration camp experiences prevented many women from speaking about the sexualized violence they had experienced.

Conclusions

The many forms of sexualized violence against women in concentration camps were partly determined by so-called Nazi "racial" ideology. This violence affected Jewish women, and it is clear that the supposedly serious crime of *Rassenschande* did not protect them from sexual assault. Some forms of sexualized violence in concentration camps (such as forced abortion, forced sterilization, and "medical" experiments) especially concerned Jewish women: the Nazis considered their lives worthless and wanted to prevent them from reproducing "inferior" people.

My focus on sexualized violence in concentration camps should not lead to the conclusion that this issue was the sole concern of the imprisoned women. Daily life in concentration camps was marked by extreme hunger, thirst, exhaustion, forced labor, illness, and catastrophic hygienic conditions, as well as by brutality and unrelenting insults from the SS and guards. There was sometimes torture, and there was often death. The violent acts with sexual connotations were just one horrific element among many. In no way is my purpose in this work to sexualize life in the camps or to defuse the crime scene of the concentration and extermination camps as an extraterritorial place of terror completely removed from any norm.[41] Nor is my analysis of female experiences of sexualized violence an attempt to claim that women held only the status of victims. My intent has been to convey specific experiences by women within their societal and political context. The crimes committed in Nazi concentration camps were conceived in the civilian realm. Nevertheless, sexualized violence today is still seen as part of the accepted norms of warfare and continues to be tolerated as a component of patriarchal attitudes toward gender.

Notes

1. Resolution 1820 was adopted by the United Nations Security Council at its 5,916th meeting on June 19, 2008.

2. Insa Eschebach and Regina Mühlhäuser, "Sexuelle Gewalt im Krieg und Sex-Zwangsarbeit in NS-Konzentrationslagern. Deutungen, Darstellungen, Begriffe" [Sexual violence in war and sex-slave labor in NS-concentration camps. Interpretations, analyses, terminology], in *Krieg und Geschlecht. Sexuelle Gewalt im Krieg und Sex-Zwangsarbeit in NS-Konzentrationslagern* [War and gender. Sexual violence in war and forced sex labor], ed. Insa Eschebach and Regina Mühlhäuser (Berlin: Metropol Verlag, 2008), 30.

3. My colleagues and I first formulated this term in 2004 in our monograph on sexualized violence. See Helga Amesberger et al., *Sexualisierte Gewalt. Weibliche Erfahrungen in NS-Konzentrationslagern* [Sexualized violence. Women's experiences in National Socialist concentration camps] (Vienna: Mandelbaum Verlag, 2004).

4. Johan Galtung, *Strukturelle Gewalt. Beiträge zur Friedensforschung* [Structural violence. Essays on peace research] (Reinbek bei Hamburg: Rowohlt, 1975), 9.

5. Forced pregnancies, used as a strategy of war in the former Yugoslavia and in Rwanda, are another serious form of physical sexualized violence. This form of violence was not relevant in the context of Nazi concentration camps.

6. Wajdi Mouawad, *Scorched*, trans. Linda Gaboriau (Toronto: Playwrights Canada Press, 2005), 62.

7. Kirsty Chatwood, "(Re)-Interpreting Stories of Sexual Violence: The Multiple Testimonies of Lucille Eichengreen," in *Life, Death and Sacrifice: Women and Family in the Holocaust*, ed. Esther Hertzog (Jerusalem/New York: Gefen Publishing House, 2008), 161–180, specifically 162. The many sexual attacks on Jewish and Soviet women by the Wehrmacht and SS on the Eastern Front, however, suggest the deliberate use of rape as part of warfare.

8. Miranda Alison, "Sexuelle Gewalt in Zeiten des Kriegs. Menschenrechte für Frauen und Vorstellungen von Männlichkeit" [Sexual violence in times of war. Human rights for women and concepts of masculinity], in *Krieg und Geschlecht*, ed. Eschebach and Mühlhäuser, 35–54, specifically 41.

9. Ruth Seifert, "Krieg und Vergewaltigung. Ansätze zu einer Analyse" [War and rape: Attempts at an analysis], in *Massenvergewaltigung. Krieg gegen die Frauen* [Mass rape. War against women], ed. Alexandra Stiglmayer (Frankfurt: Fischer, 1993), 87–113, here 101, quoted in Alison, "Sexuelle Gewalt," 42.

10. Regina Mühlhäuser, "Handlungsräume. Sexuelle Gewalt durch Wehrmacht und SS in den besetzten Gebieten der Sowjetunion 1941–1945" [Places of action. Sexual violence by the Wehrmacht and SS in the occupied regions of the Soviet Union, 1941–1945], in *Krieg und Geschlecht*, ed. Eschebach and Mühlhäuser, 167–186, 185.

11. Susan Brownmiller, *Against Our Will: Men, Women and Rape* (New York: Fawcett Books, 1975), 15, emphasis in the original.

12. Alison, "Sexuelle Gewalt," 39–40. For a discussion of the different levels of sexualized violence during and after World War II, see Elisabeth Jean Wood, "Sexuelle Gewalt im Krieg. Zum Verständnis unterschiedlicher Formen" in *Krieg und Geschlecht*, ed. Eschebach and Mühlhäuser, 75–102, published in English as "Sexual Violence during War: Toward an Understanding of Variation," in Ian Shapiro, Stathis Kalyvas, and Tarek Masoud, eds., *Order, Conflict, and Violence* (Cambridge: Cambridge University Press, 2008), 321–351. Between 1935 and 1945, some 50,000–200,000 women, most of whom were Korean, were put into brothels by the Imperial Japanese Army. The women became known by the euphemism of "comfort women," a term that completely negates the violence used against them.

13. The term "concentration camp" is used here as an overriding term for concentration and extermination camps; in some ghettos similar conditions of absolute terror prevailed. Sources are primarily biographical interviews with Austrian survivors of Ravensbrück women's concentration camp (hereafter IKF-Rav-Int.), as well as with women who survived the Mauthausen concentration camp (hereafter AMM OH/ZP1).

14. Wolfgang Sofsky, *Die Ordnung des Terrors: Das Konzentrationslager* [The order of terror: The concentration camp] (Frankfurt/Main: Fischer Taschenbuch Verlag, 1999), 27.

15. Because I am mainly concerned with showing the dominance of racist ideology and its propagation in Nazi society, I will use the general term "racism" throughout this chapter, but without equating racism with anti-Semitism or with anti-Gypsy sentiment. As "race" was a Nazi designation, I am placing quotation marks around it. For a comparative analysis of European forms of racism, see Helga Amesberger and Brigitte

Halbmayr, *Das Privileg der Unsichtbarkeit. Rassismus unter dem Blickwinkel von Weißsein und Dominanzkultur* [The privilege of invisibility. Racism from the viewpoint of being white and of the dominant culture] (Vienna: Braumüller, 2008), chapter 3, 41–72. My discussion centers on the fate of Jewish women, but one should keep in mind that the Roma and Sinti were also persecuted based on "race" and were often subjected to similar acts of violence.

16. Marie-José Chombart de Lauwe, France, testimony, AMM OH/ZP1/541, 61.

17. Sofsky, *Die Ordnung des Terrors*, 258. Sofsky calls the network of perpetrators, the relationship of the perpetrators to the victims, and the methods of violence essential factors that determined the nature and course of a violent act in the concentration camp. However, regarding sexualized violence, the difference in gender between perpetrators and victims—here male perpetrators and female victims—has to be seen as yet another determining factor for the form and degree of violence.

18. Sarah Rath and Esther Barko, Israel, testimony, AMM OH/ZP1/46, 12.

19. Zipora Nir, Israel, testimony, AMM OH/ZP1/709, 35.

20. Irma Trksak, testimony, IKF-Rav-Int. 35_3, 7.

21. Regine Chum, testimony, IKF-Rav-Int. 25_1, 16.

22. Slava Primozic, Italy, testimony, AMM OH/ZP1/517, 13.

23. See chapter 5 by Monika J. Flaschka in this volume.

24. See examples from interviews in Amesberger et al., *Sexualisierte Gewalt*, 142–143.

25. Regina Anna Langsam Lewkowicz, Netherlands, testimony, AMM OH/ZP1/547, 30.

26. Irena Liebman, Israel, testimony, AMM OH/ZP1/291, 57.

27. See, for example, chapter 1 by Nomi Levenkron and chapter 7 by Helene Sinnreich in this volume for various testimonies about Jewish men's sexualized violence against Jewish women in ghettos and camps.

28. IKF-Rav-Int. 7_1, 18; see: Amesberger et al., *Sexualisierte Gewalt*, 81.

29. Marta Kos, *Frauenschicksale in Konzentrationslagern* [Destinies of women in concentration camps] (Vienna: Passagen, 1998), 65.

30. Zipora Nir, Israel, testimony, AMM OH/ZP1/709, 14.

31. Loretta Walz, *"Und dann kommst du dahin an einem schönen Sommertag." Die Frauen von Ravensbrück* ["And then they take you there on a fine summer's day." The women of Ravensbrück] (Munich: Kunstmann, 2005), 149.

32. See Janet Anschütz et al., "'. . . dieses leere Gefühl, und die Blicke der anderen . . . ' Sexuelle Gewalt gegen Frauen," ["'. . . this empty feeling and the stares of the others . . .'" Sexual violence against women], in *Frauen in Konzentrationslagern. Bergen-Belsen, Ravensbrück* [Women in concentration camps: Bergen-Belsen, Ravensbrück], ed. Claus Füllberg-Stollberg et al. (Bremen: Edition Temmen, 1994), 123–133.

33. Ibid., 128. The speaker quoted is *Gauhauptstellenleiter* Dr. Fehringer.

34. Forced abortions were also a significant eugenic measure, especially within the walls of the concentration camps. The *Gesetze zur Verhütung erbkranken Nachwuchses* (Laws Preventing Progeny with Hereditary Diseases) of 1934, opened wide possibilities for forced sterilization, including an often undefined group of people with "hereditary dis-

eases." In keeping with this law, at least 40,000 people were forcibly sterilized, a number that represents 1 percent of the reproductive-age population of the German Reich. Approximately 5,500 women and 600 men died following the procedure. See Gisela Bock, "Sterilisationspolitik im Nationalsocialismus. Die Planung einer heilen Gesellschaft durch Prävention" [Sterilization under National Socialism. Planning a healthy society through prevention], in *Fortschritte der Psychiatrie im Umgang mit Menschen. Wert und Verwertung im 20. Jahrhundert* [Advances in psychiatry in dealing with people. Worth and utilization in the 20th century], ed. Klaus Dörner (Rehburg-Loccum: Psychiatrie-Verlag, 1985), 88–104, specifically 88 and 101.

35. See Anja Lundholm, *Das Höllentor, Bericht einer Überlebenden* [The gate to hell, Report of a survivor] (Reinbeck bei Hamburg: Rowohlt, 1988), 182–183.

36. For more information, see chapter 10 by Ellen Ben-Sefer in this volume.

37. Abortions, including forced abortions, on grounds of eugenics were permitted beginning in 1935. After March 1943 these "permitted abortions" also applied to women workers from the East and Polish women. However, according to the *Verordnung zum Schutz von Ehe, Familie und Mutterschaft* (Decree for the Protection of Marriage, Family, and Motherhood), a German woman could be given a death sentence for having an abortion.

38. See Dunja Martin, "Menschenversuche im Krankenrevier des KZ Ravensbrück" [Human experimentation in the sickbay of the Ravensbrück concentration camp], in *Frauen in Konzentrationslagern*, ed. Füllberg-Stollberg et al., as well as chapter 9 by Helga Amesberger in this volume.

39. See chapter 3 by Robert Sommer in this volume. See the following on further aspects of forced sex labor in Nazi concentration camps: Brigitte Halbmayr, "Arbeitskommado 'Sonderbau.' Zur Bedeutung und Funktion von Bordellen im KZ" [Work commando *Sonderbau*. The meaning and function of brothels in the concentration camp], in *Dachauer Hefte. Studien und Dokumente zur Geschichte der nationalsozialistischen Konzentrationslager* [Dachau annual publications. Studies and documents on the history of National Socialist concentration camps], vol. 21, no. 21 (Dachau: Häftlingsgesellschaft, 2005), 217–236; Brigitte Halbmayr, "Sex-Zwangsarbeit in NS-Konzentrationslagern. Fakten, Mythen und Positionen" [Forced sex-labor in Nazi concentration camps: Facts, myths and views], in *Krieg und Geschlecht*, ed. Eschebach and Mühlhäuser, 127–146. In the same publication also see Robert Sommer, "Warum das Schweigen? Berichte von ehemaligen Häftlingen über Sex-Zwangsarbeit in nationalsozialistischen Konzentrationslagern" [Why the silence? Reports of former prisoners about forced sex-labor in Nazi concentration camps], 147–166, as well as Insa Eschebach and Katharina Jedermann, "Sex-Zwangsarbeit in NS-Konzentrationslagern. Anmerkungen zu einer Werkstatt-Ausstellung der Gedenkstätte Ravensbrück" [Forced sex-labor in Nazi concentration camps. Notes on an exhibit of a workshop at the Ravensbrück memorial site], 269–78.

40. See Helga Amesberger and Brigitte Halbmayr, *Vom Leben und Überleben—Wege nach Ravensbrück. Das Frauenkonzentrationslager in der Erinnerung* [Of life and survival—Paths to Ravensbrück. The women's concentration camp in memory), vol. 1, *Dokumentation und*

Analyse [Documentation and analysis] (Vienna: Promedia, 2001), especially the chapter on trauma, 33–51, and on the consequences of persecution and sexualized violence on partnership and motherhood, 301–325.

41. Concerning the problem of sexualizing daily camp life and the extraterritorialization of violent crimes, see Eschebach and Mühlhäuser, "Sexuelle Gewalt im Krieg," 25–26.

3

Sexual Exploitation of Women in Nazi Concentration Camp Brothels

ROBERT SOMMER

The Establishment of Brothels in Concentration Camps

The history of brothels in National Socialist concentration camps has for many years been ignored by historians. Various novels and movies have referred to brothels for SS guards in which Jewish women were raped,[1] but the notion of brothel barracks created for prisoners has seemed completely absurd. Since the 1990s, however, scholars have begun to discover and analyze the so-called *Sonderbauten* (special buildings), the SS euphemism for these brothels.[2]

In the summer of 1941 Heinrich Himmler, together with Oswald Pohl, chief of the *Wirtschafts- und Verwaltungshauptamt* (WVHA)—the economic and administrative main office of the SS[3]—visited the Mauthausen concentration camp and its sub-camp Gusen, near Linz in annexed Austria. There they visited two nearby quarries where camp prisoners extracted granite for Hitler's megalomaniacal construction projects.[4] In October 1941, following that visit, Himmler ordered the establishment of two brothel barracks in those camps. The first was opened in July 1942.[5] The reason for this decision can be found in the desperate need for building material to realize the *Führer's* plans to redesign the major German cities, such as Berlin, Hamburg, Munich, Linz, and Weimar. Himmler's idea was to increase production efficiency by granting selected prisoners the right to frequent a brothel.

In April 1942, Himmler discussed with Hans Kammler (head of the construction branch *Amtsgruppe C* of the WVHA) the productivity of prisoners used as construction workers in the *SS-Baubrigaden*. They were building brigades, which were intended to be used to realize Himmler's construction plans in the context of the *Germanisierung* (Germanizing) of occupied Eastern Europe.

Himmler did not want to accept that the efficiency of camp prisoners was only 50 percent compared to civilian workers. To improve this, he suggested granting in *der freiesten Form* (most free manner) certain privileges to hardworking camp prisoners, such as access to *Weiber in Bordellen* (women in brothels) and *Akkordlohn* (small piecework pay). In his opinion, denying the necessity to "provide" women to satisfy sexual needs of male camp prisoners would be *welt- und lebensfremd* (out of touch with the world and life).[6]

At the same time, IG Farben was building a gigantic chemical factory in Auschwitz-Monowitz, exploiting concentration camp prisoners. The IG Farben management complained to the SS about the low efficiency of the slave workers. Together they discussed the outlines of a *Prämiensystem* (bonus system) for the prisoners working on IG Farben premises. Such bonuses included *Verpflegungszulage* (extra food rations), *Inaussichtstellung der Freiheit* (the promise of an early release from the camp), and the possibility of visiting women in brothels.[7] Soon after that, they introduced a piecework system to the factory construction site. The privilege of early release was neglected by the SS. Instead, in the autumn of 1943 a prisoner brothel was built in Monowitz. In March 1943, the Reichsführer-SS visited Buchenwald, the biggest concentration camp on the territory of the pre-war German Reich, and inspected a nearby rifle factory where camp prisoners worked. In a letter following that visit, he complained to Pohl about the absence of a prisoner brothel in the camp and demanded the design of an *Akkordsystem* (piecework wage system), which he wanted introduced into the entire concentration camp network.[8]

Such a piecework wage system was initiated by the WVHA just a few weeks later in the form of an official order called the *Prämien-Vorschrift* (bonus order).[9] The preface of the bonus order stressed that slave labor in munitions factories was necessary in order to win the war. Over four pages, the SS granted special premiums and privileges to hardworking prisoners, including more frequent mail, (military) haircuts, vouchers for cigarettes, extra food rations, and the right to visit a brothel. These were thought to be effective incentives for boosting the prisoners' performance. According to the bonus order, the prisoners would receive bonus coupons if they fulfilled the work quota. These could then be used to buy cigarettes, food at the camp canteen, or to pay for a visit to the brothel. The brothel visit, a maximum of one per week, was, however, available only to *Spitzenkräfte* (top-notch workers). To go to the brothel, they had to write a short application to the camp commander, who then had to grant permission. The prisoners had to pay two *Reichsmark* in bonus coupons, out of which the forced sex worker in the brothel would receive 0.45, the guarding prisoner 0.05, and the SS 1.50 *Reichsmark*.[10]

The *Prämien-Vorschrift* became a binding order for the camp commanders as well as the companies employing prisoners. The procedure for buying bonus vouchers from the SS and distributing them to the prisoners was agreed upon contractually. In February 1944, the bonus order was modified, and other privileges, such as attending camp movie theaters and sports events, were granted. In addition, the price of a visit to the brothel was reduced to one *Reichsmark*. Despite the fact that neither the SS commanders nor the company's management believed that the bonus system was especially effective in raising productivity, the SS gave clear orders and was adamant in enforcing its implementation.[11] By the end of the Third Reich, camp brothels had been opened in ten of the major concentration camps—Mauthausen and Gusen (July and October 1942), Flossenbürg and Buchenwald (July 1943),[12] Auschwitz-*Stammlager* (main camp) (October 1943),[13] Auschwitz-Monowitz (November 1943),[14] Neuengamme (May 1944),[15] Dachau (April 1944),[16] Sachsenhausen (August 1944),[17] and Mittelbau-Dora (February 1945).[18]

Since the end of the 1930s, the labor of prisoners in Nazi concentration camps had become an increasingly important issue for the SS. Slave labor had been the backbone not only of the commercial enterprises of the SS but also of various major state projects of the Nazis, such as the construction of monumental buildings, German settlement projects in occupied Eastern Europe, and arms production in a time of "total war." Because the time frames for these projects were extremely narrow and the production plans absolutely unrealistic, the low productivity of camp prisoners became a major issue.

The reasons for the low efficiency rates in the concentration camps were the camps' inhuman conditions, low food rations, poor hygiene, and the daily violence. In addition, high productivity was contrary to the survival strategies of prisoners, which included working as little as possible.[19] The solution to the productivity dilemma could have been easily effected through increased food rations for the prisoners, better hygienic conditions, and abrogation of the daily terror. The *Prämiensystem* was destined for failure because it did not seriously improve living conditions. Himmler, however, saw in the bonus system a solution to the efficiency dilemma, and until the end of the war, he ordered the opening of brothel barracks in most of the major concentration camps. Introducing the frequenting of brothels as part of an incentive system to concentration camp prisoners gave the brutal camp reality a new dimension: women were forced to serve as sex laborers as an incentive and privilege for some male prisoners.

The Recruitment of Women for Camp Brothels

Beginning with the construction of the first camp brothels in Mauthausen and Gusen in 1942, the SS selected female prisoners mainly from the female concentration camp of Ravensbrück,[20] but also—in the case of the brothels in Monowitz, Auschwitz-Stammlager, and Mittelbau-Dora—from Auschwitz-Birkenau. The SS used two primary selection strategies. In Ravensbrück and Auschwitz, SS officers asked women who were working in very difficult Kommandos (work squads), such as surface-level construction, to enroll for brothel Kommandos on the false promise that they would be released from the camp after six months of work there. This offer was made especially to young German women who were confined in concentration camps as asozial (asocial) and, preferably, to imprisoned former prostitutes.[21] To them, the so-called freiwillige Meldung (voluntary enlistment) became a decision between life and death and as such must be defined as coerced enlistment.

Polish Auschwitz survivor Krystyna Zywulska describes such a "recruitment." According to her account, the prisoner-overseer and a guard came into her barrack by night and went from one bunk to the next. She recalled, "The female guard asked loudly: 'Who wants to go to Auschwitz, to the town, to the men's camp? There's easy work, civilian clothing, and good food.' She gave an evil and deceitful smile. 'Well, where are the volunteers?'"[22] The infamous head of the protective custody camp, Franz Hössler, also personally recruited women for the camp brothels. He ordered young girls who had to carry out hard physical labor in the open air to report to him, telling them that those who volunteered would get their own rooms, clean clothing, sufficient food and cigarettes, and a daily bath. The women were also promised their release after six months in the brothel—although this promise was never kept.[23] Bearing in mind the catastrophic conditions in the women's camps, it is easy to imagine how attractive the promise of sufficient food and hygiene must have been for the starving, dirty, and sick women, particularly the false promise of release. Many prisoners would have done anything to escape the hell of the concentration camps and their inevitable deaths. A former Auschwitz inmate stated: "Look, if you were in Birkenau, I bet, if they asked you: cut off your four fingers and you'll be free, you would do it."[24] Romek Dubitzki (pseudonym), another Polish survivor, remembered having heard the story of a young woman from Auschwitz-Birkenau who volunteered for a brothel Kommando. She had been working in outdoor work squads and knew she would not be able to survive another winter doing such work. She justified her decision with the words: "Winter is coming and I work in the fields!"[25]

Besides recruitments for prisoner brothels, the SS also searched in Ravens-brück for Polish women whom they exploited sexually in brothels for Ukrainian SS-guardsmen serving at various concentration camps.[26] According to German "race laws," Ukrainian guardsmen were not allowed to have sexual intercourse with German women. That is why the SS established small broth-els especially for them at the concentration camp sites of Flossenbürg, Buch-enwald, the sub-camp Gusen, and possibly at Sachsenhausen.[27] With the opening of these and other prisoner brothels, the SS needed more women for sexual exploitation and employed more drastic recruitment measures. During roll calls, SS officers would walk down the columns of the lined-up prisoners and pick out women they found suitable for a brothel *Kommando*.[28]

A German prisoner, Magdalena Walter (pseudonym) was selected in 1943 at the *Zellenbau* (camp prison) of Ravensbrück for the camp brothel of Buchen-wald.[29] One day the SS told her and other women not to go to work. Instead, Ravensbrück commander Max Koegel and the camp *Oberaufseherin* (female head of guards), as well as the camp commander of Buchenwald, Hermann Pister, lined up the women. They picked out those whom they found suitable for a brothel and wrote down their serial numbers. The selected women were then brought to the camp infirmary, where they had to undress in front of the SS and the camp doctor.[30] After some weeks of quarantine, the women were dressed in their civilian clothes and transported to Weimar in a regular pas-senger train and later in military trucks. When they arrived at the Buchenwald brothel barrack, they were told by the SS that they would receive better food and not be harmed as long as they complied. Magdalena Walter was relieved that she was abducted to a brothel for prisoners, rather than for the SS. She preferred being in the *Sonderbau* to starvation, physically hard work in a road-construction *Kommando*, and being beaten every day by the SS.[31]

Living Conditions and Coping Strategies of Women in Camp Brothels

For many years it was impossible to find out how women selected for camp brothels dealt with their fate. In the 1990s, German activist and writer Christa Paul managed to interview women who had been forced into sexual exploita-tion in concentration camps. Thanks to these interviews, we know more about the living conditions in brothels. The *Sonderbau* in Buchenwald, to which Mag-dalena Walter was abducted, was a wooden barrack in the peripheral area of the prisoners' camp. It was divided into a day room, a room for the SS guard, a medical room, small brothel rooms, and bedrooms, in each of which two forced sex workers slept. The clothing of the women in the Buchenwald brothel consisted of a white plaid skirt, under which they were allowed to wear panties, and a bra. Every morning the women were required to get up at 7:30, wash themselves, and get dressed. During the day they were occupied with cleaning up the barracks and airing the rooms. They could also read nonpolitical books from the camp library, according to Magdalena Walter.[32] This routine suggests a level of civilian normality inside the brothel, but this picture is deceptive. The daily routine was monotonous and consisted of waiting for the "terrible two hours" in the evening, after the male prisoners had finished their daily work.[33] Then, as if she were part of an assembly line, Magdalena Walter had to let the male prisoners use her.

> Now, every night we had to let the men get on top of us for two hours. That meant they could come into the brothel barrack, had to go to the medical room to get an injection, could go to the number—to the prisoner, could do their thing, into the room, on top, down, out, back to the medical room, where they again got an injection. The prisoner had to leave the brothel. We had a bathroom with a certain number of water closets. It didn't lack cleanliness there. And then right away there came the next one. Non-stop. And they didn't have more than a quarter of an hour.[34]

In the beginning, Magdalena Walter tried to fight against her destiny and threatened to stab the first man she had to accept with a pair of nail scissors, but she did not have any choice other than to submit to the forced sex labor. The terror in the Ravensbrück concentration camp had broken her will to resist, and her life did not count anymore. Her reaction showed the typical concentration camp apathy. Her feelings were deadened. Magdalena Walter was released from the Buchenwald camp at the end of 1944. The reason for that release is unknown.[35]

In another interview by Christa Paul, with a woman who had to suffer in the camp brothel of Mittelbau-Dora, the survivor explains that the women had few opportunities to resist. There was often nothing they could do but bear their fate, as they were already mentally broken by their long imprisonment in concentration camps and faced almost certain death if they rebelled. Linda Bachmann (pseudonym), who was abducted to the Mittelbau-Dora camp brothel in 1945, reported:

> We put up with our fate. We always said: it's still better than in Ravensbrück or Bergen-Belsen. What can you do? Do you want to stand up against it? We did so

much. Well, deep down, of course, it was a shock, that's understandable, isn't it? You know, we were so deadened by the whole thing and everything. We practically had—you know, even in Ravensbrück, when you woke up in the morning, you were lying next to a dead body. You know, it's all so. And if you said to the senior prisoner, there's a dead body here, then she just said: "yes, throw it down." You see? And you know—you only look out for yourself. I never thought I'd survive or anything. I was so deadened by the whole thing, and I'd practically said goodbye to my life.[36]

In an attempt to at least partially escape the omnipotence and control of the SS, some women from the camp brothels maintained personal relationships with a male, usually a privileged prisoner.[37] Such "rational relationships," as the historian Anna Hájková called them, were a well-known survival strategy in ghettos such as Theresienstadt, as well as in camps where male and female prisoners could meet, such as, especially, Auschwitz-Birkenau.[38] In such "rational relationships," men would provide women with food and protection and receive sexual services in exchange. In the case of the camp brothels (not only in Auschwitz but in other camps such as Buchenwald),[39] in addition to giving their chosen women extra food rations and protection, men would seek to spare them by bribing other men not to have sex with them The SS tried to hinder these closer contacts by making the women change rooms constantly so the male prisoners could not know to which woman they were to be assigned. In Auschwitz, black marketeering increased with the opening of the camp brothel. Prisoners smuggled clothes and valuable items from *Kanada*, where the belongings of the gassed Jews were stored, to the brothel in Auschwitz to attract the attention of a particular woman.[40] Some prisoners went and visited their "lover" at night.[41] If the SS caught them, it usually meant their death. Since such punishments were unable to prevent these relationships, the SS repeatedly exchanged the women in camp brothels.[42]

The Dimension of Sex Slave Work in Nazi Concentration Camps

The camp brothels were organized with high-level bureaucratic effort. Women were regularly tested for sexually transmitted diseases, and their stay in a brothel *Kommando* was marked in their *Häftlings-Personal-Karten* (prisoner personnel cards). The money the SS collected as vouchers from the brothel visitors was accounted for daily. Many of those documents survived the war. Thanks to the existence of digital databases and the capacity to access archives that collected those documents—such as the United States Holocaust Memorial Museum Archives, the United States National Archives, and, especially, the Archives of the International Tracing Service of the Red Cross—it is possible to reconstruct the history of the ten concentration camp brothels. Furthermore, it is possible to make confident statements about the number, nationality, and reasons for detainment of almost all of the forced sex workers in the Nazi concentration camps.[43]

The names of a total of 174 forced sex workers can be identified: 168 of them were in prisoner brothels, and eight in brothels for Ukrainian SS guards.[44] According to testimonies and SS documents, the total number of all women in brothels in Nazi concentration camps may be estimated at 210 (190 in prisoner brothels and 20 in brothels for Ukrainian SS men). In addition, 11 female prisoners can be identified as prisoner guards and accountants for the brothels. The SS called these women *Puffmütter* (brothel madams). Thus we have information on 83 percent of all forced sex workers in the concentration camps.

Of the forced sex workers known by name, 114 were of German nationality.[45] Of those women, 88 were registered as asocial prisoners, nine as political prisoners,[46] and four as criminals. The SS changed the registered reason of imprisonment during two prisoners' camp internment.[47] Forty-six women were Polish (26 percent), while three others (2 percent) had—according to different documents—either Polish or German citizenship. Six women (4 percent) were classified as Russian, but according to their names or birthplaces, were in fact of Ukrainian or Belorussian descent. In four other cases (2 percent), the names do not give precise information on the women's heritage, but they were surely of Slavic origin—probably Polish, Ukrainian, or Belorussian. The SS usually classified citizens of the Soviet Union as Russian. One woman was Dutch (1 percent). In the cases of four other sex slave workers, nationality cannot be identified. However, according to their names, they were surely Eastern Europeans.

SS documents give additional information in the case of 149 women regarding the reasons for their detainment. Ninety-eight of them were classified as asocial (66 percent); 44 women were political prisoners (30 percent); and 4, criminals (3 percent).[48] All women whom the SS sexually exploited in a brothel for Ukrainian guards had, according to analyzed documents, Polish nationality. Most of them were categorized as asocial prisoners. At least one of them was sent to a concentration camp because she had had a prohibited sexual relationship with a German man.[49]

There is only one known case of a Jewish woman connected to an official camp brothel. On a slip that accompanied blood samples to be tested for syphilis at the Weimar-Buchenwald Hygiene Institute, taken by the Mittelbau-Dora concentration camp doctor, eleven names of women were listed. Nine of them were German, one was Dutch, and one was classified as Jewish.[50] The document does not explicitly mention that those women were from the brothel, but other documents—such as camp infirmary access lists—state that those women were in the camp's *Sonderbau*.[51] Berta G., the Jewish woman, probably was not a sex slave worker but had to work as a *Puffmutter* at the brothel. Before she was forced to do that job, a woman who had been sent to a concentration camp as a Jehovah's Witness had done the accounting. Since there was much corruption among the SS in Mittelbau-Dora, SS leaders probably wanted to use prisoners whom they found reliable to work as accountants. Jehovah's Witnesses, in particular, had the reputation of being honest and trustworthy. Berta G. was most likely chosen because of the centuries-old stereotype of Jews being capable bankers.[52]

Although it is not 100 percent certain that no Jewish women were inside an official concentration camp brothel, chances are slim. First, more than 80 percent of all women who had to serve in a camp brothel are known to us, and among them there is no evidence of a Jewish woman being sexually exploited. It might be possible that among the Polish women there were Jewish women hiding their identity. Officially, the SS did not recruit or select Jewish women to be sexually exploited in camp brothels. However, there is evidence that Jewish women were sexually abused or raped by SS guards in extermination camps such as Treblinka, Sobibor, or Bełżec, where there existed an atmosphere of mass murder, corruption, and insanity.[53] In addition, we know of sexual relationships between Jewish women and non-Jewish men in Auschwitz, and they, too, could have the character of sexual exploitation.[54]

In contrast to the extermination camps, concentration camp brothels were strictly regulated and supervised. They even were organized according to valid prostitution laws in Nazi Germany. On September 9, 1939, a few days after the German invasion of Poland, the interior minister enacted an order regarding the police treatment of prostitution. Prostitutes were obliged to register, be confined in brothels, and tested for gonorrhea and syphilis by state health authorities. Furthermore, Germans were strictly prohibited from visiting foreign prostitutes, who in turn were prohibited from servicing Germans. Even Nazi race laws applied. It became illegal for Jewish women to work as prostitutes, as well as for Jewish men to visit "Aryan" prostitutes.[55] Those rules also applied in the camp brothels. Only "Aryan" prisoners were allowed to visit a *Sonderbau*.[56] Jews and Soviet POWs were at all times excluded.[57] Most of the visitors were prisoner-functionaries, such as *Lagerälteste* (senior camp prisoners), block elders, *Kapos* (supervising prisoners), but also prisoners from privileged work squads such as the *Lagerschutz* (camp police), *Lagerfeuerwehr* (camp fire brigade), *Küche* (kitchen), *Frisör* (camp barber), *Krankenbau* (camp infirmary), or *Metzgerei* (butcher). Those prisoners were very often Germans, and in the case of Auschwitz, often Polish. Since they were the visitors to camp brothels and the SS enforced the laws of ethnic segregation as is known from testimonies, it is logical that the SS selected mostly German or Polish women.[58]

Conclusions

Setting up prisoners' brothels in concentration camps and recruiting women for these brothels brought a shocking new dimension to the violence in concentration camps. Not only did the Nazis exploit prisoners until their deaths (and beyond), they now also forced women to make their bodies available to maximize this exploitation. The SS consciously tried to find women who "volunteered" for the brothels, in order to conceal the element of force behind the prostitution. This shifted the blame to the victims, and thus away from themselves.[59] However, the brothels did not operate on a voluntary basis by any means. The French philosopher Norbert Campagna defines the element of force in prostitution according to three points: the decision in favor of prostitution, the choice of practices and customers, and the freedom to give up prostitution.[60] Even the indirect element of force through the inhumane conditions in the women's camp and the false promises of release show that women's decisions to join the brothels were not made voluntarily. Additionally, the forced character is particularly clear in the organization of the brothels: the SS had absolute power over the women, determining their daily routine and the men with whom they were forced to have intercourse. The sex slave workers could not reject these men. Nor could women leave the brothels voluntarily. The SS alone determined how long each woman spent working in a brothel.

It is also apparent that women in camp brothels had higher chances of survival than women in the outdoor work details in Birkenau. As yet, we have no evidence of a woman who died in a brothel *Kommando*.[61] Thus, sexual forced labor in a concentration camp brothel can certainly be described as a survival strategy. Yet the price for this survival was high. Not only did it require accepting one's own sexual exploitation, but camp brothels also meant a lifelong stigma. The subject of sexual exploitation in concentration camps was excluded from the collective memory. Women who had been sent to a concentration camp by the National Socialists because they were considered asocial did not receive recognition or restitution after the war. In West Germany, those who were persecuted as asocials during the Third Reich were not accepted as victims of National Socialist injustice according to the 1953 *Bundesentschädigungsgesetz* (federal compensation law). Only at the end of the 1980s were victims able to ask for money on the basis of extralegal regulations for instances of hardship, and then only on an individual basis. In East Germany, they were excluded from the group of "political and racial" victims of the Nazi regime and could only expect compensation payments if they integrated into the socialist society of the Soviet occupation zone and the German Democratic Republic. In the 1990s former "asocial" prisoners were accorded recognition as victims of the National Socialist regime. It is due to the outstanding work of researchers such as Christa Paul that we are now aware of these women's situations. The subject of concentration camp brothels is now openly discussed in Germany, yet more than sixty years after the end of the war, very few of these women have received public recognition or rehabilitation. These are unlikely to be granted in the future, as we can assume that almost all of the women are now dead.

The magnitude of sexual exploitation in camp brothels, compared to the enormity of the violence generally present in the camps, was rather small. The fact that there were only about two hundred women in all concentration camp brothels shows that the possibility of surviving the brothel *Kommando* was very high and, furthermore, that camp brothels had little relevance for most of camp prisoners. But one must look at the quality, rather than the quantity, of this type of exploitation. It reveals a new cynical dimension of the Nazi terror: to exploit the labor of male prisoners, a few were granted the right to sexually exploit women who were forced into prostitution. In that way, the SS brought perfidy to a new extreme in which victims themselves became perpetrators.

Notes

1. See the most prominent example: Ka-Tzetnik 135633, *House of Dolls*, 1st ed. (London: Panther, 1958). For more about Ka-Tzetnik, see chapter 12 by Miryam Sivan in this volume.

2. See Christa Schulz, "Weibliche Häftlinge aus Ravensbrück in den Bordellen der Männerkonzentrationslager" [Female prisoners from Ravensbrück in brothels of concentration camps for males], in *Frauen in Konzentrationslagern: Bergen-Belsen Ravensbrück* [Women in concentration camps: Bergen-Belsen Ravensbrück], ed. Claus Füllberg–Stolberg, Martina Jung, Renate Riebe, and Martina Scheitenberger (Bremen: Edition

Temmen, 1994), 135–146; Christa Paul, *Zwangsprostitution. Staatlich errichtete Bordelle im Nationalsozialismus* [Forced prostitution. Brothels established by the Nazi German state] (Berlin: Edition Hentrich, 1994); Christa Schikorra, "Prostitution weiblicher Häftlinge als Zwangsarbeit. Zur Situation 'asozialer' Häftlinge im Frauen-KZ Ravensbrück" [Prostitution of female concentration camp prisoners as slave labor. On the situation of "asocial" prisoners in the Ravensbrück women's concentration camp], *Dachauer Hefte*, no. 16 (2000): 112–124; Robert Sommer, "Der Sonderbau. Die Errichtung von Bordellen in nationalsozialistischen Konzentrationslagern" [The Sonderbau. The establishment of brothels in National Socialist concentration camps] (master's thesis, Humboldt University, Berlin, 2003, and Morrisville: Lulu.com, 2006); Helga Amesberger, Karin Auer, and Brigitte Halbmayr, *Sexualisierte Gewalt. Weibliche Erfahrungen in NS-Konzentrationslager* [Sexualized violence: Female experiences in Nazi concentration camps] (Vienna: Mandelbaum, 2004); Robert Sommer, *Das KZ-Bordell. Sexuelle Zwangsarbeit in nationalsozialistischen Konzentrationslagern* [The camp brothel: Sexual forced labor in National Socialist concentration camps] (Paderborn: Schöningh, 2009).

3. The WVHA was the primary administrative office of all commercial and industrial enterprises of the SS, including the concentration camp system.

4. See Hans Maršálek, *Die Geschichte des Konzentrationslagers Mauthausen. Dokumentation* [The history of the concentration camp Mauthausen. Documentation] (Vienna: Österreichische Lagergemeinschaft Mauthausen, 1980), 177.

5. Entry of Tätigkeitsbericht Nr. 2 (duty report), October 8, 1941, in Archives of the Mauthausen Memorial (AMM), without signature; *Bordellbuch Block 3* (visitor lists), in AMM K2–1.

6. Himmler to Pohl, April 23, 1942, in Archive of the Institut für Zeitgeschichte (Munich), MA 30/0812.

7. See *Wochenbericht Nr. 54* (weekly report) of IG Farben for the time between June 1–7, 1942 , in Archive of the State Museum Auschwitz-Birkenau (APMO), D-Au III/4/2.

8. Himmler to Pohl, March 23, 1942, in Bundesarchiv Berlin-Lichterfelde (BArch), NS 19/2065.

9. See *Dienstvorschrift für die Gewährung von Vergünstigungen an Häftlinge. Prämien-Vorschrift* [Official regulations granting prisoner privileges. Bonus regulations], May 15, 1943, in BArch, NS 3/426.

10. Ibid.

11. See *1. Nachtrag zur Dienstvorschrift für die Gewährung von Vergünstigungen an Häftlinge* [1. Addendum to official regulations granting prisoner privileges], February 14, 1944, in BArch, NS 3/427.

12. See *Vollzugsmeldung Errichtung Sonderbau* [Report on construction of special buildings], March 25, 1944, BArch, NS 4 Fl/185. In Buchenwald, the first daily financial account of the camp dates from July 11, 1943. See "Daily financial accounts of camp brothel," in BArch, NS 4 Bu/41.

13. The first VD examination of 21 women of brothel block 24a began on October 4, 1943. See test-tube information slips for blood and cervical smear samples of block 24a, in Archive of the State Museum of Auschwitz-Birkenau (APMO), Akta HI 391/20a.

14. The first known VD examination of eight women from the Monowitz brothel *Kommando* is dated November 15, 1943. See test-tube information slips for blood and cervical smear samples of Monowitz, in APMO, Akta HI 1201/23.

15. See Hermann Kaienburg, 'Vernichtung durch Arbeit.' Der Fall Neuengamme ["Extermination through labor." The case of Neuengamme] (Bonn: J. H. W. Dietz, 1991), 411.

16. See Kerstin Engelhardt, "Frauen im Konzentrationslager Dachau" [Women in the Dachau concentration camp], Dachauer Hefte, no. 14 (1998): 223.

17. See Odd Nansen, Von Tag zu Tag. Ein Tagebuch [From day to day: A diary] (Hamburg: Hans Dulk, 1949), 187–188.

18. See transport list of women for the camp brothel from KZ Bergen-Belsen to Mittelbau-Dora, February 18, 1945, in Archive of the Memorial Mittelbau-Dora, DMD, D1b, Bd.5, 113.

19. See Sommer, "Der Sonderbau," 30–33.

20. From May 1939 to April 1945, Ravensbrück, located north of Berlin, was the main women's concentration camp. Over 130,000 female prisoners passed through the Ravensbrück camp system by the end of the war. Only about 40,000 survived. The inmates came from every country in German-occupied Europe, and about 20 percent were Jewish. On the history of Ravensbrück see Bernd Strebel, Das KZ Ravensbrück. Geschichte eines Lagerkomplexes [The concentration camp Ravensbrück: History of a camp complex] (Paderborn: Schöningh, 2003); Rochelle G. Saidel, The Jewish Women of Ravensbrück Concentration Camp (Madison: University of Wisconsin Press, 2004).

21. See secret letter, Himmler to Pohl, November 15, 1942 (document 1583-PS), in Internationaler Militärgerichtshof Nürnberg, Der Prozess gegen die Hauptkriegsverbrecher. Urkunden und anderes Beweismaterial [Trial of the major war criminals before the International Military Tribunal. Documents and other means of evidence], vols. 3–9 (Nuremberg: Komet MA-Service- u. Verlags-GmbH, 1948), 349.

22. Krystina Zywulska, Wo vorher Birken standen. Überlebensbericht einer jungen Frau aus Auschwitz-Birkenau [Where birch trees used to stand. Survivor testimony of a young woman from Auschwitz-Birkenau] (Darmstadt: Verlag Darmstädter Blätter, 1980), 58.

23. Ella Lingens, quoted in Hermann Langbein, Menschen in Auschwitz [People in Auschwitz] (Vienna/Munich: Europaverlag, 1995), 595. The pseudonymous former prisoner and camp fireman Romek Dubitzki discovered this promise from a friend who had to interpret for Hössler. See Dubitzki, interviewed by Robert Sommer, 2004–04–06 D., pt. 2, min 01.00 (all Sommer interviews are in the archive of the author); see also Roy Tanenbaum, Prisoner 88: The Man in Stripes (Calgary: University of Calgary Press, 1998), 44.

24. Interview, Sommer 2005–01–28 S., pt. 1, 00.24.00.

25. Interview, Sommer 2004–04–06 D., pt. 1, 00.44.0.

26. Ukrainian guardsmen, also called Trawniki men, were recruited among Soviet POWs and trained at Trawniki camp. As foreign racial-ethnic (fremdvölkische) SS men, they served as guards in extermination camps of the Aktion Reinhardt, as well as in concentrations camps. See Israel Gutman, ed., Enzyklopädie des Holocaust. Die Verfolgung und Ermordung der europäischen Juden [Encyclopedia of the Holocaust. The persecution and

murder of the Jews of Europe] (Munich: Piper, 1998), 1425. (Also available in English, New York: Macmillan, 1995.)

27. See Christa Paul and Robert Sommer, "SS-Bordelle und Oral History. Problematische Quellen und die Existenz von Bordellen für die SS in Konzentrationslagern" [SS brothels and oral history: Problematic sources and the existence of brothels for SS men in concentration camps], BIOS, no. 19 (1/2006): 134–137; Sommer, Das KZ-Bordell, 46.

28. See Henryka O. testimony, in interview, Sommer, 2002–03–16 O., 00.08.00.

29. She was in the prison because she had been caught stealing potatoes in Ravensbrück. See Paul, Zwangsprostitution, 49.

30. See M. W. interview, 15 November 1988, in Werkstatt der Erinnerung Hamburg (WdE) [Workshop of Remembrance Hamburg], Sig. 295, 20. Passages from the interview are in Paul, Zwangsprostitution, 51.

31. Ibid.

32. See M. W. testimony in Rosemarie Mieder and Geslinde Schwarz, Alles für zwei Mark. Das Häftlingsbordell von Buchenwald [All of that for only two Reichsmark: The prisoner brothel of Buchenwald], Radio feature of the MDR 2002, http://www.mdr.de/DL/4051258.pdf (accessed 11 November 2007).

33. Paul, Zwangsprostitution, 56.

34. M. W. testimony in Mieder and Schwarz, Alles für zwei Mark.

35. See Paul, Zwangsprostitution, 54, 57; M. W. testimony in Christa Paul and Reinhild Kassing; L. B. testimony in Werkstatt der Erinnerung Hamburg (WdE), Sig. 295, 10.

36. L. B. interview in WdE, Sign. 294T, 21.

37. See L. B. and M. W. testimony in Paul, Zwangsprostitution, 48; Anna Hájková, "Strukturen weiblichen Verhaltens in Theresienstadt" [The structures of women's behavior in Terezin], in Genozid und Geschlecht. Jüdische Frauen im nationalsozialistischen Lagersystem [Genocide and gender: Jewish women in the concentration camp system], ed. Gisela Bock (Frankfurt/Main: Campus Verlag, 2005).

38. See Na'ama Shik, "Weibliche Erfahrung in Auschwitz-Birkenau" [Female experience in Auschwitz-Birkenau], in Bock, Genozid und Geschlecht, 103–122.

39. See Paul, Zwangsprostitution, 56.

40. This was also the case in other concentration camps. In June 1944, the Dachau brothel was searched by the SS. An investigation eventually led to the closing of the brothel at the end of 1944. See Edgar Kupfer-Koberwitz, Dachauer Tagebücher. Die Aufzeichnungen des Häftlings 24814 [Dachau diaries. The notes of prisoner 24814] (Munich: Kindler, 1997), 293.

41. Stephan Szymanski (pseudonym) explained how he visited his "lover," a Polish girl, at the Auschwitz brothel a few times at night. See interview, Sommer, 2005–01–28 S., pt.1, 00.51.00–01.08.00.

42. In one case the SS exchanged the sex slave workers of the Dachau camp brothel with women from the camp brothel in Gusen. See Sommer, Das KZ-Bordell, 143–145.

43. The types of documents in which we can find detailed information are transport lists, brothel invoice sheets, test-tube information slips for blood and cervical smear samples, brothel visitor lists, WVHA prisoner cards, and, in particular, prisoners' per-

sonnel cards. Robert Sommer, Forced Sex Labor in Nazi Concentration Camps, database, update January 2009, personal files of the author.

44. Two of these Polish women were forced to work in the camp brothel of Mauthausen as well as in the brothel for Ukrainian guards in Gusen. See International Tracing Service of the Red Cross, Bad Arolsen (ITS), envelope T/D 1033117 and T/D 1948659. Nine other sex slave workers can be identified by their camp serial number as well as by the logic of the distribution of serial numbers. Sommer, Forced Sex Labor, database.

45. This number includes women from annexed Austria. One woman was a native of Lorraine.

46. Three of them were imprisoned in a concentration camp because of sexual intercourse with a Polish man. Sommer, Forced Sex Labor, database.

47. See Sommer, Das KZ-Bordell, 145, 226.

48. The prisoners' category cannot be identified in the cases of only eleven German women. In three cases they and their given nationality vary from "asocial German" to "political Poles." Sommer, Forced Sex Labor, database. These numbers differ from previously published numbers, such as those in Robert Sommer, "Camp Brothels: Forced Sex Labour in Nazi Concentration Camps," in Brutality and Desire: War and Sexuality in Europe's Twentieth Century, ed. Dagmar Herzog (New York: Palgrave Macmillan, 2009), 175. Those numbers are based on knowledge of only 145 women's reasons for detainment. After analyzing records from the ITS at Bad Arolsen, more detailed information concerning four other forced sex laborers is now known.

49. Sommer, Forced Sex Labor, database.

50. See Begleitzettel, 24.3.1945, ITS, Ablage, T/D 1012870. Another woman who was forced to work in the Dachau camp brothel was classified on a WVHA prisoner card as a Jew but on three other documents as a German "political" prisoner. The classification as a Jew was most likely a mistake. See Sommer, Das KZ-Bordell, 158.

51. See Zugangsliste Krankenbau Mittelbau-Dora [Hospital admission list Mittelbau-Dora], 27 and 28.3.1945, USHMM, RG 04.006M Reel 18.

52. A few arguments support this theory. First, eleven women were mentioned on the list. The brothel had only ten rooms, so the maximum number of sex slave workers had to be ten. All the other women fit due to their age and nationality in the selection grid for sex slave workers. Moreover, this is the only case known in which the name of a Jewish woman is found on a list mentioning the camp brothel. See Sommer, Das KZ-Bordell, 158.

53. See account of Jankiel Wiernik, in The Death Camp Treblinka: A Documentary, ed. Alexander Donat (New York: Holocaust Library, 1979).

54. See Langbein, Menschen in Auschwitz, 598.

55. It is stated: "Therein we have to take the general race policies into account . . . Thus Jewish prostitutes are categorically excluded [from prostitution]." See Vertrauliches Rundschreiben [Confidential report] 9.9.1939, in Generallandesarchiv Karlsruhe (GLAK), 330 Zug. 1991/34/Nr. 136. Today there is only one known case of a state-run brothel for Jews in the Third Reich. The Gestapo organized a brothel in Hamburg near Valentins-kamp with money from the Jewish community, but it soon closed because of too few

requests. See Michaela Freund-Widder, *Frauen unter Kontrolle. Prostitution und ihre staatliche Bekämpfung in Hamburg vom Ende des Kaiserreiches bis zu den Anfängen der Bundesrepublik* [Women under control: Prostitution and governmental restrictions in Hamburg from the end of the German Empire until the beginning of the Federal Republic of Germany] (Münster: LIT Verlag, 2003), 176.

56. See Paul, *Zwangsprostitution*, 76; Robert Sommer, "'Sonderbau' und Lagergesellschaft. Die Bedeutung von Bordellen in den KZ," ["Sonderbau" and prisoner society: The significance of brothels in concentration camps], in *Theresienstädter Studien und Dokumente 2006*, ed. Jaroslava Milotová, Michael Wögerbauer, and Anna Hájková (Prague: Sefer, 2007), 303; Sommer, *Das KZ-Bordell*, 175.

57. For example, see Halbreich testimony in APMO, Ośw/Halbreich/1939, 108; interview, Sommer 2004–06–15 D., 00.07.00; interview, Sommer 2003–05–05 P. 2, 20.

58. See interview, Sommer 2005–01–28 S., 00. 54.00.

59. For example, the former camp commander Franz Hössler stated: "The girls for these brothels were chosen by doctors in the camp. To the best of my knowledge, Dr. Klein and Dr. Mengele carried out this selection from volunteers whom I had chosen." Statement by Franz Hössler in APMO/Ośw./Hössler/329/ 152.

60. See Norbert Campagna, *Prostitution. Eine philosophische Untersuchung* [Prostitution: A philosophical analysis] (Berlin: Parerga Verlag, 2005), 176.

61. For detailed information see Sommer, *Das KZ-Bordell*, 346.

4

Schillinger and the Dancer

Representing Agency and Sexual Violence in Holocaust Testimonies

KIRSTY CHATWOOD

The story of the death of SS *Oberscharführer* Josef Schillinger, who was shot by a female inmate in the undressing room of the Birkenau gas chamber on October 23, 1943, occupies an interesting space in terms of Holocaust literature. At the most basic "factual" level, the story of Schillinger and the dancer is the story of the death of SS man Josef Schillinger and the wounding of SS man Wilhelm Emmerich by a female prisoner, generally described as a dancer on her way to the gas chamber in Birkenau. It appears in numerous witness testimonies under the rubric of "resistance" and is a very important signifier of resistance within Auschwitz. Reading the multiple, and frequently conflicting, testimonies reveals a subtext of sexual violence, where Schillinger is identified not only as a brutal SS officer but also as a sexual predator.[1] At the same time, the dancer's sexuality is itself presented as a source of power since, as a story of resistance, the key point is the way in which the dancer uses her sexual identity to lull the SS officer into a false sense of his own masculine superiority. By displaying her femininity to disarm and kill him, she is effectively reversing the rape narrative.

The tension between competing discourses of sexual violence and resistance makes this an interesting starting point for an analysis not only of sexual violence and agency but also of stories of "sex for survival" (a form of coercive prostitution whereby food and other basic necessities are paid for with sexual acts), which is usually understood in terms of the victimization of women.[2] In this chapter I seek to complicate both the representation of "Schillinger and the Dancer" as a story and the idea of sex for survival by exploring the way in which they intersect with the concept of resistance. I suggest that in both the dancer's situation and in employing sex for survival, agency (and therefore resistance) consists of choosing compliance or noncompliance. Comparing the representations of resistance and sexual violence in the narrative of the death of SS man Schillinger to the representations of resistance and sexual violence in stories of sex for survival demonstrates the complexities of defining both sexual violence and resistance when they are dependent on multiple and conflicting witness testimonies.

To demonstrate the complexity of the relationships between resistance, agency, and sexual violence, it is worth exploring in detail the contrasting versions of the story that appear in the testimonies of countless survivors. I am aware, however, of only four testimonies from prisoners who were actually working in the Sonderkommando (gas chamber and crematoria crew) when the incident happened: those of Filip Müller, Shlomo Dragon, Ya'akow Silderberg, and Stanislaw Jankowski. (Jankowski's brief mention of the incident makes it difficult to establish whether he was actually in the undressing room at the time of the incident or simply working for the Sonderkommando in the vicinity.[3])

Witnesses to Sexual Violence and Resistance

These four stories, while possibly the most factually correct, are not the only testimonies to tell the story of the death of Schillinger. Indeed, while the exact number of actual witnesses to this event is small, the event itself became a part of camp lore within Auschwitz, and it is mentioned by survivors Kitty Hart-Moxon, Benjamin Jacobs, Wieslaw Kielar, Petro Mirchuk, and Sara Nomberg-Przytyk, to name but a few. Kommandant Rudolf Höss and SS Rottenführer Perry Broad also recalled the event, although the latter, a functionary of the Politische Abteilung in the Auschwitz complex, mentions it only in passing.[4] The importance of this story for witnesses is evident in its strength as it passed by word of mouth throughout the camp, as well as the number of witnesses (who clearly outnumber the actual witnesses) who have included it in their testimonies as a part of their experience. Because of the trajectory of the story throughout the camp, not all witnesses are factually correct in their interpretation, but their representations in terms of either resistance or sexual violence remain similar.

Stanislaw Jankowski, who survived three years in the Sonderkommando, mentions the fate of 1,750 people who had thought they were being transferred from Warsaw to Switzerland, but instead ended up in Auschwitz-Birkenau.

When informed of their imminent deaths by a member of the *Kanada Kommando* (unit that sorted inmates' clothing and possessions), all rose up against the SS guards.[5] In Jankowski's telling, the unidentified young woman who stole the gun was simply one of these people.[6] Ya'akow Silderberg describes the woman "as a dancer, a beautiful woman," but says he does not know how she managed to get a gun and shoot an unnamed SS man.[7] Shlomo Dragon, who was working in the undressing hall at the time of the incident, states that the woman simply refused to get undressed, infuriating SS Schillinger, and that when he turned his weapon on her she hit him with her bra and then grabbed the gun off the floor.[8] Dragon describes the tumult in the room but says that all the prisoners, including the *Sonderkommando*, were removed from the undressing room. And when they were sent back to continue their work, the bodies of the woman and SS Schillinger were lying on the floor. Dragon did not know the identity of the woman but later was told that she was an actress. In Dragon's testimony, the act of resistance does not necessarily involve the use of sexuality as a form of agency but is simply presented as the panicked reaction of a woman in a death camp. However, it is notable that she uses a bra to assault Schillinger, implying that she had just bared her breasts.

The Web site Women and the Holocaust: A Cyberspace of Their Own places this story firmly within a paradigm of resistance, publishing it in its "Women of Valor: Partisans and Resistance Fighters" section.[9] According to this account, the woman, who is identified as Polish music-hall dancer Franceska Mann, arrived in Auschwitz-Birkenau from Bergen-Belsen in a transport of 1,700 people, many of whom had foreign passports and thought they were being traded for German soldiers. Mann does shoot SS Schillinger to death, but she uses her feminine, and implicitly sexualized, pre-war identity as a music-hall dancer to commit the act. The implication is that SS Schillinger was more likely to have perceived Mann as nonthreatening because she was a woman. Mann's resistance is defined in terms of (male) military violence: her identity as a woman enticed the SS officer, but she committed the act of resistance as a Jew. Using her sexuality to commit (male) violence allows Mann to transgress her gendered identities, but the competing contexts of sexual violence and agency subsume the transgression under the rubric of male resistance.

The actual identity of the women is open to question as different witness testimonies identify her in different ways. For instance, Ukrainian survivor-witness Petro Mirchuk refers to the woman as a "Greek Jewish girl [who] was a dancer and physically fit." K. T. Czelny describes the woman as a Polish-Jewish actress and places the event on the unloading ramp in Auschwitz-

Birkenau, while Kitty Hart-Moxon claims the woman arrived on a Polish transport and does not name Schillinger but refers to him as a *Rapportführer*.[10]
Furthermore, in Hart-Moxon's story, the woman is not exceptional but only
one of many who rebel against their imminent death, a view that coincides
with that of Benjamin Jacobs, who briefly refers to this story as one of resistance that brought hope to the other prisoners.[11] Neither Mirchuk, Czelny,
Hart-Moxon, nor Jacobs perceived the event in terms of sexual violence. However, Wieslaw Kielar, who was arrested as a member of the Polish resistance
and was a relatively privileged prisoner in the Auschwitz complex, tells the
story of Schillinger and the dancer not only in terms of resistance but also in
terms of the sexual vulnerability of women in the camp. According to Kielar:

> This is what was supposed to have happened: Schillinger, eager as always, was
> assisting that night on the ramp during the reception of a new transport of Jews,
> in the company of his crony *Hauptscharführer* Emmerich. Both of them, slightly
> drunk, accompanied the transport to the crematorium. They even entered the
> changing room, guided either by thoughts of a little stealing or in anticipation of
> the sadistic enjoyment of watching the timid, defenseless, undressed women
> who moments later were to die a painful death in the gas chamber.
>
> The latter version seemed to me to be the more likely, if one considered Schil-
> linger's predilections, particularly when he was drunk. His attention was drawn
> to a young and reputedly beautiful woman who refused to undress in the pres-
> ence of the SS men. Incensed, Schillinger went up to the woman and tried to pull
> down her brassiere. In the struggle she managed to snatch his pistol, with which
> she shot Schillinger dead and injured Emmerich, who had come to Schillinger's
> aid, in the leg. Simultaneously, the other Jews tried to lock the doors from the
> inside. Upon hearing shots, the SS men who had been standing outside rushed
> into the changing room and, realizing what had happened, began to massacre
> everybody. Of this group of Jews, none died in the gas chamber; the enraged SS
> men shot them all.[12]

Like Hart-Moxon and Jacobs, Kielar emphasizes the importance of Schillinger's death for the growth of the camp's resistance movement. However, it
is notable that he stresses the sexual vulnerability of women while juxtaposing
it to their ability to use their sexuality as a form of individual agency, even at the
final stage of murder. Given that Kielar did not work in the *Sonderkommando*
and that his interpretation of the event is based on second-hand knowledge
passed around the camp, it is perhaps unsurprising that he also stressed the
story's importance for the prisoners' morale. Kielar's implications about
Schillinger's behavior while drunk and the way in which he expresses some

understanding of the sexual vulnerability of the women in the camp, stand in contrast to the lack of insight or empathy in his numerous other stories of sexual relationships between prisoners and the particular vulnerability of women in the Birkenau Gypsy camp. Elsewhere in his text, however, he demonstrates a similarly empathetic tone as he enumerates several stories of rapes committed by the SS in the camp.[13]

Filip Müller, as one of the few eyewitnesses to the event, explicitly places the story within a complicated paradigm of sexual violence and resistance. The woman is depicted as having arrived on a transport of privileged prisoners who were not identified with a Star of David but who spoke Yiddish. In Müller's text, as in Kielar's, SS Schillinger is defined as a sexual predator, along with a second SS officer Quackernack:

> Quackernack and Schillinger were strutting back and forth in front of the humiliated crowd with a self-important swagger. Suddenly they stopped in their tracks, attracted to a strikingly handsome woman with blue-black hair who was taking off her right shoe. The woman, as soon as she noticed that the two men were ogling her, launched into what appeared to be a titillating and seductive strip-tease act. She lifted her skirt to allow a glimpse of thigh and suspender. Slowly she undid her stocking and peeled it off her foot. From out of the corner of her eye she carefully observed what was going on [a]round her. The two SS men were fascinated by her performance and paid no attention to anything else. They were standing there with their arms akimbo, their whips dangling from their wrists, and their eyes firmly glued on the woman.
>
> She had taken off her blouse and was standing in front of her lecherous audience in her brassiere. Then she steadied herself against a concrete pillar with her left arm and bent down, slightly lifting her foot, in order to take off her shoe. What happened next took place with lightning speed: quick as a flash she grabbed her shoe and slammed its high heel violently against Quackernack's forehead. He winced with pain and covered his face with both hands. At this moment the young woman flung herself at him and made a quick grab for his pistol. Then there was a shot. Schillinger cried out and fell to the ground. Seconds later there was a second shot aimed at Quackernack which narrowly missed him.[14]

In Müller's witness testimony, the woman is sexually vulnerable to the predation of the SS officers, but she uses her sexuality as a form of resistance. This testimony is the most explicit in its effective reversal of the rape narrative: she is not raped because she uses her sexual vulnerability to entice the SS men. Given the way in which both popular and legal definitions of rape usually refer to penetration, the shoe that is slammed into SS Quackernack's head might also be seen as symbolic of rape.

Like Kielar and Müller, Michel Mielnicki testifies to Schillinger's reputation for sexual interest in the prisoners and places the events within a paradigm of sexual violence. However, for Mielnicki the story is not so much about Schillinger or the dancer (whom he identifies as a Belgian actress named Horowitz), but instead about the inner workings of the camp administration.[15] Nonetheless, Mielnicki does question Schillinger's motivations and considers rape as one possible reason for his interest in the dancer. Ultimately he believes the event was about humiliation and torture, an analysis that at the very least suggests that his reading contained conflicting structures of (sexual) violence.

Mythology and Fact

Another contrasting reading can be found in Sara Nomberg-Przytyk's testimony, *Auschwitz: True Tales from a Grotesque Land*, which is not so much a biographical memoir as a collection of short stories, one of which she labels "Revenge of the Dancer." In this story the narrator (not clearly identified but representative of Nomberg-Przytyk) learns the story of the death of an unnamed SS officer from the sole survivor of the transport, a young girl. This girl described the dancer as a "beautiful" woman who attracted the attention of the SS officer because she refused to strip when ordered to do so, committing the first important act of resistance. The mention of her beauty, however, suggests that the SS officer was also enticed by her sexuality. For Nomberg-Przytyk, "Schillinger and the Dancer" is a story of resistance with the subtext of sexual violence. However, her text is in fact far more complex than most Holocaust witness testimonies and deserves further consideration.

James Young describes Nomberg-Przytyk's text as "simultaneously relat[ing] and creat[ing] historical truth in the legends of Auschwitz, which she simultaneously writes and rewrites," a project particularly highlighted by her utilization of this piece of camp lore.[16] Nomberg-Przytyk did not arrive in Auschwitz-Birkenau until January 1944 and cannot have been a witness to the event itself (nor does she claim to be). Nonetheless, by choosing to include this iconic story in her text, mediated as it is through retelling by a witness, she is effectively incorporating the story, if not the event, into her experience of Auschwitz. She may not have been present for the "act of resistance," but it clearly becomes part of her remembered experience, part of camp lore. This fact does not make Nomberg-Przytyk's text inauthentic. Instead it demonstrates that we must take a multilayered textual reading regarding the facts of "Schillinger and the Dancer" and its numerous representations throughout Holocaust witness testimonies. The story is part of Nomberg-Przytyk's experience not because she herself viewed the event through an objective historical lens or bore witness to another's bearing witness to it. The story is part of her experience because it permeated Auschwitz and established itself as a tale of resistance, of (sexual) violence, both within and beyond the literal historical representation of Auschwitz, and of the countervailing power of sexuality. This story is both mythology and fact.

Although myths may not be construed as historically objective, what is important in this case is the way in which the deployment of a mythologized truth reveals stories of (sexual) violence. That the representation of sexual violence and resistance in "Schillinger and the Dancer" is significant is made clear by the number of Auschwitz inmates who felt it was important enough to acknowledge in their testimonies.

Sex for Survival as Active Resistance

These same themes appear in stories of sex for survival, yet sex for survival is not considered a form of active resistance, even when the exchange of sex for a commodity ends with survival. In most versions of "Schillinger and the Dancer," the woman uses her sexuality to effectively subvert the rape narrative in order to kill an SS officer; in stories of sex for survival, female sexuality is manipulated and exploited by both participants. Obviously, the female prisoners are participating from a weakened position, and in some cases, they had no choice regarding whether to participate in sexual relationships with privileged prisoners or camp guards.[17] Although these stories do not present the violent resistance exemplified in "Schillinger and the Dancer," they can nonetheless complicate further definitions of sexual violence and resistance. It is beyond question that life and death hinged on the "choice" of trading sex for food—hardly a choice at all. In this sense, sex for survival must always be seen as a form of sexual violence in which some degree of personal agency is involved. Yet, however much this agency may be curtailed by the context of the choice, there is also always an extent to which it can function as an act of resistance. If we do not acknowledge the evidence of choice in some testimonies, we risk disenfranchising the very women whose stories we seek to bring to the forefront.

Such equations are made clear in the recollections of Magda Herzberger, a Hungarian deportee who describes the relationship she developed with a

Polish prisoner who used to sneak into her barracks to give her extra bread. At first she felt he was a friend, until the fifth occasion when he began to tell her "how pretty and attractive" she was and then proceeded to move closer, wrapping his arms around her and trying to, as she puts it, "caress my body all over." Herzberger recalls: "I was shocked and disappointed, realizing that he had an ulterior motive in his mind, giving me the bread and trying to get close to me. I felt humiliated and disrespected." Yet realizing that he expected her to "prostitute" herself in exchange for food—to perform sex for survival—also leads her to a far deeper realization: "I came to the conclusion that maybe true and pure friendship didn't exist in an environment where there was such a fearsome fight for survival, where a piece of bread becomes a cheap commodity for buying and using a person."[18] Herzberger also states that she was "suspicious of his intentions," and while we cannot know if she was uneasy because such relationships were so common or because of her pre- or postwar socialization, it is certainly suggestive of the former. (We should keep in mind that at the time of writing Herzberger would most likely have been aware of this trope in other witness testimonies and of the ways in which sexual predators "groom" potential victims.) What is evident, however, is that the extra rations of bread had helped to maintain her. Therefore, by refusing to participate in exchanging sex for food—what seemed to her to be "prostitution"— she was denying herself extra rations of bread, which could have meant the difference between life and death. While we must recognize that the negative connotations of prostitution in pre- and postwar society could have changed how Herzberger represented her lived experience, her act could also have been a way for her to assert her agency in a situation where she was denied it, to retain her "humanity" by refusing to engage in sex for survival. Yet we must be careful not to read too much into Herzberger's act as a form of agency or we risk making moral judgments against those who did engage in sex for survival. Both dynamics can be defined in terms of resistance.

Suzanne Birnbaum's testimony contains two distinct stories in which a male prisoner brings food to a female prisoner. In the first of these stories, Birnbaum mentions a French-Polish inmate who brought Birnbaum and four other French women extra food while they were incarcerated in the hospital barracks, apparently requiring nothing in return.[19] The second story involves members of the *Kanada Kommando* who were actively involved in the camp black market, trading goods with other prisoners and members of the SS. As such, these inmates were also well placed for participating in the system of sex for survival.[20] The scenario is similar to the one described by Herzberger.

In a memoir by survivor Louis J. Micheels, the representation of sex for survival is further complicated because it involves an SS officer:

> Then there was Fuggert, who was in charge of an analytic laboratory staffed by two women, the wives of chemistry professors who also worked in the laboratory. The women were escorted to the lab by guards. . . . Fuggert was perhaps the most dangerous of this group of SS men, and something of a Don Juan. There was a rumor that he was carrying on an affair with one of the two women in the hayloft of one of the buildings. In exchange for her favors she was rumored to receive special privileges.[21]

The emphasis in this story is obviously on the SS officer and the crimes he committed. The woman is almost incidental to the story, and nothing is said of how she came to be involved in the relationship. Was it simply rape? Was it sex for survival, whereby the woman exercised some form of agency in "choosing" to participate? With so very little information, we cannot extrapolate too much, although it is important to recognize that Micheels felt that SS Fuggert was especially dangerous precisely because of his identification as a sexual predator. The women are not specifically identified as Jewish. If they were Jewish, and Fuggert a violent anti-Semite, then surely the laws of *Rassenschande* (race defilement) should have applied. Yet Micheels assumes they did not. Because we are not talking about rape per se, but one literary representation of "sex for survival," the nationalist-gendered discourses involved in defining sexual violence are further complicated.

Just as nationalist and gendered discourses shape the representation of sex for survival, so too can sexuality itself be deployed as a signifier for the deviance of women engaged in such acts. All three of these tropes intersect in Fania Fénelon's description of the character of "Clara" in her autobiographical text *Playing for Time*.[22] Clara is described as "a girl about twenty with a ravishing head set upon an enormous, deformed body . . . a body deformed in the transit camp by starvation, . . . a well-brought up girl who was engaged to a boy she loved," but also as "lazy, gluttonous, and selfish . . . us[ing] her sexuality in order to survive."[23] In Fénelon's telling, the situation is rendered yet more obscene by the fact that Clara was apparently still a virgin, a fact important to Fénelon's use of her as a literary foil. The destruction of Clara's humanity provides a stark contrast to Fénelon's representation of herself as maintaining her own humanity, which in turn serves to justify her self-appointed role as moral guide for the other members of the women's orchestra.[24]

Sexual Exploitation and Perceived Loss of Dignity

Fénelon and Clara's first encounter with the concept of sex for survival happens quite soon after their arrival in Auschwitz, when a soldier offers to trade them coffee for sex.[25] The two girls ignore him and the subject is not brought up again. But the soldier's statement, so soon upon arrival, and after several days trapped in a cattle car, is a lesson about Birkenau. As Fénelon comments: "Coffee? Either a woman wasn't worth much around here, or else coffee was priceless. She said nothing and he let it drop."[26] We do not know if either girl had some prior experience with witnessing sex for survival in Drancy; both were there for an extended period, so it is quite likely that they did, but this is assumption rather than factual knowledge. In any case, the more experienced girls in the orchestra are quick to point out how cheap a woman's body is in the camp: Jenny tells them, "All you need to do is find yourself a man; here sausage replaces flowers."[27]

Fénelon testifies to the sexual vulnerability of the "privileged" women prisoners, but what she ignores is the question of agency. By engaging in acts of sex for survival, these women were actively increasing their chances of survival by diminishing their starvation. In terms of Fénelon's construction of herself as a moral guide, it is important to note that Jenny's comment is directed at Clara and that Fénelon defined Clara as "violently animal" in her desperation for extra food. By way of contrast, Fénelon did not participate in sex for survival because of her belief in her own humanity.[28] Sexuality was a tool to be used, but not a tool that a "good" female prisoner would use. With this simple example, Fénelon constructs sexuality as a way to signify negative behavior and to chart the destruction of the "virginal" Clara's humanity.

This construction of sex for survival is further complicated because it intersects with Fénelon's deployment of nationalist discourse. Speaking of a German prisoner named Lotte, who is engaged in a "love relationship" with a male prisoner with whom she exchanges gifts, Fénelon is only offended by their degenerate behavior. When it comes to Clara, however, more is at stake, because she not only contravened her status as a French woman by participating in sex for survival but also refused to share the food, an act of generosity that would have written Clara in positive terms of "sisterhood." Indeed, the combination of these factors is crucial to Fénelon's critique of Clara, for it is not only that Clara quite quickly makes the "decision" that food is so important that sex can be traded for it. Fénelon also singles her out for opprobrium because she hoards the food and is not particular about whom she takes as a sexual partner. In fact, Fénelon is extremely dismissive of Clara's "choice," claiming she was more interested in food than remaining female. However, it is unclear whether Fénelon's disgust stems from her ideas on sexual, gender, or national identity. Is she disgusted with Clara because of the sexual act and her consequent loss of her womanly dignity? Because by refusing to engage in communal survival and share the extra food, Clara failed to honor her sex and gender identity by recognizing "sisterhood"? Or because, as Hutton suggests, Clara had transgressed her national identity as a Frenchwoman by refusing to share the food? The discussion of Clara's sexuality is a plot device to chart the destruction of the "good" Clara within Birkenau, replacing her with a debased sexualized animal, particularly after Clara takes a German *Kapo* (supervising prisoner) as a lover, contravening nationalist lines of behavior. It may also be the case that had Clara chosen to share some of the food received through engaging in sex for survival, Fénelon might not have used her as a literary foil.[29]

What is particularly interesting is Fénelon's construction of Clara's changing identity, and the way in which she contrasts her transformation from a good virginal girl to a prostitute is the way in which it relates to Fénelon's understanding of the behavior of "real" prostitutes in France. While Fénelon defends as a form of heroism the behavior of French prostitutes who engaged in sexual acts with German soldiers to gather information for the French Resistance, Clara's attempt to survive through sex is viewed with disgust. This contrast is highlighted in Fénelon's description of Clara's outrage, during deportation, at Fénelon's participation in cabarets where German officers were the major clientele.[30]

But the question remains: Why is Clara's transformation into a "prostitute" to save her own life portrayed so negatively? Partly, it is because Fénelon uses the character of Clara to delineate between "good" collaboration and "bad" collaboration. When Clara is given the job as a *Kapo*, Fénelon claims she behaves with ruthless and vicious violence, beating the block inmates sadistically for various rule infractions. But this did not happen until after the girls were transferred to Bergen-Belsen; Clara's "prostitution" occurred in the Auschwitz-Birkenau concentration camp. Is this negative representation of Clara as a prostitute different because she contravened a gendered narrative of women as nurturers, a narrative that has become incorporated into the collective memory of sisterhood amongst female victims of the Holocaust? If Clara had shared the food earned through the act of sex, would Fénelon have been so critical of her? If Clara had not become a *Kapo* in Bergen-Belsen, would Fénelon's representation of her have differed? Perhaps Fénelon's representation of Clara as negative in contrast to her own behavior is not a response to Clara but to postwar criticisms of the behavior of the "privileged" prisoners levied by those who did not have access to extra food or clothing, a guilty reflex on the part of Fénelon to attempt to exculpate her guilt. These criticisms of collaboration made it difficult for those prisoners who became *Kapos* to record their own experiences, so we can only investigate their experience through the mediated representations of other, nonprivileged prisoners.

These are the types of questions we need to be asking about witness testimonies, even if we cannot find adequate responses to them. More generally, Fénelon's story reveals the complexity of sexual violence during the Holocaust in that at a certain point she forgets Clara's identity as victim and recasts her as a perpetrator. In so doing, she makes the sexual exploitation of Clara a footnote to the dehumanizing effects of their situation. In order to "re-humanize" her (and many other victims of the Holocaust), we must acknowledge and recognize the way in which sexual vulnerability is accentuated by and essential to genocide, particularly because those women and men who found themselves in Clara's place and faced with her "choice" are the ones least likely to record their testimonies.[31] But more important, these "choices" of compliance and noncompliance functioned in such a way that the female prisoners were able to negotiate their sexuality in order to increase their chances of survival, just as the dancer did when she assassinated Schillinger.

Conclusions

"Schillinger and the Dancer" contains a subtext of sexual violence, but it is also a straightforward signifier of resistance, a "masculine," violent resistance. Stories of sex for survival are stories of sexual violence. The women would not have had to participate if they were not in situations that made them sexually vulnerable to predation, but these stories do include constructions of resistance if we expand the definition of resistance beyond violence. The dancer could not have committed an act of resistance if she had not been sexually vulnerable or if Schillinger had not perceived her as sexually vulnerable. However, because she utilized her female sexuality to challenge her abusers, that which made her vulnerable also became a source of power, the power to enact violent resistance. These competing discourses are dependent on multiple and conflicting witness testimonies and together demonstrate the complexities in defining both resistance and sex for survival. Moreover, individual readings of compliance and noncompliance are dependent on the multiple and conflicting witness testimonies that outline such stories, yet these disparities are themselves revealing of the ways in which different witnesses provide specifically gendered accounts of sexual vulnerability and its exploitation, and also of resistance and agency.

Notes

1. Wieslaw Kielar, *Anus Mundi: Five Years in Auschwitz*, trans. Susanne Flatauer (London: Penguin Books, 1982,); Kitty Hart-Moxon, *Return to Auschwitz: The Remarkable Story of a Girl Who Survived the Holocaust* (New York: Atheneum, 1982); Benjamin Jacobs, *The Dentist of Auschwitz: A Memoir* (Lexington: University Press of Kentucky, 1995); Filip Müller, *Eyewitness Auschwitz: Three Years in the Gas Chambers*, trans. Susanne Flatauer, (Chicago: Ivan Dee, 1979).

2. Myrna Goldenberg, "Rape in the Holocaust," in *The Legacy of the Holocaust: Women and the Holocaust*, ed. Zygmunt Mazur et al. (Kraków: Jagiellonian University Press, 2007), 159–169. Elizabeth Heineman refers to sex for survival as "hunger prostitution" in "Sexuality and Nazism: The Doubly Unspeakable?" *Journal of the History of Sexuality* 11, no. 1/2, (January/April 2002): 30, 54. Also see Ruth Elias, *Triumph of Hope: From Theresienstadt and Auschwitz to Israel*, trans. Margot Bettauer Dembo (New York: John Wiley & Sons with the United States Holocaust Memorial Museum, 1998), 114.

3. Müller, *Eyewitness Auschwitz*; see also Jadwiga Bezwinska and Danuta Czech, eds., *Amidst a Nightmare of Crime: Manuscripts of the Sonderkommando* (New York: H. Fertig, 1992), 31. Jankowski (also known as Alter Feinsilber) gave his testimony to the Commission for Investigating German-Nazi Crimes at Auschwitz on April 16, 1945. The testimonies of Shlomo Dragon and Ya'akow Silderberg appear in Gideon Greif, *We Wept Without Tears: Testimonies of the Jewish Sonderkommando from Auschwitz* (New Haven: Yale University Press, 2005), 162–163, 325, 359n51.

4. Kitty Hart-Moxon, *I Am Alive* (Great Britain: Corgi Books, 1974); Jacobs, *Dentist of Auschwitz*; Kielar, *Anus Mundi*; Petro Mirchuk, *In the German Mills of Death, 1941–1945* (Washington: Survivors of the Holocaust, 1976); Sara Nomberg-Przytyk, *Auschwitz: True Tales from a Grotesque Land*, trans. Roslyn Hirsch (Chapel Hill: University of North Carolina Press, 1985); Rudolf Höss, *Commandant of Auschwitz: The Autobiography of Rudolf Hoess*, trans. Constantine Fitzgibbon and Joachim Neugroschel (Great Britain: Phoenix, 2000); Perry Broad, "The Reminisces of Perry Broad," in *KL Auschwitz as Seen by the SS: Höss, Broad, Kremer*, ed. Jadwiga Bezwinska and Danuta Czech, 2nd ed., (Kraków: Panstowe Muzeum w Oswiecimiu, 2000), 179.

5. Bezwinska and Czech, *Amidst a Nightmare of Crime*, 55–56.

6. Ibid., 55 and note 67.

7. Ya'akow Silderberg, interview in Greif, *We Wept Without Tears*, 163.

8. Shlomo Dragon, interview in ibid., 162–63.

9. Yaffa Eliach, "Franceska Mann," in "Women of Valor: Partisans and Resistance Fighters: Biographical Sketches," Women and the Holocaust: A Cyberspace of Their Own, http://www.theverylongview.com/WATH/ (accessed February 10, 2010). Franceska Mann, who probably got her passport at the "Hotel Polski" in Warsaw, was arrested there with six hundred other Jews, some of whom were murdered in Pawiak prison before the transfer to Bergen-Belsen; all survivors were murdered in Auschwitz-

Birkenau in October 1943. The Web site is the initiative of Hungarian survivor Judy Weiszenberg Cohen of Toronto.

10. Mirchuk, *German Mills of Death*, 127; K.T. Czelny, *My Journey from Auschwitz to Buckingham Palace* (London: self-published, 1994), 51; Hart-Moxon, *I Am Alive*, 103.

11. Hart-Moxon, *I Am Alive*, 103; Jacobs, *Dentist of Auschwitz*, 140.

12. Kielar, *Anus Mundi*, 177–178.

13. Ibid., 132, 134–135, 147–148.

14. Müller, *Eyewitness Auschwitz*, 87–88. SS Walter Quackernack was misidentified as the other victim. It was SS Emmerich who was shot but survived. It is entirely possible that Quackernack was there for the event as, at one point, he did function as *Oberscharführer* of the crematorium. Quackernack was hanged on October 11, 1946, for his crimes. See Bezwinska and Czech, *Amidst A Nightmare of Crime*, 42 and note 27.

15. As told to John Munro, *Bialystok to Birkenau: The Holocaust Journey of Michel Mielnicki* (Vancouver: Ronsdale Press and Vancouver Holocaust Education Centre, 2000), 149–150.

16. James Young, *Writing and Rewriting the Holocaust: Narrative and the Consequences of Interpretation* (Bloomington: Indiana University Press, 1990), 43.

17. While I am referring here only to female prisoners, similar situations arose among the male prisoners. See Thomas Geve, *Youth in Chains* (Jerusalem: Rubin Mass, 1981); Kielar, *Anus Mundi*.

18. Magda Herzberger, *Survival* (Austin: 1st World Library, Inc., 2005), 219–222.

19. Suzanne Birnbaum, *Une Française juive est revenue* (The return of a French Jewish woman) (Paris: Le Livre Français, 1946), 55–56.

20. Ibid., 91.

21. Louis J. Micheels, *Doctor # 117641: A Holocaust Memoir* (New Haven: Yale University Press, 1989), 102.

22. For another interpretation of Clara's behavior, see chapter 11 by S. Lillian Kremer in this volume.

23. Fania Fénelon with Marcelle Routier, *Playing for Time*, trans. Judith Landry (Syracuse, NY: Syracuse University Press, 1997), 12; Anna Hardman, *Women and Holocaust*, Holocaust Educational Trust Research Papers, 2000.

24. Marlene E. Heinemann, *Gender and Destiny: Women Writers and the Holocaust* (New York: Greenwood Press, 1986), 31.

25. Fénelon, *Playing for Time*, 18.

26. Ibid., 18.

27. Ibid., 66.

28. Margaret-Anne Hutton, *Testimony from the Nazi Camps: French Women's Voices* (London: Routledge, 2005), 66.

29. Ibid., 81; Fénelon, *Playing for Time*, 189–190.

30. Fénelon, *Playing for Time*, 15.

31. Zoë Waxman, *Writing the Holocaust: Identity, Testimony, Representation* (Oxford: Oxford University Press, 2006), 124–125.

RAPE
# of Jewish Women

5

"Only Pretty Women Were Raped"

The Effect of Sexual Violence on Gender Identities in Concentration Camps

MONIKA J. FLASCHKA

Toward the end of the war, Holocaust survivor Pearl Gottesmann found herself imprisoned in the Auschwitz concentration and extermination camp, about which she later said the following: it was "the most horrible. You know you don't hear about the other concentration camps so much, you hear about Auschwitz because I think that was the worst, worst camp . . . I mean that was [the] darkest, darkest era."[1]

While in Auschwitz, Gottesmann witnessed the rape of a fellow concentration camp inmate by a Ukrainian soldier. As other survivors have also testified, she associated being raped with being pretty. She described her friend as follows: "[S]he was beautiful, and her hair grew in, started to grow in very nice, so they picked her out to rape her." The importance of hair to a woman's gender and human identity is something several Holocaust survivors have mentioned in their recollections. When describing their physical appearance without hair, survivors refer to themselves as indistinguishable from one another, as a "monolithic mass,"[2] as "animals,"[3] or as "sub-human."[4] One survivor, describing the German reaction to women with shaved heads, wrote: "They think we are some kind of animal, a species they have never seen before. No wonder. Whoever saw a woman without hair?"[5]

Gottesmann also associated the presence of hair with attractiveness, and she drew upon this association to explain the rape of her fellow inmate. What Gottesmann's quote about witnessing the rape demonstrates is the relationship between a characteristic associated with physical attractiveness particularly noticeable in the concentration camp environment—the presence of hair—and how women explained the occurrence of rape. In examining rape in the concentration camps, this chapter explores the connection between attractiveness, femininity, and rape, as perceived by the historical subjects themselves.[6]

Theories of Rape

According to scholars of rape, the act of rape is one of both feminization and masculinization—the violation feminizes the victim, male or female, and enhances the perpetrator's masculinity. Sharon Marcus writes: "Masculine power and feminine powerlessness neither simply precede nor cause rape; rather, rape is one of culture's many modes of feminizing women. A rapist chooses his target because he recognizes her to be a woman, but a rapist also strives to imprint the gender identity of 'feminine victim' on his target."[7]

Beyond the concept of feminization, philosopher Ann Cahill argues that "the threat of rape is a formative moment in the construction of the distinctly feminine body, such that even bodies of women who have not been raped are likely to carry themselves in such a way as to express the truths and values of a rape culture."[8] She also writes that "[r]ape not only happens to women; it is a fundamental moment in the production of women qua women."[9] If we accept that rape does, in some fashion, reinforce, "imprint," or "script" gender identity for women,[10] then it makes theoretical sense to ask whether women of the camps themselves understood the act of rape as such—as a reminder that they were women, particularly in an environment, the concentration camp, which challenged their identities as women.[11]

Scholars are in agreement that rape functions to reinforce masculine gender identity in cases of ethnic cleansings and genocide,[12] that it may act as a statement of "hetero-nationality,"[13] or that it may serve as an attack on the "nation's culture" of the woman.[14] Lisa S. Price most clearly articulates how rape functioned to reinforce masculine gender identity in former Yugoslavia when she writes that rape, for the man, expresses the following: "I AM only to the extent that you are not—male because you are female, Serb because you are Muslim, soldier because you are civilian. Your absence marks, verifies my presence and your pain becomes my power."[15] What is less clear, however, from these works on ethnic cleansing and genocide is what rape means to the woman. If rape functions in this manner to reinforce the masculine identity of the rapist, then, as stated above, conceivably it also reinforces the identity of woman to the rape victim. Thus Price's explanation in this context could be reconfigured as: I AM female because you are male, Jewish because you are not

Jewish, civilian because you are soldier. We do not know the various degrees to which women raped in concentration camps perceived the assault as an attack on them as women, as Jews (when applicable), as yet another manifestation of the power differential in the camps, or as further evidence of the inhumanity of the Nazi regime. However, if Price's axiom applies, then rape, as explained as a product of traits associated with femininity and womanhood, may have reminded women in the camps that they were women.

I operate under the assumption that gender identities are constructed, are constantly under the process of construction, and are performed in social environments.[16] Thus, there is nothing inherent or given about the effect of rape on the development or maintenance of gender identities. Rather, rape is assigned a specific meaning by particular societies, and one effect of rape, according to scholars, is that it serves to mark women as women. This chapter not only presumes that gender identities are constructed, fluid, and performed in a theoretical sense but also attempts to demonstrate that the historical subjects themselves understood their gender identities as malleable, and that the experience of sexual violence affected the individual's conception of her own gender identity.

At this point, it would be prudent to address the issue of geographical and temporal discontinuity. Marcus and Cahill write about rape in an American context, and Price's work analyzes rape in the former Yugoslavia. It would be fallacious to assume that rape means the same thing in the American and Yugoslavian contexts or that it followed the same "script," as Marcus calls it, during the Holocaust as it does today. This disparity in meaning is especially pertinent because this chapter deals with sexual violence committed during a time period and location (the camps) of obvious power inequity. My intention is not to present rape as a "transhistorical mechanism of women's oppression,"[17] or as the "conscious process of intimidation by which *all* men keep *all* women in a state of fear."[18] The fact remains that we do not, as scholars, know a great deal about rape committed in ghettos and concentration camps, or more generally, about rape committed by German soldiers during World War II.[19] My intention, then, is to analyze the language used by Holocaust survivors to explain their own rape or the sexual violence they witnessed while in the camps. At the same time, this methodological approach allows the evaluation of existing theories of rape through the lens of sexual violence committed during the Holocaust.

The purpose of this chapter is twofold. First, it demonstrates that female survivors explained rape as a result of attractiveness—a relatively straightforward endeavor. The language used to describe male-male rape will also be examined. As will become clear through an analysis of how men described their experiences of sexual violence, male victims less frequently invoked physical attractiveness as an explanation for having been abused. Second, and more difficult, this chapter suggests that rape may have functioned to remind women that they were women in an environment that challenged their identities as women. In this instance, the social environment was the concentration camp, in which women were stripped of their identities as women, and, as they often recounted, of their human identities as well. Rape, as an act that disproportionately targets women, may have functioned to reinforce feminine identity, and this relationship is hinted at when witnesses invoke a particular kind of physical appearance as an explanation for rape.

Scholars also suggest that rape reinforces the masculine identities of men assaulting other men, while feminizing the abused man. In writing about male-male rape, Adam Jones argues that "[o]ne of the most intriguing elements of male-on-male rape and sexual violence is the gendered positioning of rapist and victim: the way in which victims are feminized while *rapists are confirmed in their heterosexual, hegemonic masculinity.*"[20] As will become clear, it is more difficult to determine how sexual abuse challenged men's identities because we know less about how the camps affected men's identities as men. Obviously, the process called feminization does not produce an individual who is inherently inferior. Rather, cultures assign the meaning of "weak" to that which is construed as feminine, and thus to refer to the act of rape as feminizing for the victim is to relegate that individual to the weaker position, the dominated position. This is why even in cases of male-male rape, the masculinity of the individual in control is ostensibly affirmed and the victim is feminized, placed in the weaker, dominated, feminine subject position. What will become clear throughout this chapter, however, is that in the testimonies I viewed, men who abused other men were not in any way referred to as more masculine than other men, contrary to what scholars have suggested.

The Camp Environment

Before examining how the historical subjects attempted to explain sexual violence in the concentration camps, it is important to understand that the camp environment very much challenged women's identities as women. Upon entry into the camp, their heads were shaved, they were given formless clothing, and starvation frequently caused cessation of menstruation and loss of body weight, including in the breast and hips, two regions stereotypically associated with femininity and attractiveness. Memoirs and oral testimonies indicate that all of these changes prompted women to question their own identities. For example, one survivor described her starving state by saying, "We were all like men. Flat."[21] Anna Heilman, a survivor of Auschwitz, referred to the women around her as "shapeless," like "rag dolls made by the clumsy hand of a young child."[22]

After being told that there was something in the food that would halt menstruation, one survivor, Erna Rubinstein, wrote: "Some said that we would lose our womanhood completely. We didn't understand what that meant, but we knew it was bad."[23] Rubinstein also described her feelings about the myriad ways she no longer felt like a woman: "Auschwitz left a mark outside, too, after all what is a woman without her glory on her head, without hair?" she asked. "A woman who doesn't menstruate? We had lost our dignity in Auschwitz. We had no clothes that looked feminine and no desire to act like ladies."[24] Yet another survivor, describing the relationship between starvation and the cessation of menstruation, wrote: "Having lost their menstruations as a result of malnutrition and shock, the women no longer felt they were women."[25]

As an example of this challenge to identity, and the relationship between sexualized violence and the affirmation of gender identity, we can look at the writing of Isabelle Choko. Recounting her entry into the camp, Choko wrote, "One [of the guards] pointed at me and said to his cohort, 'Look at those beautiful breasts.'" She then noted that this "was the last remark about my physical appearance that I would hear for a long time to come. At the precise time my head was shaved, I ceased to exist as a human being."[26] In this case, Choko understood her status as a human being as reinforced by the sexualized comments of the guard. She knew she was human because she knew she was a woman, and she knew she was a woman because the guards commented on her physical appearance and attractiveness.

If we predicate our analysis on this point, that the concentration camp environment posed particular challenges to women's identities, then the argument that rape and fear of rape functioned to reinforce those challenged identities becomes more tangible. We can pose the following question: Did the association between rape and femininity result in the actual reinforcement of a gender identity ostensibly challenged by the camp environment, which stripped individuals of a gender, and, I might add, human identity?

The Evidence

The testimony by Pearl Gottesman, presented at the beginning of the chapter, demonstrates that particular physical characteristics were considered indicative of femininity and feminine beauty. She explained that the woman about whom she was speaking was not a victim of sexual violence until her hair started to grow back in. If having one's head shaved challenged concepts of feminine identity, as survivors have suggested, then the regrowth of hair would, and did, function as the reclamation of femininity.

Isabella Leitner, a survivor of Auschwitz, also described the regrowth of her hair as the return of her identity as a woman. She said the following about her entry into Auschwitz: "Our heads are shaved. We look like neither boys nor girls."[27] Leitner wrote the following about her appearance and identity after liberation. Note how she herself related the presence of hair to a return of her feminine identity:

> Our hair has grown a bit. We can actually begin to use a comb. We have not had any use for one in nearly a year. It is an uncanny sensation. We stroll beside the train displaying our short crowns of an inch of hair. *With our newly found woman-hood, we attract the attention of the men of our world.* We are our very attractive selves again.[28]

The return of her hair made Leitner feel like a woman again and was the explanation she invoked for any male attention she received.

This relationship between hair and feminine identity is repeated in several testimonies, and some survivors specifically associated the presence of hair with selection for sexual violence. When asked by the interviewer about what kind of woman was chosen for sexual abuse, Erica Betts, interned in Dachau, said: "I think on the whole I was picked more because I was the youngest, and I should not say so, quite good looking."[29] Helene Shiver, also speaking of her time Dachau, said the following about her own rape:

> I was raped, at the beginning of it. Must have been in either '42 or '43, wasn't very long after we were there. Yeah, the young girls who were young and pretty, so to speak, in those days, they were taken to different barracks. And sometimes right in front of the barracks, where everybody can see.[30]

Notice that Shiver qualifies her description of the "young and pretty" girls by saying that they were "young and pretty, so to speak, in those days," a qualification that can be read as an implication that there existed a different concept of "young and pretty" in the camp environment. We should, at this point, examine the relationship between attractiveness and femininity in the concentration camp environment. Outside the camp, markers of femininity and attractiveness may have included clothing, hair, marital and motherhood status, use of cosmetics, and so on.[31] Within the camp however, there were fewer external markers of femininity. Therefore, the very presence of hair, for some women, would have been enough to mark an individual as female in an environment of bald individuals. The very fact of looking healthy, of having body weight, of looking human, or looking remotely feminine was considered a source of attractiveness and, thus, was remarked upon by women who were raped or witnessed rape in the camps.

When she wrote about the process of shaving heads upon entry into the concentration camp, memoirist and physician Gisella Perl provided evidence for what was considered beautiful and feminine before entry into the camp:

> The floor was littered with dresses, coats, underwear and many lovely things so essential to true femininity . . . A moment later we felt the heavy, blunt shears in our hair, and when we looked up again we hardly knew one another any longer . . . There lay the crown of our female beauty, our hair.[32]

This is just one of Perl's descriptions of how the camp challenged her identity. She referred to the area in which women were shaved and forced to don camp clothing as the "beauty parlor," whose purpose was to "deprive its unwilling clients of even their last remnants of beauty, freshness, and human appearance."[33] She went on to describe the challenges posed to women's gender identities:

> When we finally emerged at the other end of the "beauty parlor" building, the street looked like a ghostly carnival. Sisters, friends did not recognize each other any longer, and the prettiest girls and most beautiful women looked like a bunch of grisly monsters, ridiculous, and sub-human.[34]

Perl's reference to "sub-humanity" suggests that losing one's gender identity also made women feel less than fully human. She further highlights this dehumanizing aspect of the "beauty parlor" when she writes that, before entering the changing and hair-cutting room:

> [W]e were still human beings, women, wearing our own clothes, our own shoes, our own underwear . . . We still had hair on our heads . . . Above all, we still had our identity, our individuality which made us different from the other women around us, and our pride which, as we learned, gets most of its support from outer appearance . . . When we entered the second room we had nothing left of our former identity . . .[35]

Keeping in mind that Perl considered her hair to be the marker of femininity, and the way in which she described not feeling like a woman while in the concentration camp, her description of sexual violence becomes particularly important. She wrote the following about an incidence of sexual violation: "His hand, filthy with the human excrement he was working in, reached out for my womanhood, rudely, insistently."[36] Perl is using the word "womanhood" to refer to her vagina, but it is important to note how she understood and explained the source of her womanhood—her vagina. With her choice of words, Perl demonstrated that the assault on her, on her "womanhood," actually reinforced her identity in an environment that she herself construed as challenging her feminine identity.

Several survivors, when recounting experiences or observations of sexual abuse, comment on the presence of hair. Eve Gabori explained why she thinks she and another woman were taken into a barrack where the other woman was raped: "[T]hey looked at me, and I was a beautiful girl . . . I was all sunburned, even my hair grew about half an inch, I looked healthy and my face was red and brown, because the sun was beating down."[37] Gabori goes on to say that she heard rumors that "very, very good-looking and pretty young women were taken to a certain house where they were used as prostitutes."

Ana Cymerman explained almost being raped by a German soldier in similar terms: "I was a pretty girl, really. No makeup, no nothing."[38] What is interesting is that she called herself pretty despite the absence of additive markers of attractiveness like makeup. She considered herself attractive, and that, in her opinion, is why the German soldier wanted to rape her. Lya Cohen, describing her rape by a German soldier while in a concentration camp in Greece said: "He used to pick the most pretty girls . . . and I was fourteen, but very, very well developed, unfortunately, for that time."[39] It is very clear in this case that Cohen, the historical subject herself, believed her rape was a function of her physical beauty, as measured by her well-developed, sex-specific figure, which was most likely particularly noticeable in an environment in which the majority of women were starving.

Debora Sessler also commented on physical appearance when describing the rape of a Dutch woman by a German guard. In this case, however, she referred to the health rather than the attractiveness of the woman: "We know for a fact she was taken away. She was quite a big woman, so she [didn't look malnourished] or anything."[40] Even though Sessler did not make the explicit connection between attractiveness and rape, she did implicitly connect attractiveness to looking healthy in a place where few did. To look human was to be attractive and this was the explanation for rape.

In a particularly interesting case, survivor Olga Astor described women selected to be used as prostitutes: "[S]ome of the SS selected women for the soldiers, and there were two girls from our barrack, who were the selected ones . . . they were well fed, they had clothes, they had their hair grow [sic], and it was shiny."[41] It was not unusual that women would be rewarded, however briefly, for work as prostitutes in the concentration camps. However, what is of note is that Astor described these women as retaining, or being provided, the means to ensure their feminine attractiveness. This may suggest that the guards wanted these women to look like women or that, to continue to be exploited for sex, the women had to look more like women than those around them. Witnesses imply that the women working as prostitutes had to remain attractive to the men in order to continue working. My point here is not to discuss whether Jewish women actually worked as prostitutes, but rather how those women were described by others in the camp. For an analysis of the gendered language used to describe the individuals who experienced rape and sexual violence in the camps, the truth of the event is less important than the language used to describe it.[42]

Women also invoked appearance to explain how they avoided sexual violence. Gucia Ferst suggested that she was not raped by soldiers because: "I was not pretty . . . they picked up especially nice looking girls."[43] Ursula Schwadron described how she avoided selection to be used as a prostitute:

They told all the girls to stand up, and told them to come—except me. Because these girls looked quite womanly and they took all these girls and used them as prostitutes in the whorehouses for the soldiers . . . but . . . I was a little underdeveloped, I was skinny, I looked like a ten-year old, I guess.[44]

Note again the importance of looking womanly, which meant to look sexually developed. Since so many witnesses invoked this explanation for sexual abuse, it is possible, because the women believed sexual assault was a result of physical attractiveness, that selection for sexual abuse on the basis of these physical attributes served to reinforce the gender identity of the women. These quotes demonstrate the frequency with which women raped by German soldiers or living under the threat of rape offered attractiveness or the presence of stereotypically feminine body shapes as the explanation for sexual violence.

Just as women almost always mentioned physical attractiveness when describing their own rape or a rape they witnessed, so too did the men recounting the assault of women. Harry Koltun, describing the selection, sexual abuse, and murder of a group of girls, said the following:

[T]here were a lot of girls, beautiful girls, and they were worked, and [there] was a selection one day, the Gestapo SS came in and took out a few Jewish girls, they took them into a forest, and they never came back. They did what they had to do sexually, and they killed them. Nice, nice looking girls.[45]

Gottfried Bloch described a meeting with a young woman who was raped by an SS soldier: "Now, one of these girls spoke a little German, and explained to me that she was, when she was sent to the wash room . . . was raped by one of the SS people. A really beautiful, even shorn and desperate, young woman and she thought that this was the worst thing."[46] Interestingly, this woman did not have hair, which in the camps was considered an important part of women's gender identity. Nonetheless, it was her beauty, however it was described, that was mobilized as the explanation for rape.

Male-Male Rape

We may be able to glean more information about the role of appearance and the understanding of feminine attractiveness if we briefly examine cases of male-male rape. When survivors recount the sexual abuse of men, the victims are also described as attractive or even feminine, though not with the same frequency as were the women. For example, Gilbert Metz, describing the sexual abuse of his friend by a *Kapo* (supervising prisoner) said: "And [he] was [a] very thin, bright, young kid, my age . . . He was sort of effeminate looking compared to everybody else. He had very thin, beautiful hands, had a beautiful chiseled face."[47]

Eugene Lipschutz was approached by a *Blockältester* (senior block inmate), who told him that he looked German, and was "very good-looking."[48] Auschwitz survivor Elsa Breuer described a group of young boys she believed were going to be used for sexual purposes: "[A]nd from the windows, young, beautiful boys were looking at us. Full faces, not starved, not in rags, clean, neat, well-fed young boys, twelve, fourteen, from all the windows."[49] Note that the boys were referred to as "beautiful," as well as healthy, and as clean, all characteristics the majority of camp inmates did not exhibit. This emphasis on the attractiveness of the men abused by other men points to the association between characteristics considered feminine and sexual violence. Metz clearly referred to his abused friend as "effeminate," which can be read as evidence of the posited relationship between the feminization of rape victims, male and female. At the same time, however, there are testimonies by men describing their own rape without mentioning attractiveness. Women more often invoked attractiveness as an explanation for rape than did men.

Men more frequently commented on their perpetrators as well. Men recounting sexual abuse at the hands of another man or having witnessed sexual abuse by another man frequently referred to the abuser as homosexual. Jack I.

Salzberg suggested that "ninety percent of the *Kapos* were homosexuals [who] selected . . . good-looking kids."[50] Herbert Kolischer also called the *Kapos* homosexual,[51] as did Marc Rubenstein, who described the selection of "fairly good-looking" boys for sexual abuse by *Kapos*.[52]

This is the one primary difference between the descriptions of sexual abuse provided by male and female survivors. In cases of male-male abuse, the perpetrators are usually referred to as homosexuals, as being in some way different. Men who assaulted women were not presented as abnormal, which indicates that the survivors understood heterosexual rape as something more normal, something explicable in a landscape of heterosexual normativity. This discrepancy provides evidence of what scholars refer to as the inherent rapability of women, the idea that women are always susceptible to rape and that this affects their behavior.[53]

While some scholars would like to see the discussion moved from an acceptance of the inherent rapability of women to an analysis of the meaning of rape, the fact remains that the survivor testimony examined in this chapter demonstrates that rape was assumed to be something that happened primarily to women and that women could, at any point in time, be sexually assaulted. The historical subjects themselves assumed that women, especially more attractive women, were constantly rapable. The belief on the part of the survivors that rape was something that happened primarily to women, and that people are more willing to discuss that rape as more normal than the rape of a man, is demonstrated by the interesting testimony of Elsa Breuer. She says:

> Now, now it is 1998, nobody ever, ever talks, writes about this block full of young boys. And nobody ever told you in books, I read everything, all the history books [t]hat I could, you know, I don't want to have names. All. And the writers, and the survivors, nobody ever tells you that the German officers use young boys. Nobody. Now it is 1998, today it is still a taboo to talk about it? I am absolutely horrified.[54]

Survivor Gilbert Metz also comments on the absence of attention devoted to same-sex contact or sexual abuse in the camps: "I don't think there have been many stories or books or research done on the amount of homosexuality and abuse of children at Auschwitz or the other camps. At least, I have not seen any, and there needs to be a study made, because it's a big hidden secret, people don't admit to it."[55] Analyses of homosexuality within the context of the Holocaust exist, of course, but there appears to be more willingness to discuss the abuse of women than of men. Interviewers more frequently express a sense of surprise when a male survivor recounts his own sexual abuse or describes witnessing the abuse of another man. Such is not the case in interviews with women.

The men and women describing the sexual abuse of women understood women to be rapable, to be living in an environment in which rape was a constant threat, and they attempted to explain rape as a function of physical attractiveness, however it was measured at the time. That men often mobilized the homosexuality of the rapist as an explanation for male-male sexual violence suggests that men did not consider themselves inherently rapable, but rather victims of someone else's "perversion."

Both men and women who were sexually abused were referred to as attractive in some way. In some cases, the physical attractiveness of young men was presented as feminine; some are described as "effeminate," and some as "beautiful." At this point, based on the testimonies available, it is unclear whether the majority of witnesses believed that good-looking young men were more feminine and that this explained why they were selected for sexual abuse. Witnesses explaining the rape of women, however, very clearly invoked features associated with feminine beauty—hair, breasts, or looking "womanly." For a woman to look "womanly" was enough to catch the attention of rapists. A man had to be attractive in some way, but his abuser also had to be of a particular sexual orientation.

This suggests that even though it seems that more women than men were sexually assaulted in the camps it is the men who are presented as "true" victims: the fault of their sexual abuse stems more from the abuser's "abnormality" than is the case in women's abuse. Women assaulted in the camps were believed, by the victims themselves and by witnesses, to have possessed something that caught the attention of the abuser. In the testimonies examined in this chapter, that something was some degree of noticeable physical attractiveness, some retention of feminine characteristics. Taken alone, these findings do not mean that women blame themselves, or are blamed by others, for sexual assault. However, it is noteworthy that the assault of men is explained away as the fault of the perpetrator's sexual orientation, and the assault of women is explained as a function of something the female victims possess.

The analysis of male-male rape also calls into question the idea that men who rape other men are considered more masculine, as reinforcing their masculine identity despite the fact that the contact was homosexual. We do not know, based on available evidence, whether men who abused other men felt themselves to be more masculine, as the literature would suggest, but we do know that the witnesses did not refer to abusers as more manly, but rather as homosexuals.[56]

Conclusions

All of these memoirs and oral testimonies suggest that the survivors, as historical subjects, linked rape, of men or women, with some concept of femininity. The sexual abuse of men was explained in two ways: first, by the presence of a kind of attractiveness, a soft beauty, more frequently used to describe women, that in a sense created an identity of "feminine victim" or "feminized victim," at least to observers; second, as a function of the sexual orientation of the perpetrator. The latter explanation was not invoked when describing the rape of women, primarily, I argue, because the rape of women was assumed to be a more natural occurrence: it was heterosexual and was something that happened to women—they were perceived as rapable.

In the case of women in particular, given the challenges posed to gender identity by the concentration camp, it seems likely that being selected for sexual violence on the basis of physical attractiveness or some physical aspect associated with being a woman functioned to reinforce women's identities as women. The characteristics remarked upon by victims and witnesses in the concentration camps were all publicly readable. They were markers associated with the external presentation of femininity—the presence of hair, greater weight, the presence of breasts. Insofar as it is possible to determine with these sources, *the historical subjects themselves* seem to suggest that rape, as explained by physical attractiveness and the retention of feminine characteristics, "produced" women in an environment in which women, as they had been known before, no longer existed.

Notes

I would like to thank the University of Southern California Shoah Foundation Institute for Visual History and Education for the fellowship that allowed me to view the testimonies, and the Charles H. Revson Foundation Fellowship from the United States Holocaust Memorial Museum for providing the opportunity and space to read the memoirs and work on very early drafts of this work. I also thank all those individuals who read and made comments on early drafts of this work.

1. Pearl Gottesmann, interview 6992 by the University of Southern California Shoah Foundation Institute for Visual History and Education (USC Shoah Foundation testimony).

2. Livia E. Bitton Jackson, "Coming of Age," in *Different Voices: Women and the Holocaust*, ed. Carol Rittner and John K. Roth (St. Paul, MN: Paragon House, 1993), 78–79.

3. Erna F. Rubinstein, *The Survivor in Us All: A Memoir of the Holocaust* (Hamden, Connecticut: Archon Books, 1983), 143.

4. Gisella Perl, *I Was a Doctor in Auschwitz* (New York: International Universities Press, 1948), 46–47.

5. Erna Rubinstein, *Survivor in Us All*, 152.

6. Jonathan Friedman, "Togetherness and Isolation: Holocaust Survivor Memories of Intimacy and Sexuality in the Ghettos," *Oral History Review* 28, no. 1 (Winter/Spring 2001): 1–16, mentions the relationship between attractiveness and rape in his analysis of sexual violence in the ghettos but does not examine the relationship or its possible meanings to survivors in any detail. Wendy Jo Gertjejanssen, "Victims, Heroes, Survivors: Sexual Violence on the Eastern Front during World War II," (Ph.D. dissertation, University of Minnesota, 2004), describes a number of strategies women used in attempts to avoid rape by soldiers. Among these strategies was the attempt to make themselves "unattractive" or "ugly" (274).

7. Sharon Marcus, "Fighting Bodies, Fighting Words: A Theory and Politics of Rape Prevention," in *Feminists Theorize the Political*, ed. Judith Butler and Joan W. Scott (New York: Routledge, 1992), 391.

8. Ann J. Cahill, *Rethinking Rape* (Ithaca: Cornell University Press, 2001), 143. The latter reference to the effect of rape on the behavior of women will become particularly important toward the end of the chapter, where the rapability of women is discussed. Cahill also writes that "the act of rape is distinct from other types of assault not solely because of the body parts involved in the act, but more importantly, because of the role rape—or, more precisely, the threat of rape—plays in the production of the specifically (and socially recognizable) feminine body" (147).

9. Ibid., 126.

10. Marcus, "Fighting Bodies, Fighting Words," 391.

11. It is important to note at this point that neither Marcus nor Cahill suggests that rape is the only way in which women are created. Further, neither scholar suggests that the concepts of masculinization and feminization are natural, and in fact, Marcus spends the majority of her chapter explaining how what she calls the "rape script" (390) can be changed so that rape ceases to be a way to define what it means to be a woman.

12. See, for example, Miranda Alison, "Wartime Sexual Violence: Women's Human Rights and Questions of Masculinity," *Review of International Studies* 33, no. 1 (January 2007): 75–90; Lisa S. Price, "Finding the Man in the Soldier-Rapist: Some Reflections on Comprehension and Accountability," *Women's Studies International Forum* 24, no. 2 (2001): 211–227. See also Allison Ruby Reid-Cunningham, "Rape as a Weapon of Genocide," *Genocide Studies and Prevention* 3, no. 3 (December 2008): 279–296, for a recent discussion of the meaning of rape during instances of genocide.

13. Euan Hague, "Rape, Power and Masculinity: The Construction of Gender and National Identities in the War in Bosnia-Herzegovina," in *Gender and Catastrophe*, ed. Ronit Lentin (London: Zed Books, 1997), 50–63.

14. Ruth Seifert, "The Second Front: The Logic of Sexual Violence in Wars," *Women's Studies International Forum* 19, no. 1/2 (1996): 39.

15. Price, "Finding the Man in the Soldier-Rapist," 213, emphasis in the original.

16. See Judith Butler, *Undoing Gender* (New York and London: Routledge, 2004), and Joan W. Scott, "Gender: A Useful Category of Historical Analysis," *American Historical Review* 91 (December 1986): 1053–1075, for analyses of the constructedness and performativity of gender.

17. Hazel Carby, *Reconstructing Womanhood: The Emergence of the Afro-American Woman Novelist* (New York and Oxford: Oxford University Press, 1987), 18.

18. Susan Brownmiller, *Against Our Will: Men, Women and Rape* (New York: Fawcett Columbine, 1975), 15, emphasis in the original.

19. There are exceptions to this, however. For the first analyses of sexual violence in the camps, see Joan Ringelheim, "Women and the Holocaust: A Reconsideration of Research," in *Feminism and Community*, ed. Penny A. Weiss and Marilyn Friedman (Philadelphia: Temple University Press, 1995), 317–340; "The Split between Gender and the Holocaust," in *Women in the Holocaust*, ed. Dalia Ofer and Lenore J. Weitzman (New Haven: Yale University Press, 1998), 340–350. See also Myrna Goldenberg, "Different Horrors, Same Hell: Women Remembering the Holocaust," in *Thinking the Unthinkable: Meanings of the Holocaust*, ed. Roger S. Gottlieb (New York: Paulist Press, 1990), 150–166; "Lessons Learned from Gentle Heroism: Women's Holocaust Narratives," *Annals of the American Academy of Political and Social Science* 548 (November 1996): 78–93. For sexual violence committed by German soldiers, see Birgit Beck, *Wehrmacht und sexuelle Gewalt: Sexualverbrechen vor deutschen Militärgerichten 1939–1945* [Wehrmacht and sexual violence: Sex crimes prosecuted in German military courts, 1939–1945] (Paderborn: Ferdinand Schöningh, 2004); David Raub Snyder, *Sex Crimes under the Wehrmacht* (Lincoln: University of Nebraska Press, 2007), as well as works on prostitution, for example, Christa Paul, *Zwangsprostitution: Staatlich Errichtete Bordelle im Nationalsozialismus* [Forced prostitution: State-sanctioned brothels under National Socialism] (Berlin: Edition Hentrich, 1994); Insa Meinen, *Wehrmacht und Prostitution im besetzten Frankreich* [Wehrmacht and prostitution in occupied France] (Bremen: Ed. Temmen, 2002).

20. Adam Jones in "Straight as a Rule: Heteronormativity, Gendercide, and the Noncombatant Male," *Men and Masculinities* 8, no. 4 (2006): 459, emphasis in the original. See also Alison, "Wartime Sexual Violence."

21. Bitton Jackson, "Coming of Age," 81.

22. Anna Heilman, *Never Far Away: The Auschwitz Chronicles of Anna Heilman*, ed. Sheldon Schwartz (Calgary: University of Calgary Press, 2001), 88.

23. Rubinstein, *Survivor in Us All*, 125.

24. Ibid., 152.

25. Giuliana Tedeschi, *There Is a Place on Earth: A Woman in Birkenau*, trans. Tim Parks (New York: Pantheon Books, 1992), 97.

26. Isabelle Choko, *Stolen Youth: Five Women's Survival in the Holocaust* (New York: Yad Vashem, Holocaust Survivors' Memoirs Project, 2005), 42.

27. Isabella Leitner and Irving A. Leitner. *Isabella: From Auschwitz to Freedom* (New York: Anchor Books, 1994), 19.

28. Ibid., 133, emphasis added.

29. Erica Betts, interview 20825, USC Shoah Foundation testimony.

30. Helene Shiver, interview 36035, USC Shoah Foundation testimony.

31. Definitions of femininity and attractiveness varied according to identification with religious status and geographical location. What I mean by this is that strongly religious women, for example, may have had a concept of femininity that differed from non-religious women. Additionally, women living in an urban environment were likely to have a different concept of femininity than a woman living in an isolated rural environment. These differences will require further examination in future research. I thank Dr. Elizabeth Heineman for reminding me of the importance of these differences in her comments on another project.

32. Perl, A Doctor in Auschwitz, 44.

33. Ibid., 42.

34. Ibid., 46–47.

35. Ibid., 43–44.

36. Ibid., 109.

37. Eve Gabori, interview 1544, USC Shoah Foundation testimony.

38. Ana Cymerman, interview 8641, USC Shoah Foundation testimony.

39. Lya Cohen, interview 450, USC Shoah Foundation testimony.

40. Debora Sessler, interview 25384, USC Shoah Foundation testimony.

41. Olga Astor, interview 35621, USC Shoah Foundation testimony.

42. Regardless of whether or not one believes that Jewish women were, in appreciable numbers, forced to work in the camp brothels, the number of testimonies recounting sexual contact, observed and experienced, suggests that some degree of sexual contact between Jewish women and German soldiers did occur. This is further demonstrated by some documents from the Nazi regime itself, including numerous Rassenschande cases; see Patricia Szobar, "Telling Sexual Stories in the Nazi Courts of Law: Race Defilement in Germany, 1933–1945," The Journal of the History of Sexuality 11, no. 1/2 (January/April 2002): 131–163, for an analysis of Rassenschande cases.

43. Gucia Ferst, interview 34207, USC Shoah Foundation testimony.

44. Ursula Schwadron, interview 14982, USC Shoah Foundation testimony.

45. Harry Koltun, interview 19656, USC Shoah Foundation testimony.

46. Gottfried Bloch, interview 107, USC Shoah Foundation testimony.

47. Gilbert Metz, interview 45926, USC Shoah Foundation testimony. See also the testimonies by Jack I. Salzberg, interview 3956, USC Shoah Foundation testimony, and Marc Rubenstein, interview 34387, USC Shoah Foundation testimony. Male survivors recounting sexual abuse seem to have been more frequently abused by male Kapos than by guards, whereas women were more often sexually abused by guards. There are some references to female inmates being sexually abused by female guards and Kapos, a topic that will be further explored in a future project.

48. Eugene Lipschutz, interview 28052, USC Shoah Foundation testimony. Lipschutz ultimately talked his way out of being sexually abused by the Blockältester.

49. Elsa Breuer, interview 44511, USC Shoah Foundation testimony.

50. Jack I. Salzberg, interview 3956, USC Shoah Foundation testimony.

51. Herbert Kolischer, interview 20003, USC Shoah Foundation testimony.

52. Marc Rubenstein, interview 34387, USC Shoah Foundation testimony.

53. See Marcus, "Fighting Bodies, Fighting Words," for a discussion of rapability. Marcus argues that scholars should "understand rape as a language and use this insight to imagine women as neither already raped nor inherently rapable" (387).

54. Elsa Breuer, interview 44511, USC Shoah Foundation testimony.

55. Gilbert Metz, interview 45926, USC Shoah Foundation testimony.

56. Historically and generally, although there are culturally specific exceptions, homosexuals have been considered less masculine than heterosexual men; they have been perceived as exhibiting a masculinity subordinate to a heterosexual hegemonic masculinity. See Jones, "Straight as a Rule," for a discussion of subordinate and hegemonic masculinities. See also, Alison, "Wartime Sexual Violence."

CHAPTER

6

The Tragic Fate of Ukrainian Jewish Women under Nazi Occupation, 1941–1944

ANATOLY PODOLSKY

During the past ten years, Western European and American historiographers have actively studied various issues concerning the events in Ukraine during the Holocaust. Such studies include the history of persecution and extermination of Jews and the Jewish communities in different districts of occupied Ukraine, the Ukrainian-Jewish relationship during that period, collaboration issues, and other aspects of Holocaust history.[1] The resulting publications have only occasionally mentioned the specifics of the fate of Ukrainian Jewish women, usually in the context of research on the Holocaust in a particular region of occupied Ukraine.

The tragic fate of Ukrainian Jewish women during the Holocaust, and especially their sexual abuse, has never before been investigated as a separate study. This chapter is a preliminary investigation within the framework of the study of the Holocaust in Ukrainian territory between 1941 and 1944. These women died tragically only because they were Jewish. However, they suffered both as women and as Jews, and there were few survivors. Part of the tragedy of these women's desperate conditions was the sexual violence and rape inflicted on them by the Nazis, along with their Ukrainian collaborators.

Ukrainian Historiography of the Holocaust

Although sexual abuse of women has not been studied as part of research on the Holocaust in modern Ukrainian historiography or received attention as a separate research area, a few fragments about the subject can be found in papers by Ukrainian historians. Since the Ukrainian historiography of the Holocaust is only beginning to develop, I will first briefly analyze its progress as it directly concerns the subject of this chapter.

Before the collapse of the Soviet Union in 1991, issues concerning the Holocaust were virtually disregarded in Soviet Ukrainian historiography, and they definitely were not considered as a subject for independent historical study. The historiography of the so-called Great Patriotic War (World War II) does not include any research describing the policy of the genocide of Jews executed by Nazi Germany in the occupied Soviet Ukrainian territories.[2] No doctoral dissertations were ever defended in relation to these issues. Nevertheless, some Soviet academic institutions published collections of documents during that period,[3] and among these one can find materials on the history of the Holocaust, including documentation and testimonies that registered the places of mass executions of Jews in the occupied territories. However, this entire corpus of materials and papers was strictly censored, and any information about the fate of the Jewish population was brutally withdrawn. The euphemism "peaceful Soviet citizens" (those who had not been targeted by the Nazis) was introduced into the scientific, pedagogic, and popular literature—mainly to avoid separately mentioning Jewish victims. Therefore, during the years when all of the history of World War II was falsified, any historiography of the Holocaust was out of the question. One of the main ideological postulates of Soviet historical science was the claim that Soviet citizens were murdered regardless of their nationality or religion.

Radical changes came after the collapse of the Soviet system. Since then, the history of the Holocaust has become the object of study and research in modern Ukrainian historical science. During the last eighteen years a new trend in Ukrainian historiography has developed. Holocaust studies now includes a number of research papers, publications, monographs, source studies, documentaries, and memoir collections and studies.[4] More important, the conceptual approach has changed. The Holocaust is now considered the deliberate genocide against the Jews, a systematic policy of the Nazis directed at extermination of people solely because of what the Nazis called their race. There have been a number of publications on this subject.[5] Holocaust studies in Ukraine has developed from the publishing of a few regional studies and editions of memoirs to the synthesizing of scholarly research on various aspects and publishing fundamental collections of documents. Doctoral dissertations are still quite rare, but some have already been defended.[6]

The Fate of the Jewish Women of Ukraine
during the Holocaust

Because of these recent developments, we have been able to find material concerning the fate of Jewish women during the years of Nazism and World War II. Besides the historical papers, the main sources used for this chapter are the recollections, memoirs, and diaries of Jewish women who survived the Holocaust in the territory of Ukraine, as well as those of non-Jewish witnesses, recorded since 1991 in various regions. These testimonies were recorded thanks to the initiative of the Jewish communities, regional charitable organizations, and individual professional and amateur researchers. Most were published in Russian or Ukrainian as very limited editions, with no translation into other languages.[7] Therefore, those who study the fate of Jewish women during the Holocaust but cannot read these languages know little about some of the most relevant and important sources of information. Some of these memoirs, unlike most found in Soviet and German files, contain information about rape and humiliation that the women experienced. An additional source, which will be available to researchers soon, will without a doubt add to the picture of the suffering of Jewish women during the Holocaust in Ukraine. The video testimonies collected by the University of Southern California Shoah Foundation Institute for Visual History and Education in the territory of Ukraine include testimonies from the non-Jewish population who survived the Nazi occupation of their towns and villages, and who, among others facts, remembered the rape of Jewish women.[8]

Another recent study, not intended for the purpose at hand, also provides glimpses about sexual abuse of women in Ukraine. When Father Patrick Desbois interviewed Ukrainian witnesses to the mass murders in killing fields, several of them offered evidence that beautiful Jewish women were not always immediately murdered. Petrivina was a young barefoot Ukrainian girl in Ternivka when the Nazis ordered her and others to walk on the killing fields and pack down the bodies of Jews. She remembered that the Nazi in charge was named Hummel. According to her testimony, he "took two Jewish girls out of the line [on the way to be murdered], a seamstress and a very pretty young woman who were to his liking. They were taken to Hummel's house and were not killed that day."[9] Anna Dychkant, from Busk (in the Lviv region), told Father Desbois what the Nazis did there to her Jewish classmate and others:

> The young [Jewish] girls—there was one who went to school with me, Silva, who were very beautiful—they weren't killed straight away. Silva had to live with

the German commander. The other girls waited on the other soldiers. When the girls got pregnant, they were killed, because they couldn't have children with these people. They asked the Sokal police to take these girls, who were really beautiful, to a place 10 kilometers from Busk and to kill them because they didn't want to do it themselves. There was half a truck-load of them.[10]

Another witness from Busk, Anton Davidovski, gave similar testimony. Father Desbois wrote that Davidovski testified:

The Germans kept 30 or so very pretty Jewish women that they put to work in the offices of the Gestapo but whom they also used as "sex objects" for the police and the Germans. [Davidovski] explained that these women were not killed in Busk but 5 kilometers away, in a forest. When the Germans had left the town, the Jewish women had all been pregnant. The Germans in Busk hadn't the courage to kill them themselves. They had called on another commando, from nearby Sokal, to assassinate them.[11]

Within the radical anti-Semitic Nazi ideology that doomed all Jews to destruction, the fate of some Jewish women in Ukraine thus had the added tragedy of rape and sexual abuse. These crimes took place within the context of the extermination of 1.5 million Jews during the period of the Nazi occupation of Ukraine from 1941 to 1944. The only Jews who managed to survive were those who escaped to the Eastern parts of the Soviet Union and those who were rescued and hidden by Russians, Ukrainians, or Poles, who risked their own lives to save them.

The methods for murdering Jews were not the same throughout Ukraine. The Nazis, together with their Romanian and Hungarian allies, divided the territory of Ukraine into various occupied zones: *Reichskommissariat Ukraine*, the eastern Galicia District, Transnistria, Bukovina, Transcarpathia, and the War Zone. For example, in the *Reichskommissariat Ukraine* zone, which included the Kiev area, there were generally no ghettos. Jewish women, men, and children were rounded up, made to undress, and shot at the edges of huge mass graves. There is evidence that women were sometimes raped during this brutal process. In the eastern Galicia District (part of Poland in the *Generalgouvernement* during most of World War II and behind Soviet lines at the beginning and end of the war), there were ghettos and extermination camps.[12] Ukrainian Jews living in this district often ended their lives in the Bełżec extermination camp. And in Transnistria the Nazis and their Romanian allies accompanied mass murder with mass rape.

Rape in the Ravine

Reichskommissariat Ukraine was the largest part of Ukraine, the central, eastern, and partly southern regions that were under direct control of the German civil administration and the SS police. First of all, the murders here were committed by Einsatzgruppe C (a mobile killing unit), often with the help of the local Ukrainian police. From the end of 1941 to the beginning of 1942, there were around 150,000 policemen in the Reichskommissariat Ukraine.[13] This Reichskommissariat was the location of infamous murderous events such as those at Babi Yar in Kiev, Drobitzki Yar in Kharkov, Gagarin Park in Dnepropetrovsk, Chorni Yar in Radomishl, and an airbase field in Berdychev. Here the Nazis and their collaborators destroyed the absolute majority of the Jews by mass executions from fall 1941 to winter 1942.

In the eastern part of Ukraine, rather than placing the Jewish population in ghettos, the Nazis and their collaborators subjected them to quick violent mass executions. Populations were rounded up in their homes, usually marched to a specially dug ravine outside of town, told to undress, and then shot at the edge of these pits. People fell into the ravines in layers, as groups were executed in succession. Women were among the most defenseless victims. Their murders were accompanied by unprecedented persecution, harassment, humiliation, and violation of their human dignity. Almost always, in these places, the women were stripped naked regardless of their age, illness, or pregnancy, and sometimes, before they were executed, they were raped and subjected to unthinkably violent torture. We are able to reconstruct some of the horrible scenes through a number of survivors' and witnesses' reports.

There are numerous accounts of the terrible deaths of Kiev Jewish women in Babi Yar in September 1941. One of them that includes an eyewitness account of rape was narrated by Dina Pronicheva, an actress in the Kiev Theater. She was married to a Russian and went to Babi Yar with her parents. Pronicheva recounted how she saw the groups of women getting undressed, one after another, and led to an execution site, an open pit, and shot by submachine gunners. One naked woman was breastfeeding her naked baby when a policeman pulled the baby away from her breast and threw him alive into the pit. Pronicheva claimed to be Russian, but one of the policemen said she was Jewish and had a Jewish name. She was then ordered to disrobe and was pushed to the edge of the mass grave, where another group of women was waiting to be murdered. However, before the shooting started, Pronicheva fell into the pit. Landing on the dead and dying, and with more people being shot and falling on top of her, she kept still and pretended to be dead. When it became completely dark and quiet, she opened her eyes and saw that the killers had left.[14]

Later, Pronicheva witnessed rape:

[A]t the opposite side of the ravine, seven or so Germans brought two young Jewish women. They went down lower to the ravine, chose an even place and began to rape these women by turns. When they became satisfied, they stabbed the women with daggers, so that they even did not cry out. And they left the bodies like this, naked, with their legs open.[15]

Such sexual abuse and mass executions of Jewish women were typical for the central and eastern regions of Ukraine (e.g., Kiev, Cherkassy, Vinnitsa, Kharkov, Dnepropetrovsk, and Zaporozhye), which were united by the Nazis in the so-called *Reichskommissariat Ukraine*. The first wave of mass executions in the *Reichskommissariat* took place during the fall and the early winter of 1941–1942. Those Jewish women who by luck managed to survive the first round of executions were cruelly exploited by the Nazi-occupied authorities and the Ukrainian police in humiliating activities such as cleaning toilets, washing cars, and household service for the Germans and the police. We can only conjecture that the "household service" sometimes included sexual slavery, yet almost all of these women were murdered during the second and the third actions of mass executions, which took place during 1942. Hundreds of thousands of Jewish women died the death of the "execution pits" in the territory of central, eastern, and southern Ukraine, and only a few survived this hell.

Furthermore, at any moment a Nazi or a Ukrainian policeman could kill a Jewish woman with impunity. The groundless murder of a Jewish woman in the territory of the *Reichskommissariat Ukraine* was rarely punished, even administratively. For example, Naum Epelfeld of Berdychev provided the following testimony:

The Germans took Berdychev. Sometime later two soldiers entered the basement where we stayed. They lit their way with torches and kept saying something, but we couldn't understand them. Then they started walking among people sitting on the floor and shining torches into their faces. Then they stopped near a girl and a woman, and ordered them to follow. They took them into an empty office and raped them. The girl's name was Gusta; she was our neighbour's daughter. Gusta Glozman was fourteen or fifteen years old. Soon she would be killed, together with her parents."[16]

In addition, policemen received a supplementary food ration or bonus for finding unregistered Jewish women in hiding.[17]

Women's diaries are some of the most important sources revealing the fate of Jewish women in the eastern part of Ukraine. In the 1990s, some women's diaries found in archives and private collections were published[18]; however, I have not so far found any diary testimonies by women that refer specifically to sexual abuse or rape. I believe that not all of the materials have yet been discovered. Furthermore, it is extremely likely that most of the victims of rape were subsequently murdered and could not have left testimony.

The Ghettos and Extermination Camps of Eastern Galicia

The Galicia District was included by the Nazis in the Polish *Generalgouvernement*. At least a half million Jews lived in this region, and many were more connected to Ukraine than Poland. During the time of the Holocaust, the Jewish population spoke Polish, Yiddish, Ukrainian, and Russian. Today part of this area is Western Ukraine (the Lviv, Ivano-Frankovsk, and Ternopol regions). The Nazis and their local collaborators did not organize mass executions in this region as they did in Kiev at Babi Yar or the rest of the *Reichskommissariat Ukraine*. Here, as in other areas of the *Generalgouvernement*, they created ghettos where many Jews died of unbearable conditions. The rest (except for the small number in hiding) were subsequently murdered in extermination camps.

This area's history during World War II is complicated because under the terms of the August 23, 1939, Molotov-Ribbentrop Pact it was under Soviet control for part of the time. On September 1, 1939, Germany invaded the area of Western Poland allotted it by the pact, and on September 17, the Soviet Army likewise invaded and occupied part of Eastern Poland. When Nazi Germany invaded the Soviet Union on June 22, 1941, the Molotov-Ribbentrop Pact was terminated, and Nazi Germany took over the area of Eastern Poland/Western Ukraine. As can be imagined, there was much movement of the Jewish population and non-Jewish Poles back and forth across the lines as they shifted.

Shortly after the Nazi occupation of these territories in July–August 1941, even before ghettos were created, there were pogroms against local Jewish populations in cities and small towns. They were provoked by the German occupying government and performed by the local non-Jewish population—Ukrainians, as well as Poles and Russians.

The Lvov ghetto and the Yanov camp (also situated in Lvov) are the most well-known sites in the part of the *Generalgouvernement* that was then Eastern Poland and is now Western Ukraine. However, there were also many small towns with ghettos. Often the able-bodied men were sent to forced labor camps, leaving the women behind to survive on their own and take care of their children in the unbearable conditions of a Nazi ghetto. These ghettos were organized in fall–winter 1941, and some lasted until spring–summer 1943, when the last Jews of Eastern Galicia were exterminated or deported. The Bełżec extermination camp, which began operating in the spring of 1942, was the final destination for many of these women.

Rosa Wagner, a Jewish woman who lived in Lvov (now called Lviv in Ukraine), provided an eyewitness testimony of rape there.[19] She lived in Lvov and survived a pogrom in that city on June 30–July 1, 1941. Her twenty-four-page typed Polish manuscript was submitted to the Jewish Historical Institute in Warsaw in 1945. She wrote:

It was 11 o'clock in the morning [of June 30, 1941]. We were told that Ukrainians were leading a column of Jewish women along the street. We did not yet realize what was going on. Suddenly a teenager with a gangster face appeared at the gates. "Let's go, ladies, to put in some work," he said to me and my neighbor with an expression full of sarcasm and hatred. I was gripped by fear that we were going to be dead now. As soon as we passed the gates we were surrounded by a gang of youths. They started to push and then beat us . . . At some point I lost consciousness, then someone called me and I came to . . . A beaten mass of persecuted and degraded people was now watching every movement of the pogrom initiators, waiting tensely for the further course of events.

However, for some reason, they were not in a hurry to finish with us. An irrepressible crowd wanted our blood and humiliation. They wanted to gain a financial profit from this entertainment. The prostitutes came up in front of [us] poor women. . . . and like the rulers ordered us to take off our shoes and other items of clothing that they liked. Then they ordered us to give away our documents. . . . One of the criminals announced that if they found out that anyone of us had any money or jewelry, we would be in trouble. A scoundrel did not even expect such fruitful results which were brought by his evil command.

And while the greedy killers took all the clothes off one of the women and were mercilessly beating her naked body with a stick, the German soldiers who were passing by and who we asked to get involved, answered: "Das ist die Rache der Ukrainer" (This is the revenge of the Ukrainians), in a tone full of approval of their actions. They were passing by with a look of masters and taking pictures of the naked women who were raped and violently beaten: "Das wird im Stürmer sein" (This is going to be in Der Stürmer [the Nazi newspaper]), they remarked gladly.

They were looking forward to their fellow countrymen being able to see their men and sons who were waging war to change the world for the better.[20]

Transnistria and the Romanians

Transnistria, the area between the Dniester and Bug rivers and the Black Sea coast, was controlled by the Germans and their Romanian allies from August 19, 1941, until January 29, 1944. Before the war, this area had a Jewish population of 300,000. Tens of thousands of them were slaughtered by *Einsatzgruppe* D, and by German and Romanian forces. When Transnistria was occupied, the pre-war Jewish population was increased by about 150,000 Jews who had been expelled from Bessarabia, Bukovina, and northern Moldavia. These deportations began on September 15, 1941, and continued until the Romanians halted them on October 13, 1942. Most accounts of the Holocaust in Transnistria mention mass rapes, perpetrated especially by Romanian troops, but no details are provided. The fact that the women were usually murdered after they were raped or otherwise sexually abused contributes to the dearth of eyewitness testimony. However, three Jewish survivors, one woman and two men, gave testimonies about rape to Boris Zabarko.

Golda Wasserman provided an eyewitness account of seeing girls selected to be raped and then returned to the ghetto. She described the selection for mass rape using the euphemism "work" and finally said that she herself was also chosen:

In the autumn of 1942, there were more than 3,000 Jewish families from the Ukraine, Bukovina, and Bessarabia resettled to the Tulchin ghetto. . . . About fifteen kilometers from the ghetto, there were Italian and Hungarian reserve divisions. As demanded by the commissariat-officers of these divisions, the Romanian gendarme who was the Kommandant of Tulchin selected healthy young girls from the ghetto and sent them away, under the official pretense of working in the kitchen and bakery of those divisions. The girls returned from there having been raped, ill with venereal diseases. Many committed suicide back in the barracks, while some of them were killed when resisting or attempting to flee. Then the Kommandant selected new girls for "work." Selection was carried out every fifteen to twenty days. It is impossible to describe what was happening in the ghetto—the desperate screams of the girls, the pleas of their parents. Some girls tried to run away along the road. The Fascists shot them in the back. Only a few managed to hide in the villages, pretending to be locals, or were saved by the partisans after long wanderings in the forests. I belonged to the latter group. Among twenty-five other girls, I was picked to be sent to "work."[21]

Two Jewish men also provided testimony about rape of young Jewish women by Romanians. Alexander Kuperman described what he saw in the Bershad ghetto:

> The Romanians were not much better than Germans. The ghetto was located in the territory occupied by Romanians, who tortured the ghetto prisoners day and night. On one summer day of 1942, a group of Romanians led by their "platooner" [lieutenant] entered the ghetto, where the Jewish marketplace was established and where there were many people. They selected three or four young, very beautiful, Jewish girls, took them to their barracks, and made them go "through their ranks." The girls died.[22]

Arkady Khassin, who lived in Odessa, added: "But the nights were terrible! Drunk Romanians, lighting their way with torches, roamed the workshops in search of young girls. The latter would hide under the pieces of equipment and the Romanians pulled them out. Screams, weeping, and sometimes shots, filled the building with echoes throughout the night."[23]

The Suffering Continued Afterward

About one and a half million Jews were exterminated by the Nazis in Ukrainian territory during the Holocaust years, not less than a half of whom were women. Only a small number were fortunate enough to survive the Nazi occupation, either because of sheer luck, their willpower and courage, those who risked helping them, or a combination of these factors. However, most survivors were not able to live full lives after what they had been through. Some women who had been raped felt that they could not marry, some were shunned, and often they could not bear children as a result of the assaults. Some suffered from various diseases and soon died.

Elizabeth Kremer, a Jewish woman who survived, managed to get out of an execution pit in Mariupol (on the Sea of Azov, now at the Russia–Ukraine border). She lived in Kiev after the war, and was treated with distrust, as was everyone who had been in the Nazi-occupied territories. In the Stalinist Soviet Union in the 1940s and 1950s, those who survived the Nazi occupation were constantly suspected of collaboration and held in contempt. Elizabeth worked for the city doing construction, had no documents, suffered from ill health, and married only in 1960. The doctors said she would never be able to have children after everything she had been through, implying that she had been brutally raped. She adopted a girl from an orphanage, who became her beloved daughter. However, at the beginning of the 1990s this daughter, then a grown woman, created unbearable living conditions for her adoptive mother that ultimately contributed to her death.[24]

Another female survivor, Sima Kuritskaya from Priluki in the Chernigov region, poignantly described her fate. She, too, had to hide the fact that she had survived the Nazis:

> My later life was spent wandering around. Under an assumed Ukrainian name I would beg on the streets, apply for different jobs, too difficult for my age, always hungry. I had no clothes, no shoes, and was in constant fear that somebody would find out and give me away. I even cried when nobody could see me. I cried for my parents. Because I told everybody that I did not know my parents, and that I was from an orphanage. My hardships during two years of [Nazi] occupation had done their part. At the age of thirty I became disabled, and when I was thirty-two, I endured a difficult heart surgery.[25]

Conclusions

After the Holocaust, only 4 percent of the earlier Jewish population remained in Ukraine, including eastern Ukraine. In recent years efforts have begun in Ukraine to introduce Jewish culture and history into the public consciousness as a part of Ukrainian identity. So far, progress has been very slow. Studying the fate of Jewish women during the Holocaust years could be one of the most important factors in realizing that the history of the Holocaust in Ukrainian territory is a part of the national history of the country and in taking up our responsibility for the memory of the past. As Father Patrick Desbois states regarding the Nazi mass murder in Ukraine:

> The Jewish women selected by the Germans as sex slaves and assassinated at the end of the war are not mentioned in any of the archives. Yet [non-Jewish] witnesses often mentioned them. They knew them before the occupation and were often present at their assassination. The Holocaust of Jewish women in Eastern Europe constitutes a chapter of history that has barely been opened.[26]

Notes

Translated by Elena Yurchenko.

1. See, for example, Omer Bartov, *Erased: Vanishing traces of Jewish Galicia in Present-day Ukraine* (Princeton: Princeton University Press, 2007); Karel Berkhoff, *Harvest of Despair: Life and Death in Ukraine under Nazi Rule* (Cambridge: Belknap Press of Harvard University Press, 2004); Ray Brandon and Wendy Lower, eds., *The Shoah in Ukraine: History, Testimony, Memorialization* (Bloomington: Indiana University Press with the United States Holocaust Memorial Museum, 2008); Father Patrick Desbois, *The Holocaust by Bullets* (New York: Palgrave Macmillan, 2008); Wendy Lower, *Nazi Empire-Building and the Holocaust in Ukraine* (Chapel Hill: University of North Carolina Press, 2005); Dieter Pohl, "Anti-Jewish Pogroms in Western Ukraine—A Research Agenda," in *Shared History-Divided Memory: Jews and Others in Soviet-Occupied Poland, 1939–1941*, ed. Elazar Barkan, Elisabeth Cole, and Kai Struve (Leipzig: Leipziger Universitätsverlag, 2007); Dieter Pohl, *Judenverfolgung in Ostgalizien 1941–1944. Organisation und Durchführung eines staatlichen Massenverbrechens* [Persecution of Jews in East Galicia, 1941–1944. Organization and implementation of a systematic mass murder] (Munich: Oldenbourg, 1997).

2. The term "Great Patriotic War" was introduced into scientific and sociocultural terminology to define the events of World War II on the Soviet–German (Eastern) front from June 22, 1941, until May 9, 1945. It was often a synonym for World War II. In modern Ukrainian historiography and Ukrainian society the term is used much less often, but it can be still applied in scientific and cultural discourse.

3. *SS v deistvii. Documenti i materiali* [SS in action. Documents and materials] (Moscow: Progress, 1969); *"Sovershenno secretno! Tolko dlya komandovaniya!" Documenti i materiali* ["Top secret! Only for command!" Documents and materials], ed. V. I. Dashichev (Moscow: Nauka, 1967). In the 1940s and 1950s, the collections of documents on the Nazi occupation were published in different regions of Ukraine, such as Kiev, Vinnitsa, Zhitomir, Dnepropetrovsk.

4. These include monographs and papers by such Ukrainian historians as Faina Vinokurova, Ster Yelisavetsky, Viktor Koval, Mikhail Koval, Zhanna Kovba, Viktor Korol, Alexander Kruglov, Vladimir Kucher, Felix Levitas, Anatoly Podolsky, Mikhail Tyaglyy, and Yaroslav Honigsman.

5. See, for example, Anatoly Podolsky, "Tema Holocostu v suchasniy ukrayinskiy istoriografiyi: problemy naukovyh doslidzhen ta interpretatsiy" [The Holocaust subject in the modern Ukrainian historiography: Problems of the scholarly research and interpretation], in *Druga svitova viyna i dolya narodiv Ukrainy: Materialy Vseukrainskoyi naukovoi konferentsiyi* [The Second World War and the fate of the Ukrainian people: Materials from the all-Ukrainian scholarly conference] (Kiev: Sfera, 2005), 32–34; and Podolsky, "Doslidzhennya z istoriyi Holocostu v suchasniy ukrainskiy istoriografiyi: novi pidhody" [Research of Holocaust history in the modern Ukrainian historiography: New approaches], in *Katastrofa i opir ukrainskogo yevreistva: Narysy z istoriyi Holocostu i Oporu v Ukraini* [The catastrophe and the opposition of the Jewry: Essays on the history of the

Holocaust and opposition in Ukraine] (Kiev: Institute of Politic and Ethnic Studies, National Academy of Science of Ukraine, 1999), 26–38.

6. Between 1991 and 2008, six dissertations on the history of the Holocaust in Ukraine were defended in Ukraine. Their authors are Anatoly Podolsky, Felix Levitas, Faina Vinokurova, Alexander Goncharenko, Oleg Surovtsev, and Natalia Sugatskaya. The dissertations of Maxim Gon, Vladislav Grinevich, and Dmitro Titarenko were also partially concerned with the problems of Holocaust history in Ukraine. There are some dissertation researchers who are currently investigating the history of the Holocaust in the territory of the Stanislavsky (Ivano-Frankovsk) region (by Lubov Solovka). Yuril Radchenko is studying the genocide against Jews in the zone of the German military administration (Eastern Ukraine). Mikhail Tyaglyy is researching the Holocaust in the Crimea.

7. See, for example: Vinnitskaya oblast. Katastrofa (SHOA) i soprotivleniye. Svidetelstva yevreev—uznikov konclagerei i getto, uchastnikov partizanskogo dvizheniya i podpolnoi borbi [Vinnitsa region. The Catastrophe (Shoah) and the opposition. Accounts of the Jews—Prisoners of the concentration camps and ghettos, members of the partisan movement and the underground war] (Tel Aviv/Kiev: Ghetto Fighters House and RIF, 1994); David Starodinsky, Odesskoye getto [Odessa ghetto] (Odessa: Khaitekh, 1991); Tsinoyu vlasnogo zhytta [At a price of their own life] (Rivne: Rivne Region Publishing House, 1995); Peredaite detam nashim o nashei sudbe. Sbornik documentov, dnevnikov i vospominaniy. [Tell our children about our fate. Collection of documents, diaries and memoirs] (Simferopol: Charitable Foundation Khesed Shimon, 2001); Shodennyk Lvivskogo getto. Spogadi rabina Davida Kahane [The diary of the Lviv ghetto. Memories of Rabbi David Kahane] (Kiev: Dukh i Litera, 2003).

8. From 1994 to 1998, the University of Southern California Shoah Foundation Institute for Visual History and Education collected more than 3,500 video interviews with Jews who survived the Holocaust in the territory of Ukraine. A considerable number of these interviews were given by Jewish women. Other oral history projects interviewing non-Jews who remember Holocaust events have also been carried out in Ukraine in the last few years. For example, in 2006 and 2007 the Ukrainian Center for Holocaust Studies conducted two student field studies in the Khmelnitsk region and in the Crimea. As a result, sixty interviews were collected in these regions. See also the work of Father Patrick Desbois, The Holocaust by Bullets (New York: Palgrave Macmillan, 2008).

9. Desbois, Holocaust by Bullets, 85.

10. Ibid., 126.

11. Ibid., 167. This region was part of the Austro-Hungarian Empire, and was then divided between Poland and Ukraine.

12. The history of Galicia, especially in the east, is complicated and has been disputed. In 1918, Poland proclaimed national independence, captured western Galicia from Austria, and fought against the newly established Ukrainian republic in eastern Galicia. The Paris Peace Conference (1919) assigned eastern Galicia to Poland pending a plebiscite scheduled for 1944. However, in a treaty (1920) with the Ukrainians, upheld by the Polish-Soviet Treaty of Riga (1921), Poland obtained full title to eastern Galicia. Then, in 1939 most of eastern Galicia was incorporated into Ukraine, an act later upheld by the Polish-Soviet Treaty of 1945.

13. Alexander Prusin, "The Ukrainian Police and the Holocaust in the General-bezirk Kiew, 1941–1943: Activities and Motivations," in *Holocaust and Modernity* 1, no. 2 (2007): 35.

14. See Yitzhak Arad, *Katastrofa yevreev na occupirovannih territoriah Sovetskogo Soyuza (1941–1945)* [The catastrophe of the Jews in the occupied territories of the Soviet Union (1941–1945)] (Dnepropetrovsk: Tkuma Center, Moscow Holocaust Center, 2007), 253.

15. *Babi Yar. K patidesatiletiyu tragedii 29, 30 sentabra 1941 goda* [Babi Yar: For the fiftieth anniversary of the tragedy of September 29–30, 1941], (Jerusalem: Biblioteka-Aliya, 1991), 58.

16. Boris Zabarko, ed. *Holocaust in the Ukraine*, trans. Marina Guba (London: Vallentine Mitchell, 2005), 366.

17. For more on the motives of Ukrainian policemen to track down Jews, see Martin Dean, *Collaboration in the Holocaust: Crimes of the Local Police in Belorussia and Ukraine, 1941–44* (St. Martin's Press: New York, 2000), 101–102.

18. The majority of these diaries were found in the archives of Ilya Erenburg and Vasiliy Grossman, as well as the Jewish Anti-Fascist Committee Funds. They were not included in the edition of the *Chornaya Kniga* [Black book] (Jerusalem: Tarbut, 1980). In 1993, the *Neizvestnaya Chornaya Kniga* [Unknown black book] (Moscow: GARF—Gosudarstvennyi Arkhiv Rossiyskoi Federacii—State Archive of Russian Federation, 1993) was published in Jerusalem in Russian, and the texts of these diaries can be found there.

19. John (Ivan) Himka, "Dostovirnist svidchenna: relacia Ruzi Vagner pro lvivsky pogrom vlitku 1941r" [Veracity of testimony: Roza Wagner's story of the Lviv pogrom of the summer of 1941], in *Naukovy chasopys Holocost i suchasnist. Studii v Ukraini i sviti* [Scholarly journal of Holocaust and modernity. Studies in Ukraine and the world], no. 2(4), 2008: 43–81.

20. Ibid., 46–47.

21. Boris Zabarko, ed., *Holocaust in the Ukraine*, 51–52.

22. Ibid., 153–154.

23. Ibid., 311.

24. Elizaveta Kremer-Zagoruiko, testimony recorded by the author, 1994.

25. *Zhivimi ostalis tolko mi. Svidetelstva i documenti* [We were the only ones who had survived. Testimonies and documents] (Kiev: Dukh i Litera and Institute of Jewish Studies, 1999), 234.

26. Desbois, *Holocaust by Bullets*, 168.

The Rape of Jewish Women during the Holocaust

HELENE J. SINNREICH

While many uncomfortable components of the Holocaust have been analyzed in minute detail, the rape of Jewish women during this era persists as a subject that scholars and victims alike are reticent to explore.[1] In part, this is the result of erroneous perceptions shared by victims and early Holocaust scholars, such as the idea that rape victims have cause for shame or somehow partially bear responsibility. Some scholars may also have denied the possibility that their grandmothers, mothers, sisters, or wives had been raped. As a result, the testimonies of victims who had the courage to mention personal or other prisoners' sexual abuse in diaries, memoirs, oral testimonies, or other documents were ignored or relegated to footnotes.

Embarrassment, shame, fear, and especially a desire to hide the events from family members are motives for many victims of rape to remain silent. Nechama Tec, when interviewing women for her book *Resilience and Courage*, noted that when the issue of sexual abuse was raised, the women were reluctant to share their experiences. She wrote: "Judging by the hesitation I encountered among interviewees to recount these coercive sexual experiences, I have to assume that most of these stories will die with the victims."[2] However, not all victims of sexual abuse during the Holocaust have been silent. A number of these women reported what happened to them, or witnesses to the victims' ordeals described their experiences. These testimonies, along with some corroborating evidence, provide a picture of this aspect of Jewish women's Holocaust experience.

This chapter examines some of the cases that reveal that despite contradicting central policy regarding *Rassenschande* (race defilement), rape of Jewish women did occur during the Holocaust. Numerous regional studies on the

Final Solution have focused on the role of center-periphery relations and concluded that the timing and method of Nazi anti-Jewish practice varied based on location and in many cases on local leadership.[3] In some cases, individuals at the lowest levels did not follow the policy dictated by superiors,[4] sometimes resulting in brutality, and at other times in disobedience that took the form of saving Jews. Wendy Lower has suggested that actions on the periphery were less directly scrutinized and therefore could be more brutal. She notes, "The commissars and regional police forces did not carry out the Nazi goal of genocide in a banal fashion: they fulfilled it barbarically, often encouraging sadistic methods that exceeded the expectations of their superiors, who wanted to maintain order, a measure of control, and secrecy."[5] However, citing the case of an official who hid Jews during the war, she also pointed out that this same secrecy allowed those at the periphery to carry out actions not allowed by Nazi central authorities.[6] Whether due to excess as a result of the overall culture of violence or to a recognition of the humanity of those the regime deemed undeserving of life, it is clear that what took place on the ground during the Holocaust did not always match the directed racial policy.

This phenomenon meant that the experiences of individual victims—including those who were sexually violated—did not always coincide with the Nazis' central policies. In some cases, deviations were reported back to Berlin, but in other cases, we can uncover departures from Nazi orthodoxy only through victim testimony.[7] For example, Christopher Browning's *Nazi Policy, Jewish Workers, German Killers* relies heavily on survivor testimony to reconstruct the Starachowice labor camp's internal operations and expose the German camp administration's indiscretions, demonstrating how the leadership of particular labor camps affected the experiences of their Jewish laborers. Nazis in charge of localities were sometimes at odds with central Nazi policy not only with regard to accepting bribes or other indiscretions but also in relation to creating an atmosphere conducive to sexual abuse.

Cases of Rape of Jewish Women throughout Nazi-occupied Europe

Rape committed alongside theft of private property is not unusual during war. It is the first of the five patterns of rape identified by the United Nations Commission of Experts in their final report on the rapes in the former Yugoslavia: "In the first pattern, sexual violence occurred with looting and intimidation . . . people would break into homes, steal property, and torture and sexually assault the inhabitants, oftentimes in front of other family members or the public."[8] Katharine Derderian, in her work on women during the Armenian genocide, notes a pattern of rape and robbing of victims: "After systematic despoliation of the deportees, sexual and gender-based violence predominated, including rape, sexual slavery, and forced marriage."[9] And writing about the Rape of Nanking, Iris Chang states that soldiers went door to door "demanding money and *hua gu niang*—[meaning] young girls."[10]

During the Holocaust, Jewish women were raped throughout Nazi-occupied Europe, usually where individuals could carry out such abuse without their superiors' knowledge. Germans were not supposed to loot Jewish homes, but in wartime conditions and in the absence of their civil rights, Jews were subjected to mass looting. In this atmosphere, rape was also possible. As one testimony from Poland reveals: "The Jews of Włocławek were driven out of their homes, robbed, tortured, and forced to do hard labor. Jewish women were raped. Finally, nearly all Jews were driven out of town in separate groups until by March 1940 there was hardly a Jew left."[11] Sometimes soldiers broke into homes just so they could demand victims to sexually abuse. As a Warsaw doctor testified: "One continually hears of the raping of Jewish girls in Warsaw. The Germans suddenly enter a house and rape 15- or 16-year-old girls in the presence of their parents and relatives."[12]

There is also testimony that German soldiers raped Jewish girls in their homes in Grodzisk Mazowiecki, as Jezechiel F. of that location testified to a representative of the World Jewish Congress in Vilna: "At night the Germans would force their way into Jewish homes and rape women and girls. The other members of the household would be locked up in another room. Some of the girls, those of the more educated type, would be taken by the Germans to their barracks where they were raped and killed."[13]

Sometimes women were first taken from their homes, ostensibly for forced labor, and then raped. According to one account of rape that took place in Warsaw: "In February 1940 the Germans began rounding up Jewish women for forced labor. . . . Girls would disappear for several days and come home after having been attacked. The attractive wife of a Jew on the Iron Gate Place was abducted and permitted to return home after she had been raped."[14]

Jewish women were raped not only in their homes but also later, after they had been forced into ghettos and concentration camps. Kraków ghetto survivor Jan Rożański described an incident during one of the mass deportations from that ghetto. He and his mother were called downstairs by a German SS officer and ordered to clear a stairwell. Rozansi described what he and his mother found at the foot of the stairs: "a young girl. She was dead. Her dress lifted and pants torn off her body. She was raped, illegally, and then killed, legally, by the representants [sic] of the 'high race.' She was shot directly in the face."[15]

Testimony that rape was a part of the Holocaust experiences of some Jewish women comes also from Telsiai (Telz), Lithuania. A number of survivors testify that Lithuanian collaborators both took women away for "work" during the daytime and made selections from the barracks at night. The work was in reality rape at the hands of their "employers."[16] During the period when these rapes occurred, one famed scholar requested that one of his daughters read several texts, including Maimonides's Hilchot Yesodei HaTorah (The Laws of the Foundations of the Torah). One reason for his recommendation may have been to remind her that it was an act of great faith to choose death over forbidden sexual relations.[17]

Regarding rape in concentration camps, a survivor related that her aunt and cousin were raped: "There were all these rules about German men and Jewish girls—they were not allowed to be together. Well, Nazis raped this girl [her cousin Ruth] and my aunt. It is unbelievable. Where could I have gotten that information back then? The two of them were not allowed to disclose it. They only told me. That's how it was."[18]

Survivor Paula N. related an incident that took place in Bruss-Sophienwalde concentration camp. A woman in the camp became pregnant. She felt that the commandant of the camp was kind-hearted and confided in him about her pregnancy. Rather than the sympathetic treatment she expected, he put her on a list to be deported to Stutthof. The girl hid to avoid deportation, but was eventually found by four German guards. In front of everyone in the camp— mostly young girls—this pregnant woman was gang-raped and then thrown onto the truck to Stutthof.[19]

Women in other concentration camps were also raped, either by fellow prisoners or German guards. Several survivors of Auschwitz, for example, have testified that women were dragged from their barracks by guards and raped.[20] A Greek Jewish woman, Laura Varon, reported that she and her friend were raped by three SS officers at Auschwitz. She described them suddenly throwing open the door, violently assaulting the women and raping them.[21] Emil G. reported that while he was in Auschwitz-Birkenau, the Germans arranged a "show" in which they took twenty Jewish women prisoners and raped them in front of one of the labor groups. Emil added that the male prisoners were supposed to stand and applaud. He knew one of the raped women from his hometown. She survived the war but committed suicide soon afterward.[22]

Similarly, survivor Sara M. was a very young girl when she was raped at Ravensbrück concentration camp. She was taken from the barracks by a woman, given candy, and led to a small room. She testified:

> [T]here were two men there and there were some other people in the room I think. I was put on a table. From what I remember, [it was] a table or it could have been a high table. I was very little so it seemed like it was very high up from where I was and I was very violently sexually abused. And I remember being hit, I remember crying and I wanted to get out of there. And I was calling people and screaming and I remember one thing that stands out in my mind that one of them told me that they would stand me up on my head and cut me right in half. And they wanted me to stop screaming and I've had nightmares about that most of my life.[23]

Sara M. was returned to her aunt after the brutal abuse, and afterward there was no discussion about what had happened to her. The rape of young girls such as Sara M. in Ravensbrück was possibly carried out without the knowledge of the concentration camp's administration.

In the Glöwen concentration camp, German guards dragged women from their beds at night for sex. Rose S. noted that, "at night, the time was ours alone except for some of us—they had to go out and attend the Germans. They just came and picked the girls, whoever they felt like and took them away to their barracks. Sometimes they had to stay overnight."[24] Paula K. offered similar testimony regarding the Tschenstochau-Pelzery concentration camp. She testified that a *Wehrmacht* soldier came into the women's barracks and started talking to her and some of her female family members. Four or five weeks later, when they were all asleep, this same soldier, who was very drunk, came and started to pull the blanket off Paula. One of her family members stood between her and the German and told her to run. Frustrated by his inability to find the first woman he had selected, he grabbed a girl who was sleeping near the entrance to the barrack. He dragged her off and raped her. The girl came back at four o'clock in the morning, bleeding, screaming, and crying. She was taken to the hospital.[25]

Rape in a Ghetto: The Case of Hans Biebow in the Łódź (Litzmannstadt) Ghetto

The Łódź (Litzmannstadt) ghetto was among the places where the local Nazi ruler's deviation from central policy led to a culture of sexual abuse and widespread rape. The *Chronicle* written in the Łódź ghetto reported that a man named Ordinanz had been found guilty of rape in the ghetto court system, and the rapist was appealing his conviction. The *Chronicle* mentioned the case not because it was the only rape conviction in the ghetto court system's history, but because Jewish ghetto leader Mordechai Rumkowski's wife, attorney Regina Rumkowska, served as co-council in the appeal.[26] Not only the ordinary ghetto dweller was accused of sexual abuse in the ghetto. Postwar testimonies point to the Jewish ghetto leadership in the form of Rumkowski himself, as well as German ghetto head Hans Biebow, as having engaged in sexual abuse.[27]

Biebow, in charge of the German Ghetto Administration of the Łódź ghetto, raped a number of Jewish women during the last years of World War II. He has primarily been depicted by scholars and others as a bureaucrat more concerned with the profitable running of the ghetto than with playing out sadistic tendencies. Christopher Browning describes Biebow and another German official as "neither hard-core party activists nor fanatic anti-Semites."[28] Similarly, Primo Levi wrote, "Biebow was not a wild animal: he was not interested in causing suffering or punishing the Jews for their sin of being Jewish, but in making money on his contracts."[29] However, Biebow did have a violent streak, as reflected in victim testimony from the ghetto, which manifested itself in beating Jews and raping Jewish women. For example, Biebow beat the elderly Rumkowski so severely that the more than seventy-year-old Jewish leader was in the hospital for several weeks.[30] Declaring this the first severe beating delivered by Biebow to Rumkowski, the *Chronicle* nevertheless hinted that it was not the first time Biebow had engaged in beating someone. The comment by the *Chronicle* was: "Anyone who knows the *Amtsleiter* [head official] knows that this is one of his fits of rage which he will later regret."[31]

Evidence of at least one of the rapes has been in public circulation since 1960, when Jakub Poznanski's *Pamiętnik z getta łódzkiego* (Diary from the Łódź ghetto) was first published. As evidenced by other more neutral descriptions about Biebow, this account of his temper and that in the *Chronicle* have largely been ignored by most historians writing about him. However, Poznanski, in a diary entry dated September 2, 1944, wrote of the rape of a Jewish girl by Biebow. He reported:

> Ejbuszyc and Blachowski told us about something horrible that happened at 36 Lagiewnicka Street. Dr. Sima Mandels, a pediatrician, was there with her engineer husband and her two children. The tragedy occurred when Hans Biebow noticed their beautiful 16-year-old daughter. One evening when he was drunk, he grabbed her in the hallway, dragged her into his office, and tried to rape her.

The girl tried to defend herself and started screaming. It was then that "the master of life and death" shot her in the eye. The mother started crying in despair. In order to silence her, Biebow ordered the entire family shipped out immediately. The same happened to the chief physician Dr. Miller, who spoke up for the Mandels family. He was deported with his wife and little son.[32]

The rape of Sima Mandels's daughter was not the only instance in which Biebow was accused of rape. There are at least two oral testimonies in which Biebow was also so accused. Esther H. was in Dresden during the war when Biebow arrived. At one point, he ordered her to move a mattress into his office.[33] He then accused her of moving the wrong mattress and beat her with a rubber whip. While her proximity to Biebow left her vulnerable to this beating, it also enabled her to learn of Rita, a woman described by Esther as being a beautiful Czech girl whom Biebow and another German kept. According to Esther, Rita was raped by both men, and the SS knew about it but did nothing. When the prisoners were being evacuated from the camp to escape the advancing front, the woman was murdered.[34] Not all of Biebow's victims were killed. Bina W. was among those few who were left in the Łódź ghetto to clean it up after its final liquidation. One night, she was raped by Hans Biebow.[35]

Although scholars might doubt one testimony, it is hard to dismiss three of them about the same individual. In one case, a ghetto diarist reported what might be called hearsay. Some may dismiss this type of evidence as unsubstantiated, as the writer was not an actual witness. The second testimony comes from a woman who was witness to the incarceration of one of Biebow's rape victims, and the third is from a woman who had actually been raped by him. It might be argued that discipline had broken down at the end of the war, providing circumstances that allowed Biebow to commit rape. Alternatively, I believe that rape was part of a larger pattern of violence that Biebow exhibited, a pattern that escalated as it became apparent that the Germans were losing the war.

Rape in a Concentration Camp: The Case of Skarżysko-Kamienna

In Skarżysko-Kamienna, a labor camp in Poland to which numerous Łódź and Kraków ghetto inhabitants were sent, we know that German officers engaged in the rape of Jewish women. The leadership of this camp regularly raped the prisoner population, and survivors have identified numerous German officers at the camp as having taken part. The officers include Kurt Krause, Otto Eisenschmidt, and, mentioned by virtually all of the victims, notorious Fritz Bartenschlager.[36] The sexual abuse there was so pervasive that it went on in the open, as a part of the camp culture. In her book on Skarżysko-Kamienna, Felicja Karay described the camp as a place where "the 'rites of manhood' were expressed in orgies of drunkenness and gang rapes of Jewish girls."[37] Most of the men chose newly arrived Jewish women to serve them as room cleaners or meal servers, and then raped the women and killed them immediately afterward.[38] At times the prisoners learned what was happening from others in the camp. For example, Bronia S. reported that a *Volksdeutscher* (Pole with German roots) at the factory told her that the disappearing girls were being raped.[39] Milla D. testified that a girl was taken away from her machine and raped by five or six Germans in the office in the center of the factory. She noted that there were many such incidents.[40] At other times, prisoners were witness to the women being dragged out of their beds at night. Luba M. testified that one night a few Germans came and took away twenty girls under the age of fifteen, including her cousin.[41] Some women, such as Ester G., escaped rape and death. She was reported as a thief to Bartenschlager when she refused to become the mistress of a Ukrainian named Edik. Bartenschlager twisted her breast and assigned her three days of hard labor, but she ultimately survived the war.[42]

The archive of the University of Southern California Shoah Foundation Institute for Visual History and Education and the Yad Vashem archive both have eyewitness accounts of sexual abuse perpetrated against female inmates at Skarżysko-Kamienna. The sheer number of accusations against the same group of people in the same place lends weight to the argument that these abuses were perpetrated. Whether permitted by German law or not, there were German functionaries at concentration camps who took sexual advantage of women who did not have the ability to refuse them. In the cases described above, German officials in charge of large prisoner populations engaged in gross sexual abuse. Sometimes this was done in secret, sometimes it was an open secret, and sometimes it was done in full view of other prisoners. These exceptional cases have the benefit of multiple voices attesting to the same phenomenon.

Jewish Women in Forced Prostitution

Jewish women were also sometimes among the women forced to serve as prostitutes in brothels for soldiers. This, too, can be defined as a form of organized rape. Slavic women, those women marked as "asocial" (often lesbians or prostitutes in civilian life) and Gypsy (Sinti and Roma) women also fell victim to these rape camps set up by the Germans. Early in his regime, Hitler had professed himself and the Nazi party to be against prostitution. However, "by 1936, the Military Supreme Command declared that the construction of military brothels [was] 'an urgent necessity' and insisted that health authorities should cooperate."[43] Brothels were created not only for the military, SS, and civilian population, but even for foreign workers.[44] Jewish women served in all of these categories of brothels.[45] According to German regulations, Jewish women were not supposed to work in official brothels servicing Germans. Although this had been made explicit in 1939 when the brothels were set up, it was reiterated in another order in March of 1942.[46] This reissuing of the regulation is an indication that it was probably not being followed. In fact, there is sufficient evidence to suggest that despite ideological conflicts, Jewish women were subjected to sexual enslavement in Nazi brothels.

Testimonies by survivors provide ample indications that Germans heading ghettos made requests of the Jewish ghetto councils for lists of names of young Jewish women to serve in brothels, and that Jewish women were also taken for this "service" in another way.[47] Numerous survivors testified that just as Jewish men were rounded up from the street for forced labor, so, too, Jewish women were rounded up and put into brothels.[48] A. A. Ruzkensky testified that Jewish girls were rounded up in 1941 in the streets of Lvov and put into a brothel. A few days later they were shot.[49] Recruitment into military brothels from roundups on the street was a common means of obtaining women for forced sexual slavery. Many non-Jewish Slavic women were similarly abducted.

There is also documentation that Jewish women served in brothels in France.[50] These testimonies of Jewish women being forced into sexual slavery for the German military call into question the assertion of Doris Bergen that "the wartime dread that some Jewish women expressed of 'girls' battalions' sent east to service the troops may have been a symptom of how much they misunderstood the Nazi genocidal project."[51] In fact, some historians' mistaken belief about the unwavering German implementation of both *Rassenschande* and their genocidal policy has caused them to turn a blind eye to numerous sources, German and Jewish, that testify to the realities of Jewish women's experiences during the war.

Fela F. testified that two of her friends were taken to the prostitution block, where they acquired venereal diseases. She lamented, "they made from them a mess."[52] Another second-hand account of Jewish women being forced into sexual slavery in a military brothel is provided by Ilse B., a woman who was part Jewish and thus saved from incarceration in a concentration camp. She testified that Jewish women were field prostitutes and that she obtained this knowledge from her Jewish aunt and cousin, who had been imprisoned in a concentration camp.[53]

The effects of service in military brothels were devastating. The multiple rapes that women endured there damaged them psychologically and physically. In some cases, women's reproductive organs were so damaged that they could not bear children afterward.[54]

Conclusions

Although the rape of Jewish women was not part of German genocidal policy or what became known as the Final Solution, it nevertheless occurred and was a form of torture that was part of some Jewish women's experiences during the Holocaust. Ruth Seifert has described rape as a "violent invasion into the interior of one's body that represents the most severe attack imaginable upon the intimate self and the dignity of a human being: by any measure it is a mark of severe torture."[55] Jewish women, as Jews during the Holocaust, were placed in situations that made them particularly vulnerable to any type of violence, including rape. Additionally, they were vulnerable to rape because a war was raging. In the words of Rhonda Copelon, "War tends to intensify the brutality, repetitiveness, public spectacle, and likelihood of rape. War diminishes sensitivity to human suffering and intensifies men's sense of entitlement, superiority, avidity, and social license to rape."[56]

Although this chapter primarily focuses on Jewish women being raped by German men, there were numerous other rapes made possible by the genocidal conditions of the Holocaust. Rape victims included Jewish and non-Jewish men, women, and children. Victims were variously sexually abused in their homes before deportation, in hiding, in ghettos, in prisons, in brothels, and in concentration camps. The perpetrators of these sexual crimes during the war included German soldiers, guards, and SS members, non-German allies and collaborators, and civilians, as well as fellow prisoners. Sexual abuses were committed as part of semi-legal institutionalized structures such as brothels and included unsanctioned rapes accompanying the looting of homes. Victims of various ages, genders, and geographical locations were assaulted in public and private. Some survived and testified about their own experiences, while others testified about abuses perpetrated against third parties. Yet others remained silent, or were silenced by murder.

Despite the circulation of testimonies since the early days following World War II, this story has been largely ignored by most scholars—in part, possibly, because the data about rape during the Holocaust, like most non-physical rape evidence, relies heavily on testimony. Some historians' reluctance to utilize victim testimony in their construction of Holocaust history may be a result of a prejudice among them to utilize only "official documents" or to combat accusations of Holocaust deniers by being able to demonstrate the facts through the words of the Nazis themselves.[57] Favoring German documentation over victim documentation is problematic in general, and in rape cases, where Nazi documentation is scarce or nonexistent, it is even more so.

However, despite the scarcity of Nazi documents, sufficient data from both perpetrator and victim testimony exists to indicate that Jewish women were exploited sexually during the Holocaust. Taken together, these testimonies clearly substantiate one another's claims and demonstrate that rapes were perpetrated by Germans against Jewish victims. In some cases, the rapes were clustered in places where the German leadership was particularly lenient about sexual abuse, while in other areas incidents took place out of sight of the authorities.

During the last twenty-five years, scholars such as Joan Ringelheim, Susan Brownmiller, and Sara Horowitz began to ask questions about sexual abuse during the Holocaust. In response, most scholars have cited Nazi "racial" theory and laws as proof that Jewish women could not have been sexually abused and have thus dismissed the existence of rape of Jewish women. Yet the belief that Nazis would not commit *Rassenschande* by engaging in sexual relations with a Jewish woman is as absurd as any other argument that the existence of rules against an action are proof that the action could or would not take place. While it is true that sexual relations with all women deemed racially inferior, including Jewish women, were against Nazi policy, nevertheless, sexual relations between Germans and non-Germans—including Jews—persisted. In recent years, some scholars have begun to study this perplexity.[58] The emerging focus on the topic of rape during the Holocaust may in part be due to the increase of research on rape in other areas of genocide scholarship, as well as to the recognition that genocidal conditions contribute to the likelihood that those women targeted for extermination are also likely to be raped.[59]

Notes

1. For more on the reluctance of Holocaust scholars to address the topic of rape, please see Helene Sinnreich, "'And it was something we didn't talk about': Rape of Jewish Women during the Holocaust," *Holocaust Studies* 14, no. 2 (December 2008): 1–22.

2. Nechama Tec, *Resilience and Courage: Women, Men, and the Holocaust* (New Haven: Yale University Press, 2003), 231.

3. Scholars such as Christian Gerlach, *Kalulierte Morde: Die deutsche Wirtschafts- und Vernichtungspolitik in Weissrussland 1941–1944* [Calculated murder: German economic and extermination policies in White Russia, 1941–1944] (Hamburg: Hamburger Edition, 1999); Dieter Pohl, *Von der "Judenpolitik" zum Judenmord. Der Distrikt Lublin des Generalgouvernements 1939–1944* [From Jewish politics to Jewish death: The General Government's Lublin District, 1939–1944] (Frankfurt am Main: Peter Lang, 1993); and Bodgan Musial, *Deutsche Zivilverwaltung unter Judenverfolgung im Generalgouvernement: Eine Fallstudie zum Distrikt Lublin 1939–1944* [German civil administration and Jewish persecution in the General Government: A case study of the Lublin District] (Wiesbaden: Harrowitz Verlag, 1999) have published regional studies. In English, see Ulrich Herbert, ed., *National Socialist Extermination Policies: Contemporary German Perspectives and Controversies* (New York: Berghahn, 2000).

4. There are many such cases. For example, see Christopher R. Browning, *Nazi Policy, Jewish Workers, German Killers* (Cambridge: Cambridge University Press, 2000), 148, 149.

5. Wendy Lower, "'Anticipatory Obedience' and the Nazi Implementation of the Holocaust in the Ukraine: A Case Study of Central and Peripheral Forces in the Generalbezirk Zhytomyr, 1941–1944," *Holocaust and Genocide Studies* 16, no. 1 (Spring 2002): 8.

6. Ibid., 10.

7. Ulrich Herbert, "Extermination Policy: New Answers and Questions about the History of the 'Holocaust' in German Historiography," in Herbert, *National-Socialist Extermination Policies*, 17.

8. Todd Salzmann, "'Rape Camps,' Forced Impregnation and Ethnic Cleansing: Religious, Cultural, and Ethical Responses to Rape Victims in the Former Yugoslavia," in *War's Dirty Secret: Rape, Prostitution, and other Crimes Against Women*, ed. Anne Llewellyn Barstow (Cleveland: Pilgrim Press, 2000), 72.

9. Katharine Derderian, "Common Fate, Different Experience: Gender Specific Aspects of the Armenian Genocide, 1915–1917," in *Holocaust and Genocide Studies* (Spring 2005): 2, 7.

10. Iris Chang, "The Rape of Nanking," in Barstow, *War's Dirty Secret*, 49.

11. Jacob Apenszlak, ed., *The Black Book of Polish Jewry: An Account of the Martyrdom of Polish Jewry* (New York: Roy Publishers, 1943), 12. This testimony, given before a representative of the World Jewish Congress in Vilna, seems credible because of the other details that it provides. See Helene Sinnreich, "The Supply and Distribution of Food to the Łódź Ghetto: A Case Study in Nazi Jewish Policy, 1939–1945" (Ph.D. dissertation, Brandeis University, 2004), 51. The single line about rape was not needed to indicate that great injustices had been done. In fact the one line nearly goes unnoticed among the more detailed descriptions of atrocities.

12. Apenszlak, *Black Book of Polish Jewry*, 29.

13. Ibid., 9. The preference for "educated types" might suggest that these women were from the upper class and were for that reason more desirable than those "merely"

raped at home. In the Japanese system during World War II, there were three classes of women: those of upper and middle class and educated, favored as the future mothers of the state; those from middle and lower classes, encouraged to be good workers; and those from the lowest class, used to provide "comfort." See Hyun-Kyung Chung, "'Your Comfort Versus My Death': Korean Comfort Women," in Barstow, War's Dirty Secret, 20, 21.

14. Apenszlak, Black Book of Polish Jewry, 28.

15. Jan Różański, In Your Blood I Live (self-published, 1980). The book and microfiche (RG 02.079*01) are available in the United States Holocaust Memorial Museum.

16. Malke Giles, testimony, Yad Vashem archive O.71 file 34; Dvoyre Zif, testimony, Yad Vashem archive O.71 file 38; Khane Pelts, testimony, Yad Vashem archive O.71 file 35; Yente Alter-Gershovitz, testimony, Yad Vashem archive O.71 file 36.

17. Gershon Greenberg, "Holocaust and Musar for the Telsiai Yeshivah: Avraham Yitzhak and Eliyahu Meir Bloch," in The Vanished World of Lithuanian Jews, ed. Alvydas Nikžentaitis et al. (Amsterdam: Rodopi, 2004), 239.

18. Ilse B., testimony, in Cynthia Crane, Divided Lives: The Untold Stories of Jewish-Christian Women in Nazi Germany (New York: St. Martin's Press, 2000), 210–211.

19. Paula N., interview 4788, USC Shoah Foundation testimony.

20. See, for example, O.3 6537, Yad Vashem archive; O.3 12782, Yad Vashem archive; O.3 10423, Yad Vashem archive; and Ruth Elias, Triumph of Hope: From Theresienstadt and Auschwitz to Israel (New York: John Wiley, 1998), 120.

21. Na'ama Shik, "Weibliche Erfahrung in Auschwitz-Birkenau" [Female experience in Auschwitz-Birkenau], in Genozid und Geschlecht: Jüdische Frauen im nationalsozialistischen Lagersystem [Genocide and gender: Jewish women in the National Socialist camp system], ed. Gisela Bock (Frankfurt: Campus Verlaine, 2005), 112.

22. Emil G., interview 19178, USC Shoah Foundation testimony.

23. Sara M., interview 29016, USC Shoah Foundation testimony. Compare this testimony with that of Doris Roe (interview 23687, USC Shoah Foundation testimony) in chapter 15 by Eva Fogelman, in this volume. For more on sexual abuse at Ravensbrück, see Rochelle Saidel, The Jewish Women of Ravensbrück Concentration Camp (Madison: University of Wisconsin Press, 2004).

24. See Rose S., interview 10119, USC Shoah Foundation testimony.

25. See Paula K., interview 7952, USC Shoah Foundation testimony.

26. Lucjan Dobroszycki, ed. The Chronicle of the Łódź Ghetto, 1941–1944 (New Haven: Yale University Press, 1984), 384–385, entry for September 24, 1943.

27. Rumkowski was not the only ghetto leader accused of improper sexual behavior. Rita H. reported that once, when she went to ask for help from Rubinstein, one of the members of the Pabianice ghetto Judenrat (whom she had known before the war), he sexually molested her. See Rita H., interview 30717, USC Shoah Foundation testimony. For more on Rumkowski's sexual abuse during the war, see Lucille Eichengreen, Rumkowski and the Orphans of Łódź (San Francisco: Mercury House, 2000); Michal Unger, Reassessment of the Image of Mordechai Chaim Rumkowski (Jerusalem: Yad Vashem, 2004); Yitzhak Zuckerman, A Surplus of Memory: Chronicle of the Warsaw Ghetto Uprising (Berkley: Univer-

sity of California Press, 1993), 108; Solomon Bloom, "Dictator of the Łódź Ghetto," in *Commentary* 7 (1949); and Philip Friedman, "Pseudo-Saviors in the Polish Ghettos: Mordechai Chaim Rumkowski of Łódź," in *Roads to Extinction: Essays on the Holocaust* (New York: Jewish Publication Society of America, 1980), 333–352.

28. Christopher Browning, *The Path to Genocide: Essays on the Launching of the Final Solution* (Cambridge: Cambridge University Press, 1995), 56.

29. Primo Levi, *Moments of Reprieve: A Memoir of Auschwitz* (New York: Penguin Classics, 1995), 125.

30. Lucjan Dobroszycki, ed. *Chronicle of the Łódź Ghetto*, 504, entry for June 16, 1944.

31. Ibid.

32. Alan Adelson and Robert Lapides, eds., *Łódź Ghetto: Inside a Community Under Siege* (New York: Viking Press, 1989), 464. Wendy Jo Gertjejanssen notes that many reports of German rape of non-German women included notations of the drunken state of the violator. See Wendy Jo Gertjejanssen, "Victims, Heroes, Survivors: Sexual Violence on the Eastern Front During World War II" (Ph.D. dissertation, University of Minnesota, 2004), 65.

33. Esther H., interview 506, USC Shoah Foundation testimony.

34. Ibid. The killing of a camp guard's mistress in his absence was not unique to this case. Moshe Bahir testified that *Scharführer* Paul Grot, leader of the Ukrainian columns at Sobibor, had a Jewish mistress named Ruth, who apparently was murdered the day after Grot was transferred to another death camp. See Miriam Novitch, *Sobibor: Martyrdom and Revolt* (New York: Walden Press, 1980), 151.

35. Bina W., interview 33960, USC Shoah Foundation testimony.

36. Testimony mentioning Otto Eisenschmidt: Sonia N., interview 1832, USC Shoah Foundation testimony. Testimonies mentioning Bartenschlager by name: Eva L., interview 51181, USC Shoah Foundation testimony; Sonia N., interview 1832, USC Shoah Foundation testimony.

37. Felicja Karay, *Death Comes in Yellow: Skarżysko-Kamienna Slave Labor Camp* (Amsterdam: Overseas Publishers Association, 1996), 80.

38. For testimonies on this, see Karay, *Death Comes in Yellow*, 80, 81. For testimonies on survivors' awareness of newly arrived women being taken away and not seen again, see Marta C., interview 2790, USC Shoah Foundation testimony; Pola K., interview 32812, USC Shoah Foundation testimony; Harry K., interview 19656, USC Shoah Foundation testimony; Saul M., interview 6145, USC Shoah Foundation testimony. Using women as room cleaners and raping them was not confined to Skarżysko-Kamienna. Lya C. noted that every morning the commandant of the Haidari concentration camp in Greece would select the most attractive women prisoners to clean the rooms. One day Lya was selected for this duty and a young German approached her. He sent her to clean the bathroom, and then raped her there. She was sent back to the camp and there consulted a doctor about the pain. He could only try to calm her and her mother. See Lya C., interview 450, USC Shoah Foundation testimony.

39. Bronia S., interview 10747, USC Shoah Foundation testimony.

40. Milla D., interview 15012, USC Shoah Foundation testimony.

41. Luba M., interview 35267, USC Shoah Foundation testimony.

42. Ester G., interview 23436, USC Shoah Foundation testimony.

43. Annette F. Timm, "The Ambivalent Outsider: Prostitution, Promiscuity, and VD Control in Nazi Berlin," in Social Outsiders in Nazi Germany, ed. Robert Gellately and Nathan Stoltzfus (Princeton: Princeton University Press, 2001), 195.

44. Timm, "The Ambivalent Outsider," 201. Zdeněk Tmej, a Czech forced laborer sent to Wroclaw, photographed a brothel with prostitutes employed to service the foreign laborers there. A series of portraits of one woman included the following captions: "This Czech woman was given a choice: brothel or concentration camp . . . Years later I bumped into her in Prague; she was drinking herself to death." For more of these photographs, see Ana Fárová, Tomáě Jelínek, and Blanka Chocholova, Zdeněk Tmej: Totaleinsatz [Zdeněk Tmej: Total employment] (Prague: Torst, 2001). Thank you to Krista Hegberg for pointing out this source to me.

45. Birgit Beck, "Rape: The Military Trials of Sexual Crimes Committed by Soldiers in the Wehrmacht, 1939–1944," in Home/Front: The Military, War and Gender in Twentieth-Century Germany, ed. Karen Hagemann and Stefanie Schueler-Springorum (Oxford: Berg, 2002), 267. For a different interpretation, see chapter 3 by Robert Sommer in this volume.

46. Christa Paul, Zwangsprostitution: Staatlich errichtete Bordelle im Nationalsozialismus [Forced prostitution: State brothels under National Socialism] (Berlin: Hentrich, 1995). See 23 and 131 for exact reference. Timm, "The Ambivalent Outsider," 201.

47. See, for example, Apenszlak, Black Book of Polish Jewry, 26, 27; William Samelson, "Piotrkow Trybunalski: My Ancestral Home," in Life in the Ghettos During the Holocaust (Syracuse: Syracuse University Press, 2005), 9, 10; Doris L. Bergen, "Sex, Blood and Vulnerability: Women Outsiders in Nazi-Occupied Europe," in Gellately and Stoltzfus, Social Outsiders in Nazi Germany, 276; Ana C., interview 864, USC Shoah Foundation testimony; Judit Z., interview 41162, USC Shoah Foundation testimony; Michael J., interview 26142, USC Shoah Foundation testimony.

48. Gertjejanssen, "Victims, Heroes, Survivors," 191, 192.

49. Ibid.

50. Ibid., 191.

51. Bergen, "Sex, Blood and Vulnerability," 278.

52. Fela F., interview 39064, USC Shoah Foundation testimony.

53. Ilse B., testimony, in Crane, Divided Lives, 211.

54. Regarding the physical results of forced military prostitution by the Japanese Army during World War II, see Chung, "'Your Comfort Versus My Death,'" 16; and Anne Llewellyn Barstow, "Taiwan: 'Money Can't Buy Our Youth Back; Apology Can't Make up for Our Fate,'" 41, both in War's Dirty Secret.

55. Quoted in Salzmann, "'Rape Camps,'" 70.

56. Rhonda Copelon, quoted in the introduction to Barstow, War's Dirty Secret, 8.

57. For more on arguments in favor of using victim testimony in combination with perpetrator documentation, see Christopher Browning, Collected Memories: Holocaust History and Postwar Testimony (Madison: University of Wisconsin Press, 2003).

58. See, for example, Gisela Bock, ed., *Genozid und Geschlecht. Jüdische Frauen im nationalsozialistischen Lagersystem* [Genocide and gender: Jewish women in the National Socialist camp system] (Frankfurt am Main: Campus, 2005); Birgit Beck, *Wehrmacht und sexuelle Gewalt: Sexualverbrechen vor deutschen Militärgerichten 1939–1945* [The Wehrmacht and sexual violence: Sex crimes prosecuted in German military courts, 1939–1945] (Paderborn: Schöningh, 2004); Baris Alakus, Katharina Kniefacz, and Robert Vorberg, eds. *Sex-Zwangsarbeit in Nationalsozialistischen Konzentrationslagern* [Forced sex labor in National Socialist concentration camps] (Vienna: Mandelbaum, 2006); Gertjejanssen, "Victims, Heroes, Survivors"; Dagmar Herzog, ed., *Sexuality and German Fascism* (Austin: University of Texas Press, 2002) and Herzog, ed., *Brutality and Desire: War and Sexuality in Europe's Twentieth Century* (London: Palgrave MacMillan, 2009); as well as chapter 5 by Monika J. Flaschka in this volume.

59. See, for example, Barstow, *War's Dirty Secret*; Katharine Derderian, "Common Fate, Different Experience: Gender Specific Aspects of the Armenian Genocide, 1915–1917," in *Holocaust and Genocide Studies* 19, no. 1 (Spring 2005); Alexandra Stiglmayer, ed., *Mass Rape: The War against Women in Bosnia-Herzegovina* (Lincoln: University of Nebraska Press, 1994); Christoph Schiessl, "An Element of Genocide: Rape, Total War, and International Law in the Twentieth Century," in *Journal of Genocide Research* 4, no. 2 (2002): 197–210; Lisa Sharlach, "Gender and Genocide in Rwanda: Women as Agents and Objects of Genocide," in *Journal of Genocide Research* 1, no. 3 (1999): 387–399; Roger W. Smith, "Women and Genocide: Notes on an Unwritten History," in *Holocaust and Genocide Studies* 8, no. 3 (Winter 1994): 315–334.

8

Rape and Sexual Abuse in Hiding

ZOË WAXMAN

"Thousands of women were raped during the war, but no one hears about them. . . . The Anne Franks who survived rape don't write their stories," as Hungarian Holocaust survivor Judith Magyar Isaacson told her daughter.[1] This chapter explores the largely overlooked issues faced by women in hiding or open hiding—especially the very real danger of rape and sexual abuse. Unlike Anne Frank and her family, hiding together in an attic with the help of Gentile friends, most Jewish women did not literally hide themselves away, but instead attempted to imitate the lives of normal citizens by passing as "Aryan," some alone and others with family members. Some acquired forged documents and moved from place to place, both in cities and small villages, hiding in convents and monasteries, in factories, and sometimes posing as non-Jews in forced labor or concentration camps. Others lived without documents and survived by concealing themselves in fields, forests, attics, and stables. The fact that Anne Frank's story has become the paradigm of hiding has meant it is widely assumed that the only danger people in hiding faced was being caught and deported.[2] However, women in hiding also faced other dangers, including threats or acts of sexual assault against them.

Although ignored by most historians, the situation of Jewish women in hiding or open hiding during the Holocaust was strikingly precarious—they were surviving on the margins of society, and this made them extremely vulnerable. These women were uniquely dependent on the support and "sympathy" of the local populations to spare them from physical, emotional, and sexual vulnerability. Not only were their families and communities unable to protect them, but in many cases they had to break any contact with them in order to survive. They both lived outside the law and were fugitives from it. This circumstance provided openings for encounters leading to rape and sexual abuse. Jewish women were abused not only by Nazis, but also by their collaborators and by Jewish men in positions of power.

Factors Affecting the Ability to Hide

When it came to passing as "Aryan," women had certain advantages over men. A particular physical one is obvious, because in Eastern Europe usually only Jewish men were circumcised. If a man was suspected of being Jewish, he was ordered to undress. In his novel *Blood from the Sky*, Piotr Rawicz, who attempted to flee the Nazis with his wife Anna, describes his constant fear that his circumcision would betray his Jewishness.[3] Women at least knew they could not be discovered by physical examination. In Warsaw, where it is thought that more Jews went into hiding than in any other European city, it is estimated that about two-thirds of Jews in hiding on the "Aryan" side were women.[4] Writing of the predominance of women among those who lived in open hiding in Poland, Lenore Weitzman noted that "it may be explained, at least in part, by the fact that women were more likely to believe that they could pass initially, and were more self-confident when they embarked on their new lives. Men, by contrast, were more reluctant to try." She compares being circumcised to "other distinguishing physical or social characteristics, such as dark hair, or a prominent nose, or a distinctive accent."[5] In addition to stereotypically Jewish features, the markings of emotional and physical suffering and a lack of financial resources limited men and women's ability to pass as "Aryan."

In addition, women themselves had varying backgrounds that either facilitated or hindered their ability to hide. Their socioeconomic status, education, work experience, linguistic ability, and religious background were all relevant. The country in which they were trying to hide or "pass" mattered, insofar as knowledge of local language and culture was key. Paula Hyman writes regarding Eastern Europe: "[T]he same families that chose for their sons various forms of private Jewish education, whether of traditional or modernized curriculum, often sent their daughters to public primary schools, where they were introduced to secular culture"[6]—which unknowingly better prepared them to survive.

Weitzman offers a similar explanation regarding religious Jewish girls in Poland, who were not permitted to study in the exclusively male religious schools. She writes:

> Ironically, the "inferior" non-Jewish education that Jewish girls were more likely
> to receive provided them with knowledge and contacts that helped them to

pass—such as the ability to speak colloquial Polish, familiarity with Polish customs (and Catholic prayers and rituals), a sense of the patterns and nuances of social interaction, personal networks and contacts in the non-Jewish world of their Polish classmates, and sometimes a few friends to whom they might be able to turn for help.[7]

In Germany, the situation was somewhat different. There were more Jews who were either partially or completely assimilated into the non-Jewish culture (although there were also a substantial number of observant Jews). Here, too, the Jewish women seemed to have a better pulse on the society and culture than did the men. According to Marion Kaplan, some estimates suggest that between ten thousand and twelve thousand German Jews went into hiding, and only about 25 percent survived. "Men in hiding were in greater danger of being caught than women," she wrote, explaining that most German men of military age had been drafted. She continues:

> Jewish women could blend in among German women more easily as servants or nannies. Indeed, one Jewish woman, introduced as the hider's aunt, had an ersatz coffee now and then with the Nazi block warden, while another, introduced as the hider's fiancée, had to accept the suspicious and dangerous friendship of a leader of the Nazi women's organization.[8]

Kaplan also points to other perils of going into hiding in Germany: "Some young women even resorted to exchanging sex for shelter, including working in brothels in Berlin." But she also notes a *Rassenschande* (race defilement) court case involving Jewish women in hiding and reports that the women convicted of exchanging sex for shelter were then murdered.[9]

Testimonies by Survivors Who Were in Hiding

Although many testimonies refer to the vulnerability of women in the concentration camps and in hiding, there is no way of knowing how widespread the rape of women actually was. Typical is the rather ambiguous testimony of a young woman, "A. G. (maiden name R.)," who escaped from the Warsaw ghetto with her grandfather. She describes seeking refuge in a flat belonging to Roman, a Polish sailor, but, she says, she "only stayed there a short while" because "Roman was always bothering me and we were afraid his jealous wife would denounce us to the police."[10] In other testimonies, we are told that it was the fear of rape that prompted the decision to flee and hide. In Tylicz, Poland, Rena Kornreich Gelissen was observed walking to work by a German soldier who later that night, very drunk, decided to go looking for her. Her parents covered her with straw and were forced to stand by and watch as the solider poked through the straw with his rifle threatening, "'Perhaps you want to tell me before I stab her through her pretty eye!'"[11] As a result of this encounter, her parents decided that it was too dangerous for Rena to remain at home and arranged for her to be smuggled across the border into Slovakia.

Women were sometimes encouraged to take extreme measures to avoid rape; some women were lucky enough to outwit their enemies. For example, Lawrence Langer cites a woman named "Celia K." who at eighteen fled the ghetto and left her mother, brothers, sisters, nephews, and nieces to go into hiding with one of her sisters. Her brother, a partisan, brings the two young girls a gun, warning them, "[T]his gun is more valuable than anything I have. I am giving it to you and I want you to use it if the Germans ever capture you. You must never, never under any circumstances get caught alive." To underscore this point he tells them what the Germans are doing to the Jewish women they catch, reminding them once more, "If you know the Germans are going to catch you, one of you must shoot the other and then shoot yourself."[12] In another memoir, a young woman named Eva Safszycka, at seventeen years old, escaped the Siedlce ghetto and hid in an empty brick factory. There she encountered a watchman who, she said, "probably understood who I was." She reports: "[R]oughly he tried to rape me, threatening that if I did not go along, he would denounce me." Eva fought back saying, "'Take me to the Germans,'" and after that, she said, "he gave up and left."[13]

One hardship for Jewish women in open hiding in towns and cities was learning to enter places with the placard "No Jews Allowed," without showing any signs of fear. Yet, in rural areas things were not necessarily any easier. Alicia Appelman-Jurman, while a young girl, hid with her mother in Podole—a part of the Ukraine annexed by Poland after World War I. She did not specifically cite fear of sexual abuse, but fear of it is implicit in her memories of dreading separation from her mother, passing as a non-Jew, and being caught:

> My mother and I decided on a plan that called for her to remain hidden in the ravine while I worked on building up a rapport with the local farmers. It wasn't enough just to work for them in the summer; I also had to earn their fondness and sympathy for the wintertime, when there would be no work and I would have to go begging. It was out of the question for my mother to try to work; she would be too easily recognized as a Jewess. The sadness and pain that had settled permanently in her eyes would betray her.

We agreed that she would hide in the wheat fields or in the ravine during the day, and I would bring food for her after my work was through. When I thought of my mother hiding day in day out in the wheat—trembling at every sound, wondering if I would come back or if I had been found out and caught, and waiting, waiting all day with nothing to do, totally dependent on her child for survival—my heart ached for her. But that was how it had to be if we were to survive.[14]

Whole families rarely hid together. Although Alicia Appelman-Jurman was still with her mother, like most of those in hiding she had already experienced many losses. For her, it was the loss of her father and brothers that prompted her and her mother's attempt to escape the Gestapo. Unlike Appelman-Jurman, the majority of those who survived the war by passing as "Aryan" were alone. Their suffering from feelings of isolation, of being able to trust no one—not even other Jews in hiding—greatly defined their experiences. For them, the fear of potential abuse or discovery, rather than the fear of the gas chamber, was always present. The double bind of being dependent on others, yet at the same time being able to trust or confide in no one, created the perfect climate for rape and sexual abuse to occur. And its unfortunate legacy has continued long after the end of World War II.

Suffering during the Holocaust and Afterward

Women who experienced sexual violence during the Holocaust are faced with the dilemma of attempting to relate their experiences in a context that insists that rape and sexual abuse do not belong to the history of the Holocaust, or remaining imprisoned by memories they cannot share. They may feel obliged to stay silent about certain aspects of their experiences for fear that they do not belong to the history of the Holocaust, or that the experiences will not be easily understood. Their silence can prevent us from challenging traditional narratives, or adding to them by acquiring further information about the diversity of experiences during the Holocaust.

Joan Ringelheim presents the experiences of a Jewish survivor called Pauline who was molested by male relatives of the people hiding her. Because Pauline was told that if she complained they would denounce her, she didn't tell her twin sister who was hiding with her. Nor did she tell the young Jewish woman who checked on them from time to time.[15] The effects of this on her life are, unsurprisingly, enduring. In an interview she told Ringelheim: "I can still feel the fear. . . . Sometimes I think it was equally as frightening as the Germans. It became within me a tremendous. . . . I [didn't] know how to [deal with it] . . . what to do with it. I had nobody to talk [to] about it. Nobody to turn to."[16] It was an experience that, as Pauline herself realizes, is not easily reconciled with traditional Holocaust narratives. She asks: "In respect of what happened, [what we] suffered and saw—the humiliation in the ghetto, seeing people jumping out and burned—is this [molestation] important?"[17] After the war she didn't tell her husband or daughter what had happened. In the words of Ringelheim: "Her memory was split between traditional versions of Holocaust history and her own experiences."[18] Only when comprehension of the Holocaust is broadened to acknowledge types of experiences that stand outside traditional narratives will stories such as this be explored. Particular experiences of sexual violence can then be connected to the broader suffering of the Holocaust.

In the few testimonies that do break the taboo by talking about actual rape and sexual abuse in hiding, the experiences are still mostly hinted at or given to another person—a friend or an aunt, for example. These feints, of course, mirror the difficulties of talking or writing about being raped in civilian society and then being believed. For example, Fanya Gottesfeld Heller waited fifty years before writing about the rape of her aunt in front of her husband, after a Gestapo raid:

> Unable to find me, Gottschalk and his henchmen left and went looking for me at the home of one of my aunts. When they didn't find me there, they raped her and forced her husband to watch. The rape had to be kept secret because if the Gestapo [presumably she is referring to the higher ranks] found out about it they would have killed her immediately, since Germans were forbidden to "fraternize" with "subhuman" Jews. My aunt told a few members of the family but they didn't believe her—they didn't want to hear or know about it. She never told her children, and for that reason, I have not disclosed her name.[19]

As perpetrators of rape know all too well, rape silences women in a way that deliberately alienates them from their families and communities.[20] Historically, a victorious army will rape the women of the conquered people as a permanent mark of their victory. By forcing Gottesfeld Heller's aunt's husband to watch the rape, the aggressors were reinforcing what they considered to be the passivity of their Jewish victims. This points to another area of silence: the shame of Jewish men who were unable to prevent the rape or sexual exploitation of their mothers, sisters, and daughters.

In the same testimony, Gottesfeld Heller describes what she classifies as a consensual sexual relationship between herself as a teenager and Jan, a

Ukrainian militia man who rescued and protected her family—both from the Nazis and from the anti-Semitic Ukrainian villagers who hounded them. (He was later accused by her family of murdering her father upon liberation by the Soviet Army.) Her parents knew that it was the man's feelings for their daughter that motivated him to hide them, feed them, and protect them. Her testimony is clear that her parents did not verbally acknowledge the relationship, but they were well aware that their daughter was sexually involved with this non-Jewish man from a lower social class. Gottesfeld Heller has clearly had time to consider the relationship and ultimately must be allowed to interpret it in a way that makes sense to her. Nevertheless, whether such a relationship based on such an extreme power imbalance can be understood in terms of consent is surely questionable, despite Gottesfeld Heller's insistence on its reciprocity.

Indeed, the shame and guilt of having to resort to her sexuality in order to survive continued to haunt Gottesfeld Heller after her liberation. Trying to envisage a life married to Jan and as the mother of his children, she focused on the impossibility of finding a home. She wrote:

> How could I condemn my babies to grow up in Poland, or the Ukraine, the graveyard for millions of Jews? No, not a graveyard, for there were no graves. The Jews had been burned to ashes and the ashes had turned to dust which was in the air we breathed and the water we drank . . . I saw myself holding a baby to my breast, and my breast and the baby were black with the ashes of their murdered relatives. Black milk came out of my breast.[21]

To resolve this impossible conflict she decided instead to bury her experiences and enter into a hastily arranged marriage with a young Jewish man named Joseph:

> He was told that I was a very nice girl, intelligent, educated, and from a fine family, but that I'd had an affair with a *goy* [non-Jew]. "You know," he said to me, "if you tell me that you're a virgin, I'll buy you the nicest Persian lamb coat." I told him, "you can save yourself the coat." He said nothing more and never asked me about Jan, not then and not ever, and I respected him for this.[22]

It appears from her testimony that Gottesfeld Heller interpreted her ability to build a life for herself after the Holocaust as dependent on her ability to suppress her difficult and often ambiguous wartime experiences, and it was important for her to find a partner who could support her in this. The pejorative use of the term "goy" clearly indicates the potential and ongoing stigma of a young Jewish woman who had entered into a sexual relationship with a non-

Jewish man. By marrying a Jewish man, Gottesfeld Heller was able to avoid this fate by reabsorbing herself into the respectable Jewish community, thereby drawing a line between her present and her past. At the same time, however, it is equally obvious that Gottesfeld Heller was ultimately unable to bury the experience. She began therapy in 1969, and it was this process that very gradually led her to be able to write her memoir, in which the enduring silence of her family is a key theme.

Interpreting Survivor Stories of Sexual Abuse while Hiding

Those who have explored the experiences of women in hiding have in some cases tended to disregard the issue of rape and sexual abuse. Once again, an exclusive—if understandable—emphasis on heroic resistance and Jewish solidarity has inadvertently silenced alternative voices. Thus, the research that does exist on Jewish Holocaust survivors in hiding typically focuses on the partisan groups who hid in the forests rather than on individual experiences of hiding. What Gunnar S. Paulsson terms "evasion" as a means of survival has for the most part been neglected. Paulsson suggests that this neglect can be partly explained by the "stigma attached to flight" as well as to the consequent "'survivors' guilt' for abandoning relatives."[23] Yet this neglected area of Holocaust research is, it can be argued, particularly significant for female survivors, especially in Poland, where the majority of Jews who survived by passing as "Aryan" were women.

A refusal to pursue gender as a line of inquiry has meant ignoring the often gendered nature of lived experience. This avoidance of gender analysis is particularly evident when exploring the question of hiding during the Holocaust. A study of women's testimonies not only reveals different types of experiences, but also shows that women's memories and the treatment of women's memories are specifically organized by gendered expectations. Rather than calling attention to sexual violence to retrieve women's Holocaust experiences from oblivion, researchers have instead been eager to emphasize the myriad ways in which women attempted to resist their fate and hold onto to their dignity by exhibiting moral, heroic, or noble behavior.[24]

Even this initiative, of course, is not without its risks. For example, Lenore Weitzman, who carried out pioneering research on women in hiding during the Holocaust, argues that passing as "Aryan" as a means of survival should be understood as a form of resistance and that many of the Jewish women living under false identities "were consciously defying Nazi orders and deliberately trying to subvert the murderous intentions of the Nazis."[25] The problem with this approach is not only that it is likely that the majority of women were solely intent on trying to save themselves from an increasingly frightening fate but also that survivors may feel pressure to present their experiences of hiding through the lens of heroism. Ironically, then, even some attempts to recapture experiences of women in hiding have tended to silence those who were raped.

Experiences of sexual exploitation—or negotiated sex—are a particularly vulnerable area of women's experience. For survivors and their families there is an understandable reluctance to confront the fact that a family member or friend might have been raped or, perhaps more uncomfortable still, engaged in sexual activity for the procurement of food or protection.[26] That Jewish women were sometimes forced to succumb to the sexual demands of Jewish men to survive has unsurprisingly remained a largely silent chapter of Holocaust history. This discussion is not intended to expose survivors' most personal or humiliating moments or to suggest that survivors of the Holocaust are concealing aspects of their survival. Instead, it points to the possible implications of "the unsaid" and "the unspeakable,"[27] in making sense of narratives of lived experience. Arguably, rape and sexual abuse—the violation of one's body at the hands of someone seeking to cause both physical and mental pain—is one of the loneliest and most alienating things that can happen to a person. As the perpetrator is usually all too aware, it silences the victims and leaves them alone in a world they can no longer recognize. The experience of rape in particular shows the victim that the world is not as it seems. Sex is transformed from an act of intimacy into a tool of violence or coercion and even language is destroyed as "no" becomes "yes," and "stop" gives rise to further pain.[28]

In this way, rape is synonymous with torture and, as Jean Améry has famously argued, "Whoever has succumbed to torture can no longer feel at home in the world. . . . That one's fellow man was experienced as the antiman remains in the tortured person as accumulated horror."[29] To feel excruciating pain meted out at the hands of another is to lose control over one's body, mind, and ultimately one's life. In her study of torture, which is clearly informed by her reading of Améry, Elaine Scarry explains: "Physical pain does not simply resist language but actively destroys it, bringing about an immediate reversion to a state anterior to language to the sounds and cries a human being makes before language is learned."[30] Such a vocabulary does not speak of shared experiences, of being part of history, but of agony and humiliation. And as Lawrence Langer goes even further to argue, victims of the Holocaust who experienced physical torture have often felt shame at their inability to prevent that torture. He cites one survivor who explains, "I was ashamed . . . and when I'm ashamed, I don't like to talk about it."[31] If the torture involves sexual violence, then it becomes even harder to discuss.

Writing about rape should have the potential to write the victim back into the world.[32] This has proved to be difficult in the case of the Holocaust, where rape and sexual abuse have tended to be written out of its history. Survivors of rape have been ignored. The role of gender in mediating the experience of the Holocaust has been overlooked—or even denied. The result has been that rape during the Holocaust—and particularly the rape of women in hiding during the Holocaust—remains underexplored and increasingly hard to un-cover. What is more, this silence is fueled by the emergence of an unintended hierarchy of suffering during the Holocaust—structured by possible factors such as time spent in particular ghettos and concentration camps, or survival in hiding—and this has inevitably affected how survivors have interpreted the Holocaust in their postwar lives.

Notes

1. Judith Magyar Isaacson, *Seed of Sarah: Memoirs of a Survivor* (Chicago: University of Illinois Press, 1990), 143–144.

2. The same point is made by Joan Ringelheim, "The Split between Gender and the Holocaust," in *Women in the Holocaust*, ed. Dalia Ofer and Lenore J. Weitzman (New Haven: Yale University Press, 1998), 345.

3. Piotr Rawicz, *Blood from the Sky*, trans. Peter Wiles (New York: Harcourt, Brace & World, 1964).

4. Gunnar S. Paulsson, *Secret City: The Hidden Jews of Warsaw, 1940–1945* (New Haven: Yale University Press, 2002). See also, Paulsson, "The Demography of Jews in Hiding in Warsaw, 1943–1945," in *Polin. Studies in Polish Jewry, XIII. Focusing on the Holocaust and its Aftermath*, ed. Antony Polonsky (London: Littman Library, 2000), 78–103.

5. Lenore Weitzman, "Living on the Aryan Side in Poland," in *Women in the Holocaust*, ed. Ofer and Weitzman, 203. For an excellent discussion of the myriad ways women had to blend linguistically and culturally with the non-Jewish population, see Nechama Tec, "Sex Distinctions and Passing as Christians during the Holocaust," *East European Quarterly* 18, no. 1 (March 1984): 113–123.

6. Paula E. Hyman, "Gender in the Jewish Family in Modern Europe," in *Women in the Holocaust*, ed. Ofer and Weitzman, 33.

7. Weitzman, "Living on the Aryan Side in Poland," 204. On French Jews in hiding, see Susan Zuccotti, *The Holocaust, the French, and the Jews* (Lincoln: University of Nebraska Press, 1993). On Dutch Jews who went into hiding, see Bob Moore, *Victims and Survivors* (London: Arnold, 1997).

8. Marion Kaplan, *Between Dignity and Despair: Jewish Life in Nazi Germany* (New York: Oxford University Press, 1998), 203.

9. Ibid., 209. In a note attached to the quoted material (note 15), Kaplan cites Konrad Kwiet, who told her that brothels in Berlin are mentioned in several Wiener Library memoirs: "See also: Kwiet, *Widerstand*, 155. In the Brandenburgisches Landeshauptarchiv: PrBr Rep 12 B St Potsdam 80, a *Rassenschande* case involved exchanges of sex for shelter. The Jewish women were sent to their deaths. Voigt reports that 'sex was demanded of a whole slew of Jewish women.' *Die Zeit*, April 8, 1994, 7."

10. "Eyewitness Testimony 26. On Both Sides of the Ghetto Wall." in Isaiah Trunk, *Jewish Responses to Nazi Persecution* (New York: Stein & Day, 1982), 183.

11. Rena Kornreich Gelissen with Heather Dune Macadam, *Rena's Promise: A Story of Sisters in Auschwitz* (London: Weidenfeld and Nicolson, 1996), 30–31.

12. Lawrence Langer, *Holocaust Testimonies: The Ruins of Memory* (New Haven: Yale University Press, 1991), 10.

13. Cited in Nechama Tec, *Resilience and Courage: Women, Men and the Holocaust* (New Haven: Yale University Press, 2003), 224.

14. Alicia Appelman-Jurman, *Alicia: My Story* (New York: Bantam, 1990), 134.

15. Ringelheim, "Split between Gender and the Holocaust," 343. Also see Myrna Goldenberg's excellent essay "Rape During the Holocaust," in *The Legacy of the Holocaust: Women and the Holocaust*, ed. Zygmunt Mazur et al. (Krakow: Jagiellonian University Press, 2007), 159–169.

16. Ringelheim, "The Split between Gender and the Holocaust," 343.

17. Ibid.

18. Ibid., 344.

19. Fanya Gottesfeld Heller, *Strange and Unexpected Love: A Teenage Girl's Holocaust Memoirs* (Hoboken: Ktav, 1993), 81.

20. See Susan Brownmiller, *Against Our Will: Men, Women, and Rape* (New York: Simon and Schuster, 1975), 35. See also Christoph Schiessl, "An Element of Genocide: Rape, Total War, and International Law in the Twentieth Century," *Journal of Genocide Research* 4, no. 2 (2002): 198.

21. Gottesfeld Heller, *Strange and Unexpected Love*, 275.

22. Ibid., 278.

23. See Gunnar S. Paulsson, *Secret City*, 10. See also Michal Borwicz's classic study, *Arishe papirn*, [Aryan papers], 3 vols. (Buenos Aires: Tsentral-Farband fun Poilishe Yidn, 1955).

24. See, for example, Judith Tydor Baumel, *Double Jeopardy: Gender and the Holocaust* (London: Vallentine Mitchell, 1998); and Brana Gurewitsch, ed., *Mothers, Sisters, Resisters: Oral Histories of Women who Survived the Holocaust* (Tuscaloosa: University of Alabama Press, 1998), xii.

25. Weitzman, "Living on the Aryan Side in Poland," 217.

26. See Joan Ringelheim, "Gender and Genocide: A Split Memory," in *Gender and Catastrophe*, ed. Ronit Lentin (London: Zed Books, 1997), 25. On this subject see also the research of Nechama Tec revealing the expectations of male partisans and Red Army soldiers that they would receive sex in exchange for protection, and women's responses to "sexual advances were motivated by the promise of food." See Tec, *Resilience and Cour-*

age, 205–335, 146; and *Defiance. The Bielski Partisans: The Story of the Largest Armed Rescue of Jews by Jews During World War II* (New York: Oxford University Press, 1993), 126–70.

27. See Annie G. Rogers et al., "An Interpretative Poetics of Languages of the Unsayable," in *Making Meaning of Narratives*, ed. Ruthellen Josselson and Amia Lieblich (London: Sage, 1997), 77–106. For Rogers et al., "What is unspeakable exists as a deep and haunting sense of something that begs for words but is also forbidden to be spoken," 86.

28. On the debate over rape as an act of violence or a sexual act (or both), see C. Chinkin, "Rape and Sexual Abuse of Women in International Law," *European Journal of International Law* 5 (1994): 50–74. See also chapter 2 by Brigitte Halbmayer in this volume.

29. Jean Améry, *At the Mind's Limits: Contemplations by a Survivor on Auschwitz and Its Realities*, trans. Sidney Rosenfeld and Stella P. Rosenfeld (Bloomington: Indiana University Press, 1980), 40.

30. Elaine Scarry, *The Body in Pain: The Making and Unmaking of the World* (Oxford: Oxford University Press, 1985), 4.

31. Lawrence Langer, *Holocaust Testimonies*, 88.

32. See Roberta Culbertson, "Embodied Memory, Transcendence, and Telling: Recounting Trauma, Re-establishing the Self," *New Literary History* 26 (1995): 169–195.

PART

III

ASSAULTS
on Motherhood

9

Reproduction under the Swastika

The Other Side of the Nazi Glorification of Motherhood

HELGA AMESBERGER

Images of grieving and suffering mothers are a familiar motif on memorials for the victims of Nazi atrocities. As this chapter details, these symbols mask a history that has overlooked gender-specific experiences, and such representations accentuate and transmit "unexamined mythical images of womanhood."[1] My focus is on the Nazi policies governing sexuality and population issues. These mandates permeated practically all spheres of women's and men's lives, as well as the social family unit, and substantially determined the chances for survival of those who were persecuted. I take into account various measures that denied women the rights to give birth and experience motherhood, especially aspects of pregnancy, birth, and maternity in the context of the concentration camp and ghetto. Both the camps and ghettos were areas of physical confinement as well as spheres of absolute power.

In her analysis of how women are portrayed in Holocaust research, Sara R. Horowitz points to the danger of falling back on gender stereotypes and identifies two approaches taken by most scholars: the first stresses the equality between men and women and neglects sexism as a component of persecution; the second, which emphasizes the distinctiveness of women's experiences (such as pregnancy, motherhood, and rape), makes women seem homogeneous.[2] Horowitz adds: "The related tropes of pregnancy and motherhood have led later scholars to focus on one of two distinct forms of narrative: those of atrocity and those of heroism."[3] This chapter aims to avoid both of these approaches. My examination seeks to delineate stories of pregnancy and motherhood according to specific reasons for persecution, neither shaping a uniform narrative nor viewing persecuted women as a homogeneous group. The experiences, perceptions, and memories of women within a given persecuted group are not the same, and it is important to heed the polyphonic chorus of voices and their complexity, even if this sometimes yields conflicting testimonies.

Narratives by survivors regarding their own pregnancy and motherhood reflect their culturally and socially determined norms of womanhood and their notions about the role of mothers. Motherhood is never considered outside of the context of society. It is fundamentally determined by social, economic, political, and cultural frameworks, a point that I can only briefly touch on here.[4]

I am not attempting to prove that women suffered more than men, but rather to clarify the specific situations in which women found themselves. Nor do I want to give the impression that motherhood equals infinite goodness or that it should serve to symbolize the atrocities committed by the Nazis. My purpose is to gain insight into experiences particular to women, those different horrors of the same hell, to paraphrase Myrna Goldenberg.[5] I also want to emphasize that even though the thematic focus here is on pregnancy and motherhood, men were also affected by population and sexual policies. They, too, were governed by the Nazi principles of "racial politics" and "racial hygiene." To date there has been no specific research on men as fathers, which suggests that researchers have not yet asked detailed questions about this and have continued to produce traditional images of gender roles.

My sources are primarily biographical accounts taken from interviews with Austrian survivors belonging to various prisoner groups incarcerated at Ravensbrück women's concentration camp. I also draw on interviews that David P. Boder conducted with Jewish women survivors in 1946, as well as an interview I conducted with a Jewish survivor of Auschwitz and Mauthausen who gave birth to two children during the time that she was incarcerated by the Nazis.

Pregnancy and Birth

The Nazis dealt with pregnancy according to their system of "racial" classification. The deportation of pregnant women was commonly carried out, as evidenced by the enactment of a decree forbidding the admission of pregnant inmates into Ravensbrück, Auschwitz, and Lublin concentration camps.[6] The reason given for this prohibition was that concentration camps were not equipped to aid women giving birth. The decree further stated that before deportation to a concentration camp, women had to be examined not only for sexually transmitted diseases but for evidence of pregnancy. It is highly unlikely that this proscription ever applied to Jews and Roma and Sinti women, and I know of no such case.[7]

Pregnant Jewish women were generally sent to their deaths immediately in concentration camps, unless they became the subject of heinous "medical" experiments. The interruption of a German (non-Jewish) pregnant woman's prison term was in many cases possible,[8] but all stories about and by pregnant Jewish women taken to a concentration camp or ghetto mention that they tried to hide their pregnancy from the SS, and sometimes from the other prisoners, for as long as possible because they were afraid of forced interventions and further deportation. Such was the case of Anka Bergman, a Czech Jewish survivor who brought her first child into the world in Theresienstadt.[9]

Unlike other concentration camps, Theresienstadt allowed Jewish women who arrived at the camp already pregnant to give birth, though becoming pregnant once in the camp was forbidden. Anka Bergman therefore had to choose whether to abort her pregnancy at a very late stage or to hand over her child to the Nazis at birth. As pregnant women and subsequent deliveries were not rare in Theresienstadt, Anka's pregnancy there in 1943 should not have been anything out of the ordinary. However, when she became pregnant again while in Theresienstadt, she and her husband violated not only camp regulations regarding the segregation of females and males but also the racial population policies of the National Socialists. They had committed a crime. In a world governed by policies designed to effect the total annihilation of the Jewish populace, Jewish women and men had no right to self-determination regarding their own reproduction. In short, reproductive rights were revoked for Jews. The fact that the Nazis pretended to require the "permission" of the parents, whether they "chose" to abort or to relinquish a child, further points to the treachery involved.[10] The Nazis made the victims legitimize their actions so the public would have the impression that the parents had acted of their own free will. The expectant mothers or parents were thus turned into accomplices, if not made into perpetrators themselves.[11]

Anka Bergman tried to conceal her second pregnancy as long as possible. She was pregnant at the time of her deportation from Theresienstadt to Auschwitz in October 1944, before being transferred to Freiberg, a sub-camp of Flossenbürg. Luckily, her pregnancy was discovered only after Auschwitz had been liquidated. Most women—Jewish and non-Jewish—had to work until the day they gave birth, and often, to survive, they had to do forced manual labor again a few days afterward. In Freiberg, Anka Bergman was assigned the "light" work of sweeping the factory floors (not all pregnant women there were given such consideration).[12] From Freiberg, she was sent to Mauthausen, where gassing had been terminated one day before her arrival.

Bergman's second delivery was very different from her first. On April 29, 1945, she brought her daughter Eva into the world on a cart while on the way to the Mauthausen concentration camp. The following passage from her interview tells us of her emotional state and the hygienic conditions that existed:

> I tell you something. My second delivery, which was spectacular, really, but it was so very easy. But that's neither here nor there. But all through the time it was going on, I was thinking of my mother. Not that she would be sorry for me; she would say, "How dare you have a child under those circumstances!" That's what I was thinking about, because nothing was good enough for us at home. I mean, the best was only just good enough. And now, I dare to have a child on a cart! I don't know why I thought like that because my mother would have done anything for me and would have taken the pain or whatever. We had a beautiful relationship. But that's what I thought—my mother would be so cross that I dared have a baby under those circumstances. Well, that's what I was thinking of, and it turned out all right because she [my baby] wasn't moving or crying for about ten minutes, until we got there, and it was cold, and these women with typhus. The lice were running around in millions, and I was sitting up and not having been washed for three weeks and not having eaten properly for three weeks. And just sitting there. And I couldn't care less really at the moment when the baby came out if it cries or doesn't cry.[13]

Anka arrived with the other prisoners from Freiberg after a fifteen-day meandering journey in an open railway wagon.[14] Her daughter survived because the Mauthausen concentration camp was liberated just one week after her delivery.

How and where births took place depended on the setting. Thus Anka Bergman believed that there was nothing special to report about her first delivery in the hospital of Theresienstadt, because all had gone as "normal." Before a so-called delivery block was established in the Ravensbrück concentration camp, expectant mothers were either taken to the hospital in nearby Templin or remained in the concentration camp for the delivery of their babies.[15]

Beginning in fall 1944, very pregnant women and women who had just given birth in Ravensbrück were housed in the delivery block. According to Ilse Reibmayer, an inmate doctor, by comparison to camp conditions this block was almost a "sanatorium" where the women could recover for several days, though when the rate of births rose due to an influx of pregnant (non-Jewish) Polish women who had been arrested in the August 1944 Warsaw Uprising, women had to return to their old barracks within one day of giving birth.[16]

Regardless of a camp's structural capacity to meet the needs of birthing women, very pregnant women were not spared from being transferred to other places. The "pregnant women's transports" from Ravensbrück and Mauthausen to Bergen-Belsen are an example.[17] This was the final destination for many pregnant women and mothers with small children, whose chances of survival there were nil. According to Thomas Rahe:

> That Bergen-Belsen had intentionally become a camp for receiving pregnant concentration camp inmates at the beginning of 1945 is only surprising at first glance. These transports of pregnant women continued a development that had already begun in spring of 1944, when Bergen-Belsen had become the final destination for transports of sick camp prisoners who were no longer able to work. It is precisely in this category that pregnant women fell out of the purview of the SS—for them they no longer could be used fully for forced labor.[18]

Like Anka Bergman, women about to give birth were part of "regular" transports of prisoners being "evacuated" from concentration camps. The unthinkable conditions under which these women delivered children while being transferred were also described in Edith Serras's 1946 testimony that tells of five non-Jewish Yugoslavian women prisoners giving birth during a death march from Auschwitz to Ravensbrück:

> We traveled 120 kilometers on foot. . . . Those who could walk, walked. And those who remained behind were shot. The majority were shot. And that is how we arrived in Breslau. Breslau is the border [town] between Poland and Germany. We were loaded into open railroad cars. That was January 18 [1945]. . . . It snowed all over us for three days and three nights. I found myself in a car, in an open one, with the five women, with sick little children, and with sick women, because I had the people from the sickroom. The five women gave birth to their babies. That was a picture which I shall not be able to forget in my lifetime. . . . They came down in labor. . . . They were lying stretched out, half-naked, to give birth to their babies. They could not be active [proceed with labor], and so were not able to give birth to the babies. . . . [W]oman about to have a baby must be active, she must expel the child from her body. The woman had no strength; she was frozen. It snowed over her—it snowed over her body [abdomen]. The babies—there were moments when we pleaded with the women. . . . We took off our dresses and threw them over her, over the sick woman, so she could . . . she was frozen. . . . And we pleaded with the women! "Be active, deliver your child, gather strength," but the woman [women] was so weakened and said, "I /We/ can't. I . . . we are cold." We saw the baby emerging with a half-head outside and

it goes back. The baby is . . . cannot come out. Finally, it lasted three days and three nights, and the women gave birth to their children—live children on the snow. . . . All alive. It lasted three days and three nights. And in a corner of the car little children were lying and saw how women have children.[19]

By and large, most children born in the camps did not survive. Due to hard labor and little nourishment, the mothers did not have enough milk, and the camp overseers did not provide enough nourishment for babies. Most babies starved, but many were also murdered by the SS with injections of air or gasoline, or they were drowned or beaten to death. The number of children born or living in the camps will always remain a mystery, but a record of births in Ravensbrück from fall 1944 to April 1945 can give us a vague notion. The records tell us that 560 children were born, 23 women delivered prematurely, 20 had stillborn babies, and 5 suffered miscarriages. For 266 children a date of death is given in the same book that records their birth.[20] According to my analysis of the birth records, 22 Jewish women (from Hungary, Poland, Slovakia, and stateless) gave birth in the Ravensbrück delivery block. Most of these women came to Ravensbrück in the last months of 1944 or at the beginning of 1945, some of them from Auschwitz. Eleven newborn babies definitely did not survive; most of them died after two to four weeks. The fate of the other newborn children is not clear. In total, perhaps only about one hundred children survived,[21] thanks to the solidarity among the prisoners and the timing of the births during the last weeks of the war.

Hopeless Hope

The older children in the camps relied on biological as well as surrogate mothers. Many women came into the camps with their children of different ages, but other children and adolescents arrived alone or lost their mothers to disease or starvation. The age of the children was a decisive factor in determining the survival of mother and child. Mothers with children under the age of sixteen (unless they falsified their children's ages to make them seem older) were especially targeted to be selected for annihilation. Their children were regarded by the Nazis as "useless eaters," whose ability to perform work was too low.

Most mothers used their limited sphere of influence to reduce the children's suffering as much as possible, which sometimes meant turning norms and beliefs held in a civil society on their heads. For example, if women tried to protect their children from performing forced labor in order to keep them from suffering the harsh conditions, they were in fact signing their children's death sentences. Mothers who made sacrifices for the sake of their children adhered to the traditional expectations that mothers will place their child's life before their own. Women whose actions ran counter to this model, who placed their own life above that of the child and had an abortion, or who took newborn babies away from their mothers and killed them to save the mother's life, were sometimes stigmatized after World War II, their actions categorized as morally reprehensible.[22]

According to bourgeois patriarchal notions, motherhood is to be understood as the fulfillment of a woman's life, as the source of happiness. Other feelings that mothers may have, such as doubt about their role or dissatisfaction with it, the inability to establish a relationship with the child, or even having an aversion to the child, do not fit concepts promoted by this patriarchal world. A mother with these feelings is regarded in a negative light and as worthy of contempt. Societal expectations regarding "correct" or "proper" feelings and nurturing behavior are projected onto mothers (and to a far lesser extent onto fathers).

Because they are part of society, women themselves sometimes share such normative notions and often suffer when they cannot meet society's expectations. Values shared in a civil society are not automatically thrown overboard at the gates of ghettos or concentration and death camps. Even during persecution they remain valid and continue to influence the actions and attitudes of women regarding pregnancy and motherhood. What did it mean in psychological terms for women persecuted by the Nazis to become mothers and not be able to experience the ideal life of motherhood?

Interviews with persecuted women who were pregnant or who were mothers incarcerated with or without their children reveal a wide spectrum of emotions that include hope, fear, grief, anger, hatred, impotence, helplessness, disappointment, willingness to make sacrifices, love, affection, shame, despair, and hopelessness.[23] These emotions might sometimes be directed toward the woman's child, other people, or herself. The women's psychological makeup and their motives and opportunities for taking action depended on many personal and structural factors, as is shown by the following quote from the interview with Anna Kovitzka:

Later I reported to the "police" that I was a Jewess. I wanted to die together with the Jews rather than to live this way. They did not believe me. They thought I must have gone crazy because my husband was taken away. After that they held me for a month in a Königsberg prison, and then I was sent to Auschwitz. By the time of our arrival at Auschwitz, I had lost all semblance of a human being. Now when I encountered people who have seen me in Auschwitz, they tell me . . . [Here she begins to sob violently.][24]

Anna's spirits improved when she heard that two of her relatives were also in the camp:

I was taken by hope that I would see them. And that gave me some courage, in spite of the fact that in Auschwitz I was a complete so-called *Muselmann* [walking dead], . . . In Auschwitz I had a change of mind. I decided again to live. One day a distant cousin of mine, a girl, Nelly Kovitzka, a seventeen-year-old girl appeared in my block. Her face was that of my little girl. And I was overcome with hope that I would return. Maybe she is alive. . . . I started to fight again, to struggle for life, in Auschwitz. I became a—I was cleaning the block. A block that housed thirteen hundred people. I cleaned it, I scrubbed it, and for that I would get another helping of soup, and at times I would get a little piece of bread that the *blokova* [prisoner in charge of a block] would leave uneaten. Then in spite of curfew I dressed up. In Auschwitz there was enough to wear. There was the clothing of the dead.

After Anna Kovitzka lost her will to live because of separation from her child and other factors, the child alone was not enough motivation to fight for survival. The uncertainty about the fate of her whole family and the destruction of the Jewish community of Grodno at first led her to choose to give up. However, after being reminded of her abandoned daughter by the resemblance of her cousin, she found the strength to fight to survive, a strength that was reinforced by her realization, she said later in her interview, that she had become responsible for her family's lineage. "They [her relatives] . . . told me that I am the oldest in our family and that I must survive," she said.[25] Anna made a conscious decision to try to live. She did not give over her life to fate but grasped the opportunities within her reach in order to fight against the will of the Nazis to destroy her.

While being a mother sometimes strengthened the will to live, at other times it was a cause for despair and hopelessness. Time played a significant role, according to various interviews. For instance, the longer the separation from the child, the less relevant was the child as a motive for remaining alive. Interviewed mothers often mentioned their children only as an aside in their interviews, discussing neither the actual separation (the breaking of the mother-child bond) nor their inability to care for the child as a consequence of their incarceration. These women seem to have forgotten their children, or perhaps they were repressing the all-too-painful memory. The reasons for these gaps are manifold and can often be construed from the stories the women tell. For example, an incarcerated woman may not have been raising the child herself, having placed him or her in the care of a loving person; the mother-child relationship may have been problematic, and the mother experienced it as the source of her anguish; shame at not having met societal norms or expectations may explain the scant mention of a child.[26] The survivor Aloisa Hofinger expressed her feelings about her dead daughter as follows:

> Well, I stood at the grave, like a lump, like a stone. What can you do? I stood there a long time until I even shed one tear. Because I told myself the whole time over and over: Why, how come, how come, why is it that way? You had to suffer so much and had to put up with so much. And then it all was still for nothing. Then it finally came to me, that I thought: "It is better that she died. At least I don't have any responsibility anymore and no one can blame me. I am still so young. I don't know what the future holds for me." And that was the point I had reached. And it was also all right that way.[27]

Women imprisoned for engaging in a "forbidden sexual relationship" felt especially guilty for having committed such a "crime." They even feared renewed accusations from potential husbands or their neighbors, which increased their sense of culpability.[28] The death of a child or relegation of child rearing to someone else thus could have been a relief for some women. The horrible fate of most children in concentration camps, as well as the stigma felt before, during, and after persecution, makes these mothers' relief all too understandable.

Dina Wardi, however, points to another condition that has to be taken into account in the analysis of interviews—the trauma that was experienced:

> The fact that survivors say very little about their separation from their parents, siblings and other family members can be misleading. The topic of separation is indeed often omitted from the story of what happened to them during the Holocaust, or drowned in a sea of events that seem more important. Sometimes, after many years have passed, some of them are ready to talk about the separation from their families (generally in answer to their own children's direct questions), but even then their descriptions are usually short and narrated in a monotonous voice. However, this appearance is misleading. A deeper look shows that the trauma accompanying the survivors' separation from their families is very deep—perhaps the most difficult trauma to cure.[29]

In no society is motherhood only the individual's concern, and this was also true in the context of the concentration camp. Despite their misery, the children were again and again the source of hope and strength. The small children often roused the prisoners to take action, stirring them to compassion and solidarity. For example, women who had a second undershirt would donate it for baby clothes.[30] In 1944, a Christmas party was organized for the children in Ravensbrück,[31] and some women took care of children who were on their own. So-called camp mothers "adopted" a child and cared for her or him as best they could.[32]

Johanna Bodenstab explains that pregnancies led fellow prisoners to have a series of expectations that totally contradicted the reality of the camp. Other female inmates pinned numerous hopes onto expectant mothers and children, and such hopes were paradoxically among the worst memories of many survivors.[33] Their anticipation of the birth would first of all be connected to hope for their own survival and the future. In addition, pregnancies and births represented a type of "normal" life in face of the horrors of everyday concentration camp life.[34] Yet the murder of a child in sight of a prisoner illustrated the inmate's utter powerlessness—the fact that the SS decided the end of the story. In the eyes of Lawrence L. Langer, the solidarity among prisoners could have only little influence on the situation.[35]

Bodenstab's analysis, which emphasizes the expectations of the interviewees, is based on an excerpt from an interview citing the case of a pregnant woman, the delivery of her baby, and the subsequent murder of the newborn by an SS soldier. Langer quotes the same passage. However, he places the emphasis on the women's helplessness, on the idea that the murder of the child demonstrates that the SS decided the outcome of that event. It's important to note that the intentions of the two researchers differ. While Bodenstab wants to show what pregnancy and birth could mean for fellow prisoners, Langer is concerned with demonstrating that the Holocaust does not have a gender-specific dimension we must consider because the "end result" was the same for men and women. "[They] were victimized by events beyond their control that mocked their efforts to create for themselves a gendered part," he wrote.[36] To my mind, one paradigm does not preclude the other.

Almost all stories of pregnancy, birth, and children during the Holocaust are closely linked with narratives of death. The hope of a new beginning, a future, some "normalcy" symbolized by pregnancy and children, is destroyed by the arbitrary murder of children by the SS and replaced by hopelessness, despair, and the wish that one would also die. At the same time, many women had no illusions. Their realism is the only way to understand the active engagement of women in secret deliveries of babies and subsequent removal of the child from the mother. They brought about the death of the newborn in order to allow the mother to live.

The After-effects

The end of the war and liberation did not end most survivors' trauma. In most cases, Jewish survivors had to come to grips with the facts that their relatives had been murdered and they had been robbed of their possessions. They were faced with having absolutely nothing at all. The traumatic events of persecution influenced many spheres of their lives, including their attempts to build families and their relationships with children born afterward. However, persecution itself was not the only factor. A person's age at the time of victimization, her social environment and class, the reason for her persecution, and her personal experiences during the war also matter.[37] Likewise, psychological examinations of the interviews reveal a variety of after-effects, and here I will present some that survivors themselves have identified. Rather than identifying pathological problems, I am merely pointing out the long shadow cast by National Socialist persecution.

It is mainly non-Jewish women whose children were left behind in their homeland who tell of the difficulties of being accepted as the mother by the child upon their return. The children had viewed a substitute mother as their mother, and sometimes very young children no longer had any memory of their birth mother. Some mothers also reveal their own sense of alienation from their child. It often took years to overcome such estrangement, and sometimes the children secretly never forgave their mothers for having abandoned them. Erna Musik, for example, reports that her relationship with her daughter—an infant at the time of Erna's arrest—only improved after they visited the Auschwitz memorial site together:

> It was only then that I had a real daughter. One that calls at least once a day: "How are you? What's going on? Should I get something for you?" But before that I was just more or less there, a mother in name only, but I felt as though I was a stranger. She regarded my sister-in-law as her mother.[38]

In addition, there were the expected conflicts with foster mothers who, on one hand, often didn't want to relinquish their responsibilities and, on the other hand, felt more competent in caring for a child than the returning mothers. In some cases, women who returned had to leave their children in the care of foster mothers because they had no means of subsistence, no income or place to live, or they were not in good health.

The assertion is often made that Jewish survivors especially wanted to create new families in order to defy the systematic mass murder that had destroyed their homes, families, and communities. For some, the birth of new children became a symbol of triumph over the Nazis. For others, loneliness, coincidence, emptiness, social norms, the insistence of the partner, lack of contraception, and much more may have played a role in the creation of new families after the Holocaust.[39] My own research shows that among survivors, Roma women and women from rural areas had many children, while survivors from an urban environment, regardless of the reason for their persecution, often had no more than two.[40]

In fact, many women mentioned that they and their partners did not want to have any (more) children. They often justified this choice—even when it was not the only reason for their decision—with their experiences during their persecution. The fate of the children in concentration camps was present in their minds, and to a certain extent they were afraid that the same fate might also await their children. For example, immediately after her return from Mauthausen concentration camp, Anka Bergman had her Jewish daughter, born in the concentration camp, baptized by a priest. Later she sent the daughter to Catholic schools. These acts can be interpreted as an attempt to spare her child from possible persecution as a Jew. Forced sterilization, as well as injuries resulting from forced abortions and medical experiments, destroyed many women's ability to reproduce, but harmed yet fertile women who had a new partner after liberation were nonetheless likely to bear a child.[41]

The relationship to children born after liberation varied. Some women were happy that, despite their doubts, they had decided to have a child. The children brought joy and gave purpose to having survived. They substituted for the many great losses, making life worth living again.[42] Others could not find happiness in their offspring because the memory of the murdered children was too strong, the trauma too great.[43] Yet others thought that it had been a mistake to have a child after all they had experienced. These children, who were born later, were said to have serious psychological wounds due to their mothers' trauma.[44] Many women may have felt like Sally H., of whom Langer writes:

> Sally H. cannot simply celebrate the birth of her own child because in her imagination she associates it with the doom of Rachel and her unborn infant. She suffers from what I call a tainted memory, and neither the passage of time nor an unwilled amnesia can erase it. There may be a valid text about small communi-

ties of women who survived through mutual support or some strength of gender, but it exists within a darker subtext emerging in these testimonies. To valorize the one while disregarding the other is little more than an effort to replace truth with myth.[45]

In this chapter the object has not been to create new "myths," as Langer implies, but to render as full a picture as possible of the effect of the Holocaust on motherhood. Ambivalent feelings with regard to pregnancy, birth, and one's own child can be the result of trauma, but they are also present in women who were never persecuted. Associating motherhood, before and after liberation, with only happiness and self-fulfillment assumes that the apparent natural predestined course for women is to become mothers. Such an assumption would give the tales of mass murder a positive, reconciliatory ending, as though the patriarchal values of ideal motherhood are indeed true.

Conclusions

The experience of violence, in this case the trauma of sexualized violence, has a lasting influence on people's lives. In no other political ideology has sexuality played as important a role as it did in National Socialism. To promote their racist aims, the Nazis had to control the sexual behavior of the populace of the German Reich. Women's sexuality and the reproductive capabilities of women were an integral part of the Nazis' racist agenda to create and maintain an "Aryan race" and the German *Volksgemeinschaft*, the community of the German people. The "Aryan woman" was expected to support and strengthen the project of the "Thousand-Year Reich" with regard to its moral, social, and cultural aspects. An essential characteristic of patriarchal systems is denying women self-determination over their own bodies, and under National Socialism this restriction weighed even more heavily in light of racist and anti-Semitic ideologies.

In pursuit of its goals, via the creation and enforcement of "racial" laws, the National Socialist regime created strict boundaries between women. All women were not equal to each other, just as all mothers and pregnant women were not alike. The recent focus on gender aspects of the Holocaust and victimization by the National Socialists has made it possible to identify ideological connections to sexualized violence:[46] incursions into the domain of reproduction were motivated by racism and anti-Semitism and waged against women as the childbearing representatives of their people. The Nazis took aim at women's bodies as defined by "race" and targeted the women they considered inferior. Although directed at groups of people, the Nazis' violent acts were nonetheless aimed at each woman as an individual insofar as they diminished her identity as woman or mother by inhibiting her sexual self-determination. Thus the National Socialist agenda was not only anti-Semitic and racist but also sexist.

The countervailing idealization of the "Aryan" woman as mother and keeper of society's morals may seem to contradict National Socialist practices of forced sterilization, murder, and removal of newborn babies, but these were meant to help create a healthy, racially pure *Volkskörper* (body of a people). A series of laws was enacted to help the National Socialists reach these aims, and sexual behavior became a state affair that concerned not only the populations that were being devastated but the whole of society.

Reproduction is and was both a highly personal and public political affair. Women had to make unbearable choices for their own or their children's lives, and often had no choice at all. Visibly pregnant Jewish women and mothers went along with their children to gas chambers immediately after arrival in death camps. Some women tried to regain their agency, which did not always mean that they sacrificed their lives to protect their children. To survive, women sometimes killed their newborn children, because they knew that the babies had no chance to live; others left their children behind. Pregnant women often chose abortion. From various testimonies, we also know about the ingenious and inventive strategies of women to protect and save their children. In the end, no matter how the women acted or reacted, the decision about life or death was made by the Nazis.

Notes

1. Silke Wenk and Insa Eschebach, "Soziales Gedächtnis und Geschlechterdifferenz: Eine Einführung" [Social memory and gender difference], in *Gedächtnis und Geschlecht. Deutungsmuster in Darstellungen des nationalsozialistischen Genozids* [Memory and gender. Interpreting representations of National Socialist genocide), ed. Insa Eschebach, Sigrid Jacobeit, and Silke Wenk (Frankfurt: Campus Verlag, 2002), 24.

2. Sara R. Horowitz, "Women in Holocaust Literature: Engendering Trauma Memory," in *Women in the Holocaust*, ed. Dalia Ofer and Lenore J. Weitzman (New Haven: Yale University Press, 1998), 369–370.

3. Ibid., 371.

4. For more information about the influence of social and cultural stipulations surrounding reproduction, as well as images, expectations, norms, and values concerning motherhood, please see the following: Esther Hertzog, "Past and Present in My Mother's Holocaust Memories," in *Life, Death and Sacrifice: Women and Family in the Holocaust*, ed. Esther Hertzog (Jerusalem: Gefen Publishing House, 2008), 261–285; Dalia

Ofer, "Motherhood under Siege," in *Life, Death and Sacrifice*, 41–67; Paula E. Hyman, "Gender and the Jewish Family in Modern Europe," in *Women in the Holocaust*, ed. Ofer and Weitzman, 25–38; Marion Kaplan, "Keeping Calm and Weathering the Storm: Jewish Women's Responses to Daily Life in Nazi Germany, 1933–1939," in *Women in the Holocaust*, 39–54.

5. Myrna Goldenberg, "Different Horrors/Same Hell: Women Remembering the Holocaust," in *Thinking the Unthinkable: Human Meanings of the Holocaust*, ed. Roger Gottlieb (New York: Paulist Press, 1990), 150–166.

6. This decree, "RdErl. des ChdSPud8D. vom 6.5.1943—IV C 2 Nr. 43 076 od. 43 876" (the number is almost illegible), was enacted on May 6, 1943. The full title is *Erlass zum Verbot der Einweisung schwangerer Häftlinge in die Frauenkonzentrationslager Ravensbrück bzw. in die Frauenabteilungen der Konzentrationslager Auschwitz und Lublin* [Decree forbidding the admission of pregnant inmates into the women's concentration camp Ravensbrück or the women's sections of the concentration camps Auschwitz and Lublin]. A copy can be found in the collections of the Ravensbrück Memorial in Sammlungen MGR/StBG.–RA II/3–1–16, Kopie.

7. It may have affected Jewish women who were incarcerated for political reasons before the mass deportations started.

8. Aloisa Hofinger, interview IKF-Rav.Int. 13 (Austrian survivors of Ravensbrück), conducted by Helga Amesberger on December 2, 1998, and March 8, 1999, at the Institute of Conflict Research (IKF), Vienna. Aloisa Hofinger was temporarily released from incarceration in spring 1942 to give birth. Four months after the birth, she was deported to the Ravensbrück concentration camp.

9. Anka Bergman, interview OH/ZP1/536, conducted by Helga Amesberger on January 26, 2003, Archive of the Mauthausen Memorial. Anka Bergman mentioned in the interview that she first heard about euthanasia when she and her husband had to decide whether to interrupt her pregnancy or hand the child over after delivery. The fate of the newborn was clear; it was destined for murder.

10. Anka Berman, interview with author, May 10, 2003. In this interview Anka stated that she and her husband had had to sign the document.

11. This strategy was also used in cases of forced sex labor, where the Nazis were especially successful in turning their victims into accomplices, as is conveyed by the many negative eyewitness reports about women forced into sexual labor and the public discourse surrounding this aspect of persecution. See Helga Amesberger et al., *Sexualisierte Gewalt. Weibliche Erfahrungen in NS-Konzentrationlagern* [Sexualized violence. Women's experiences in Nazi concentration camps] (Vienna: Mandelbaum, 2004), 105–114, 256.

12. Pascal Cziborra believes pregnant women's incarceration in the sub-camp Freiberg, as well as a lighter work detail, were due to two factors: the relatively late stage in the war—the impeding downfall of the Germans was becoming apparent and Auschwitz-Birkenau had already been liberated—and the influence that the *Oberkapo* Maria (Marysia), who also was pregnant, exerted on the leader of the commando, *Unterscharführer* Beck. See Pascal Cziborra, "Mutterglück und Kindestod. Schwangere KZ-Häftlinge zwischen Freiberg und Mauthausen," [Motherhood and child death. Pregnant

concentration camp prisoners between Freiberg and Mauthausen] in *Zwischen Mutter-kreuz und Gaskammer. Täterinnen und Mitläuferinnen oder Widerstand und Verfolgung?* [Between the German mother's cross and the gas chamber. Women perpetrators and collaborators or resistance and persecution?], ed. Andreas Baumgartner et al. (Vienna: Edition Mauthausen, Mauthausen Komitee Österreich, 2008), 105.

13. Bergman, interview OH/ZP1/536.

14. In this transport there were several pregnant women and some women with newborn babies. See Cziborra, "Mutterglück und Kindestod," 109–110.

15. Britta Pawelka, "Als Häftling geboren—Kinder in Ravensbrück" [Born as a prisoner—Children in Ravensbrück], in *Frauen in Konzentrationslagern. Bergen-Belsen, Ravensbrück* [Women in concentration camps. Bergen-Belsen, Ravensbrück], ed. Klaus Füllberg-Stollberg et al. (Bremen: Edition Temmen, 1994), 158. See also IKF-Rav-Int. 20_1–3; Sammlungen MGR/StBG.—15/3, 11.

16. For the procedure of giving birth and the situation in the delivery block, see citations from an interview with Dr. Reibmayr (1995) in Amesberger et al., *Sexualisierte Gewalt*, 247–250.

17. See Andreas Baumgartner, *Die vergessenen Frauen von Mauthausen. Die weiblichen Häftlinge des Konzentrationslager Mauthausen und ihre Geschichte* [The forgotten women of Mauthausen. The women prisoners of Mauthausen concentration camp and their story] (Vienna: Verlag Österreich, 1997), 173–174.

18. Thomas Rahe, "'Ich wußte nicht einmal, daß ich schwanger war.' Geburten im KZ Bergen-Belsen" ["I didn't even know that I was pregnant." Births in the Bergen-Belsen Concentration Camp], in *Frauen in Konzentrationslagern*, ed. Klaus Füllberg-Stollberg et al., 154.

19. Edith Serras interview, August 7, 1946 (David P. Boder Archive, Voices of the Holocaust, spool 34, http://voices.iit.edu/). A footnote by the translator of this interview states, "There is a constant mixture of singular and plural. She speaks of one and the five pregnant women interchangeably."

20. Pawelke, "Als Häftling geboren," 158.

21. Sammlungen MGR/StBG.—Vol. 15/3, 11.

22. See Hertzog's comments in *Life, Death and Sacrifice* (275) about the investigation by an all-male commission evaluating Dr. Gisella Perl's application for United States citizenship. She was the Jewish-Hungarian doctor who had secretly performed thousands of abortions in Birkenau.

23. Amesberger et al., *Sexualisierte Gewalt*, 279–287.

24. Kovitzka, interview, 9.

25. Ibid., 10.

26. There is a double bind in the role research plays in reinforcing the ideals of motherhood. Asking why mothers did not always mention their children implies that they should have. However, as long as the analysis is objective and not judgmental, such norms can be dismantled and examined. See Helga Amesberger, "Doing Gender within Oral History," in *The Challenges of Dialogue*, ed. Marta Kurkowska-Budzan and Krystof Zamorski (Amsterdam: John Benjamins, 2009), 63–75.

27. Hofinger, interview, 27.

28. Helga Amesberger and Brigitte Halbmayr, *Vom Leben und Überleben. Wege nach Ravensbrück—Dokumentation und Analyse* [Of life and survival. Paths to Ravensbrück—documentation and analysis], vol. 1 (Vienna: Promedia, 2001), 233–234.

29. Dina Wardi, *Memorial Candles: Children of the Holocaust*, trans. Naomi Goldblum (London: Tavistock/Routledge, 1992), 9.

30. Charlotte Dorowin-Zeissl, interview IKF-Rav-Inter. 21_1, 9, conducted by Hemma Mayerhofer on January 14, 1999.

31. See Dorowin-Zeissl, interview, 10–11; Amesberger et al., *Vom Leben und Überleben*, vol. 1, 194–195; Pawelke, "Als Häftling geboren,"162–164.

32. See Antonia Bruha, interview IKF-Rav-Int. 20_3, 18, conducted by Helga Amesberger on September 19, 2002.

33. See Amesberger et al., *Sexualisierte Gewalt*, 250–253. One should note that most female survivors, regardless of age, family status, and reason for persecution, deal with the subject of the misery of children and expectant mothers in the concentration camps in their testimonies; whereas the stories of males only seldom include mention of the fate of children. See also Amesberger, *The Challenges of Dialogue*, 68–70.

34. Johanna Bodenstab, "Under Siege: A Mother-Daughter Relationship Survives the Holocaust," *Psychoanalytic Inquiry* 24, no. 5 (2004): 731–751.

35. Lawrence L. Langer, "Gendered Suffering? Women in Holocaust Testimonies," in *Women in the Holocaust*, ed. Ofer and Weitzman, 351–363.

36. Ibid., 356.

37. See Amesberger et al., *Sexualisierte Gewalt*, 294–325.

38. Erna Musik, interview IKF-Rav-Int. 3_3, 16–17, conducted by Brigitte Halbmayr on October 2, 2002.

39. Wardi, *Memorial Candles*, 26–29.

40. Amesberger et al., *Sexualisierte Gewalt*, 320.

41. Ibid., 322.

42. Wardi, *Memorial Candles*, 30.

43. Langer, "Gendered Suffering?" 357–358.

44. Amesberger et al., *Sexualisierte Gewalt*, 296–297.

45. Langer, "Gendered Suffering?" 354–355.

46. See chapter 2 by Brigitte Halbmayr in this volume.

CHAPTER

10

Forced Sterilization and Abortion as Sexual Abuse

ELLEN BEN-SEFER

Forced sterilization and forced abortion are acts of sexual violence and gender-based discrimination as defined by the World Health Organization.[1] The procedures can be fatal, and when they are not, they can give rise to lifelong consequences ranging from physical injury, such as tearing of tissue, to trauma to permanent infertility.

Although some literature details cases of forced sterilization of both women and men, as well as the forced abortion of Jewish and Gypsy (Sinti and Roma) women's fetuses during the Holocaust, accurate numbers of victims cannot be known.[2] Abortion and forced sterilization still are not discussed in depth in historical books about the Holocaust. One reason may be that women who had forced abortions or were sterilized were subsequently murdered, and another is that the victims may have had considerable difficulty in coming to terms with such trauma and may have chosen not to speak of it. Joan Ringelheim describes as a "split memory" both leaving the issue of gender out of Holocaust research and women's ambivalence about disclosing any form of sexual abuse. She writes:

> What is meant by the notion of a "split memory"? First, gender is considered irrelevant to the Holocaust. This results in "forgotten" memories; memories that are misunderstood by the survivors or not taken as Holocaust-related and thus split from the Holocaust. Second, there is a dividing line between what is considered personal and private to women, and what has been designated as the proper collective memory of the Holocaust. These private and personal experiences are known to have happened and are sometimes mentioned. But, they are usually severed from serious talk about the Holocaust. This results in "ignored" memories which eventually also turn into forgotten memories.[3]

Although often ignored, forced sterilization and abortion relate to a central tenet of cultural norms valid during the time of the Nazi regime: women were expected to bear children. Thus, being forced to give up a fundamental function of one's defined feminine role was emotionally painful. For those who were the victims of forced abortions and were then able to bear children after the war, their ordeal may have remained a painful secret, best left private. For those who suffered permanent damage as a result of abortions performed crudely, either in concentration or death camps, the consequences of infertility may have been too shattering to discuss.

Both forced sterilization of women and forced abortion can be viewed within the context of the Nazis' plans to selectively control breeding. These procedures that negated women's rights to a sexual life that would result in pregnancy and childbirth were forms of sexual abuse, because they interfered with a woman's right to control her own body and sex life. Furthermore, forced sterilization and, sometimes, forced abortion could cause serious infection, hemorrhage, or permanent damage that later disrupted both a woman's fertility and her ability to enjoy sex. Such abuse is not only related to sex and gender but is also a fundamental violation of human rights and directly identified as an element of genocide. The United Nations' definition of genocide includes the following: "Genocide is the committing of certain acts with intent to destroy—wholly or in part—a national, ethnic, racial, or religious group."[4] The concerted effort to control human breeding and prevent the birth of children of those deemed inferior by the Nazis clearly occurred within this context.

The Aryan Master Race Versus the "Undesirables"

In July 1933, the *Gesetz zur Verhütung erbkranken Nachwuchses* (Law for the Prevention of Genetically Diseased Offspring) was enacted, initiated by Interior Minister Wilhelm Frick. Under this law, German citizens who were identified as having congenital disabilities were to be forcibly sterilized. The "diseases" included a wide range of disorders and disabilities, not all of them hereditary: congenital feeble-mindedness (perhaps a euphemism for mental retardation), schizophrenia, hereditary epilepsy, hereditary blindness or deafness, Huntington's chorea, manic depression (bipolar disorder), any obvious serious physical deformities, and chronic alcoholism.[5] From 1940 to 1941, the T4 operation, short for Tiergartenstrasse 4, the address where the program was implemented, carried out not only enforced sterilization but also euthanasia by gassing, the latter taking place at several psychiatric facilities.[6] In a parallel development, on December 12, 1935, Heinrich Himmler initiated the Lebensborn program, based on principles of racial hygiene and designed to strengthen the "Aryan race" through "pure blood" selective couplings. Therefore, one program sought to prevent births of those who were deemed inferior, while the other sought to increase birth rates for a "superior" element of the population.[7]

Sterilizations were forcibly imposed by medical practitioners and performed throughout Nazi Germany. The justification for the sterilizations, which were surgical procedures, was that any German who suffered from the types of diseases or disabilities identified in the 1933 law was very likely to pass defects to his or her children. Therefore, once a medical practitioner stated that one of these "diseases" was present, force could be used to ensure that sterilization would take place. The proceedings deciding the cases of individuals selected for sterilization took place behind closed doors in Hereditary Health Courts. Estimates indicate that up to 350,000 people were sterilized in Germany during the 1940s. According to Patricia Heberer, "In all, some 200,000 individuals perished as a result of Operation T4 ('euthanasia') and its corollaries between 1939 and the end of World War II in Europe."[8]

The indiscriminate application of the law extended to youth who were considered juvenile delinquents by the Third Reich. Juvenile delinquency encompassed a range of behaviors considered to be asocial, including truancy from school, loitering after curfew, smoking, drinking, attending dances and cabarets after 9 P.M., and, in the case of girls, consorting with soldiers.[9] Youths accused of these crimes were sent to reformatories where they were subjected to a harsh diet along with forced labor. Sometimes they were also slated to be sterilized.

Forced sterilization laws soon applied to couples if one of the partners was an "Aryan" German and the other was Jewish or a Mischling (half-Jewish). Adolf Eichmann, in particular, took a rather uncompromising view of Mischlinge and wanted all of them treated as full Jews. These discussions took place over a period of time prior to, during, and after the enactment of the 1935 Nuremberg Laws and the 1942 Wannsee Conference.[10] Eichmann, Reinhard Heydrich, and other Nazi leaders propagated sterilization as well as "forced divorce" as potential solutions to the "Jewish question," but were met with opposition. At the Wannsee Conference, a suggestion was made that Mischlinge should be permitted to remain in Germany, provided that they submit to sterilization to ensure there would be no further offspring.[11]

Johanna Lindner Krause was one victim of forced sterilization because of the Nuremberg Racial Laws. As a Jewish woman married to a non-Jewish man, Johanna violated the racial purity laws. She spent years in and out of prison and was pregnant when she was arrested in Dresden in 1943. Her condition was discovered by the SS during a period when she was imprisoned as a slave laborer, and she was forced to abort her fetus during her third trimester of pregnancy and was subsequently sterilized. Then she was sent to Ravensbrück women's concentration camp.[12]

Gypsies were also considered "racially inferior," thus they were candidates for forced sterilization. Approximately thirty thousand Gypsies were resident in Germany during the 1930s, and some number of them, though we don't know how many, were forcibly sterilized.[13] Furthermore, some individuals of African descent living in Germany faced persecution. Most of the men were former soldiers who had served in Africa during World War I and were living in territory that had been disputed between France and Germany. With the rise of the Nazis and their extremist views on racial purity, these Afro-Germans became victims, along with other "asocials" in the new Germany.[14] Those who had married or had had sexual relations with German women found themselves and their children targeted, as mixed race marriages were strictly prohibited. Their biracial children were referred to as "Rhineland bastards," and as a consequence of their "illegal" status and "racial inferiority," a number of these children were forcibly sterilized.[15] By 1937, estimates indicate that between 385 and 500 children underwent sterilization based solely on racial background. The sterilizations to prevent "racial pollution" were performed secretly.[16]

Abortion was nominally illegal in Germany, both for Germans and those deemed inferior. However, there were many exceptions to the rule, and abortion was sometimes forced on "undesirables." Furthermore, women in dire circumstances sometimes elected to have secret abortions. No reliable statistical evidence exists to provide an understanding of the scope of secret abortions within Nazi Germany, but anecdotal evidence offers some indication of Jewish women's reasons for electing to abort. For example, for many German-Jewish women, the birth of a child was not the joyful occasion that it might have been in better days. If a couple was hoping to escape Nazi Germany, waiting for the birth of a child might delay or prevent emigration. Others worried that Jewish children would be born into a hostile world surrounded by increasing hatred. Faced with grim prospects for the future, women sought physicians who would secretly perform an abortion. Marion Kaplan cites Ruth Klüger's recollections of her father, who had qualified as both an obstetrician and pediatrician, being arrested for performing abortions, including one performed on his own wife.[17] These abortions would almost certainly have been psychologically painful for women, reflecting decisions taken within the context of increasing hostility and reflected in plummeting Jewish birthrates.

Sterilization and Abortion in Camps

From about March 1941 to January 1945, sterilization experiments were conducted at the Auschwitz and Ravensbrück concentration camps and other places for the purpose of developing a method of sterilization suitable for sterilizing millions of people with a minimum of time and effort. The experiments were conducted by means of x-rays, surgery, and various drugs. At postwar crimes trials in Nuremberg, defendants Karl Brandt, Karl Gebhardt, Rudolf Brandt, Joachim Mrugowsky, Helmut Poppendick, Viktor Brack, Adolf Pokorny, and Herta Oberheuser were charged with special responsibility for and participation in these crimes.[18]

Sterilization

Oberdienstleiter Viktor Brack, one of those listed as a defendant in the Nuremberg trials, organized the Nazis' euthanasia program. He also prepared a report for Himmler in June 1942, describing how to sterilize camp inmates by using x-rays on a large scale and without the victims' knowledge. According to Brack's estimates, up to 3 million Jewish men and women out of the entire Jewish population in Germany and German-occupied regions would be physically fit to work and should, therefore, be kept alive. He added that they could only be suitable (slave) workers if they were rendered incapable of reproduction. In a link to the forced euthanasia sterilizations that had taken place earlier in Germany, Brack told Himmler:

> I reported to you about a year ago that persons under my instruction have completed the necessary experiments for this purpose. I wish to bring up these facts again. The type of sterilization which is normally carried out on persons with genetic disease is out of the question in this case, as it takes too much time and is expensive. Castration by means of x-rays however, is not only relatively cheap, but can be carried out on many thousands in a very short time. I believe that it has become unimportant at the present time whether those affected will then in the course of a few weeks or months realize by the effects that they are castrated.[19]

One of the most well-known Nazi doctors involved in mass sterilization experiments was SS physician Carl Clauberg. Clauberg, an eminent gynecologist who had joined the Nazi party in 1933, was appointed by Himmler in 1942 to undertake experiments in mass sterilization at Auschwitz that continued until 1944. In the last year of the war, Clauberg was also involved in sterilization experiments in Ravensbrück. Among Clauberg's "medical" experiments,

Jewish and Gypsy women were sterilized through direct injection into the uterus. Chosen for these experiments because of his professional reputation as an expert in fertility treatments, Clauberg reported that he would be able to sterilize hundreds, if not thousands, of women each day.[20]

At least one thousand Jewish women appear on an order for forced sterilization by Clauberg. Gypsy women and girls were no safer from Clauberg's sterilization, and this procedure continued into 1945, even when the war was drawing to a close. About 120–240 Gypsy women and adolescent girls were forcibly sterilized during the final months of the war, but the total number of Jewish and Gypsy women sterilized in Ravensbrück is not known.[21]

At the request of Brack, Horst Schumann was also appointed to conduct sterilization experiments. Brack had speculated that too low a radiation dose might cause only temporary sterility, while too high a dose would lead to burns. Of the two physicians, Clauberg became far more infamous after the war through a trial that concerned another physician. Polish prisoner physician Wladislaw Dering, accused of participating in thousands of sterilization experiments in Auschwitz, sued American novelist Leon Uris for libel in a British court after Uris made such a claim in his 1959 novel, Exodus. The trial took place in London in 1962, and perhaps the most impressive and revealing witness for the defense was French physician Adelaide Hautval, a Christian, who had also been a prisoner.

In Auschwitz, Hautval had applied herself to caring for Jewish women inmates, hiding the ill and attempting to treat them. Ordered by SS physician Edward Wirths, head doctor in Auschwitz, to participate in medical experiments including sterilizations, Hautval refused. She also refused to administer anesthesia, making it clear that she understood and was willing to accept the consequences of her refusal. Hautval survived and was able to testify at the trial that prisoner physicians could refuse to take part in sterilizations, a powerful rebuttal to Dering's claims.[22]

During the Eichmann trial in April 1961 in Jerusalem, charges from the court transcript (fourth count) documented prescribed measures for the sterilization of Mischlinge—Jews of "mixed descent of the first degree"—in Germany and in the occupied territories. Those who chose not to be sterilized were deported to concentration camps and segregated by sex to prevent further births. Sterilizations were performed secretly. During the trial, two witnesses testified about the details of their sterilization operations, but they asked to be heard in chambers and requested that the court ban photographs and not reveal their names. One of them had an adopted child, and both of them wanted to keep their condition private.[23]

In Bergen-Belsen, as Thomas Rahe reported, Sinti and Roma women who had arrived from other camps, most often from Ravensbrück, faced forced sterilization.[24] Children were also sterilized, according to Else Freiermuth, who herself had been forcibly sterilized at the age of twelve and arrived in Bergen-Belsen in a state of extreme physical and psychological distress. When Freiermuth recounted this sterilization to Rahe in 1987, she concluded that the years had not lessened the pain of never being able to have children.

Abortion

When discussing abortions performed in camps, we need to differentiate between forced abortions ordered by the Nazis and secret abortions aimed at saving the lives of mothers. In Theresienstadt, births as a result of conception within the camp were forbidden, and any woman who conceived was forced to have an abortion. With some exceptions, if a pregnant woman refused to abort, the pregnancy constituted immediate grounds for deportation of both parents to a death camp in the East.[25] Gideon Hausner stated: "Bearing children in Theresienstadt was strictly outlawed. Childbirth was visited with immediate deportation for the father, mother and child. A doctor who did not immediately report a pregnancy was regarded as an accomplice."[26]

Claude Romney points out that prisoner physicians in Auschwitz were presented with a medical practice unlike anything they had experienced prior to their deportation.[27] Some physicians were able to use their privileged position to assist their fellow prisoners, while others participated in "medical experiments." One of the most difficult decisions prisoner doctors faced was whether to perform secret abortions for pregnant prisoners. Pregnancy was a death sentence in Auschwitz-Birkenau, as women discovered to be pregnant were automatically sent to the gas chambers. If pregnancy was not immediately identified, women were able to pass selection, but newborn infants could not survive in Auschwitz, and newborns and mothers were also sent to the gas chamber. Thus, performing a secret abortion could save a woman's life.

Lucie Adelsberger, who had been a pediatrician in Berlin prior to the war, was an inmate physician at Auschwitz, and she readily admitted afterward that she performed secret abortions on inmates in the camp. She justified this practice on the basis of medical ethics, claiming that historical ethical principles dictated that when a mother and infant are both in danger, then all efforts must be utilized to save the mother's life. "The child had to die so that the life of the mother could be saved," she wrote.[28] Adelsberger cites only one mother who willingly agreed to the abortion, as she had three children who were in hiding and wished to do anything possible that would enable her to survive and be reunited with her children. Although it is impossible to completely appreciate the circumstances of inmate physicians in Auschwitz, it is still reasonable to argue that Adelsberger, who cited medical ethics as the basis for her decisions, was acting in direct contradiction of the Hippocratic Oath to "do no harm." She not only did harm by aborting a fetus, but she selectively applied personal interpretation of medical ethics to pregnant women. Furthermore, at no point did she make clear that all of the women agreed to the procedure. On the contrary, she admitted that some of the women never forgave her for killing their babies. Nor is it clear if gestational age was a consideration for her. Early-term pregnancies would be considered abortion, but late-term pregnancies involved labor and delivery and therefore can be considered infanticide. Nor did Adelsberger discuss the attitudes of any Orthodox Jewish women with regard to abortion, and the question must be raised whether she gave any of them a choice or proceeded irrespective of their personal wishes.[29]

Gisella Perl, a gynecologist imprisoned in Auschwitz, also described carrying out secret abortions in the camp. She had personally witnessed pregnant women being beaten and taken alive to the crematoria. Afterward, Perl came to the conclusion that because there was no way to save the infants she would have to kill them with the hope that she could save the mothers. She therefore warned pregnant women of their fate and then performed the abortions. In her own words:

> I ran back to camp and going from block to block told the women what I had seen. Never again was anyone to betray their condition. . . . On dark nights when everyone else was sleeping—in dark corners of the camp, in the toilet, on the floor, without a drop of water, I delivered their babies. First I took the nine-month pregnancies, I accelerated the birth by the rupture of membranes, and usually within one or two days spontaneous birth took place without further intervention. Or I produced dilatation with my fingers, inverted the embryo and thus brought it to life. In the dark, always hurried, in the midst of filth and dirt. After the child had been delivered, I quickly bandaged the mother's abdomen and sent her back to work. . . . I delivered women pregnant in the eighth, seventh, sixth, fifth month, always in a hurry, always with my five fingers, in the dark, under terrible conditions.
>
> No one will ever know what it meant to me to destroy these babies. . . . I loved those newborn babies not as a doctor but as a mother and it was again and again my own child whom I killed to save the life of a woman.[30]

Clandestine abortions were also performed in Ravensbrück, a women's concentration camp, but the information we have about them is sometimes contradictory, and conditions changed over time. Rochelle Saidel highlights the testimonies of women prisoners helping other women to abort because pregnancy was punishable by death or, at the very least, a forced abortion.[31] She has coined the term "childdeath" to accompany childbirth, as the occasion of giving birth to a child in Ravensbrück generally resulted in the death of newborns to save the mothers, secret stillbirths, or forced abortions. Likewise, Kristian Ottosen notes that giving birth to a newborn child also became a tragedy, since there was no chance for life.[32]

Susan Benedict has examined the role of nurses in Ravensbrück.[33] She notes that prior to 1942, pregnant women were sent away to give birth and returned to the camp without their babies. However, after that year, births took place in Ravensbrück, and then the infants were strangled by the prisoner nurses. One horrifying account claims that one of the nurses burned the babies' bodies in a boiler room.[34] Germaine Tillion, a French political prisoner, provided an eyewitness report from Ravensbrück, stating that women who gave birth were forced to witness their infants being smothered or drowned in a bucket.[35] Another account claims that women were forced to have abortions in the final trimester of pregnancy, and the abysmal care in the *Revier* (hospital barrack) placed the women at even greater risk from the surgery. Several physicians and nurses were tried after the war for their involvement in forcible abortion; at least one was charged with the killing of newborn babies.[36]

The Case of Westerbork

Westerbork, a transit camp in the Netherlands, provides us with an unusual case study of sterilization and abortion. First, as Jacob Presser briefly described, sterilization was performed outside the camp during the occupation of the Netherlands. He wrote:

> Sterilization is perhaps the clearest illustration of how the Germans tormented the Jews before destroying them altogether, until their victims, ground down and crushed in mind and spirit, would bow to the inevitable. . . . All that matters here is what actually happened with regard to the sterilization of Jews in Holland. On this subject we have a few, isolated documents. One dated March 20, 1943, suggests that the Germans had not yet quite made up their minds. On April 29 [Hans] Rauter apparently discussed the matter with Zöph, as part of his plan to rid Amsterdam of all Jews. The upshot was a letter sent by [Wilhelm] Harster on May 5 to various German departments offering the Jewish partner of

mixed marriages with children a choice between voluntarily sterilization and "forced sterilization in the camp at Vught."[37]

Forced sterilization was discussed in the Amsterdam Jewish hospitals, where it was thought the procedure would take place, and the Jewish Council was asked to tell the German authorities that the proposed surgery was "godless and bestial."[38] Dutch filmmaker Mirjam Bartelsman has explored this little-known aspect of the Holocaust in the Netherlands.[39]

Forced Sterilizations

Westerbork was the main transit camp in the Netherlands, and the large majority of the Dutch Jewish population passed through it on their way to death camps in Poland. Forced sterilizations took place in Westerbork from 1943 to 1944. During that time some Jews imprisoned there had to choose between sterilization and deportation. Only Jews whose spouses were non-Jews were given the choice of sterilization.

In May 1943, Jews, both men and women, all of whom were married to non-Jews, were called to a large barrack in the camp. A group of 103 eventually stayed.[40] They were met by Ferdinand Hugo aus der Fünten, who served as the director of the *Zentralstelle für Jüdische Auswanderung* (Central Office for Jewish Emigration), a branch office of the *Reichssicherheitshauptamt Referat IV B 4* (the Reich Security, or RSHA, Department IV B 4), headed by Adolf Eichmann. Aus der Fünten was accompanied by Albert Konrad Gemmeker, the commandant of the transit camp, and he announced that these Jews would be given a choice of sterilization or deportation. Those who would accept the procedure would be permitted to leave the camp and join their non-Jewish spouses. Those to be sterilized would be sent to Amsterdam for the surgery. Anyone who changed his or her mind at that point and refused the surgery would be sent to Vught, another Dutch camp, where a forced sterilization would be performed. The group was given half an hour to make a decision. Ultimately, 52 refused and 51 accepted. Out of this group, 11 were women, and they were required to declare that their sterilization was voluntary.

The Jewish doctors in Westerbork were approached to perform the procedure. They discussed the dilemma and, despite some disagreement, ultimately decided to refuse, citing professional ethics that forbade them to prevent bringing new life into the world. Fritz Spanier, the chief physician of the hospital in Westerbork, claimed to have been opposed to the procedure along with other doctors in the camp. Spanier referred to events in 1944 during which he had informed Gemmeker of the decision. At a meeting with Gemmeker, several of the doctors, including Rosalie Wijnberg, made clear the medical team's objections. The doctors stated that they felt such a procedure was in direct opposition to the Hippocratic Oath and would cause harm to their patients. Dr. Wijnberg asked what the consequences would be if the physicians refused to obey the order to sterilize anyone, and she was told by Gemmeker that refusal would constitute sabotage. The result of this discussion was Dr. Spanier's request for written orders from Gemmeker and his superior. The order was never co-signed by the SS or any other authority, and, ultimately, the physicians were neither forced to take a stand against the procedure or to forcibly sterilize any patient. Spanier's position regarding the matter was that the doctors must present a united front so that blame could not devolve onto one individual who might be forced to perform the procedure. In particular, Dr. Wijnberg's adamant refusal to take part in sterilization must be noted despite Gemmeker's threats that she should be made "to see reason."[41] For Wijnberg, this was a profound ethical dilemma to which there could only be one response—to refuse to perform sterilizations.

As a consequence, German military doctors performed the sterilizations. Hartog Druijf, one of those who was sterilized, recalled armed German soldiers at the operating table. Furthermore, he was forced to pay the costs of the procedure. Eyewitness accounts claim that at least one of the men who had been sterilized and released from Westerbork was seen back in the camp on July 26, 1943, despite promises for release made by the Germans, and this was confirmed by Aadrianus Vanas.[42] Six weeks later, the sterilized man was observed being deported to Poland.

A second group of Jewish spouses was confronted with the choice between deportation and sterilization in Westerbork in June 1943. Eventually, the surgery was undertaken by a Dutch Nazi sympathizer physician, J. van der Hoevern, and an elderly German-Jewish doctor, S. Lichtenstein. At this point, doctors and lawyers became involved in falsifying sterilization certifications that sabotaged the process. The certificates incorrectly stated that the potential candidate was infertile and did not require sterilization. Eventually, Ferdinand aus der Fünten became suspicious of these certificates, since 1,416 Jewish women had been declared infertile. Mirjam Bartelsman has claimed that 1,330 women accepted the offer of sterilization. However, the numbers are questionable because women above the age of forty-five were given a sterilization declaration on the basis of age, and yet there is no reason why some women of this age could not conceive and bear a child. As of June 5, 1944, out of a total of 8,610 Jews married to non-Jews, 2,562 had taken advantage of the sterilization offer; 1,416 were women.[43]

Abortions in Westerbork

Abortions also took place in the Westerbork transit camp, but it cannot be determined how many were due to coercion. They were performed in the camp hospital as medical procedures, according to Dr. Ellis Hertzberger.[44] In the absence of the surgical register, which did not survive, we cannot even estimate if abortions were a common procedure. However, according to two nurses, Jeanne van den Berg van Cleef and Ruth Gormans,[45] abortions also took place in the segregated women's barracks, and it is unlikely that male medical practitioners were aware of these. The lack of written documentation also makes it impossible to ascertain how many women chose abortion, or why they chose it. Any information about abortion can be derived only from scant first-hand accounts.

We do know that Westerbork had an excellent hospital, staffed by some of the best physicians in Europe, who were supported by nurses, physiotherapists, and other allied health professionals. A regular supply of medicine arrived at the hospital. These pieces were in place because Gemmeker wanted to create an illusion of well-being so that he could then orchestrate orderly and quiet deportations to Sobibor and Auschwitz-Birkenau. Thus, deportees who were ill and hospitalized were temporarily exempted from deportation to support the commandant's explanation that deportees were going to labor camps and must be healthy. The Jewish inmates believed this ruse, and designated deportees attempted to be admitted to the hospital to avoid deportation. It is possible that abortion was also used as a means to temporarily achieve a reprieve from deportation, but we have no substantive proof.

Prohibitions against Giving Birth in Lithuanian Ghettos

Giving birth was prohibited not only in some camps but also in some ghettos. For example, prohibitions were issued in the ghettos of Kovno (Kaunas), Vilna (Vilnius), and Shavli (Siaulia) in Lithuania. In 1942, Jewish women in the Kovno Ghetto were forbidden to give birth and compelled to undergo abortion in every case of pregnancy. Aharon Peretz, a gynecologist in the Kovno ghetto, recorded:

Unwittingly, they would reach advanced stages of pregnancy . . . by an order of July 1942 pregnancy in the Kaunas ghetto was punishable with death to the father, the mother, and the infant. . . . We had to start making abortions by the hundreds. . . . yet there were many women who refused abortion, for all the danger it involved, and with great courage awaited the day of giving birth.[46]

Leah Preiss's study of women's health in the ghettos of Eastern Europe found:

In the Kovno ghetto, the health department arranged the required medical services for terminating pregnancies. In addition, the medical staff was also responsible for public-relations efforts and warning women of what awaited them. Moreover, quite a few women refused to give in to the decree. They went underground in order to evade the prohibition, and with the help of the medical committee located near the ghetto labor department, they were released from their work obligations until they delivered their babies in secret. Dr. Aharon Peretz, one of the gynecologists in the ghetto, said that the widespread incidence of pregnancy was the result of amenorrhea among women who were unaware that they could still conceive. Another reason was the absence of birth-control methods. According to him, because of the intensive abortion work and the shortage of proper hospitalization and treatment supplies in the ghetto, some of the operations were performed in the strangest and most dreadful conditions. Deliveries were performed in secrecy mainly by specially trained midwives, while doctors were called only in cases of severe complications.[47]

In the Vilna ghetto in 1942, there were approximately 237 hospital beds, 12 of them allocated to gynecology. Solon Beinfeld claims that the gynecology ward's main purpose was to perform abortions.[48] Consistent with other ghettos in Lithuania, a decree was issued in February 1942 that prohibited Jewish births. Thus, giving birth to a Jewish child was a crime, punishable by death of both mother and child. Despite this decree, those women in Vilna who chose to give birth were accepted for care and hidden until the infants could be sent home as children who had been born before the decree. Although the hospital maintained a policy of assisting women to give birth despite the danger, claims have been made that a number of women were forced to abort these fetuses in cases where ghetto police found pregnant women and took them to the hospital to undergo termination. It is not clear how many women were forced to abort their unborn children, as some may have voluntarily chosen to do so. However, there is an element of coercion in even this context as women may have felt forced to give up their unborn children to save family members. According to Preiss, data on the gynecology department in the Vilna ghetto until its official closing show that in 1942, 429 women were hospitalized there, and more than 60 percent were abortion cases. Moshe Figenberg, a gynecologist in the ghetto, stated in his testimony: "Because the death penalty loomed over any woman who gave birth in the ghetto, the women's department in the hospital where I worked was loaded down with abortion cases." Because of the large number of pregnancies, the Vilna ghetto's health office provided advice about birth control and also tried to falsify records.[49]

The ghetto administration in Shavli was far more aggressive. From minutes of meetings in Shavli, it is apparent that the decree forbidding birth and the option of abortion were matters of urgent concern for the Judenrat (Jewish council), as evidenced by the following. At a July 4, 1942 meeting, "Dr. Charny drew attention of the Jewish delegation to the Order concerning births. The Order was first issued on March 5, 1942." The latest date for authorized births was August 5, 1942, extended to August 15. "In the event of a birth taking place in a Jewish family after this date the whole Jewish family would be 'removed' and the responsibility would rest with the Jewish delegates."[50] Thus, any woman who had passed the first trimester of pregnancy would still be able to give birth. For others, giving birth either in a hospital or at home had become impossible after August 15. Abortions were permitted, and the pressure to have an abortion was clearly placed on pregnant women as any woman who gave birth after that date would endanger the members of her family. The order was clear that an entire family could be executed.

The situation in Shavli was an ongoing issue, as evidenced by a discussion of the members of the Judenrat on March 24, 1943.[51] The deliberations involved how births were to be prevented, not why, and whether the Judenrat should be involved. It is clear from the notes of the meeting that communication existed between Shavli and other ghettos. Members discussed a recent birth in Kovno and its consequences—in this case, that all members of the family had been shot. Nonetheless, women were still conceiving in Shavli, and this was a matter of grave concern to the Judenrat.

Conclusions

Both sterilization and abortion remain shameful for most victims, a hidden secret too painful for them to discuss despite the passing of years. Even when women were forcibly sterilized or forced to have abortions, the victims often blame themselves and do not speak of these experiences. The self-imposed silence of some survivors who are unable to publicly bear witness is compounded by the unknown number of women who died because of the procedures or were murdered afterward. The forced sterilization and abortion inflicted on women remains an underexplored area of Holocaust research that merits further study.

Notes

1. United Nations Office for the Coordination of Human Affairs and Integrated Regional Information Networks, *The Shame of War: Sexual Violence Against Women and Girls in Conflict* (New York: United Nations, 2007).

2. The Nazis designated the Sinti and Roma, or Romani people, as Gypsies, and I am, therefore, using that term.

3. Joan Ringelheim, "Genocide and Gender: A Split Memory," in *Gender and Catastrophe*, ed. Ronit Lentin (London: Zed, 1997), 20.

4. United Nations Report of the Secretary General, *In-depth Study on All Forms of Violence Against Women* (New York: United Nations, 2006).

5. For more information, see Mark Adams, *The Wellborn Science: Eugenics in Germany, France, Brazil, and Russia* (New York: Oxford University Press, 1990); and Jonathan Friedman, "The 'Eugenic Utopia,'" in *Speaking the Unspeakable: Essays on Sexuality, Gender, and Holocaust Survivor Memory* (Lanham: University Press of America, 2002), 13–39.

6. For more information on the T4 program, see Henry Friedlander, *The Origins of Nazi Genocide: From Euthanasia to the Final Solution* (Chapel Hill: University of North Carolina Press, 1995).

7. Mark Polnoroff, "Unknown Victims—The Lebensborn Children," in *The Legacy of the Holocaust: Children and the Holocaust*, ed. Zygmunt Mazur et al. (Krakow: Jagiellonian University Press, 2002), 224–239.

8. Patricia Heberer, "The Nazis and Medical Ethics: The Context," in *Israel Medical Association Journal* 9(2007):192–193.

9. Nicholas Stargardt, *Witnesses of War: Children's Lives under the Nazis* (London: Jonathan Cape, 2005), 58, 67.

10. The Nuremberg Race Laws, enacted in 1935, institutionalized many Nazi racial theories, excluded German Jews from Reich citizenship and prohibited them from marrying or having sexual relations with Germans. The Wannsee Conference, held on January 20, 1942, discussed plans for the deportation and extermination of all Jews in German-occupied territory—the Final Solution.

11. Gideon Hausner, *Justice in Jerusalem* (New York: Harper & Row, 1966), 95.

12. See Rochelle Saidel, *The Jewish Women of Ravensbrück Concentration Camp* (Madison: University of Wisconsin Press, 2004), 211; and Johanna Krause, *Twice Persecuted: Surviving Nazi Germany and Communist East Germany*, ed. and translated by Carolyn Gammon and Christiane Hemker (Waterloo, Canada: Wilfrid Laurier University Press, 2007).

13. See Ian Hancock, "A Brief Holocaust Chronology," regarding the 1939 statement by the Office of Racial Hygiene to treat all Gypsies as "hereditarily sick" and to eliminate this "defective element in the population," http://www.osi.hu/rpp/holocaust.html

(accessed July 30, 2009). For more information on Nazi doctor Robert Ritter's genetic research on the Sinti and Roma, see *Sinti and Roma*, United States Holocaust Memorial Museum, http://www.holocaust-tre.org/sinti.htm (accessed July 30, 2009).

14. For further study, see Clarence Lusane, *Hitler's Black Victims: The Historical Experiences of European Blacks, Africans, and African Americans in the Nazi Era* (New York: Routledge, 2003) and Hans J. Massaquoi, *Destined to Witness: Growing up Black in Nazi Germany* (New York: Perennial, 2001).

15. For more information, see Clarence Lusane, "Nazi-Sterilization of Afro-Germans," in *"Mixed Race" Studies: A Reader*, ed. Jayne Ifekwunigwe (New York: Routledge, 2004), 80–96. See also Tina M. Campt, *Other Germans: Black Germans and the Politics of Race, Gender, and Memory in the Third Reich* (Ann Arbor: The University of Michigan Press, 2005), 77–80.

16. Reiner Pommerin, "The Fate of Mixed Blood Children in Germany," *German Studies Review* 5, no. 3, (1982): 315–323. See also, Tessa Chelouche, "Doctors, Pregnancy, Childbirth and Abortion during the Third Reich," in *Israel Medical Association Journal* 9 (2007):202–206. On forced abortion of foreign slave laborers after 1941 in Lower Bavaria, see Anna E. Rosmus, "Murder of the Innocent: Foreign Slave Laborers and Forced Abortion in Bavaria," in *Women in the Holocaust: Responses, Insights and Perspectives*, ed. Marcia Sachs Littell (Merion Station: Merion Westfield Press, 2001), 139–157.

17. Marion Kaplan, *Between Dignity and Despair: Jewish Life in Nazi Germany* (Oxford: Oxford University Press, 1998), 82–83; Ruth Klüger, *Still Alive: A Holocaust Girlhood Remembered* (New York: Feminist Press, 2003), 35.

18. Transcript of the so-called "Doctors' Trial" (the Medical Case of the Subsequent Nuremberg Proceedings, from the official trial record), *Trials of War Criminals before the Nuremberg Military Tribunals under Control Council Law No. 10, Nuremberg, October 1946–April 1949* (Washington, D.C.: U.S. G.P.O, 1949–1953), 13.

19. Yad Vashem, "Viktor Brack Proposal for the Sterilization of 2–3 Million Jewish Workers, June 23, 1942," http://www1.yadvashem.org.il/search/index_search.html (accessed December 4, 2008).

20. Susan Benedict and Jane Georges, "Nurses and the Sterilization Experiments of Auschwitz: A Postmodernist Perspective," *Nursing Inquiry* 13, no. 4 (2006): 277–288.

21. Saidel, *Jewish Women of Ravensbrück*, 211.

22. For a complete description of the libel trial, see Mavis Hill and L. Norman Williams, *Auschwitz in England: A Record of a Libel Action* (New York: Stein and Day, 1965). See also Moshe Bejski, "Rescue Attempts During the Shoah," in *Proceedings of the Second Yad Vashem International Historical Conference*, ed. Yisrael Gutman and Efraim Zuroff (Yad Vashem: Jerusalem, 1974), 627–647.

23. *The Trial of Adolf Eichmann, Record of Proceedings in the District Court of Jerusalem*, April, 1961 (Jerusalem: Ministry of Justice and Yad Vashem, 1961). Session 66, June 6, 1961, discusses the witness testimony to be given in private.

24. Thomas Rahe, "Aus 'rassischen' Gründen verfolgte Kinder im Konzentrationslager Bergen-Belsen: Eine erste Skizze" [Racially persecuted children in Bergen-Belsen concentration camp: A preliminary sketch], in *Kinder und Jugendliche als Opfer des Holocaust*

[Children and youths as victims of the Holocaust], ed. Edgar Bamberger and Annegret Ehmann (Berlin: Gedenkstätte Haus der Wannseekonferenz, 1995), 141. For an account of sterilization disrupting Romani family life after the war, see Otto Rosenberg, A Gypsy in Auschwitz (London: London House, 1999), 135.

25. Some babies were born in Theresienstadt. See Ruth Bondy, "Elder of the Jews": Jakob Edelstein of Theresienstadt (New York, Grove Press, 1981), 270; Ruth Schwertfeger, Women of Theresienstadt: Voices from a Concentration Camp (Oxford: Berg Publishers, 1989), 61–62; and Anna Bergman, Imperial War Museum testimony 26752, in Lyn Smith, Remembering: Voices of the Holocaust. A New History in the Words of the Men and Women Who Survived (New York: Carroll and Graf, 2006), 142. For further information on giving birth in Theresienstadt, see Anna (Anka) Bergman's testimony in chapter 9 by Helga Amesberger in this volume.

26. Gideon Hausner, Justice in Jerusalem, 159. See also Katharina von Kellenbach, "Reproduction and Resistance During the Holocaust," in Women and the Holocaust: Narrative and Representation, ed. Esther Fuchs (Lanham, MD: University Press of America, 1999), 19–32. Some women who arrived pregnant were allowed to give birth. See chapter 9 by Helga Amesberger in this volume.

27. Claude Romney, "Ethical Problems Encountered by Auschwitz Prisoner Doctors," in Remembering for the Future: The Holocaust in an Age of Genocide, vol. 1, ed. John K. Roth and Elisabeth Maxwell (London: Macmillan, 2001), 319–334.

28. Lucie Adelsberger, Auschwitz: A Doctor's Story (London: Robson Books, 1999), 101.

29. Jewish law places the utmost value on life, but when an unborn life threatens the life of the mother, the preference is given to the latter, allowing for abortion in some cases. See, for example, Avraham Steinberg, "Induced Abortion According to Jewish Law," Journal of Halacha [Jewish Law] and Contemporary Society 1, no. 1 (1981), 29–52.

30. Gisella Perl, "A Doctor in Auschwitz," in Different Voices: Women and the Holocaust, ed. Carol Rittner and John K. Roth (New York: Paragon House, 1993), 114. See also chapter 11 by S. Lillian Kremer in this volume.

31. Saidel, Jewish Women of Ravensbrück, 12, 211.

32. Kristian Ottosen, The Women's Camp: The History of the Ravensbrück Prisoners, trans. Margrit Rosenberg Stenge (Oslo: Aschehoug, 1991).

33. Susan Benedict, "The Nadir of Nursing: Nurse-perpetrators of Ravensbrück Concentration Camp," in Nursing History Review 11 (2003): 129–146.

34. Ibid.

35. Germaine Tillion, Ravensbrück—An Eyewitness Account of a Women's Concentration Camp (New York: Anchor Press, 1975), 77.

36. Benedict, "Nadir of Nursing," 129–146.

37. Jacob Presser, Ashes in the Wind: The Destruction of Dutch Jewry (London: Souvenir Press, 1965), 195–196.

38. Ibid., 197–198.

39. Mirjam Bartelsman, "Deportatie of Sterilisatie?" [Deportation or sterilization?] in De Volkskrant, January 24, 1998. In her documentary that aired on Dutch television, Bartelsman interviewed survivors or their spouses, who were just beginning to speak

about their ordeal under Nazi occupation. Only by means of sterilization could the Jewish partner in a "mixed-marriage" (with a non-Jew) escape deportation. One eighty-six-year-old interviewee said of her husband's sterilization in 1943: "I would have liked to have six children. But I loved my husband so much that I would have rather seen him come back sterilized than in a transport to Auschwitz." She added that her husband felt terribly humiliated by this operation.

40. Presser, *Ashes in the Wind*, 199.

41. Ibid., 200.

42. Aadrianus Vanas, interview with the author, September 5, 1997.

43. For more information, see "Deportation of Dutch Jews to Several Concentration Camps, Reaction of the Local Population," http://www1.yadvashem.org/odot_pdf/Microsoft%20Word%20-%205214.pdf (accessed July 21, 2009).

44. Ellis Hertzberger, letter to the author, March 22, 1998.

45. Jeanne Van den Berg van Cleeff, interview with the author, June 28, 1998; Ruth Gormans, letter to the author, May 28, 1998.

46. Hausner, *Justice in Jerusalem*, 213.

47. Leah Preiss, "Women's Health in the Ghettos of Eastern Europe," *Jewish Women, A Comprehensive Historical Encyclopedia*, Jewish Women's Archive, http://jwa.org/encyclopedia/article/womens-health-in-ghettos-of-eastern-europe (accessed July 19, 2009).

48. Solon Beinfeld, "Health Care in the Vilna Ghetto," *Holocaust and Genocide Studies* 112, no.1 (1998): 66–98.

49. Preiss, "Women's Health in the Ghettos of Eastern Europe."

50. Eliezer Yerushalmi, *Pinkas Shavli* [Records of Shavli] (Jerusalem: Yad Vashem and Mossad Bialik, 1958), 88, 188–189; "The Ban on Births in Shavli Ghetto, From the Diary of Eliezer Yerushalmi, 1942–1943," in *Documents on the Holocaust, Selected Sources on the Destruction of the Jews of Germany, Austria, Poland and the Soviet Union*, ed. Yitzchak Arad, Yisrael Gutman, and Abraham Margaliot (Jerusalem: Yad Vashem, 1996), 450–453.

51. "Ban on Births in Shavli Ghetto," 451–453.

SEXUAL VIOLENCE
in Literature and Cinema

11

Sexual Abuse in Holocaust Literature

Memoir and Fiction

S. LILLIAN KREMER

Since the late 1980s, literary scholars have become increasingly sensitive to gendered Holocaust suffering, paralleling the findings of feminist historians and social scientists about women's biological and socially gendered
suffering and coping patterns.[1] I examine themes and approaches to sexual
abuse appearing in memoir and fiction by men and women who wrote from
recollection, extensive research, or literary imagination. Among the survivor-
writers are voices of a Communist, a cabaret singer, a schoolgirl, a resistance
fighter, and health professionals. The creative writers, "witnesses through the
imagination,"[2] as Norma Rosen termed them, are clearly influenced by survivor testimony and research.

Women's wartime tribulations were complicated by biology and by pre-war
normative social constructs. Passages focusing on female anatomy and defeminized appearance reference the deterioration of and attack on women's
bodies through induced amenorrhea, sterilization, forced abortions, punishment for pregnancy and subversive childbirth, annihilation based on maternal
status, and sexual assault. Although male writers such as Elie Wiesel and
Primo Levi convey the effect of starvation and primitive sanitary facilities on
their protagonists' strength, health, and feelings of powerlessness, they do
not address the aesthetic reactions and procreational anxieties dominant in
women's writing. Representative of women writers' detailed depictions of the
deterioration of women's bodies and health problems is the testimony of Hungarian medical worker Olga Lengyel, trained to qualify as first surgical assis-
tant, deported in 1944, and assigned to an infirmary job. She writes in her early
Auschwitz memoir, *Five Chimneys*, that "prisoners looked like skeletons . . .

[having] lost from 50 to 60 percent of their original weight . . . [and had] shrunken in height." She cites a Moscow professor's report that autopsies established that "nine out of every ten internees revealed a distinct withering of the ovaries."[3]

Sexual Humiliation during Camp Induction Process

Concentration camp induction processing, among the most dehumanizing experiences for men and women, is a central motif of Holocaust literature. Prisoners are ordered to undress, subjected to rapid and brutal removal of all body hair, and drenched with harsh delousing chemicals. Perhaps because women were socialized by religious teaching and communal values to be modest, they experience and write of the induction ordeal as a sexual assault. Highlighted in women's writing are the shame and terror of facing men who make lewd remarks and obscene suggestions during delousing and shearing processes as they search women's bodily cavities for hidden valuables. Characteristic of the survivors' brief, straightforward reportage of these outrages, heightened only by occasional commentary, Lengyel writes, "[W]e were compelled to undergo a thorough examination in the Nazi manner, oral, rectal, vaginal. . . . We had to lie across a table, stark naked while they probed. All that in the presence of drunken soldiers who sat around the table, chuckling obscenely."[4]

Although she writes in great detail of the women's barrack conditions, daily humiliations, and suffering, and most effectively about resistance by political prisoners, in *Auschwitz: True Tales from a Grotesque Land*, Sara Nomberg-Przytyk—survivor of Stutthof, Auschwitz, and Ravensbrück—presents her Auschwitz induction in a dramatically different voice. The prose of her chapter titled "New Arrivals" departs from her typical somber tone as she acerbically denounces the Nazi system. The newcomer, who is later to join a camp Communist resistance group, renders the confusion of newcomers who "made themselves absurd trying to defend their human dignity." She remarks initially, in moral indignation that readers anticipate, on the wretched state of huddled naked women, shivering in an unheated room in January 1944. Her final observation captures the irrationality of the Nazi universe: Jewish women "waiting for the SS men to visit."[5]

> We jumped up from our places and stood naked in front of a large group of SS men who looked us over slowly, with disdain in their eyes. . . .

The shearing of the sheep had started, and with scissors so dull that they tore bunches of hair out of our heads. . . . The sheep bleated as they were being shorn, but we stood there in silence with tears streaming down our cheeks.

"Spread your legs," yelled the *blokowa* [prisoner in charge of a block]. And the body hair was shorn too.

All of this took place very quickly, to the accompaniment of shouts and blows, which fell thickly on our heads and shoulders. We ceased to exist as thinking, feeling entities. We were not allowed any modesty in front of these strange men. We were nothing more than objects on which they performed their duties, non-sentient things that they could examine from all angles. It did not bother them that cutting hair close to the skin with dull scissors was excruciatingly painful. It did not bother them that we were women and that without our hair we felt totally humiliated.

Nomberg-Przytyk matter-of-factly reports the demeaning order to "spread your legs" but she elects to remain silent regarding the burning sensation the delousing agent had on the genitals. Uppermost in her account is the pain and humiliation of loss of bodily hair, a central feature of social appearance coupled with the shame of public nudity. The sense of being objectified, dehumanized, and defeminized by disdainful men dominates the passage.

Auschwitz memoirists Fania Fénelon and Judith Isaacson also convey the humiliation women experienced as they were shorn, but they introduce an element of judgment against prisoner tormentors who appear complicit in causing fellow victims pain and humiliation. In *Playing for Time*, Fénelon, the French deportee, presents Polish conspiratorial inmates managing and carrying out the induction ceremonies as relishing their privileged status above the Jewish women. "I felt considerably less than human," she writes, "a peculiar, grubby object upsetting the natural order."[6]

Hungarian Judith Isaacson conveys the brutishness of the camp induction in *Seed of Sarah: Memoirs of a Survivor*, focusing on the humiliation and shame of the victim. She delineates the oppressive action in staccato bursts of commands evoking physical assault by multiple assailants:

A woman in a striped dress grabbed me by the hair and attacked me with scissors. Another drove a razor around my crown. . . . A shove in the buttocks propelled me along the assembly line. "Raise your arms!" came the command in German. Two females shaved my armpits in unison. . . . A voice barked: "Spread your legs!" A razor moved into my crotch. A shower of disinfectant hit my armpits and scalp. A sudden spray scorched my vulva. An attendant shoved me from behind. I landed outdoors.[7]

By her rhetorical adoption of the survivor's voice, echoing material obtained through copious survivor interviews, and meticulous integration of historic detail, American novelist Susan Fromberg Schaeffer establishes an authentic aura for the Kaiserwald labor camp induction. In *Anya* she boldly and graphically juxtaposes the victim's pain with the oppressor's pornographic sadism:

> "Take off all your clothes and leave them on the side of the barracks and then come outside." . . . So we stood there in the winter sunlight. . . . "So," one said approaching me, "lice, eh?" He pinched my nipples. "And how is this, after the trip, all dirty, eh?" He pulled my pubic hair. . . . My stomach was heaving and heaving. . . . "Gasoline for you," he said, "for the lice," and then the next man came along and it began again. My breasts were so sore I could feel the pain in my toes. . . . "[W]e take care of your hair. And stoop over when the men get to you; they have to check your rectums for ringworms and bleeding; it's for your own good, only for your own good." . . . Then a man began coming down the rows with a canister of gasoline and another clipper; he clipped the hair under our arms, then our pubic hair. "Why should it hurt so much?" I wondered, and then came the gasoline from the can, poured all over my hair, from head to toe. "Bend over," he ordered, pouring it down my back, then spreading my behind, pouring it in. It burned; . . . I was drenched in it. . . . I was biting my lip from the burning.[8]

Schaeffer's selection and arrangement of graphic detail dramatizes male violence and female humiliation and degradation more vividly than do the survivors' powerful but objective, less lurid accounts. Her prose specifically genders the humiliation with emphasis on women's physicality and vulnerability implicit in shorn hair, mauled breasts, probed rectums, and chemically burned vaginas—offenses that simultaneously sexually assault the victims and strip them of feminine attributes. Racism and sexism characterize the guards' strategy for forcing their victims to realize their utter loss of autonomy in the camp universe.

American novelist Marge Piercy departs from customary emphasis on physical and psychological humiliation emphasized by survivor writers to introduce psychological distancing in response to Nazi shaming tactics. Well past their entry into Auschwitz, Piercy's captured French Jewish female resistance fighters in *Gone to Soldiers* are ordered to strip and parade before SS men and Krupp entrepreneurs who add sexual mockery to economic exploitation. Unable to escape physically, the prisoner withdraws mentally and emotionally, imagining "that her body was hidden inside an imitation body. The men could only see the imitation rubber body, but she was the bones hidden inside that they could not see or touch."[9] The response of Piercy's protagonist resembles what the psychiatric literature identifies as "psychological removal. . . . insulating oneself from the outside stress, developing ways of not feeling, creating the impression of 'I'm not here,' and 'This is not happening to me.'" Psychological withdrawal from the situation allows "the 'feeling I' to be replaced by a 'photographic dispassionate I.'"[10]

"Medical" Sexual Assaults

Medical experimentation was among the most horrendous sexual assaults against women in the Nazi universe. According to survivor Lengyel, in addition to a whole series of medical experiments including vivisections and intracardiac injections of phenol, women inmates suffered sexually oriented trials. "One of the favorite experiments was conducted on newly arrived women whose menstruation was still normal. During their periods, they were told, 'You will be shot in two days.' The Germans wanted to know what effect such news would have on menstrual flow." Although she does not provide a citation, Lengyel claims "a professor of histology in Berlin published an article in a German scientific journal on his observation on hemorrhages provoked in women by such bad news."[11]

Many non-medical memoirists take up the subject of amenorrhea as well. French memoirist Fania Fénelon represents anxiety regarding loss of menstruation as a dual psychological assault on female identity, since the prisoners had no knowledge of whether fertility would return if they survived. Even while they fear permanent loss of fertility, her women fear punishment if they continue to menstruate: "[F]or those who did have their periods, the situation was extremely awkward: nothing to wash themselves with; nothing to wear. The blood ran down their thighs and dripped from between their legs. Always sticklers for cleanliness, the blockowas struck them, forced them to wipe up the stains."[12] The women's brief but carefully rendered reactions reflect their religious and cultural diversity: "Catholics crossed themselves, others [Jews] recited the Shema; everyone tried to exorcise this curse the Germans were holding over us: sterility."[13]

In her capacity as medical worker, Lengyel frequently witnessed Nazi assaults on women's bodies. In addition to her report of women subjected to artificial insemination and injection with sex hormones that caused abscesses that were lanced, she observed sterilization experiments designed to "compare the results of the surgical methods and X-ray treatments." She testifies to having seen "numerous sick women . . . [suffering] serious burns caused by the clumsy application of these rays."[14] Citing the patients and deportee doctors as the source of her information, she describes the procedure in detail:

> The subject was placed under X-ray radiation, which was made more and more intense. From time to time the treatment was interrupted in order to see if the subject could still copulate. All this took place under the vigilant eyes of the S.S. in Barrack 21. When the physician verified that the X-rays had definitely destroyed the genital faculties, this subject was dispatched to the gas chamber.[15]

Abortion and Infanticide

For many Jewish women the most tragic expression of Nazi assault was systematic violation of their maternal roles. From her perspective as an attendant in the Auschwitz infirmary, Olga Lengyel addresses the anguish she and others experienced while trying to save the lives of imperiled pregnant women:

> As soon as a baby was delivered at the infirmary, mother and child were both sent to the gas chamber. . . . Only when the infant was not likely to survive or when it was stillborn was the mother ever spared and allowed to return to her barrack. The conclusion we drew from this was simple: . . . We five, whose responsibility it was to bring these infants into the world—the world of Birkenau-Auschwitz— felt the monstrous conclusion, which defiled all human and moral law. . . . [W]e decided . . . We must at least save the mothers. To carry out our plan, we would have to make the infants pass for stillborn. . . . [I]f the Germans were ever to suspect it, we, too, would be sent to the gas chambers—and probably to the torture chamber first.[16]

Like Lengyel, Gisella Perl, a Hungarian Jewish obstetrician and gynecologist, was selected by Josef Mengele to administer a "hospital" ward within the death camp. Without proper equipment, medications, even beds, she worked tirelessly to comfort the starving, diseased, and dying. She soon understood that the Germans were deceiving arriving women by asking them to identify themselves as pregnant. Pregnant women were promised they would be sent to a camp with better living conditions and double bread rations, only to be brutalized before being dispatched to the gas chambers. Although Perl initially resisted adopting the role of secret abortionist, after witnessing a group of mothers beaten with clubs and whips, torn by dogs, dragged by their hair, and "thrown into the crematory—alive,"[17] she quickly found a reason to survive and offered her services for clandestine operations. Lengyel and Perl worked tirelessly and courageously to help the suffering women in their charge and to cheat the Nazis of their genocidal goals by saving pregnant women from the gas chambers, Perl by performing many clandestine abortions and Lengyel by helping to deliver babies and then administering a lethal injection to the infant in order to save the mother.

American writer Cynthia Ozick explores the ordeal of clandestine camp motherhood in a brilliant, frequently anthologized short story, "The Shawl." A young mother, Rosa Lublin, confronts the terrible choice encountered by many Jewish mothers: whether to entrust her infant to a stranger's goodwill or conspire to preserve its life in her own, often fatal, setting. "A walking cradle,"[18] Rosa is so frail and thin that she successfully conceals her daughter, Magda, between her breasts under a shawl. Underscoring the female character of maternal suffering, Ozick privileges breast imagery at each oppressive juncture. The mother's anxiety for her child's survival is conveyed through references to teat and nipple: "Magda relinquished Rosa's teats . . . both were cracked, not a sniff of milk. The duct-crevice extinct, a dead volcano, blind eye, chill hole."[19] Magda misses the wrap that her young aunt usurped to warm her own frozen body, toddles into the *Appellplatz* (roll call area), and "[a] tide of commands hammered in Rosa's nipples."[20] As a German guard swoops up the infant and flings her onto the electrified fence, Rosa inhibits the maternal instinct to run to her suffering child. Instead, she honors the survival instinct, for to retrieve her baby's charred corpse would assure the guard's bullet for herself. The shawl, now her life preserver, muffles Rosa's scream.

Rape

Although Jewish female memoirists rarely give attention to rape, such feared and realized abuses are treated in the writing of Elzbieta Ettinger, Ida Fink, and Judith Magyar Isaacson. Ettinger was in and out of the Warsaw ghetto, hid in "Aryan" locations, served as a partisan, and was incarcerated in Majdanek for four months. Her fictionalized women, especially those active in the resistance and in open hiding in "Aryan" districts are nevertheless vulnerable, and occasionally empowered, by virtue of their gender. Maria, a resistance worker in *Kindergarten*, is caught in a labor roundup early in the occupation, suffers harassment by a Nazi officer who finds her "*so jung . . . so schön*" (so young, so beautiful), and expresses his admiration in a manner that foreshadows rape. Although Ettinger foregoes dramatic representation of the outrage, once at home, Maria sits, "staring blankly ahead,"[21] and talks of an acquaintance who committed suicide with her two daughters. Later, her daughter, Elli, also assisting a resistance unit, outwits a Polish extortionist hiding a group of fugitives who repeatedly insists on payment in cash and sex by the women, forcing himself upon them and threatening to denounce them. Because Ettinger's women are relatively free, opportunity presents itself to benefit from male lust. When the fugitives determine to kill the extortionist who taunts them with a promise of betrayal, they not only ply him with liquor but the women are assigned to distract him by playing to his sexual desires.

Among the well-crafted stories that sketch fragments of Holocaust experience in *A Scrap of Time*, Ida Fink's compelling collection of short stories, "Aryan Papers" presents rape as a survival bargaining chip in "Aryan" sectors of Poland. Here, for a price, blackmailers and informers protected the identity of Jews in open or concealed hiding only to betray them once their money was exhausted. While this tale shares with other stories in the collection the theme of fugitive survival, it differs markedly in its intense focus on the dramatic encounter of sexual predator and victim. A Pole humiliates a desperate Jewish girl by having her meet him in a sleazy bar, insisting on sexual favors, offering a degrading comment in mockery of her sacrifice, and exposing her to arrest at any time. The story centers on the detail and process of exploitation by the perpetrator and the fear and humiliation of the victim.

The meeting places of the man and girl serve as objective correlative of the filthy transaction and as metaphor of death camp experience. "Smoke hung in the air like a dense fog and curled towards the roaring exhaust fan,"[22] evoking the crematoria. Fink's prose often concentrates on the tension of waiting—in this case, of awaiting the blackmailer's decision to deliver the false documents after accepting financial and personal payment, and the attendant uncertainty of whether he will denounce her or take his payment and withhold the documents. To foreground the victim's mounting anxiety, Fink introduces vacillations, detours, repetitiveness, and emotions ranging from fear of recognition to grief, despair, resignation, and terror. The girl's feelings alternate from relief, as she contemplates the man's failure to appear, to terror, as she observes that "if he didn't come that would be the end of everything." Without good Aryan papers, her parents are in jeopardy. When the man arrives, there is no joy, no calm, just terror: "Her legs began to tremble and she had to press her heels against the floor to steady herself." He is at ease. "She is afraid that she would pass out; she felt weak, first hot, then cold."[23]

Initially, the transaction appears to be a currency exchange for papers. The girl declares that she has the money. The blackmailer assures her that "everything is ready. Signed and sealed. No cheating—the seals, the birth certificate —*alles in Ordnung!* [everything in order]." Fink, who lived with her family in the Zbaraz ghetto until 1942 when she escaped with her sister and lived in hiding for the remainder of the war, masterfully adds German to characterize the Polish betrayer. Nazi *Deutsch*—the language of deception in which "showers" dispense gas, "work" kills rather than liberates, "special actions" lead to death rather than privileged security, and sadistic pleasure is derived from debasing Jewish women—links the Polish blackmailer to Nazism.

The Pole betrays his vile character as he speaks freely of having recognized the young woman's vulnerability early, shifting discourse from sexual innuendo to political danger: "I knew you were my type the day you came to work. And I knew right away what you were."[24] That he plays on her fear is voiced in his challenge that her papers are inferior to those he will provide. That his offer to help the desperate Jew is void of generosity becomes evident in his exploitative demand. Cash payment is insufficient for the blackmailer; only the bonus of the young innocent's virginity will suffice. The man's intent becomes more obvious as he insists they continue the transaction in his apartment and states his preference for thin girls. In contrast to the confident middle-aged man, the sixteen-year-old girl is diminutive, pale, and teary-eyed. He is handsome, suntanned, nicely dressed, but his fingernails are dirty. Her nervousness amuses him: she "looked like a child."[25] That the girl is aware of the heavy price she will pay is evident in her fear of vomiting. She must resist the will to wretch for she must not offend him. He would dismiss her "and it will all be for nothing." To overcome her fear, she remembers how dependent her mother is on her, that they would be in Warsaw already had she acted sooner, that he has been nice to her at work, "when he could have informed."[26]

The coerced coupling ends an hour after the assault began, with the arrival of the blackmailer's business associate. The extortionist orders his victim to dress, to stop looking so mournful, and acknowledges her youth and inexperience, observing, "You'll be a terrific woman some day!"[27] He delivers the papers she has worked so hard to earn, and again reverting to German, calls them *Kennkarten* (identity cards), thereby rhetorically allying himself with the Nazis once more. As he counts his money, she departs, barely able to stand, still queasy. In response to the newcomer's query about the girl's identity, the rapist articulates his utter contempt for his victim:[28]

"Oh, just a whore."
  "I thought she was a virgin . . . Pale, teary-eyed, shaky . . ."
  "Since when can't virgins be whores?"

Like other female memoirists of her generation, Judith Magyar Isaacson, deported to Auschwitz at age nineteen, refers fleetingly, but recurrently, to the terrors many young women harbored about rape. Citing her uncle as the source, her worst fear is, of "Jewish girls being dragged to the Russian front by cattle cars."[29] Isaacson alludes to the uncle's warning in her first reference. Later, in a dramatic funeral scene, he pulls Judith aside to admonish her: "[D]on't forget what I told you about the Russian front."[30] Here, he exacts her promise to "risk [her] life to escape a girls' transport," a promise she honors during an Auschwitz selection. In an earlier conversation following German intrusion in her grandparents' home, she ponders her own shame, "I wanted to ask, but I was too embarrassed: could I convince a German soldier not to rape me?"[31] So impressed was the eighteen-year-old girl with her uncle's warning that as she prepares to leave her home for the ghetto she confides to her grandmother, "I feared rape more than death and I decided to take some poison with me."[32]

Following three miserable weeks in Auschwitz, Isaacson is in the company of thousands of women for a selection conducted by a figure she assumes in retrospect to have been Josef Mengele. Soldiers randomly lash the women into lines and march them "in a gigantic curve around and around, naked" to determine one of three destinations.[33] Some women were directed "straight ahead, toward the freight train. The sick and the worn wobbled left, toward a waiting truck. A select group of young girls steered right and marched off nude, in rows of five."[34] She was nauseated by "all the nudity, the breasts, the buttocks, the pathetic pubic slits, so visible on the shaven parts."[35] Motivated by fear of rape, Isaacson defied Mengele's order to join the young girls' transport, and pushed forward with her mother and aunt to the train bound for slave labor.

Sexual Violence by Guards and *Kapos*

Although most memoirs and fiction by women focus on sexual abuse initiated by guards, *Kapos* (supervising prisoners), and lower-level ghetto and camp functionaries, Fania Fénelon recalls the sadistic behavior of an SS officer during a death selection:

> [He] had brought a thousand women out into the snow, lined them up, entirely naked, in freezing air, then, moving along their ranks, lifted their breasts with the tip of his whip. Those whose breasts sagged went to the left, those whose breasts remained firm went to the right and were spared a little longer, except of course for those who perished from the cold.[36]

While perpetrators of sexual assault against women are most often either male soldiers or camp functionaries, Dr. Gisella Perl recounts the particularly gruesome sexual violence perpetrated by Irma Grese, the notorious highest-ranking SS-affiliated woman in Auschwitz. Grese derived pleasure similar to sexual arousal while witnessing Perl operate "on a young woman's breast, cut open by whipping and subsequently infected." Perl describes this operation as without the benefit of anesthetic, a knife her only instrument and the patient screaming all through the procedure. During the operation, she observed Grese "enjoying the sight of human suffering." From that day forward, following what she clearly experienced as a titillating event, Grese wanted more opportunities:

> [Grese] went around in camp, her bejeweled whip poised, picked out the most beautiful young women and slashed their breasts open with the braided wire end of her whip. Subsequently those breasts got infected by the lice and dirt which invaded every nook and corner of the camp. They had to be cut open, if the patient was to be saved. Irma Griese [sic] invariably arrived to watch the operation, kicking the victim if her screams interfered with her pleasure and giving herself completely to the orgiastic spasms which shook her entire body and made saliva run down from the corner of her mouth.[37]

More prevalent than sexual exploitation by SS men was that by privileged prisoners or lower-level functionaries, *Kapos*, or other prisoner supervisors who demanded sex from female inmates in exchange for an extra piece of bread, medicine, a pair of boots, a better job, or escape from a selection. Polish political survivor Tadeusz Borowski's critically acclaimed Auschwitz stories, collected in *This Way for the Gas, Ladies and Gentlemen*, are written primarily in the voice of a non-Jewish Polish deputy *Kapo*, a cynical labor commando, an indifferent hospital orderly trainee, or an outraged lover, who is positioned by his camp job to witness what Primo Levi called "the grey area" of relative accommodation in the camps. Whatever empathy the male workers might have felt for the female prisoners, they had become hardened by camp conditions and thought of women as commodities, naming the female section of the camp the "Persian Market," where, from a distance, the faceless, ageless women were a mass of "bright summer dresses" and "gay kerchiefs."[38] The Dachau and Auschwitz survivor's brutally honest narrator admits that roofers work in the women's section not by order, nor with charitable intent toward the older serial numbers: "[A]n Elder had to pay. She had to pay the Kapo, the Kommandoführer, the Kommando 'bigwigs.' She could pay in various ways: with gold, food, the women in her block, or with her own body." Sex, like food or gold, is camp currency, for as the narrator condescendingly notes, "Any one of them could be had for a piece of bright silk or a shiny trinket. Since time began, never has there been such an easy market for female flesh!"[39]

Camp Brothels

In "Auschwitz, Our Home," written in the form of a letter to his fiancée, who was a political prisoner incarcerated in the women's barracks at Birkenau, Tadeusz Borowski adopts a tone that is more compassionate and more angry as he describes some of the male attitudes toward "the Puff," the camp brothel. In contrast to the distanced tone when referencing the "Persian Market," he begins by commenting on the "pretty little heads of various shades of colour, with delicate shoulders, as white and fresh as snow, emerging from their frilly blue, pink, and sea-green robes" peeking out the windows at prospective customers. The tone becomes scathingly sardonic to satirize sex as commodity as his gaze turns to the men who frequently surround the Puff:

> For every Juliet there are at least a thousand Romeos. Hence the crowd, and the competition. The Romeos stand along the windows of the barracks across the street; they shout, wave, invite. The Camp Elder and the Camp Kapo are there, and so are the doctors from the hospital and the Kapos from the Kommandos. It is not unusual for a Juliet to have a steady admirer, and, along with promises of undying love and a blissful life together after the war, along with reproaches and bickering, one is apt to hear exchanges of a more basic nature, concerning such particulars as soap, perfume, silk panties, or cigarettes.[40]

Having declined the invitation to use the facilities as a "guest from Birkenau," he defers to the report of a barrack mate who has used the facility regarding its operation: the necessary bribery for the madam, the necessary hygienic treatments, mandatory reading of the rules posted on each door "saying that such and such is forbidden, under severe penalty, that only such and such (a detailed list follows) is allowed, but for only so many minutes. He sighs at the sight of a spy-hole, which is occasionally used for peeping by the other girls, occasionally by the Madame, or the Puff's Kommandoführer, or the camp Kommandant himself."[41] In good German health practice, the prisoner-client undergoes disinfecting treatment again upon departure.

In a brief digression from the routine brothel experience, the narrator comments on extra-curricular events of barrack 10, the experimental medical block, where women are customarily "artificially inseminated, injected with typhoid and malaria germs, or operated on. . . . The women are kept behind barred and boarded-up windows, but still the place is often broken into and the women are inseminated, not at all artificially."[42] Unlike most Jewish male survivors of the *Lager* (camp), who write sparingly if at all of women's experience, as a Polish political prisoner, Borowski's job permitted his entry to the women's section, access to his lover, and the insight to write more knowingly than many male colleagues about the sexual reward system for privileged prisoners.

Arnošt Lustig, survivor of Theresienstadt, Auschwitz, and Buchenwald, simultaneously details the Nazi bureaucratic approach to prostitution and captures the sexually abused woman's point of view in *Lovely Green Eyes*. The novel is narrated by a male voice, the future husband of the woman whose history is the subject, an approach the author may have taken to acknowledge women's postwar tendency to remain silent about the sexual abuse they suffered. Lustig's fictional protagonist provides the counter voice to Judith Isaacson. Lustig's fictional fifteen-year-old Jewish girl, whose camp job is assisting a physician who sterilized women, seizes an opportunity to save her life by secretly joining a convoy of young women, assembled near her work place, for transport to a military brothel.

Far more explicit than women writers and even than Borowski's narrator, Lustig's narrator describes the brothel's conditions and operational procedures in vivid detail. Regulations posted on the cubicle doors, in the washroom, and waiting room convey the atmosphere of the field bordello:

With immediate effect, it is forbidden to provide services without a rubber sheath. Most strictly prohibited are:

Anal, oral or brutal intercourse;
To take urine or semen into the mouth or anus;
To re-use contraceptives.[43]

The brothel supervisor further instructs the women: "Anything that is not specifically permitted is forbidden . . . . The soldier is always right. Kissing is forbidden. Unconditional obedience is demanded. You must not ask for anything."

A major strength of the novel is Lustig's graphic description of the young woman's job, her revulsion and shame, and her coping mechanism. On her belly is the blue tattoo identifying her as a *Feldhure*, an army whore: "Twelve times a day . . . she let a stranger do with her body whatever he liked. She felt ashamed not only for herself, even though there were no witnesses. She must not show it. She must not think of whose turn it would be next. The second, the third, the twelfth man."[44] Throughout the text, Lustig introduces a refrain listing the names of twelve German men evoking the laborious, daunting task of serving a dozen or more soldiers every day but Sunday. The girl's thoughts alternate between guilt at the prospect of her family knowing what she is doing to a measure of psychic distancing—imagining the ocean, the darkness outside, the accompaniment of scurrying, squeaking rats. Her guilt is expressed in recurrent thoughts of anticipated paternal disapproval, wondering whether her father would rather see her dead than in the field brothel, whether she should be relieved that her family no longer exists. She struggles with ambivalence: "Had she committed a sin by wanting to live?"[45] The girl rationalizes that this work, humiliating as it is, is like the other camp jobs she had, a means of survival. Yet she ponders "whether [survival] was worth the price paid for it." When she feels sorry for herself, she remembers that she is better off than tens of thousands of others despite the fact that "[s]he was paying for her life with her crotch, her thighs, her arms, legs, lips, fingers, tongue—and her soul."[46]

Characteristic of Lustig's graphic description of sexual encounter is his protagonist's understanding of the male stare: "the path of their gaze the way it mapped out what more or less made up a girl, at least from the outside—hair, chin, eyes, breasts, hips, buttocks, legs and crotch—assessing her in a hundredth of a second usually though sometimes lingeringly. . . . a piece of colorfully decked-out flesh."[47]

Upon her return to Prague, the fictional girl, who had entered the brothel at age fifteen and a half and was liberated four months later, fears judgment for her wartime ruse, dwelling on the double irony that she had had to conceal her Jewish identity in the brothel and "now she would have to conceal that she had been an army whore." She anticipates being challenged by those who will question whether there was no other way to save herself, except by being "a whore for the Germans . . . A lot of people to whom nothing had happened in the war would think that she should have let herself be killed."[48]

Trading Sexual Favors for Survival

That all women in the camps could be subject to sexual abuse by fellow prisoners is aptly conveyed in Gisella Perl's memoir, as she recounts her humiliation at the need to trade sex for survival. After two months' shoelessness during daily roll calls, Perl had obtained ill-fitting shoes by paying two days of her bread rations to a woman who was able to steal a pair of shoes from the crematorium. She was then desperate for a bit of string to hold the shoes in place. Perl purchased this precious commodity at a high price from a Polish latrine worker who refused her bread ration and instead "grabbed [her] by the shoulder and hissed . . . 'I don't want your bread . . . You can keep your bread . . . I will give you a piece of string but first I want you . . . you . . .'"

Her response to the assault is more completely developed as she describes escaping her unlikely benefactor, "running away from the indignity that had been inflicted on me, forgetting about the string, about the shoes, about everything but the sudden realization of how deeply I had sunk . . . How high the price of a piece of string had soared."[49] It is to this degradation that she attributes her revived rebellious spirit, the decision to maintain her humanity by beginning a spiritual form of resistance encouraging barracks mates to keep up their spirits by reciting poetry, telling stories, sharing reminiscences, singing.

The latrine, it appears, was a site for assignations, where "male and female prisoners met for a furtive moment of joyless sexual intercourse in which the body was used as a commodity to trade for the badly needed items the men were able to pilfer from the warehouses" or to secure by other means.[50] Of male workers in their camp environs who ate their lunch in the washrooms or latrines the women used, Olga Lengyel writes, "it was rarely pity that made the men share their not-too-abundant food. For food was the coin that paid for sexual privileges."[51] Refraining from judging women who engaged in prostitution for food, Perl correctly blames camp administrators for the inmates' degradation and addresses the lamentable consequences of camp prostitution as an ordinary phenomenon in Birkenau. Perl writes with disgust, but understanding, that the trusted old prisoners, the latrine "Don Juans of Camp C . . . chose their women among the youngest, the prettiest, the least emaciated prisoners and in a few seconds the deal was closed."[52] She concludes her description of the sexual exchange by shifting from payment to desired object: "Openly, shamelessly, the dirty, diseased bodies clung together for a minute or two in the fetid atmosphere of the latrine—and the piece of bread, the comb, the little knife wandered from the pocket of the man into the greedy hands of the woman."[53] With great honesty, Perl charts her metamorphosis from righteous indignation, shock, and revulsion at this form of "prostitution" to understanding, relenting when she eventually understood that "the pieces of bread thus earned saved lives" or that a young girl saved herself from the crematory by earning a pair of shoes for a week's prostitution.

Because Fania Fénelon was a celebrated Parisian cabaret singer and pianist whom a Nazi officer wanted for a performance of *Madame Butterfly*, she was transferred from her original ordinary barrack to the special barrack for the Auschwitz orchestra women under the direction of Gustav Mahler's niece, Alma Rosé. While these women had slightly better living conditions than the ordinary prisoners, they too were starving and in mortal danger. That only one woman, Clara, who attached herself to Fénelon and joined the orchestra with her protector, uses her body to negotiate with guards for more food suggests the limited role such exchanges offered Jewish women.[54] Yet objection to trading sex for food or for other means of survival is voiced here by starving inmates who accuse the victim of moral degradation.

Clara's decision to trade sex with Polish *Kapos* to supplement her meager rations is dramatized as a trajectory toward moral decline. When Clara degenerates from *Kapo's* whore to sadistic *Kapo*, Fénelon's tone shifts from sympathetic protector to condemnatory antagonist. She contrasts Clara's selfishness with her own altruism and charts Clara's rapid transformation solely in terms of sexual exchange to allay hunger. When Clara abandons her shared "box" with Fénelon, to organize her own storage space (while announcing "I won't share with anyone anymore"), Fénelon mocks the self-centered Clara for her "nobly earned jam" and speculates that her tears of rage are "perhaps the last glimmer of a former morality, a remnant of dignity."[55] Although she claims to feel sorry for Clara, Fénelon's tone belies her mocking contempt: "She had become frighteningly selfish; she would do anything to get food. In the middle of all these painfully thin girls, her obesity was a wonder, a most effective lure for men, who paid court to her in butter and sugar."[56] The memoirist repeats these sentiments about Clara "who'd lost all modesty, and had become a kapo's girl; [comparing her with] Lotte, . . . her protruding stomach and hidden charms all too visibly available, sickened us all."[57] In this place, where romantic love is as scarce as food, opportunism reigned, "discreditable couplings of whores with kapos and block superintendents whose physiques were often closer to those of beasts than men."[58] With each reference to Clara's prostitution, Fénelon's condemnation grows increasingly severe: charging her with flirtation to achieve not only food but to preserve a life-saving job. "Swinging her hips complacently proffering her pallid fat," Fénelon writes, "she would go toward the highest bidder, steering a course between her two main concerns, guzzling and singing."[59]

In his screenplay based on Fénelon's memoir, the acclaimed American playwright Arthur Miller remains essentially faithful to the original. He changes the name of Fania Fénelon's friend/antagonist from "Clara" to "Marianne," but echoes the early worshipful tone of the younger woman toward the famous singer/protector and heightens Fania's condemnation of Clara's camp metamorphosis. Miller, like most male writers studied here, especially those who did not experience the camps, conveys Marianne's behavior more explicitly than did the female memoirist. Rather than articulate the sexuality in dialogue, however, Miller dramatizes Marianne's transformation primarily through stage directions: "On the toilet bowl Marianne is straddling a man, a kapo still wearing his striped prisoner's hat. In his hand are gripped two sausages. Marianne turns and sees Fania, but turns back and continues with the man who is looking straight up at Fania."[60] Similarly, while Fénelon had declared that Clara trades sex for food, we rarely see the food in the memoir. In contrast, Miller shows the food in the latrine scene and again when two *Kapos* give Marianne a chocolate bar that she begins to devour before leaving the barrack with them. Miller sharpens the critique with each iteration of Marianne's trafficking with *Kapos*. In the third reference, he juxtaposes dialogue between Fania and a male electrician working in the women's camp who reports the day's toll of 12,000 people gassed with stage directions for Marianne's entrance "eating meat off a bone. She sees Fania is slightly surprised, but goes on eating. Kapo gives her ass a squeeze and walks away."[61] The camp evacuation scene is the first instance in which Miller assigns Marianne flirtatious dialogue. She approaches a soldier, trying to discover where the women are being taken, "gives him a flirty look" and suggests, as he shows some interest in her, "[c]ause wherever it is, I know how to make a fellow forget his troubles."[62] On stage or screen, these stage directions and brief lines of dialogue make powerful impressions and are consistent with male graphic depictions of sexual activity in the camp universe.

Eroticizing the Holocaust: A Male Perspective

As shown, women's Holocaust testimony and women's Holocaust fiction rarely include explicit discussions of sexuality and eroticism. Male writing, especially fiction by men who have no Holocaust experience, tends to treat sexual abuse more fully, more graphically, and, on occasion, titillatingly, giving rise to charges of Holocaust exploitation. The English novelist D. M. Thomas, who has been criticized for such exploitative treatment of the Holocaust, has published two novels that integrate themes of psychology, sexuality, and the Holocaust. The best known and most controversial, *The White Hotel*, is about a woman who undergoes analysis with Sigmund Freud and meets a brutal death at Babi Yar.

Controversies engendered by *The White Hotel* are grounded in critical assessments of Thomas's representation of the Holocaust, allegations of plagiarism and accusations of pornography. The plagiarism charge originated with a 1982 letter from D. A. Kenrick to the *Times Literary Supplement* asserting that Thomas's sequence on Lisa's death was "a superficially reworked version of the historical accounts in Anatoli Kuznetsov's *Babi Yar*,"[63] especially Dina Pronicheva's testimony.[64]

For our purpose, the most pertinent of these controversies is Thomas's focus on the sexual life and imagination of his protagonist, Lisa Erdman, and whether by eroticizing death and sexual violence the novel's rape scene constitutes exploitive use of the Holocaust. I share Susanne Kappeler's conclusion —representative of critics who argue that the Holocaust is exploited for the novel's sexual/psychological agenda—and concur that particularly the "Don Giovanni" and "Gatstein Journal" chapters reflect male-defined sexuality and a male-defined view of female sexual hysteria.[65]

The Babi Yar scene is expansive. The narrator describes Lisa's march to a ravine to be executed, focusing largely on women and children, the response of townsfolk, bystanders who understand the fate of the Jews, some expressing sympathy, others enjoying the victims' misery. Lisa and her stepson are duped initially into anticipating transport for eventual resettlement in Palestine. Upon arrival at the killing site, the herded masses encounter open hostility. Soldiers randomly beat them and force them to strip and leave their possessions. Thomas alternates the third person perspective with Lisa's consciousness as she stands on the brink, holding Kolya's hand:

> Lisa looked down and her head swam . . . Beneath her was a sea of bodies covered in blood. . . . She did not see as much as feel the bodies falling from the ledge and the stream of bullets coming closer to them. Just before it reached them she pulled Kolya's hand, crying "Jump," and jumped with him off the edge.
>
> It seemed to her that she fell for ages—it was probably a very deep drop. When she struck the bottom she lost consciousness.[66]

As Lisa lands at the bottom of the ravine, Thomas shifts from her brief fantasy of being in her own home to realization that the sounds she hears are of fellow victims, those still living among the corpses. As she contemplates crawling out of the mass grave with Kolya after darkness falls, German soldiers appear, firing at anyone showing a sign of life, walking among and on top of the bodies, looting remaining possessions. Attracted by the glint of something, an SS man's "hand brushed her breast when he reached for the crucifix to pull it free, and he must have sensed a flicker of life. . . . He drew his leg back and sent his jackboot crashing into her left breast. . . . Still not satisfied, he swung his boot again and sent it cracking into her pelvis."[67]

Kuznetsov's work, described as a documentary novel, used real testimony from Babi Yar survivor Dina Pronicheva. While Kuznetsov did not write that Dina was sexually assaulted, Thomas does not spare Lisa. With the arrival of the Ukrainian police, who are to bury the masses, Thomas's fictional description veers on the pornographic, especially in its echo of the sexual references, diction, and imagery in the earlier chapter's *Don Giovanni* poem:

> There was a clatter of spades and then heavy thuds of earth and sand landed on the bodies, coming closer and closer to . . . [Lisa] . . . The unbearable thing was to be buried alive. She cried with a terrible and powerful voice: "I'm alive. Shoot me, please!" It came out only as a choking whisper, but Demidenko heard it. He scraped some of the earth off her face. "Hey, Semashko!" he shouted. "This one's still alive!" Semashko, . . . looked down and recognized the . . . woman who had tried to bribe her way out [by offering sex earlier when she heard another refuse the opportunity] "Then give her a fuck!" he chuckled. Demidenko grinned, and started unbuckling his belt. Semashko rested his rifle, and yanked the . . . woman into a flatter position. Her head lolled to the left and looked straight into a boy's open eyes. Then Demidenko yanked her legs apart.
>
> After a while Semashko jeered at him, and Demidenko grumbled that it was too cold, and the . . . woman was too ugly. He adjusted his clothing and picked up his rifle. With Semashko's assistance he found the opening, and they joked together as he inserted the bayonet, carefully, almost delicately. The . . . woman was not making any sound although they could see she was still breathing. Still very gently, Demidenko imitated the thrusts of intercourse; and Semashko let out a guffaw, which echoed from the ravine walls as the woman's body jerked back and relaxed, jerked and relaxed. But after those spasms there was no sign of a reaction and she seemed to have stopped breathing. . . . Demidenko twisted the blade and thrust it in deep.[68]

The scene horrifies readers, but its Holocaust impact is diminished by its unfortunate recall of similar diction from an erotic poem in which Lisa fantasizes incessant intercourse with Freud's son at the white hotel. The poem's erotic passage supplants the violent image of burning bodies falling from hotel windows. In Thomas's Babi Yar impalement scene, sadistic brutality is the overwhelming element. His representation of the ravine rape is far more explicitly detailed and sadistically titillating than any written by women. His prose is focused on the male gaze, the male-defined possession, control of, and violent battering of the female body in the context of the Ukrainian policeman's salacious jeering, and pleasure. Defending the Babi Yar scene, Thomas explains that his heroine is changing from being "Lisa an individual to Lisa in history—an anonymous victim. . . . From individual self-expression she moves to the common fate."[69] Thus, Thomas suggests Freud's misdiagnosis of Lisa's symptoms, and his intent that the reader perceive these symptoms as prophetic, for the jackboot crashing into her left breast and pelvis are not neurotic manifestations of an hysteric about her childhood psychological trauma, but her fate as part of the collective experience of twentieth-century European Jewry. Whether Thomas achieves his purpose is open to debate.

Conclusions

Collective Jewish victimization under Nazi racist policies is the primary subject of Holocaust writing. However, because the combined forces of racism and sexism violently and relentlessly assaulted women's vulnerability, the writing studied in this chapter focused intensely on sexual intimidation and trauma. These authors eschewed essentialist positions and refrained from suggesting that Jewish women were persecuted because they were female in a male-dominated universe or that gender comprised the totality of women's Holocaust experience. Yet by persuasively underscoring the gendered dimensions of women's suffering and their coping strategies, which had long been silenced or marginalized, these memoirists and creative writers significantly broadened the Holocaust canon.

Notes

1. See the following texts for examination of women's Holocaust literary expression: Judith Tydor Baumel, *Double Jeopardy: Gender and the Holocaust* (London: Vallentine Mitchell, 1998); Ellen S. Fine, "Women and the Holocaust: Strategies for Survival," in *Reflections of the Holocaust in Art and Literature*, ed. Randolph L. Braham (Boulder, CO: Social Science Monographs, 1990), 79–95; Marlene E. Heinemann, *Gender and Destiny: Women Writers and the Holocaust* (New York: Greenwood Press, 1986); Myrna Goldenberg, "Different Horrors, Same Hell: Women Remembering the Holocaust," in *Thinking the Unthinkable: Meanings of the Holocaust*, ed. Roger S. Gottlieb (New York: Paulist Press, 1990), 150–166; "Testimony, Narrative, and Nightmare: Experience of Jewish Women in the Holocaust," in *Active Voices: Women in Jewish Culture*, ed. Maurie Sacks (Urbana: University of Illinois Press, 1995), 94–108; Sara R. Horowitz, "The 'Pin with which to Stick Yourself': The Holocaust in Jewish American Women's Writing," in *Daughters of Valor: Contemporary Jewish American Women Writers*, ed. Jay L. Halio and Ben Siegel (Newark: University of Delaware Press, 1997), 141–159; "Memory and Testimony of Women Survivors of Nazi Genocide," in *Women of the Word: Jewish Women and Jewish Writing*, ed. Judith Baskin (Detroit: Wayne State University Press, 1994); "Women in Holocaust Lit-

erature: Engendering Trauma Memory," in *Women in the Holocaust*, ed. Dalia Ofer and Lenore J. Weitzman (New Haven: Yale University Press, 1998), 364–377; S. Lillian Kremer, *Women's Holocaust Writing: Memory and Imagination* (Lincoln, University of Nebraska Press, 1999); ed., *Holocaust Literature: An Encyclopedia of Writers and Their Work*, 2 vols. (New York: Routledge, 2003), includes 108 articles on women writers; "Holocaust-Wrought Women: Portraits by Four American Writers," *Studies in American Jewish Literature* 11, no. 2 (fall 1992):150–161; "An Estate of Memory: Women in the Holocaust," in *Holocaust Studies Annual*, ed. Sanford Pinsker and Jack Fischel (New York: Garland Publishing Inc., 1992), 99–11; "Holocaust Writing," in *The Oxford Companion to Women's Writing in the United States*, ed. Cathy N. Davidson and Linda Wagner-Martin (New York: Oxford University Press, 1994), 395–397; "The Holocaust and the Witnessing Imagination," in *Violence, Silence, and Anger: Women's Writing As Transgression*, ed. Deirdre Lashgari (Charlottesville: University Press of Virginia, 1995), 231–246; "Norma Rosen: An American Literary Response to the Holocaust," in *Daughters of Valor*, 160–174; "Women in the Holocaust: Representation of Gendered Suffering and Coping Strategies in American Fiction," in *Experience and Expression: Women, the Nazis, and the Holocaust*, ed. Elizabeth R. Baer and Myrna Goldenberg (Detroit: Wayne State University Press, 2003), 260–277; introduction to *A Long Labour: A Dutch Mother's Holocaust Memoir* by Rhodea Schandler (Vancouver: Ronsdale Press, 2007); Rebecca Scherr, "The Uses of Memory and Abuses of Fiction: Sexuality in Holocaust Film, Fiction, and Memoir," in *Experience and Expression*, ed. Baer and Goldenberg, 278–297.

2. Norma Rosen, "The Second Life of Holocaust Imagery," in *Accidents of Influence: Writing as a Woman and a Jew in America* (Albany: State University of New York Press, 1992), 51.

3. Olga Lengyel, *Five Chimneys: The Story of Auschwitz* (Chicago: Ziff-Davis Company, 1947), 83.

4. Ibid., 19.

5. Sara Nomberg-Przytyk, *Auschwitz: True Tales From a Grotesque Land*, trans. Roslyn Hirsch, ed. Eli Pfefferkorn and David H. Hirsch (Chapel Hill: University of North Carolina Press, 1985), 13–14.

6. Fania Fénelon with Marcelle Routier, *Playing for Time*, trans. Judith Landry (New York: Athenaeum, 1977), 19.

7. Judith Magyar Isaacson, *Seed of Sarah: Memoirs of a Survivor* (Urbana: University of Illinois Press, 1990), 66–67.

8. Susan Fromberg Schaeffer, *Anya* (New York: Macmillan Publishing Company, 1974), 221–223. For a full analysis of *Anya*, see Kremer, *Women's Holocaust Writing*, 119–148.

9. Marge Piercy, *Gone to Soldiers* (New York: Summit Books, 1987), 574. For a full analysis of *Gone to Soldiers* see Kremer, *Women's Holocaust Writing*, 176–211.

10. Joel E. Dimsdale, "The Coping Behavior of Nazi Concentration Camp Survivors," in *Survivors, Victims, Perpetrators: Essays on the Nazi Holocaust*, ed. Joel E. Dimsdale (Washington: Hemisphere Publishing, 1980), 168.

11. Lengyel, *Five Chimneys*, 173.

12. Fénelon, *Playing for Time*, 88.

13. Ibid., 88–89. The *Shema* is a Jewish affirmation of faith in one God.

14. Lengyel, *Five Chimneys*, 177.

15. Ibid., 177–178.

16. Ibid., 99.

17. Gisella Perl, "A Doctor in Auschwitz," in *Different Voices: Women and the Holocaust*, ed. Carol Rittner and John K. Roth (New York: Paragon House, 1993), 113. See also chapter 10 by Ellen Ben-Sefer in this volume.

18. Cynthia Ozick, *The Shawl* (New York: Alfred A. Knopf, 1989), 3. For a full analysis of *The Shawl* see Kremer, *Women's Holocaust Writing*, 149–175.

19. Ibid., 4.

20. Ibid., 8.

21. Elzbieta Ettinger, *Kindergarten* (Boston: Houghton Mifflin, 1970), 34. For a full analysis of Ettinger's novels see Kremer, *Women's Holocaust Writing*, 66–99.

22. Ida Fink, "Aryan Papers," in *A Scrap of Time and Other Stories*, trans. Madeline Levine and Francine Prose (New York: Random House, 1987), 63.

23. Ibid., 64.

24. Ibid., 65.

25. Ibid., 64.

26. Ibid., 66.

27. Ibid., 67.

28. Ibid., 67–68.

29. Isaacson, *Seed of Sarah*, 36.

30. Ibid., 53.

31. Ibid., 42.

32. Ibid., 47.

33. Ibid., 84.

34. Ibid., 84–85.

35. Ibid., 84.

36. Fénelon, *Playing for Time*, 158.

37. Perl, "A Doctor in Auschwitz," 117.

38. Tadeusz Borowski, *This Way for the Gas, Ladies and Gentlemen*, trans. Barbara Vedder (Middlesex, UK: Penguin Books, 1976), 86.

39. Ibid., 93.

40. Ibid., 106.

41. Ibid., 107.

42. Ibid., 108.

43. Arnošt Lustig, *Lovely Green Eyes*, trans. Ewald Osers (New York: Arcade Publishing, 2002), 5, italics in the original.

44. Ibid., 37.

45. Ibid., 56.

46. Ibid., 39.

47. Ibid., 101.

48. Ibid., 181.

49. Perl, 109.

50. Ibid., 112.

51. Lengyel, *Five Chimneys*, 182.

52. Perl, "A Doctor in Auschwitz," 112–113.

53. Ibid., 113.

54. For a different interpretation of Clara's behavior, see chapter 4 by Kirsty Chatwood in this volume.

55. Fénelon, *Playing for Time*, 105.

56. Ibid., 105–106.

57. Ibid., 115–116.

58. Ibid., 145.

59. Ibid., 189.

60. Arthur Miller, *Playing for Time* (New York: Bantam Books, 1981), 53.

61. Ibid., 81.

62. Ibid., 141.

63. D. A. Kenrick, letter to *Times Literary Supplement*, March 26, 1982, 412.

64. The Kuznetsov-Thomas parallels are fully documented in Sue Vice, *Holocaust Fiction* (New York: Routledge, 2000), 42. Of particular interest is her discussion of Thomas's conflation of Kuznetsov's scene of Dina's efforts to extricate herself from the ravine and another scene located on the far side of the ravine of six or seven German soldiers raping and then bayoneting two women. For Pronicheva's story, see chapter 6 by Anatoly Podolsky in this volume.

65. Susanne Kappeler, *The Pornography of Representation* (Cambridge: Polity Press, 1986).

66. Donald Michael Thomas, *The White Hotel* (New York: Pocket Books, 1981), 291–292.

67. Thomas, 293.

68. Ibid., 293–294.

69. Donald Michael Thomas, letter to the *Times Literary Supplement*, April 2, 1982, 383.

12

"Stoning the Messenger"

Yehiel Dinur's House of Dolls *and* Piepel

MIRYAM SIVAN

Since the end of World War II, fiction has sometimes filled the lacunae of historical documentation and discourse regarding Jewish sexual slavery and abuse during the Holocaust. Rachel Lev-Wiesel and Marianne Amir, who have studied the sexual abuse of Jewish children during the war, claim that by ignoring this critical piece of the historical puzzle, some scholars have been able to avoid their "own feelings of fear, helplessness, and horror in dealing with such life stories."[1]

Because "men of a conquered nation traditionally view the rape of 'their women' as the ultimate humiliation, a sexual *coup de grace*,"[2] according to Susan Brownmiller, rape has come to represent literally, figuratively, and allegorically the depths of an individual's and a nation's helplessness. For Jews the connection between sexual violation and existential powerlessness is seeded in the Bible. In Genesis 12:10–20, Abram takes his entourage down to Egypt during a season of famine. On the way, he instructs his beautiful wife, Sarai, to tell the Egyptians that she is his sister, for if she pleases Pharaoh, he will have the husband, Abram, killed. Taking the husband's life was acceptable in order for his wife to then be violated sexually.

Sarai was indeed taken into Pharaoh's palace, where she remained for some time, and Abram was compensated financially. The story continues that plagues descended upon Pharaoh's house. One rabbinic commentary explains that Pharaoh was struck with impotence, and his lust for Sarai was not consummated.[3] Other commentaries say Pharaoh suffered leprosy or venereal disease, medical conditions that also could have prevented him from having sex with Sarai.[4] As we see here, the obfuscation of rape is not a modern invention.

Modes of Understanding—Inside and Outside of Israel

There is a marked difference in the way writers and readers inside and outside of Israel have dealt with the fact of sexual abuse of women and children during the Holocaust. For Israelis, the allegorical model of sexual violation as an extreme form of Diaspora vulnerability seems obvious and from their reconstituted position of political and military agency, enraging, but not existentially threatening. The emphasis in the culture that raised them is not on impotence, but on durability, resilience, and fortitude. For many Jews in the Diaspora, however, rape and sexual slavery are so intimidating that they continue to be cloaked in denial, and when they are mentioned at all, even in fiction, they are referred to only euphemistically.[5]

I do not condone the reductive analysis of a "feminized," passive, and weak Diaspora and a "masculine," active, and strong Israel and, of course, do not abide by the conflation of feminization with weakness. However, I also do not think it coincidental that the image of a Jewish woman forced into sexual slavery in Palmach founder Yitzhak Sadeh's poem "My Sister on the Beach" became the symbol of Jewish ravishment in Europe, and a rallying cry in the nascent Israeli state's fight for independence.[6] Written in 1945, the poem's speaker is a young fighter who describes a young female survivor and vows to do everything in his power to protect her. The poem begins:

> Darkness. On wet sand my sister stands before me: dirty,
> Disheveled.
> Matted hair. Her feet bare and her head lowered. She
> Stands and sobs.
> I know: she is tattooed: "for officers only" . . .

The poem goes on to describe that she was sterilized (one assumes by the Germans), but in the eyes of the young Jewish officer she epitomizes femininity and motherhood. In pre-state Israel, the situation is diametrically opposed. Immediately after the war in Europe was over, the fighting between the Jews, the British, and the Arabs in Palestine raged on. Thus it is not surprising that when Yehiel Dinur first published *House of Dolls*, in Hebrew in 1953 and its English translation in 1956, and then *Piepel*,[7] in Hebrew in 1958 and its English translation in 1961, two novels that deal with sexual slavery in the concentration camps, preliminary reactions within and outside of Israel were dissimilar.[8]

For many Israelis, Dinur's realism, the way he was able to "penetrate into subtle layers of [camp] reality and reconstruct it from within" was accepted at face value.[9] His depiction of atrocities was understood to be an important act of witnessing and an indictment of Nazi abuses. Sexual slavery was seen as a problem of the Holocaust, not of the books. Writing in the Israeli daily newspaper *Haboker* soon after *House of Dolls* was published, Yosef Heftman saw that "extreme sexual abuse and [the women's] treatment as mere objects in this brothel limpidly illustrate the familiar trope of Ka-Tzetnik's [Dinur's nom de plume] series of novels—the Holocaust as the most horrifying, obscene, and unique of modern situations."[10] Outside of Israel, Dinur was and continues to be for the most part largely ignored.[11]

In recent decades, some Israeli readers and critics have begun to marginalize Dinur as well, possibly as a reaction to the extended social and political stability that Israel has experienced. Now that Israel is no longer fighting for its existence to the same degree as during the first two decades after World War II, some of its critics seem to have become rather genteel in their tastes and affectations. It is ironic that their critique coincides with the important historical research conducted in recent years on sexual abuse of women and children. To those willing to listen, Dinur seems less a mad prophet of fantasy and doom and more a reliable chronicler of another level of hell. Within Israel then, there is dissonance between some established scholars' negative responses to Ka-Tzetnik's books and the Ministry of Education's 1994 decision to reissue them and make them part of the high school curriculum.[12]

What has Dinur done to warrant such vituperation? It is not because he was the first Jew to break the silence by telling the story of Auschwitz,[13] which he did as early as 1946 with the Hebrew publication of his first novel, *Salamandra*. And it is not the lack of sophistication of his writing that accounts for such reproach, though this is a common barb hurled at his work. Rather, "Dinurbashing" is an expression of anxiety and fear. It is a reaction to his subject: sexual slavery in general, pedophilic sexual slavery in particular.

Writing about Sexual Slavery in the Camps

Yehiel Dinur, also known as Ka-Tzetnik 135633,[14] decided to focus on the fates of his younger sister and brother in *House of Dolls* and *Piepel*, his second and third novels respectively.[15] Both were children and sex slaves in concentration camps before being killed. The fear of dealing directly with such material is so great that, in Israel, Dinur has even been cast in the role of rapist. Israeli writer Haim Be'er claims that by writing about sexual horrors so directly, Ka-Tzetnik in effect "forces" the reader to face them. Be'er prefers his Holocaust described as a consensual courtship between a man and a woman.[16] One wonders if Be'er levels the same criticism at all narratives of war and atrocity, or only at those where sexual slavery is among the many crimes filling the nightmarish canvas. More importantly, one wonders where and how Be'er misplaced the prerogative of any reader to put aside a book not to his liking. Be'er must be reminded, it seems, that in the world of reality and not of metaphors, rape victims do not share the same agency or privilege.

The "need for protective boundaries,"[17] which historian Dina Porat feels are necessary when faced with Ka-Tzetnik's books, casts writing about atrocity as a kind of menace that must be censored. Innumerable horrors are told over and over again in fiction and nonfictional accounts of the Holocaust, but when it comes to sexual slavery, suddenly, according to Porat, the reader's sensibilities, the public's psychological interests, a moral imperative even, eclipse the survivors' rights to speak and be heard.

When Elie Wiesel described a child dying slowly on the gallows in *Night*, or when his protagonist confesses to wishing for his father's death, many are emotionally and morally stirred. The terror of these sights and the emotions they evoke effectively convey the enormous trauma the victims endured, and understandably, sympathy abounds. Ka-Tzetnik's terrors, however, do not seem to elicit comparable compassion in many of the same critics. The task of examining and contextualizing the extreme and even outrageous responses to Ka-Tzetnik's *House of Dolls* and *Piepel* exhumes prejudicial judgments that one may identify as expressions of a national and political anxiety so great that, to date, no one has brought attention to the important fact that these are Jewish children, not adults, who are being oppressed as sex slaves.

Dinur's inclusion of sexual slavery in the narratives he composed is seen by turns as obscene, pornographic, melodramatic, voyeuristic, vulgar, even as kitsch.[18] His technical writing skills are also decried as melodramatic and unfairly labeled as juvenile. In addition, he is personally attacked for his supposed lack of good style and his lack of literary restraint. He is even demonized for fantasizing and insidiously passing off as real the horror of institutionalized rape and sexual slavery. The pervasive animosity toward Ka-Tzetnik in critical writing is a contemporary example of an ancient ritual of repression: when you do not like what you are hearing, stone the messenger.

A Messenger of the Dead

The criticism directed against Ka-Tzetnik's naturalistic fiction is nothing short of ironic when considered in light of Theodor Adorno's dictum that to write poetry after Auschwitz is barbaric.[19] Adorno feared that art and artifice could distract from, or eclipse, documentation of murderous fanaticism. His concern has been used too often to critique many literary accounts of the Holocaust not written by survivors. A counter-chorus claims other writers have the right to explore and express the agonies of that war.

Yet Ka-Tzetnik, who fits the category of first-person witness and as such has as much "right" as anyone to write about his experiences, is condemned for producing writing that is not sufficiently aesthetic. His work is charged with being simplistic, with a "lack of complexity" both in his narrative technique and in his use of language.[20] One might think that Ka-Tzetnik's straightforward, realistic style would not offend sensibilities wary of using the Holocaust to further aesthetic agendas or egos. One might suppose that Adorno would even *approve* of the lack of poetry, the clear demarcation of intention.

Ka-Tzetnik claimed to have no literary ambitions, but to be a mere chronicler writing for the dead. He became their spokesperson because he understood, much like Harriet Tubman did one hundred years earlier, that "dead niggers tell no tales."[21] So many victims of sexual terrorism, like his younger siblings, did not survive the abuse to tell. And those who did have too often chosen silence in response to shame and guilt and social pressures to will this phenomenon away. His books were not novels, Ka-Tzetnik insisted. He wrote using the third person only because the first-person point of view was too threatening. He testified that "unless I hid behind the third person, I wouldn't have been able to write at all."[22] Jeremy Popkin points out that Ka-Tzetnik "was one of the first survivors to cast his story as a coherent narrative, and he had to invent his own literary strategy rather than follow established models."[23] Since he first published, the standard Holocaust memoir has become a first-person narrative and openly autobiographical. Ka-Tzetnik's work, not fitting the mold, has too often been cast into the "gray zone" of an unidentified genre. But he insisted on the witness stand at the Eichmann trial: "I do not regard myself as a writer and a composer of literary material." That was when he also disclosed that he, Yehiel Dinur, was the scribe Ka-Tzetnik. His books, he explained, were "a chronicle of the planet Auschwitz."[24]

There are of course many critics and readers who are not disturbed by Ka-Tzetnik's "non-judgmental, neutral manner,"[25] his "lack of complexity and his immature position,"[26] his lack of embellishment.[27] They are more concerned with the content of what is being conveyed than with the manner of conveyance, a view that I share. In fact, former Chief Rabbi of Israel Meir Israel Lau, himself a child survivor of Buchenwald, said that Ka-Tzetnik "didn't color it even in dark colors, he just presented it in the dark colors it has: the red and the black."[28] And Zvi Dror from the Ghetto Fighters' Museum at Kibbutz Lo-hamei Haghettaot calls Ka-Tzetnik "'the witness of all witnesses' because his books contain true documentation."[29] This kind of appreciation and acknowl-edgment is not unusual among survivors. The criticism of Ka-Tzetnik's output often comes from those who did not suffer the war directly.

There is something ludicrous, if not perverse, in judging a work of witness-ing against standards of literary excellence.[30] Recognizing that the writing in *House of Dolls* and *Piepel* is perhaps pedestrian does not make the works any less important. "Kitsch" is a word that is often used in critical writing about Ka-Tzetnik, such as in remarks by Omer Bartov, Tom Segev, Dvir Abramovich, and Rina Dudai, but his books are neither particularly sentimental nor imitative, two central features of kitsch. They are heavily descriptive and provide a slow photorealistic account of scenes. Their detailed realism is the opposite of the type of minimalism often lauded in the genre of Holocaust literature. One cannot help but wonder whether psychological and not artistic consider-ations prompted the aesthetic predilection for minimalism in words about the camps.

Eli Wiesel's famous opus *Night* began as an 862-page tome in Yiddish, *Un di velt hot geshvigen* (And the world was silent). Published in Buenos Aires in 1955, it was filled with accusations, recriminations, and passion. What critics may have come to call melodramatic "purple prose" was well in evidence in this version of the book. However, with the editorial help of the French writer Fran-çois Mauriac, Wiesel cut down the manuscript to 178 pages and republished it in French in 1961. Without this aesthetic makeover, the book, like so many other survivor testimonies, might not have met literary benchmarks. In fact, Bartov claims that Wiesel and Ka-Tzetnik are "uncannily alike." Yet while "Wie-sel's kitsch [sic], his bombastic utterances and exclamations about the human condition" have been embraced by a wide audience, Ka-Tzetnik's "anarchic refusal to conform to any rules of the genre have barred him from gaining attention in cultures that prefer a well-told story, insist on close attention to matters aesthetic, require some moral lesson."[31]

If Adorno claimed it is disconcerting to use beautiful language to describe atrocity, then by turn it is certainly disturbing, if not downright offensive, to use elitist aesthetic standards to condemn descriptions of atrocity. Adorno's dictum is a sword that cuts both ways and, as if to clarify this once and for all, eight years after his frequently cited line was published Adorno wrote: "Peren-nial suffering has as much right to expression as a tortured man has to scream; hence it may have been wrong to say that after Auschwitz you could no longer write poems."[32] Just as a highly gifted writer has the right to express her or his experiences, so too does one who is not as skilled. The former may inadvertently also create pleasure where only horror was intended. The latter, like Ka-Tzetnik, may use words in their utter nakedness to simply tell what was. These are worthwhile risks.

Criticism of Ka-Tzetnik's explicit language is also odd because there are no overt depictions of sexual abuse in either House of Dolls or Piepel. One wonders how many people who condemn him for this literary feature have actually read his books. In these books, the emphasis is on the characters' vulnerability and fear, and yet they, and by extension Ka-Tzetnik, their creator, are critiqued for not being models of "spiritual resistance."[33] Both Daniella in House of Dolls and Moni in Piepel are overcome in the end by their oppressors. There are no happy endings here. The few physical attacks that are recounted in the books do not relate the specific details of sexual assault alone and read no differently than scenes of violence and sadism in countless well-known and respected Holocaust narratives, including Elie Wiesel's Night, Tadeusz Borowski's This Way for the Gas, Ladies and Gentlemen, Charlotte Delbo's None of Us Will Return, and Primo Levi's If This Is a Man.

Ka-Tzetnik's later book, Star Eternal (1971), deals with much of the same material in language that is "laconic, trimmed and controlled."[34] Charges of melodrama, mediocrity, and an inability to control the material leveled at him by Omer Bartov, Rina Dudai, Irving Halperin, Dvir Abramovich, and others, as if he had been a teenage boy with raging hormones, no longer apply. However, because the subject of sexual slavery is included, some critics also consider this book to be "indelicate."

Describing Another Level of Hell

Ka-Tzetnik is certainly not the only survivor to acknowledge the existence of sexual slavery in the camps. In his memoir, Frank Stiffel mentions the boys, "usually in their teens, whom they called Piepels . . . who served the Kapo's personal needs, often including the sexual ones."[35] Arnošt Lustig's novel based on a diary, The Unloved: From the Diary of Perla S., recounts the life of a seventeen-year-old Jewish prostitute in Theresienstadt. Hanna Krall in The Subtenant talks about a child born to a Jewish woman, the product of a rape by a German soldier, and about a Jewish child hidden in the countryside who was repeatedly raped by neighboring peasants. In To Outwit God, Marek Edelman confesses to Krall how he and hundreds of other men meekly watched a young Jewish woman being gang-raped by Ukrainian guards. And Elie Wiesel in

Night, in a strange parenthetical comment, writes that "there was considerable traffic in children among homosexuals here, I learned later,"[36] distancing himself from knowledge of pedophilic rape. Yet only a few pages later he discusses *Piepels* in the camp. In fact the young boy whose slow death on the gallows brought on Wiesel's traumatic doubt in God was a *Piepel*, a beautiful boy, he wrote, who was "the little servant" of a Dutch *Kapo* (prisoner supervisor). It could be that as a naïve fourteen-year-old boy, Wiesel did not understand or could not fathom the fact that children were being used in such a horrific manner, and while he knew young boys were servants, he did not think of sexual abuse. But whatever Wiesel's motives were for citing this information in this manner, cite it he does. I have never read anywhere that Wiesel is mad and has made up the image of young boys being used in this way.

When Harriet Jacobs wrote *Incidents in the Life of a Slave Girl* in 1861, her intention in describing her white master's sexual demands and cruelty was not to voyeuristically titillate by lifting the veil on what went on behind plantation manor doors.[37] Rather, Jacobs, a young black woman born a slave in North Carolina, disclosed this painful information to rouse white women in the North to work for abolition. From a woman's point of view, the interface between sexual violation and political oppression provided a powerful call to arms. The idea, both in Jacobs's text and in Ka-Tzetnik's, was to move the reader to a position of moral outrage. Elizabeth Heineman acknowledges that "there is always a danger that sexual images, rather than helping us understand genocide, might serve a pornographic function of simultaneously disgusting and fascinating the reader, making genocide, in a perverse way, appealing." Yet, she continues, "[p]roblematic modes of representation and reception . . . should not be confused with serious attempts to understand the intersections of sexuality and genocide."[38] Women in the North were indeed outraged by Harriet Jacobs's descriptions. However, those who read Ka-Tzetnik's works as voyeuristic, like Ephraim Sicher,[39] or who feel sexual arousal and not moral outrage, or feel themselves raped, trivializing the victims' pain, do so out of choice and not because of any inherent content or quality of the text.

"Pornography"—Who Decides?

"Taste governs every free—as opposed to rote—human response," Susan Sontag wrote. "Nothing is more decisive. There is taste in people, visual taste, taste in emotion—and there is taste in acts, taste in morality. Intelligence, as well, is really a kind of taste: taste in ideas."[40] And so it is to delineations of taste that one must turn in order to define pornography, another common charge leveled at Ka-Tzetnik's books.

The word "pornography" comes from the Greek *pornè*, prostitute, and *graphein*, to write. Literally the word means the writing or the description of prostitutes and their trade. This early narrow definition has come to include descriptions of men and women of many trades involved in various kinds of sexual engagement. Today "there is no consensus" about the application of this term, as historical and cultural variables continue to shift.[41]

A frequently cited definition of pornography comes from American Supreme Court Justice Potter Stewart's 1964 ruling: "I don't know what it is, but I know it when I see it."[42] This highly reactive, non-intellectual response was by far not the final word on the matter and may, in fact, have been the opening volley of the raging debates over the subject in the late twentieth century. Since Stewart spoke, much work has been done to clarify the much-disputed categorization of pornography, and by 1989 Linda Williams was writing: "To come to terms with pornography . . . we need to not only acknowledge the force of it, but also to get beyond merely reacting to gut responses."[43] In the complex world of psyches, epochs, and tastes, one person's pornography is another person's erotica, and, I would add, one person's erotica is another person's uneventful day of present-day television viewing, especially if it includes music-video channels.

This imprecision in terminology, as Williams claims, shows that the many working definitions of pornography reveal more about dominant power groups and their desire for censorship than about the work itself.[44] Despite the ambiguities, a number of contemporary scholars do seem to agree on a number of elements that must exist if a work is to be considered pornographic. These elements include intentions: the creator's intent to endorse, condone, or encourage degrading or abusive sexual behavior; to degrade women for male sexual entertainment and gratification; to be used for effect alone; to produce sexual feelings and actions in the consumer; to elicit the release in fantasy of a compelling impulse; to constitute the practice of cultural sadism, as well as a means of diffusing it into the mainstream of accepted behavior, and therefore into the private lives of individuals.[45]

Not one of these intentions is relevant to Ka-Tzetnik's *House of Dolls* or *Piepel*. He was not interested in entertaining or degrading or socializing or encouraging any kind of sexual behavior. He was compelled to show suffering, to expose crime, to cry out with anguish. According to Diana E. H. Russell, "[R]ealistic representations of rape with the apparent intention of helping viewers [and, I would add, readers] understand the reprehensible nature of rape, as well as the agony experienced by rape victims" are not pornography.[46] When the purpose of such material is educational, when its intention is to be informative, to reveal offenses and sadism—and this is precisely what Ka-Tzetnik claims he intended when he chose to write about his siblings' experiences—it cannot be classified as pornographic.

However, talk of sexual slavery brings out conformist reactions in some researchers and readers, as does sexual abuse, rape, and to some extent pornography in general. Suddenly decorum becomes all-important, and notions of good taste are used to silence the so-called crass voices that seem to have violated the boundaries of propriety. Describing the inner process she went through before deciding to write her book *Female Sexual Slavery*, Kathleen Barry writes:

> I was moving from fear to paralysis to hiding. It was then that I realized, both for myself personally and for all the rest of us, that the only way we can come out of hiding, break through our paralyzing defenses, is to know the full extent of sexual violence and domination of women. It is knowledge from which we have pulled back, as well knowledge that has been withheld from us.[47]

Conformist reactions set certain limitations that inhibit fully understanding what sexual violence can entail. The harsh reactions to Ka-Tzetnik's subject matter fall into the category of the conservative-moralist theory that Daniel Linz and Neil Malamuth have researched. According to them, while all approaches to pornography embody values that usually cannot be tested empirically, an idea that was implicitly expressed by Justice Stewart, "the conservative-moralist approach suggests that sexually explicit materials often attack basic societal and religious values, and the reader or viewer may become desensitized to immoral acts in general."[48] For example, Dina Porat's previously cited argument that society has a right to protect itself from such overt representations of depravity falls into the conservative-moralist approach that wants to guard others "from the disorder and moral disintegration" that are caused by individuals who are "unduly pursuing their sexual self-interests."[49]

Not only does Ka-Tzetnik's work fail to fit any of the standard and quite wide definitions of pornography, but when actually examined, his work does not even fit the conservative-moralist's definition. I have already questioned whether his most severe critics have actually read his work, and this question was not asked glibly. Upon close examination, there is not one instance of a graphic description in *House of Dolls* or *Piepel* of genitals or sexual penetration. Ka-Tzetnik uses broad strokes of language, keeping the lens of his narrative tightly focused on his characters' thoughts and not on the sexual assault of the body. During the one and only description of rape in *House of Dolls*, Daniella thinks of the similarities between her posture lying underneath a drunken German soldier and the one she previously endured in the research block where she was sterilized and lay bound in a cage.

The most detailed passage, out of a handful of sexual trespasses in the entire novel, occurs in this scene: "The face of the Neanderthal mummy is lying on her, pawing her, licking her face."[50] Is this pornography, perverse in that it shows "uncontrolled energy and [a] nihilistic impulse"?[51] For critics to say that this description is pornographic is puzzling, to say the least. In *Piepel*, the level of overt sexual explication never goes beyond: "I told you not to undress. Just let your hands do the whole job. Franzl likes that. Get him hot in all the places I told you. Then he'll go right after you."[52] This, too, is but one of a few such short descriptions in the entire 284-page novel.

Even Omer Bartov, who is able to simultaneously condemn and appreciate Ka-Tzetnik's work for its "remarkable and at times quite devastating insights into the reality of Auschwitz,"[53] and who is considered one of the few sympathetic critics, claims that "providing the details of human anatomy or sexual activity generally considered too intimate or crass for public exposure" makes the novels works of pornography, as does "lingering on instances of physical and mental abuse and torture, or any other form of inflicting bodily and psychological pain."[54] One wonders how much literature he and other critics are reading from around the world, so much of which documents physical and mental abuses and torture suffered by victims of various regimes, such as works by Alexander Solzhenitsyn, Jorge Semprún, André Philippus Brink, Ariel Dorfman, Chinua Achebe, J. M. Coetzee, and Gao Xingjian.

Denying Reality

"Often in hearing about sexual slavery," Kathleen Barry writes, "some people hide in disbelief denying its reality. When we do recognize the terrorism, we may simply put it out of our minds, not wanting to acknowledge it. Or we sometimes hide it by sitting in judgment of the victim"[55]—or of the messenger. This is what happens to Ka-Tzetnik. Criticism of his work slides quite rapidly into a critique of him as a human being. He is considered mad, outlandish, uncouth, perverse, and unreliable by Dan Michman, Avraham Amir, Dan Miron, and Dina Porat—views also held by many other scholars. The suspicion begins with his insistence on publishing under the name he acquired in

Auschwitz, though according to Jeremy Popkin "many early Holocaust testimonies were published with their authors identified only by first names or initials."[56] He said he was not trying to be coy or clever by not identifying Yehiel Dinur as the author. At the Eichmann trial he insisted Ka-Tzetnik "was not a pen name,"[57] and in a later work he wrote, "my [birth] name was burned with all the rest in the crematorium in Auschwitz."[58] Ka-Tzetnik 135633, a person from the *Katzet*, or *Konzentrationslager* (concentration camp), with a number, was born in Auschwitz in 1943, and this was the "real identity of the author."[59]

Dinur's continual use of the name Ka-Tzetnik has prompted accusations of a morbid insistence on remaining in the *univers concentrationnaire*, of not being rehabilitated, of not repressing the experience enough.[60] Dan Michman, chief historian at Yad Vashem, summarizes this discomfort as follows: "Ka-Tzetnik symbolizes the unwillingness to leave it behind and move forward. He represents the desire to remain . . . in that terrible event. To drag it on."[61] Why the use of the number of a concentration camp inmate indicates more of an unwillingness to let go of the horror than the plethora of memoirs published under individual names is unclear to me. In essence, Ka-Tzetnik is criticized for continuing to insist, like the American writer William Faulkner, that "the past is never dead. It's not even past."[62]

People want their Holocaust survivors to emerge from hell intact and with a message of hope. Ka-Tzetnik's insistence on publishing under his given "war name" is seen as proof of his instability. "He was someone who chose to be a symbol,"[63] and according to Glasner-Heled, to those who do not forgive him this insistence on bringing the past into the present, he "represents madness, and maybe is even seen as a threat both to the personal mental health of the readers and to the sanity of Israeli society."[64] When he fainted at the Eichmann trial, it was convenient for those who wanted to dismiss him to use this as further proof of his psychological instability. Yet it has been suggested that Ka-Tzetnik was among the very few witnesses at the trial who had actually met Eichmann during the war.[65] Shoshana Felman claims Ka-Tzetnik fainted when the court insisted on calling him by his surname, which "plunge[d] [him] into the abyss between different planets. On the frontier between the living and the dead, between the present and the past, he f[e]ll as though he himself were a corpse."[66]

Conclusions

Too often the world Ka-Tzetnik depicts is used to indict him, meaning that there is a supposition that anyone sane would not be so "vulgar" and "gross."

Ka-Tzetnik transgressed a literary taboo when he presented to the world that which it did not want to hear about: pedophilic rape. His exposure of sexual terrorism has caused decent people to retreat from "the emotional impact of [his works that] is so fierce that they arouse the fear of insanity."[67] This fear marks Ka-Tzetnik as insane, as a mad man, and supposedly renders him an unreliable witness. His work is thus eagerly rejected by some. Yet, as Wiesel has written, "the witness has nothing but his memory. If this is impugned, what does he have left?"[68] In contrast to those who have accused the author of fantasizing about the cruelties of the concentration camps, Yechiel Szeintuch "has determined that for the most part, what Ka-Tzetnik wrote about Auschwitz is indeed anchored in what happened to him at the camp."[69]

Ka-Tzetnik is not forgiven by many of his critics for "hammer[ing] home the idea that perversity and murder were polymorphous in the Nazi phenomenon."[70] He is often accused of repelling readers, of showing too much. But as Lynn Rapaport writes about films and the Holocaust: "Although we might want to criticize the representation of Nazi evil . . . the sad truth is that the real Nazis were much worse."[71] And what can one say about the "voyeurism" of the camera? As Etti Danzinger points out, "if you look at photos you see nakedness, you see all the skeletons, the corpses, without embellishment, with nothing that stands between, no view, no metaphor."[72] Are these photographs pornographic? Are the curators who choose to display these images perverse, crazy, or unwilling to let go of the past?

Ka-Tzetnik wrote about pedophilic rape, a topic that is generally met with public outrage—all our furies rise up to protest this most heinous act, perhaps more hateful to some extent than even the murder of children. Ka-Tzetnik wrote about the sexual terrorism waged against children, what women and men are only recently willing to talk about. Only because his siblings suffered this abuse, not Ka-Tzetnik 135633 himself, could he write about it. Shame and social censorship did not stifle him. In fact, he had the courage to broach a topic that by and large no one wants to deal with. As Alan J. Yuter puts it: "Moni's Piepeldom, like Daniella's prostitution . . . represents the novel's greatest moral indictment."[73]

There are many survivors who see the truth of their own experiences recounted in Ka-Tzetnik's writings and feel grateful for his courage to immerse himself once more in the material and record it on the pages of his books, to be their messenger. So much did they feel he spoke for them that, at the Eichmann trial, the journalist Haim Shorer pleaded with state prosecutor Gideon Hausner:

Leave aside your concluding speech and take Ka-Tzetnik's latest book *Piepel* and read it aloud to the court and its listeners and don't stop . . . All of us, all of Israel, will cry and wail without end; perhaps we could wipe away with the sea of tears the great horror, whose depth we yet [do] not know. We will cry until we faint with our dear Ka-Tzetnik, with his pure and holy book.[74]

Notes

1. Rachel Lev-Wiesel and Marianne Amir, "Holocaust Child Survivors and Child Sexual Abuse," *Journal of Child Sexual Abuse* 14, no. 2 (2005): 80.

2. Susan Brownmiller, *Against Our Will: Men, Women, and Rape* (New York: Fawcett, 1975, 1993), 38.

3. *Bereshit Rabba* 41:2; *Talmud Yerushalmi Ketubot* 7:9; *Midrash Tanchuma Lech Lecha* 8. God changed Abram's name to Abraham in Genesis 17:5, and Sarai's to Sarah in Genesis 17:15.

4. Ibid.

5. For example, in Cynthia Ozick's novella *The Shawl* (New York: Vintage, 1990), sexual abuse is alluded to and even, to some extent, denied. Evidence that she was raped includes Rosa's tepid verbal admission that she was "forced," the daughter she birthed, and her niece's acrimonious testimony. But she desists from naming the horrors of her own abuse. It is the reader's responsibility to understand that she was raped. *Wartime Lies* by Louis Begley (New York: Ballantine, 1992) tells the tale of a beautiful young Jewish woman from Poland who takes a German officer as a lover to prevent herself and her young nephew from being sent to the death camps. Before the tragic denouement of this affair, the narrator says that Tania justified herself as "the perfect, selfless aunt who became a courtesan to save her little nephew, a sort of small-town, small-scale Esther" (62). An episode in Begley's novel where Tania's vulnerability to rape is recounted is riddled with the kind of euphemisms and broad strokes I claim are endemic to these types of scenes in fiction written in the Diaspora (162). Yet Begley is not sparing in graphic detail when it comes to penning lurid descriptions of the sexual abuse of Christian women. The contrast between the descriptions of the Christian women's "gaping mouths entered by penis after penis" (129) and Tania's experience convinces one of how difficult it is for a Jewish writer in the Diaspora to face the abuse of his or her women.

6. The Palmach was the regular fighting force of the Haganah, the unofficial army of the Jewish community under the British Mandate. For the full poem in English translation, see Ronit Lentin, *Israel and the Daughters of the Shoah: Reoccupying the Territories of Silence* (New York: Berghahn Books, 2000), 207.

7. *Piepel* denoted a boy-child prostitute "in the jargon of the camps, a term apparently derived from the German provincial word for lad and *penis*" and "the Hebrew term *pipi*, used by children to denote penis . . . probably from Yiddish but common in similar forms in many other European languages." See Omer Bartov, *Mirrors of Destruction: War, Genocide, and Modern Identity* (Oxford: Oxford University Press, 2000), 187, 279, and note 94.

8. Both of these novels were originally written in Yiddish and then translated by Dinur himself into Hebrew prior to publication. For English editions, see Yehiel Dinur, *House of Dolls*, trans. Moshe M. Kohn (London: Frederick Muller, 1956), and *Piepel*, trans. Moshe M. Kohn (London: Anthony Blond, 1961).

9. Iris Milner, "The 'Gray Zone' Revisited: The Concentrationary Universe in Ka-Tzetnik's Literary Testimony," in *Jewish Social Studies: History, Culture, Society* 14, no. 2 (Winter 2008): 140.

10. Yosef Heftman, "The House of Dolls," *Haboker* (Tel Aviv), April 19, 1953, 6.

11. Ka-Tzetnik's work is not mentioned in any of these important books: Edward Alexander, *Resonance of Dust: Essays on Holocaust Literature and Jewish Fate* (Columbus: Ohio State University Press, 1979); Sidra DeKoven Ezrahi, *By Words Alone, The Holocaust in Literature* (Chicago: University of Chicago Press, 1980); Lawrence Langer, *Art from Ashes* (New York: Oxford University Press, 1995); Alan Mintz, *Hurban: Responses to Catastrophe in Hebrew Literature* (New York: Columbia University Press, 1984), Alan Rosenfeld, *A Double Dying: Reflections on Holocaust Literature* (Bloomington: Indiana University Press, 1980).

12. In 2007, Israeli filmmaker Ari Libsker made the documentary *Stalags* about the phenomenon of pulp-fiction pornographic novels popular in the 1960s, which were set mainly in prisoner-of-war and labor camps. These novels were exploitative, totally fictional entrepreneurial enterprises. Not only does Libsker conflate these novels with Ka-Tzetnik's autobiographically based fictions (even though Libsker interviewed the very writers of these pulp novels, who made no pretense of having made up all the scenes and sexual interactions), but he blames Ka-Tzetnik's novels for spurring what he deems to be a slew of "copycat" books.

13. Galia Glasner-Heled, "Reader, Writer, and Holocaust Literature: The Case of Ka-Tzetnik," in *Israel Studies* 12, no. 3 (fall 2007): 111.

14. Dinur wrote his books under the name given to him in Auschwitz. The name "Dinur" reflects another postwar identity as well. The author was born Yehiel Feiner and, once in Israel, changed his last name. *Dinur* means fire in Aramaic, but it "may also be associated with the Hebrew word *din*, which can mean trial, justice, and punishment, especially with the Di-nur River mentioned in the Book of Daniel and interpreted by the *Kabbalah* as 'a river of fire in the upper reaches of hell that descends upon the evil after their death to purify them.'" Bartov, *Mirrors of Destruction*, 186.

15. Whether Dinur had a brother and sister that were in the camps is controversial. According to his later writings, Daniella, the protagonist of *House of Dolls*, was based on his twin sister's experience.

16. Glasner-Heled, "Reader, Writer, and Holocaust Literature," 127.

17. Ibid., 125.

18. Some views offered by Omer Bartov, Tom Segev, Dvir Abramovich, Ephraim Sicher, Sidra DeKoven Ezrahi, Rina Dudai, Irving Halperin, and Dan Miron, among others.

19. Theodor Adorno, *Negative Dialectics*, trans. E. B. Ashton (New York: Continuum, 1999), 362–363.

20. Glasner-Heled, "Reader, Writer, and Holocaust Literature," 121.

21. Sarah Bradford, *Harriet Tubman, the Moses of her People* (New York: Corinth, 1961), 33.

22. Ka-Tzetnik 135633, *Shivitti: A Vision*, trans. Eliyahu Nike de-Nur and Lisa Herman (San Francisco: Harper and Row, 1989), 71.

23. Jeremy D. Popkin, "Ka-Tzetnik 135633: The Survivor as Pseudonym," *New Literary History* 33 (2002): 345.

24. Trial of Adolf Eichmann, session 68, Jerusalem, June 7, 1961, http://www.nizkor.org/hweb/people/e/eichmann-adolf/transcripts/Sessions/Session-068-01.html (accessed March 22, 2010).

25. Dvir Abramovich, "The Holocaust World of Yechiel Fajner," *Nebula* 4, no. 3 (September 2007): 32.

26. Glasner-Heled, "Reader, Writer, and Holocaust Literature," 124.

27. Ibid., 117.

28. Ibid.

29. Ibid.

30. I am not alone in this view. Malka Tor, historian, teacher, and head of the Oral Testimonies Department at Yad Vashem also has "reservations about applying the techniques of literary criticism to Ka-Tzetnik's work," as does Columbus, a literary scholar, teacher, and coordinator of literature teaching in the Israel Ministry of Education's religious sector, who stated: "[T]here are some things that cannot be judged according to the usual literary criteria." Glasner-Heled, "Reader, Writer, and Holocaust Literature," 116.

31. Bartov, *Mirrors of Destruction*, 197.

32. Adorno, *Negative Dialectics*, 362–363.

33. Halperin, *Messengers from the Dead: Literature of the Holocaust* (Philadelphia: Westminster Press, 1970), 109.

34. Abramovich, "Holocaust World of Yechiel Fajner," 34.

35. Frank Stiffel, *The Tale of the Ring: A Kaddish. A Personal Memoir of the Holocaust* (Wainscott, NY: Pushcart Press, 1984), 172.

36. Elie Wiesel, *The Night Trilogy* (New York: Noonday Press, 1987), 56.

37. Harriet Jacobs, "Incidents in the Life of a Slave Girl," in *Slave Narratives* (New York: Library of America, 2000).

38. Elizabeth D. Heineman, "Sexuality and Nazism: The Doubly Unspeakable?" *Journal of the History of Sexuality* 46 (January–April 2002): 54–55.

39. Ephraim Sicher, *The Holocaust Novel* (London: Routledge, 2005), 46.

40. Susan Sontag, "Notes on Camp," in *Against Interpretation* (New York: Delta, 1966), 276.

41. Diana E. H. Russell, *Dangerous Relationships: Pornography, Misogyny, and Rape* (London: Sage, 1998), 6.

42. *Nico Jacobellis v. Ohio*, 378 U.S. 184 (1964), http://laws.findlaw.com/us/378/184.html (accessed March 22, 2010).

43. Linda Williams, *Hard Core: Power, Pleasure, and the "Frenzy of the Visible"* (Berkeley: University of California Press, 1989), 5.

44. Ibid., 12.

45. These criteria are found in the work of Linda Williams, Kathleen Barry, Daniel Linz, Neil Malamuth, Diana E. H. Russell, and Lynn Rapaport.

46. Russell, *Dangerous Relationships*, 5.

47. Kathleen Barry, *Female Sexual Slavery* (New York: New York University Press, 1979), 5.

48. Daniel Linz and Neil Malamuth, *Pornography* (London: Sage, 1993), 5.

49. Ibid., 8.

50. Dinur, *House of Dolls*, 182–183.

51. Bartov, *Mirrors of Destruction*, 189.

52. Dinur, *Piepel*, 27.

53. Bartov, *Mirrors of Destruction*, 188.

54. Ibid., 190.

55. Barry, *Female Sexual Slavery*, 11.

56. Popkin, "Ka-Tzetnik 135633," 345.

57. Trial of Adolf Eichmann, session 68, Jerusalem, June 7, 1961.

58. Ka-Tzetnik, *Kaddish* (New York: Algemeiner, 1998), 152.

59. Popkin, "Ka-Tzetnik 135633," 347.

60. David Rousset, *The Other Kingdom*, trans. Ramon Guthrie (New York: Howard Fertig, 1982), 54.

61. Glasner-Heled, "Reader, Writer, and Holocaust Literature," 123.

62. William Faulkner, *Requiem for a Nun*, (New York: Random House, 1951), 92.

63. Glasner-Heled, "Reader, Writer, and Holocaust Literature," 123.

64. Ibid., 124.

65. Coming face to face with his former torturer could, of course, explain why he was overcome with emotion at the trial. Unfortunately, there were a number of people, including Hannah Arendt, who viewed Ka-Tzetnik's fainting as an indication of vanity and instability. See Hannah Arendt, *Eichmann in Jerusalem: A Report on the Banality of Evil* (New York: Penguin, 1994), 224.

66. Shoshana Felman, *The Juridical Unconscious: Trials and Traumas in the Twentieth Century* (Cambridge: Harvard University Press, 2002), 149.

67. Glasner-Heled, "Reader, Writer, and Holocaust Literature," 128.

68. Elie Wiesel, *All Rivers Run to the Sea* (London: Harper Collins, 1997), 336.

69. Tom Segev, "Who were you, Karl Zetinski?" *Ha'aretz*, July 27, 2001, http://www.haaretz.com/hasen/pages/ShArt.jhtml?itemNo=56837&sw=Holocaust (accessed March 23, 2010).

70. Abramovich, "Holocaust World of Yechiel Fajner," 29.

71. Lynn Rapaport, "Holocaust Pornography: Profaning the Sacred in *Ilsa, She-Wolf of the SS*," *Shofar* 22, no. 1 (2003): 78.

72. Glasner-Heled, "Reader, Writer, and Holocaust Literature," 116.

73. Alan J. Yuter, *The Holocaust in Hebrew Literature: From Genocide to Rebirth* (Port Washington, NY: Associated Faulty Press, 1983), 12.

74. Abramovich, "Holocaust World of Yechiel Fajner," 28.

13

Nava Semel's And the Rat Laughed

A Tale of Sexual Violation

SONJA M. HEDGEPETH AND ROCHELLE G. SAIDEL

The Israeli writer Nava Semel boldly places the issue of sexual abuse during the Holocaust at the core of her multidimensional novel *And the Rat Laughed*. Originally in Hebrew, it is now available in English translation.[1] Semel takes the reader underground, into cyberspace, and to future intergalactic space to tell the story of a small Jewish girl hidden in a pit on a Polish farm and the sexual violence repeatedly committed against her there. Entering the black hole of time and crossing boundaries separating generations from one another, the author unlocks the psyche of the adult survivor who was sexually abused as a child, as well as that of her rescuer. Semel also reveals the complexity and challenges of remembering such a story.

A Child of Holocaust Survivors

Before she wrote *And the Rat Laughed*, Nava Semel wrote a short story that dealt with sexual abuse, "A Hat of Glass." In the beginning, as a child of Holocaust survivors, she was afraid that her writing might wound her parents. However, she simply had to "follow the instructions of her characters." She wrote "fact that is wrapped in fiction," which is what her mother needed. Much to the author's surprise, her father was very positive and supportive and her mother seemed happy about her work. Semel did not know that she was writing about the "second generation" (children of Holocaust survivors) at the time—in the 1980s this term did not exist.[2] She at first thought that she was simply writing stories about turning points in lives, but she later realized that as part of the second generation she was facing issues in her writing before doing so in her own life. And she began to see that, beyond the personal implications of "A Hat of Glass," the events in the story—the tale of a Jewish woman used as a sex slave and the role she then played in a small, all-but-forgotten forced labor camp on the German–Polish border—could become part of the record of events surrounding the Holocaust.[3]

Semel's story, while fiction, comes from her own mother's recollections. Margalit Artzi, her mother, never spoke about the Holocaust while Nava and her brother Shlomo were growing up.[4] Some of what had been shrouded in silence about her mother's past didn't emerge until Semel was about to be married. Her wedding dress, draped over a chair, compelled her mother to go to a cupboard, as if in a trance, and retrieve a photo of herself in a wedding dress with a man that was not Nava's father. Only at age twenty-two did Nava find out that her mother had had another husband and a baby before the Holocaust. As a child, she had known so little about her mother's past that she thought her mother had been born in a land called "Auschwitz." Nothing of the past was mentioned at home to ensure that this evil spirit, mentioned only in the code word "Auschwitz," would not be brought into their house.

However, "A Hat of Glass" is her mother's own story, which she only told "over Nava's head" when her daughter was seventeen. On *Yom Hashoah* (Holocaust Remembrance Day), Nava was with her boyfriend, and her mother talked to him, rather than to her. The young man, who had never met a Holocaust survivor, became the recipient of the story of Margalit's last month in a camp in Klein Schönau. Semel thinks that perhaps the Israeli army uniform her boyfriend was wearing compelled her mother to speak.

While telling her story, Margalit Artzi never made eye contact with Semel. Her mother related that she was saved by a *Kapo* (supervising prisoner), a beautiful German-Jewish woman who told the other camp inmates that she had been a *Fronthure* (a prostitute for Nazi troops at the front, sometimes called a *Feldhure*, a field prostitute). The Nazis had put this former "front whore" in charge of the other prisoners, thinking she would be sadistic, "but she was noble and vowed to bring her people through the war."[5]

"A Hat of Glass"

Nava Semel first presented the subject of sexual exploitation during the Holocaust in "A Hat of Glass." The story is told by a nameless survivor, who narrates her experiences in a forced labor camp. She recalls a *Kapo* named Clarissa, who had wanted to move to pre-Israel Palestine after the war.[6] The survivor wonders if she will ever see this *Kapo* in Tel Aviv, where she is living. Intertwined with the narrator's memories of the past and thoughts of the present is the story of the *Kapo* Clarissa and her role as a sex slave for the Nazis. Another inmate states that Clarissa had been a *Fronthure* before coming to their camp:

> A broad-framed woman, she wore a prisoner's uniform like the rest of us but she was different . . . Janine the Frenchwoman, whose pallet was next to mine, said: "This Clarissa was a 'Fronthüre' [sic]." . . . I tell my children that she was a whore sent to the front more than three years earlier as a diversion for the soldiers.[7]

The *Kapo* in Nava Semel's short story is Jewish and uses her influence to help the women prisoners, such as giving medication to the narrator when she is burning with fever and having her dismissed from *Appell* (roll call) because she is too weak to stand. In the story, the *Kapo's* influence is achieved through her lesbian relationship with Brünnhilde, a Nazi guard:

> Late one night, the door came open quietly. Clarissa got up and walked towards it, treading very carefully, as though on sizzling embers . . . I could make out the shadow of the golden-haired officer . . . As soon as Clarissa crossed the threshold, the officer turned on her heel, and Clarissa followed. The door closed silently, as though it had never moved. I fastened my head to the hardness of the pallet, and as I turned back, I found Janine's eyes, like a cat's slicing through me in the darkness. I turned away.
>
> Other times she would be gone all night. We knew well enough where she slept those nights. Nestling in the embrace of the woman officer, her gateway to the world.[8]

The reader wonders whether the relationship is really one of mutual consent, or whether Clarissa agrees to go to the Nazi woman's bed because she is commanded to do so. Or is this the price that the *Kapo* is willing to pay in order to protect the other women in her barrack? Clarissa's predicament is not simple, and the narrator is concerned about the sexual role her compassionate *Kapo* plays in the relationship with their Nazi overseer:

> One night I awoke and found that Clarissa had returned to her cot from the hidden room. But instead of stretching out, she was sitting there like a statue in whom life had frozen, staring out into the darkness . . .
>
> "Clarissa," I spoke softly, "What does she do to you?" Suddenly her face contorted with a pain so intense that I recoiled. She turned her head slowly, as though a key had been inserted in her back and said dryly:
>
> "She doesn't do me any harm." Then she touched my head. "You're so young," she said.

"Why, I almost had a child, and my youth is gone."
"You'll have other children." She touched my forehead. "I never will."[9]

This lesbian relationship between Clarissa and the Nazi guard is part of what Semel's mother had related in her story about the forced labor camp. In "A Hat of Glass," the narrator's past reflects that of the author's own mother.

After the publication of "A Hat of Glass," Semel thought that if the real-life Clarissa had indeed survived the war and come to Israel as she had planned, she might see her short story. She waited for years for the real Clarissa's phone call, which never came. Nava's mother, whom the author describes as a "rationalist," said the following: "When she vanished, I thought that she was from another world and was sent to save us." This was the only time that Nava remembers her mother as being "mystical." Her mother thought that "Clarissa" had probably committed suicide, perhaps because she couldn't bear that her Nazi partner was turned in, as one learns from the short story. Here, when the Nazi guard tries to disguise herself as one of the camp prisoners to avoid detection by the conquering Russian army, Clarissa quietly urges the narrator to point Brünnhilde out to their liberators, hesitating to turn in the Nazi guard herself. The French prisoner, Janine, gladly points her out to the Russian soldiers, who take Brünnhilde out of the ranks of the camp prisoners and shoot her.

In giving the Kapo in "A Hat of Glass" what might seem to be an unbelievable past as a Fronthure or Feldhure, Nava Semel challenges a general consensus that Jewish women were not used as forced sex laborers during the Holocaust. Although they were probably not knowingly used for supervised official camp brothels for Nazis and "privileged" prisoners, there is testimony that that they were used unofficially, and then most were murdered on the front or in the field.[10] Other Holocaust literature depicting characters of Jewish women as sex slaves for the Nazis includes Ka-Tzetnik's *House of Dolls*, Arnošt Lustig's *Lovely Green Eyes*, and Yoram Kaniuk's *Commander of the Exodus*.[11] Considering the factual basis of forced sex labor, one can argue that these authors did not seek simply to sensationalize the past by including the character of a Jewish forced sex slave in their fiction.

Representations of this figure have certainly appeared in various permutations—and have been met with resistance. For example, the authenticity of the photograph taken by Paul Goldman in Israel in 1945 of an anonymous Auschwitz survivor, whose face is not seen, showing only her chest with the tattoo "Feld-Hure" followed by her number has been questioned by some. The archivist of Goldman's photographs had to defend its veracity, as when a guest on an Israeli talk television program suggested that it was a fake: "'How dare he,' [David] Rubinger thunders into the phone in his office. 'Listen, I have the negative right here. The negative! How could anyone suggest that Goldman faked anything?!'"[12] In this case, even seeing and believing were not enough—suspicion of an altered picture of the past persists.

The Genesis of *And the Rat Laughed*

After Nava Semel had boldly addressed the question of *Kapos* and lesbian sexual abuse in "A Hat of Glass," she went on to write about an even darker subject, the story of a sexually violated hidden girl. The trigger for Semel's decision to write her novel *And the Rat Laughed* was a gathering in New York in the late 1980s of Holocaust survivors who had been hidden as children.[13] At that meeting, she heard accounts by the hidden children, and a voice in her head told her that someone should write on their behalf. At the time, she was not yet aware that she would be the person to do the job.

Semel began to collect the hidden children's stories to take them out of the "cemented pit where memory is locked." Drawing from the people she had heard tell their stories at the New York gathering, Semel the novelist presented her main character as a seemingly normal and successful adult Holocaust survivor, despite an inner memory of childhood trauma. In so doing, she set the stage to explore uncharted but very real territory in survivors' lives. A former hidden child wrote of the difficulty in dealing with this Holocaust experience as an adult: "Normal people! We became obsessed with what the life of normal people felt like . . . Some of us even tamed our memories to tame the rage at all cost. After all, how to live a 'normal' life with inappropriate memories?"[14] The novelist would give her protagonist the most extreme fate possible, that of being raped as a little Jewish girl hidden in a pit, in order to examine what enabled the child to overcome her fictional biography.

The effects of Semel's character's memories on her own daughter and granddaughter in the novel, and on the readers who bear witness by proxy, all interconnect in *And the Rat Laughed*. As a writer, Semel says, she was compelled to conjure up a horrific past that is present as an undercurrent of contemporary Jewish life in general, and of Israeli society in particular. For Semel, "Memory is alive, [like] a live animal banging at my door."[15]

Semel's father, Itzhak Artzi, a survivor from Romania, started gathering orphans who had been hidden in Transnistria in 1944. It was her father who gave Nava "her first baton for the relay race," and told her to do volunteer work, which she has been doing for many years at Massuah, an institute dedicated to the study of the Holocaust that specializes in educational activities for young people and teachers in Israel and abroad. When Semel began writing her novel, she remembered the relay race and envisioned one character handing the story over to another character. Among the many elements, fragments, appendages, and associations the author uses to fuse her story is the rat that never appears, lurking always in the background but central to the novel. The grandmother disguises her story as a legend featuring the rat, the only creature that had shown her any affection in the pit. She tells of a legend about a rat that wanted to laugh like humans, but God would give him this gift only if he could get another creature to laugh with him beneath the ground:

> The rat tried everything he could to make her laugh. He hopped around in the pit, he crawled out of the tunnel, he climbed back in, he sniffed at her smooth skin covering, he ate out of her hand, and she almost laughed, till the rat was convinced that pretty soon he'd succeed in laughing along with her. That's how he figured he'd prove to God that promises should always be kept.[16]

With this legend, the grandmother is able to push memory into the future, much like memory is conveyed embedded in a folktale or *midrash*, a particular way of interpreting or reading a biblical verse. Something happened in the pit, but the secret is buried in the tale that future generations have to ferret out and interpret for themselves. Like other survivors of sexual abuse, Nava Semel's protagonist will never speak of it. Only on a symbolic level will she tell her granddaughter, because otherwise "the house will be crushed." Yet the grandmother also knows that if she says nothing, provides no information about what happened to her, people may say that she never existed, her story never occurred, and everything will be erased from memory. Nevertheless, she doesn't want to destroy her own house. If she tells, she will no longer have the persona of mother or grandmother.

Re-membering the Past

When Nava Semel began to write *And the Rat Laughed*, she thought she was writing a children's book, but as she kept "raising the bar," something quite different emerged. In her novel, the author pushes at the limits of possible discourse about the Holocaust and demands that readers consider the issue of rape. She told us: "The fact that women were raped is ignored. They were prey.

All that is left as a child is your body and that is destroyed, too. Even with this she [the protagonist] still survived, still had a reason to live in this world. This salutes the survivors."[17] Holocaust survivors today might be perceived as old, poor, sick, or in need of social welfare, but with her book, Semel wanted to illustrate their courage and resilience.

As in "A Hat of Glass," the nameless female protagonist of *And the Rat Laughed* is a sixty-year-old grandmother who has a twelve-year-old granddaughter. The granddaughter, now the third generation after the Holocaust, is interviewing the grandmother for a school project but is disappointed because her notebook remains empty. What her grandmother tells her seems all mixed up, making no sense to her. The granddaughter complains to her teacher: "I was even more upset that my mother never bothered to find out all these details when Grandma was much younger and her brain was much sharper, because then I might at least have been able to hear the story from my mother—organized and clear, with a beginning, a middle and an end."[18] The intergenerational conflict portrayed in the novel, the fact that the second generation did not hear their parents' Holocaust stories, and thus could not retell them to their own children, reveals a rupture in the family narrative of survivors and their descendants. According to one analysis, "The conflicts of the survivors of trauma between the wish to forget and need to tell their stories interface and correspond to their children's conflicted wishes to know the unspoken stories and feeling that they are too dangerous to know."[19]

The main character in Semel's book cannot tell her story to her daughter, but makes the attempt to relate to her granddaughter at least some of it in bits and pieces, even if in an incoherent way. Hadas Wiseman and Jacques Barber identify such "conflicts between talk and silence," citing from Nava Semel's novel to illustrate their point:

> . . . [the idea] that the "toxic" elements in the survivors' unbearable stories may affect their children and, therefore, endanger the continuation of the family is a strong one. The grandchildren indeed are often perceived as the proof for the ability to overcome this danger. Not only did the survivors bear healthy children but these children in turn continued the chain of the generations.[20]

The second generation had an especially difficult burden to bear. Semel says that children of survivors knew they had to be "the curtain between their parents and their past," and that children of the 1950s are "the mother and father of their parents." Yossi Hadar's remarks at a 1988 Israeli conference corroborate Nava's insights about her generation growing up in Israel:

Dr. Hadar stood up in the audience and said that his parents' generation and all the previous generations had lived in a world without the Shoah; then came the shock of experiencing it with its great losses.

However, the second generation who were not there, are directly affected all the time, because from the day they were born and every day since they have lived in a world of Holocaust, with all its associated myths and taboos.[21]

In the novel, the daughter has no role to play in remembering her mother's past. Semel left her out, because "[s]urvivors of sexual abuse will not talk about it to anyone, only on a symbolic level to their grandchildren—otherwise the house will be crushed." Here, the link to the grandmother's past, no matter how weak, is through the granddaughter. Anna Reading has remarked on the importance of "(grand)mothers" as conveyors of family history:

> It is not that mothers and grandmothers essentially have authoritative interpretative roles to play in the early construction of Holocaust memory, but that their place and role with the community and their living memory of the past means they are more likely to be in a position to have acted as a memory bridge for younger people.[22]

In *And the Rat Laughed*, the intergenerational link is weak, if not broken, and only the completion of a homework assignment given in an Israeli school, the memory work of the third generation, can possibly mend this fracture. The story is one that no one wants to hear: "It's not," as the grandmother remarks, "one of those stories that audiences love."[23] In fact, the grandmother doesn't even want her story to be revealed: "Deep inside, the old woman is hoping for a hostile reaction that will wipe out the story once and for all." If her granddaughter simply dismisses the past and gives up on trying to find out what happened, or if we as readers simply put down the book and say to ourselves that no such thing could ever have happened to a child, then the grandmother can also continue to suppress her own childhood memories of the Holocaust. However, the granddaughter presses forward, although she has nothing on paper to show for her interview with her grandmother. In speaking with her teacher at school, she continues to try to puzzle out her grandmother's past, though she misconstrues the facts, as a twelve-year-old may very well do:

> I tried every way I know. I asked the simplest things, but it didn't work. Because if the story is stuck, how am I supposed to know how to get it free? . . . because even though my grandmother really was in the Holocaust, I'm not sure it counts, because she was a little girl and she didn't go through any of the big, horrifying things we learn about in history or read about or see in the movies . . . But me, all

I've managed to get out of her was that they hid her with a couple of farmers in some small village. She couldn't even remember its name because she was so little then, and considering that she can't say anything about a ghetto or about concentration camps, her story doesn't add up to much.[24]

Even the granddaughter cannot break through the silence to find out about her grandmother's rape as a child. Only the grandmother's inner monologue tells the truth about the survival of "the little-girl-who-once-was," her only name in the novel. The granddaughter assumes that the farmers must have been kind to her grandmother and made a nice room for her, with toys and her clothes, in the potato pit where she was hidden. As she doesn't know that they were actually her grandmother's tormentors, she considers finding out their names and nominating them to be honored as rescuers by Yad Vashem, the Holocaust Martyrs' and Heroes' Remembrance Authority in Israel. Semel drives home the point that the imagination of subsequent generations about survival during the Holocaust, as well as those preconceived notions of readers and perceptions in general, can effectively block important, if seemingly small, events from surfacing. The sexual abuse of a child in hiding is certainly not insignificant, even if it is misunderstood, even if it is what no one wants to talk about or wants to hear.

Jewish Girls Violated while in Hiding

Jewish children were hidden more often in urban areas of Poland than on farms in the countryside because relationships between Jews and Poles were closer in larger towns and cities. Though many children were also hidden in the countryside, there were added difficulties, as Nahum Bogner describes:

> Given the Germans' lax control in the villages and the sheer size of rural Poland, more Jews could have found refuge there if not for the ingrained antisemitism in most of the villages . . . There were indeed peasants who took Jews into their homes and saved them, in some cases paying with their lives for their kindness. The Germans usually found out about such cases from neighbors of the rescuers . . . In general, though, the attitude of most of the peasants toward the Jewish fugitives ranged from indifference to hostility.[25]

It was much easier for girls to hide than for boys, as Jewish boys could not hide their circumcision and children sometimes engaged in a type of "sex game" with each other to expose a boy's genitals to reveal whether or not he was a

Jew: "Eros was not absent from the intimate way of life in the villages, and sex games among children in the pastures were commonplace."[26]

In *And the Rat Laughed*, the peasants' son, Stefan, makes frequent visits to the potato pit to rape the small girl, acts undertaken with his parents' knowledge, as one later learns from the diary of the village priest. The priest feels that he has become culpable in the crime being committed against the child, because he has heard Stefan's confession and has forgiven all of the young man's sins, though the perpetrator had not mentioned his gravest transgression. The silence remains profound. Even in the confessional, the sin of rape is not heard; the sin is one of omission, as if merely an "oversight." The priest reflects:

> A girl-child. He never mentioned her. What he did to her in the dark was with the knowledge of his father and mother. Perhaps he bought their silence. Do not forgive me Father for my sinful thoughts . . . They pushed this little girl along the path to her death, wrenching her away from her mother and father, and from everyone who loved her. I cannot fight off this despair. Tonight I will be the message-bearer.[27]

The "little-girl-that-was" did not understand why her mother and father did not come to rescue her from "the Stefan," as she has named her tormentor. As a five-year-old, she doesn't understand that they may no longer be alive. Even as an adult, she still waits for them to contact her. The little girl's torture at the hands of the peasants' son is condoned by his parents because they are no longer receiving payment for hiding her. As incredible as it may seem that a little girl being hidden from the Nazis could be raped, there is testimony regarding such incidents. Possibly one of the most terrible accounts is that of "Anne," who went to live in Australia after the war. In an interview with psychotherapist Paul Valent, she tells about her humiliation, degradation, and violation as she was hidden in different homes in France between the ages of four and eight. She was raped in various households that hid her, but she didn't even know what to call what had happened to her. She recounts:

> In addition to the usual couple and an old woman, there was a younger man in this family. He was big, and was always friendly and laughing.
>
> I liked the fact that he took notice of me, while the others hated me . . . Then at nights he took my singlet [undershirt] off and brushed himself against me. And he took my pants off. I did not think there was harm in that . . .
>
> But, I don't know, he had no clothes on, and I had never been near anyone naked. I did not like the feel . . . I do not know how he did not squash me to

death. I came to hate the whole thing, him . . . And he . . . wanted me to play with him, his penis, and every part of him . . .

I remember saying something to the lady about him squashing me. She yelled and screamed at me. She called me a liar, and said she would punish me by putting me in the oven. She took me to the oven, opened it, lifted me, and I thought I was going into the roaring fire . . . Sometimes I wished that she had put me in there . . . because now it meant that this man would continue as before. And he did.[28]

Anne was between four and five years old when this occurred. Placed in another household, she was raped again:

He was a big person. I can see him, me, the room, the surroundings. He was determined to penetrate me, and he did. I certainly wanted to die then . . . I still did not think there was anything wrong in what was done. No one told me it was wrong. As a child, you have to be told something is wrong, otherwise it is not wrong.[29]

Anne told Valent she was raped over and over again. In one household, a man even used to urinate in her mouth. She says of her memories of sexual abuse as a Jewish child in hiding: "I would like to think that what is in my head is not true, I would love it if someone could say that some of it is wrong, that I imagined or read it, it is someone else's story."[30] The fictional grandmother in *And the Rat Laughed* may not wish to tell her story, but the real-life Anne does. Unlike the grandmother in Semel's novel, Anne chooses to tell her story to a psychotherapist so that her family would finally know about her past.

Rescue in *And the Rat Laughed*

In Nava Semel's novel, one adult does take notice of the girl's plight and helps her. Stanislaw, the village priest, finally becomes aware of the child's torture and buys her from the farmers, giving them church ceremonial ornaments as payment. He hopes that they will not reveal the secret to the other villagers, who would gladly turn the girl over to the Nazis. The girl's story and slow recovery from her ordeal in the pit is at this point told from the priest's perspective in diary entries that document his feelings and fears in hiding her. To coax the girl back to life, he pretends to be a rat, imitating the rat that she had befriended in the pit, the only creature she trusted. In the process of rehabilitating the girl and ensuring her safety, the priest loses his own faith.

Here Semel heightens the tension between hiding and discovery, since the child is hidden almost out in the open, in the church and the rectory, instinctively knowing when to melt into the shadows and when to be quiet.

Debórah Dwork has pointed out the great psychological difficulty for the children: "Children in hiding and hidden were burdened with terrible isolation and deprivation. Their lot was to live as if they were not living, to exist without a trace."[31] She adds that this "unnatural situation preclude[d] a healthy relationship between hider and hidden, [and] reinforced the prevailing ethos that to be a Jew was despicable and dangerous."[32]

Toward the end of Semel's novel, we find out that the priest himself was shunned as a child. He was born out of wedlock, "conceived in sin," and for this was rejected by his community. To be an unwanted child is an experience he shares with the little girl. He says that he will be the child's "rememberer," becoming her "Stash," who is kind to her like the rat that shared her pit. As he turns the girl over to a soldier of the liberating Russian army, who is a Jew, he renounces his own religion, saying:

> "The Jewish officer followed me to the churchyard and waited at the gate. I took the little girl to him.
> Don't be afraid. This man is your brother.
> She clutched at the edge of my robe, started tugging at my body.
> Make him leave, she cried . . .
> I knelt before her. I said: I am a Jew too. Forever a Jew.
> Frantically she [the girl] kissed the cross around her neck. I removed my own and put it on the ground . . .
> The officer said: The Zionists are going through the orphanages now. Go hand over the girl.[33]

This child, who came back to life, who had been protected among the icons in a Catholic church, does not want to go into the unknown, to a faith and people that she does not know anything about. Her experience mirrors that of many Jewish children in hiding, who learned to closely identify with their Christian surroundings. According to Nahum Bogner: "Most children, and the girls in particular, adopted the Christian way of life enthusiastically. They were charmed by the church ritual and by the stories of the saints, which they took to their hearts."[34] And, as in Semel's novel, the process of finding Jewish orphans was undertaken in order to return them to their families or Jewish organizations: "The first stage in tracking down the children was inevitably individual and impromptu. Within a short time, however, the situation changed.

In several liberated areas, groups of survivors began to act in order to locate and gather together Jewish children in villages in the vicinity."[35]

Reconciling the Past and the Future

Semel gives the grandmother, the "little-girl-who-once-was," a sophisticated way to keep her life and family intact, by pushing memory into the future. Her granddaughter only has the legend of the rat's search for laughter to record in her notebook. Everything else remains hidden behind this tale of the rat. For Nava Semel, the rat is a metaphor of memory, and the author has come to understand that people's memories change to protect them.[36] Semel's plot leaps through time, between present, past, and future, to piece together fragments of the memories and thoughts of her characters, human and animal, to "re-member" what can be related and mended only with great emotional difficulty.

Haim Dasberg has said about remembering the Holocaust that "[t]here are no observers, only participants. We are all either second-generation or first-generation or bystanders who are never innocent, or admirers of heroes, for instance, or accusers of the weak, for instance. We feel either guilty or unavenged, or have other claims."[37] Similarly, Nava Semel activates and involves her readers, making them feel that everyone has a stake in knowing the story of the girl in hiding—that one didn't have to be there to care. She allows for additional voices, those of a third generation and generations into a hundred years in the future to blend with the narrative, thus creating new and somewhat different accounts and perspectives.

In the novel, the narrative that the grandmother cannot really disclose to her granddaughter in Tel Aviv in 1999 makes its way onto the Internet, and poetry about the hidden girl begins to appear: "Listen, Cookie, last night I hit on this site—really weird, horrible, disgusting—you've got to check it out. The poems are totally crazy . . . I was surfing house-pet sites . . . and I tried to figure out who was behind the little girl and the rat, but I couldn't."[38] We cannot be sure who has introduced the story on the Web, but the grandmother has been learning how to use the computer and is becoming "Internet savvy." Maybe the granddaughter's teacher wrote the poems? Or the granddaughter and her classmates wrote them? There are many turns of the plot that intentionally elude precise interpretations by readers, and Semel contends that hers is an open text. An explanation by the author herself is not more valid than that made by anyone else, and she says she doesn't know more than others, "especially anyone who was writing in 1999," she adds with a sly grin.

In the novel, there is much Web activity after 1999 as Internet users seek to deconstruct the tale about the girl and the rat, and interest remains active a full century later. In the year 2099, a female anthropologist from the future, Y-mee Prana K-0005275–149, is trying to reconstruct the story of the girl and the rat by means of a REMaker, a dream machine, belonging to "Stash," the director of the Pan-Euro Anthropological Institute, who coincidentally bears the name that the girl used to call Father Stanislaw, her rescuer. This "Stash," however is not helpful in providing Y-mee with access to information, so she has had to break into his dreams to steal information necessary to voyage to other places to collect more information. The story has by this point undergone many permutations, and by 2099, "Girl & Rat" has become a popular myth in many countries, prompting even the Disney Studios to turn Mickey Mouse into "Mickey Rat." But Y-mee has a difficult time figuring out the meaning of "the Stefan" and his relationship to the story. She asks:

> Who is the Stefan . . . Are there many more Stefans?
>
> I'll spare you the polemic about the Holocaust . . . A large part of the sub-memoryfolder is devoted to question marks, casting doubt on the many testimonies within. Most of the films are presented as reenactments, and many of the documents as forgeries or misrepresentations. With the gradual disappearance of the survivors and the dwindling of the *Remembearers*, the controversy surrounding the authenticity of these testimonies has died down.[39]

According to Nava Semel, when *And the Rat Laughed* appeared in Hebrew in 2001, the futuristic part of the novel was rather controversial because some readers in Israel saw it as making a connection between science fiction and the Holocaust. However, it was popular among young readers. The novel has also been translated into German, and the author said that the controversy about the book in Germany was that generations should not have to remember so far into the future.

Conclusions

The opera *And the Rat Laughed* had its world premiere in 2005 at the Cameri Theater in Tel Aviv.[40] Composer Ella Milch-Sheriff, together with Nava Semel, added voice and music to stage the story about the hidden girl. Milch-Sheriff, also part of the second generation, purposely wanted to blend beautiful music with the story's brutality. When the opera was staged in Warsaw, Poland, it was very well received, though one audience member commented that the Cameri

Theater should come again—but not with such an "anti-Polish" production.[41] As this and other reactions to Nava Semel's work have shown, it is still difficult to reconcile the past with the present. Yet her writing encourages us to work toward the future so the past will be properly remembered.

People in the future may forget what happened during the Holocaust, and there is danger that the perpetrator may be recast as the victim. The Holocaust survivors may be forgotten, and whether or not they ever existed may not matter in 2099 unless a daring renegade anthropologist, such as Semel's Y-mee, tries to find out the truth. Semel cleverly uses the broken continuity of the legend of the girl and the rat in the future to show us today that we have not fully accepted or understood the past. We must become better listeners and "Remembearers" of the stories that survivors tell about the Holocaust. We are invited to become part of a bridge between the past and the future, listeners who, with the aid of technological innovations and our creative minds, can record and document stories, revealing a more permanent and true account for future generations. The past and the future may be reconciled through our memories.

With her dynamic and innovative novel *And the Rat Laughed*, Israeli author Nava Semel challenges us to search for the truth that has strangely been relegated to the realm of silence. She encourages us to pay close attention to the most nuanced details so that we may discover and approach the past with more precision and depth, accepting that the fantastic may indeed be fact, not fiction. Beyond this, Nava Semel's writings are an essential tool for promoting a growing awareness and willingness to include, discuss, and accept rape and forced prostitution as aspects of women's Holocaust experience.

Notes

1. Nava Semel's novel was originally published in Hebrew as *Tsehok shel Akhbarosh* [The rat's laughter] (Tel Aviv: Yediot Aharonot, 2001). The English publication is Nava Semel, *And the Rat Laughed*, trans. Miriam Shlesinger (Melbourne: Hybrid Publishers, 2008.) The cadence of the English-language title reminded the author of a line in a Yiddish song, "*az der Rebbe lacht*" (when the rabbi laughs).

2. Background information and quotes by Nava Semel about her writing process are taken from an interview she gave to co-authors Sonja Hedgepeth and Rochelle Saidel on July 4, 2008, in Tel Aviv.

3. Semel, interview, July 4, 2008. Semel recalled how her mother had drawn a map for her before she went to see the former camp site at Zittau/Klein Schönau in 1988. When Semel arrived, she found the compound had been turned into a mental institution. Her mother's map was exact, and Semel found the hangar, which had simply been closed. She even found the crematorium. Semel said that "the blocked tunnels were

like a time machine to 1945." Only through her book did anyone come to know about the place—there was no plaque marking it as a former Nazi labor camp.

4. Nava Semel, interview, July 4, 2008. For more about "A Hat of Glass," as well as conversations between Ronit Lentin and Nava Semel throughout the 1990s about her work, see Ronit Lentin, *Israel and the Daughters of the Shoah: Reoccupying the Territories of Silence* (New York: Berghahn Books, 2000), 27–67. Shlomo Artzi, Nava Semel's brother, is the famous Israeli singer and recording artist.

5. Semel, interview, July 4, 2008.

6. "A Hat of Glass" was first published in Hebrew in *Kova Zekhukhit* [A hat of glass] (Tel Aviv: Sifriat Poalim, 1985), a collection of short stories by Nava Semel. It was republished in Hebrew in 1998. The English translation of the short story "A Hat of Glass" can be found in Risa Domb, ed., *New Women's Writing from Israel*, trans. Miriam Shlesinger (London: Vallentine Mitchell, 1996), 186–201. Semel speaks about being a second generation writer and the controversy surrounding her short stories before such writing had become acceptable. For more on Israeli reader reactions to her stories, hear her in a podcast interview with Nitza Lowenstein, December 9, 2008, on SBS Radio at http://www20.sbs.com.au/podcasting/index.php?action=feeddetails&feedid =23&id=19466 (accessed August 2, 2009).

7. Semel, "A Hat of Glass," 191.

8. Ibid., 193.

9. Ibid., 193–194.

10. See, for example, testimonies collected by Father Patrick Desbois in Ukraine, in chapter 6 by Anatoly Podolsky in this volume.

11. See Yehiel Dinur, *House of Dolls*, trans. Moshe M. Kohn (London: Frederick Muller, 1956); Arnošt Lustig, *Lovely Green Eyes*, trans. Ewald Osers (New York: Arcade Publishing, 2002); Yoram Kaniuk, *Commander of the Exodus*, trans. Seymour Simckes (New York: Grove Press, 2001). For more about sexual slavery in Dinur's (Ka-Tzetnik's) novels, *House of Dolls*, and *Piepel*, see chapter 12 by Miryam Sivan in this volume. For more about *Lovely Green Eyes* by Arnošt Lustig, see chapter 11 by S. Lillian Kremer in this volume.

12. Sam Ser, "Resurrection," *The Jerusalem Post*, July 20, 2007, features section. The photograph is in the Paul Goldman collection and can be viewed at http://www.paul goldmanphotographs.com/ (accessed August 4, 2009). David Rubinger told co-author Saidel on July 14, 2010, that there are still unresolved questions about the photograph.

13. Semel, interview, July 4, 2008. The gathering took place at the Waldorf-Astoria in New York City.

14. André Stein, *Hidden Children: Forgotten Survivors of the Holocaust* (New York: Penguin Books, 1994), 272.

15. Semel, interview, July 4, 2008.

16. Semel, *And the Rat Laughed*, 87.

17. Semel, interview, July 4, 2008.

18. Semel, *And the Rat Laughed*, 66.

19. Hadas Wiseman and Jacques P. Barber, *Echoes of the Trauma: Relational Themes and Emotions in Children of Holocaust Survivors* (Cambridge: Cambridge University Press, 2008), 236.

20. Ibid., 237–238.

21. Haim Dasberg, *Trauma, Loss and Renewal in Israel: Selected Papers*, Haim Dasberg and Gaby Shefler, eds., (Jerusalem: Temmy and Albert Latner Institute, Herzog Hospital, 2007), 43.

22. Anna Reading, *The Social Inheritance of the Holocaust: Gender, Culture and Memory* (London: Palgrave Macmillan, 2002), 150.

23. Semel, *And the Rat Laughed*, 6.

24. Ibid., 54–55.

25. Nahum Bogner, *At the Mercy of Strangers: The Rescue of Jewish Children with Assumed Identities in Poland*, trans. Ralph Mandel (Jerusalem: Yad Vashem, 2009), 79–80.

26. Ibid., 97.

27. Semel, *And the Rat Laughed*, 169.

28. Paul Valent, *Child Survivors of the Holocaust* (New York: Brunner-Routledge, 2002), 253–254.

29. Ibid., 255.

30. Ibid., 263.

31. Debórah Dwork, *Children With a Star: Jewish Youth in Nazi Europe* (New Haven: Yale University Press, 1991), 96.

32. Ibid., 80–81.

33. Semel, *And the Rat Laughed*, 225–226.

34. Nahum Bogner, *At the Mercy of Strangers*, 65.

35. Emunah Nachmany Gafny, *Dividing Hearts: The Removal of Jewish Children from Gentile Families in Poland in the Immediate Post-Holocaust Years* (Jerusalem: Yad Vashem, 2009), 87.

36. Semel, interview, July 4, 2008. For more on the reconstruction and construction of memories of hidden children, see Suzanne Kaplan, *Children in Genocide: Extreme Traumatization and Affect Regulation* (London: The International Psychoanalysis Library, 2008).

37. Haim Dasberg, 44.

38. Semel, *And the Rat Laughed*, 95.

39. Ibid., 153.

40. For more about the opera in the canon of Israeli creative works about the Holocaust, see Dalia Ofer, "The Past That Does Not Pass: Israelis and Holocaust Memory," *Israel Studies* 14, no. 1 (Spring 2009): 21.

41. Reactions to the staging in Warsaw and other reviews, as well as other audio and video clips of the opera, can be found on Ella Milch-Sheriff's Web site at http://www.ellasheriff.com/evideoplayer.asp?clip=rat-roim-olam (accessed August 8, 2009).

14

"Public Property"

Sexual Abuse of Women and Girls in Cinematic Memory

YVONNE KOZLOVSKY-GOLAN

The cinematic medium commemorated the events of the twentieth century in various ways, reaching a new level during World War II. During this period, feature filmmaking transformed itself from depicting the century's events descriptively to documenting all of the stages of the war. The cameramen/directors were among the troops that liberated the death camps of central Europe. They documented the events of the initial days of liberation, traces of the Nazis' deeds, and the *"she'erit hapleita,"* the surviving remnant saved from the flames. Filming was realistic-naturalistic without censorship or considerations of bias. Shots portrayed prisoners and guards alike behind a single fence encircling them. These images, constituting a visual document, served as the proof that brought Nazis and their collaborators to judgment, despite the fact that the cameras were unable to capture the horrors that took place but a moment before the liberators came through the gates.

The documentary material comprising these horror stories and their background was almost immediately translated into the language of the feature film to form a visual language that linked form and content. Film bonded the implicit to the explicit to create a meaningful narrative, with scenes from documentary films integrated into feature films, including footage of terror and abuse. Conventions of the feature film usually include dramatization of reality integrated with a fictional story. The cinematic narrative takes a historical perspective, referring to events that took place during a defined period, and the plot is always dramatic.[1] For example, the protagonist is ripped away from family and home, presenting a story of loss, suffering, torture, death of family and friends, and survival. Through narrative, the event described in a film becomes understandable to viewers, although perhaps difficult to watch.

Death is a motif that commonly deepens viewers' understanding of and identification with the plot.[2] At the same time, the spirit of early Holocaust films was humanistic and usually touched upon human ability to overcome pain and suffering. What nevertheless stands out in these films is the absence of any serious attempt to grapple with the physical and sexual abuse of women,[3] whose role in advancing the plot was significant. Such missing elements include exploitation, forced or "consensual" sexual and mental humiliation, torture, and death in the concentration and extermination camps. An overall survey of the films that refer to sexual abuse shows that very few Holocaust films address such themes, and that the national, religious, and ethnic origin of a film does not seem to play a part in the cinematic treatment of the young women.

The Female Body as "Public Property:"
Through the Documentary Prism

The German troops themselves had already been documenting the sexual abuse of women during the course of the war. The documentary film *My Private War* (Dirs. Harriet Eder and Thomas Kufus, Germany, 1989) interviewed five Wehrmacht soldiers who had used their still camera and 8 mm movie camera to document their unit's journey into Eastern Europe and the plains of Russia in 1942. The five documented their lives: becoming soldiers, the invasion of Russia, impressions of the weather, and their encounter with the Red Army and local population. In conversations about the cultural differences between them and the local people, they stated in their own defense that this did not allow too much emotional closeness because they considered the Russians base, too connected to nature itself, and therefore a sub-race to be feared.

From the photographs taken on the Eastern Front and incorporated into the documentary, a terrible picture emerges of an army advancing into a civilian area—burning its synagogues, houses, and pasture lands—as well as revealing women carrying packages and tiny infants in their arms. Facing the scene with equanimity, one of the soldiers films a group of young Ukrainian women separated from the rest, standing at the entrance to a spacious hut. At the top of the staircase stand three officers, examining the woman whose turn it is to enter. She is dressed as a typical villager, covered from head to toe. One of the officers stretches out a hand toward her breasts, his face like that of his fellow officers, split by an amused, lecherous grin. Two young women stand with their backs to these women, their faces looking right in the camera. Despite the cold, they are dressed in lightweight clothing, and it looks as if they were peeled out of their clothing for the officers. Their collars are open, with breast-bones visible. The braids of one woman are undone. She stands with lowered gaze, looking ashamed, as she hungrily chews a piece of bread that the soldiers have given her. Her friend is dressed carelessly in equally light clothing, combing her disarrayed hair. The women's faces show mental anguish, tear marks clearly visible on their sooty cheeks. Their blouses are open. The camera faces another girl, who is in a modeling stance, dressed only in a skirt, her upper torso bare. She is embarrassed and vainly attempts to cover herself with a shawl, but she is asked to remove it and bare her breasts. She is ordered to wriggle in "exotic" movements for the camera. She ties a scarf around her head as a makeshift Oriental headdress and makes belly-dancing motions as the soldiers greedily watch the spectacle, photographing her while they chuckle with pleasure.

In the lower part of the frame sits a little girl of about three or four years old, watching the soldiers with interest. It seems her turn will come in a moment. The camera does not set out her fate in detail, or what was done to the young women at the structure's entrance, although the hints are clearly there.

The next scene takes place directly in front of the camera: soldiers steal animals from a home belonging to two women. Two others are asked "to clean up" the killing fields left by the Wehrmacht, to take out the corpses, concentrate them in a mass grave, and burn them.

The order of the images in this film makes it clear to us how events unfolded: first the soldiers occupied the villages; then they raped, abused, and defiled the women and young girls of the village, looted their property, and finally forced them to hide the evidence of the deeds of the soldiers who "protected" them and their villages.

We can assume that the women who suffered the embraces of the Wehrmacht were not Jewish, but this scene reveals the attitude of the units toward the civilian population in general and the local women in particular. From here, we can draw conclusions about the treatment by the Wehrmacht and Einsatzgruppen (mobile killing units) and their collaborators who assisted in "purifying" the region of Jewish women and girls.[4] This 1989 documentary was not distributed widely and soon sank into the oblivion of video libraries.

In a surprising move, directors Oliver Axer and Susanne Benze merged these scenes into their troubling film Hitler's Hit Parade (Germany, 2003), which aroused many reactions. It is difficult to categorize this film as either a feature or documentary. The filmmakers deliberately did not want it neatly pigeonholed, as their goal was to portray life in Germany as it was seen through the eyes of Germans who lived under the Nazi regime. Through clips of daily life during the Third Reich, the viewer sees two sides of a mirror image: on one side, German self-satisfaction and national pride, portrayed through film and diaries; on the other, the "Big Lie" perpetrated on the souls of civilians and soldiers—a lie that the film exposes by contrasting patriotic photographs of soldiers in the East and photographs of sexual abuse of women in Eastern Europe and identifying them as part of the same patriotism. The film is considered extremely subversive.

During the first viewing of *Hitler's Hit Parade*, one is likely to miss the directors' cynical irony. On a second and third examination, the sensation of nausea intensifies as the scenes take on their historical significance and contextual value. The documentary photographs were taken by Germans themselves in 1942, as well as from material found by the Allies after the war. Not many photographs actually depict rape of women. Nevertheless, when the concentration camps in Western Europe were liberated by the Allies in 1945, first-hand evidence of sexual abuse was filmed.[5]

For example, the Allies' camera entered Breedonk, a torture camp that was explicitly designed for "special handling" of those who opposed the Nazi regime in Belgium. Ex-prisoners there demonstrated for the camera the tortures they underwent with the instruments left on site. The men were dressed in a dignified manner in gabardine trousers and buttoned-down white shirts. The witnesses in the film take off their shirts. Others roll up their trouser legs to show signs of burns and beatings. Men who underwent surgical tortures to their groin are photographed from the neck down, without showing their faces. The audience receives the impression that the cinematographer was preserving the dignity of the survivors, rather than revealing their injuries provocatively or with an intent to humiliate.

As this sequence ends, a young woman appears in an unusual location: on the roof balcony of a building overlooking the destroyed city, where she is asked to show the result of the tortures she underwent. However, in contrast to the respectful representation of the men's tortures, apparently at a signal from the director, she raises her skirt in one sweep, and exposes her underwear. She turns her back to the camera and displays her buttocks pocked from blows. The camera focuses on her buttocks as the narrator dryly explains that this is "a woman who suffered beatings."

Scholar Lawrence Douglas strongly condemned this shot, stating that it is unworthy to be screened because it is semi-pornographic, in an unlikely setting, and seems staged.[6] Douglas's statement correctly takes into account the way the young woman is placed facing the camera. The setting in which a lovely young girl is made to pose for the camera on the roof of a building over-looking the city seems a poor choice, if not cynical. It expresses lack of consideration and basic understanding of what victims suffered in general, and what women endured in the camps in particular. However, I do think that this scene has narrative importance and gives us hints about information concealed from view.

The entry into the camps and the authentic photographs of what was done there moments prior to liberation enables the Allies to represent their covert partners: those who were left alive and those who paid with their lives for the liberation. Filming just the men who experienced torture only partially reflects the events of the war; filming a woman who was physically tortured is no less important. Even portraying a woman whose intimate organs were abused to humiliate her can be seen as contributing to completing the missing pieces of the story regarding the sexual abuse of women.

Another fact revealed in this short scene is the type of torture experienced by members of the Resistance. Among the men who were filmed, 90 percent testified to physical torture, such as cigarette burns, broken fingers, being scraped with barbed wire, and receiving beatings on their back, and beatings of their upper and lower limbs without breakage. As the film continues, it portrays another type of torture, one more of the nature of sexual abuse—the young woman whose signs of torture are shown in the close-up of her buttocks pockmarked from beatings. Although the narrator does not state anything about sexual abuse, it does not require a great leap of imagination to span the short distance from the site of the beatings to the woman's sexual organs. However, the way in which the young woman is filmed swallows up her narrative in a wave of details transmitted to the shocked viewers, due perhaps to the director's lack of attention or lack of sensitivity toward the women in the camp.

As the film continues, after many transitions between the camps, a woman doctor who had been incarcerated in 1945 in Bergen-Belsen women's camp stands before the camp. She testifies to the camera, with numerous women standing behind her. She is talking in German while the narrator only partially translates her words into English. The woman doctor tells about life in the camp explicitly, including lack of food and cannibalism. She describes her work as a doctor and tells how some doctors abused the prisoners under the guise of "medical experiments." Her testimony is lengthy, and her voice is often muffled by the narrator who translates her words. When she begins to tell about the gynecological "experiments" on women, the way they were executed and their essential nature, her voice is entirely silenced by the narrator's voiceover on another subject. His speech deliberately follows hers by only a few seconds. When she speaks in German of the details of what was done to the women, her voice is drowned out by the narrator speaking about the injections of kerosene into prisoners' bodies. The woman doctor's testimony is swallowed up in the bigger story of the war and the horrors perpetrated by human beings on other human beings, some of which can be described in words and others by silence.

Later Evidence

The tendencies to conceal and repress the abuse of women in general and sexual abuse in particular also took root in postwar cinema. The most outstanding examples of concealment were perpetuated precisely by the survivors themselves, many of whom were interviewed in Israel decades later. In interviews conducted as part of the project founded by Steven Spielberg, now an ongoing project of the University of Southern California Shoah Foundation Institute for Visual History and Education, women survivors extensively describe their past according to a particular order of topics, as if illustrating the Nazis' orderly mechanism of destruction.[7] They describe their parents and family and conditions under which they lived, which included hunger, fear, hard labor, abuse by those in control, and death. They tell only in hints of the painful events that damaged their bodies and their femininity. Some of these testimonies were later incorporated into films.

In Tor Ben-Mayor's documentary Love in Auschwitz (Ahava b'Auschwitz, Israel, 2003), the protagonist describes an affair between an SS officer and a Jewish prisoner in the camp, through which the woman and her sister's lives were saved. The description of the relationship and the site of the event raise reasonable suspicions that this so-called love takes place on the thin seam between an emotional relationship and sexual exploitation. The survivor claims that the woman did not love the officer but had a sexual relationship with him in circumstances that saved her life. The context of exploitation did not prevent the officer from later asking "his survivor" to testify on his behalf before an Austrian war crimes tribunal. She did so, despite her distaste, out of a feeling of obligation and gratitude.

Marco Carmel's documentary film constituting part 1 of A Matter of Time (Israel, 2005) relates the destruction of the Jews of Libya, based on interviews and factual research. A survivor who had been a young girl at the time of World War II states only one sentence: "They did terrible things to them [the mothers and daughters in the camp] . . . I don't know . . . I was just a little girl . . ." The elderly narrator blushes, and refuses to continue her testimony.

Through the Cinematic Prism of the Feature Film

As suggested above, in order to create the fictional world of concentration camps for postwar feature films, filmmakers used iconographic imagery of the survivors who appeared in the footage of liberation films.[8] These documentaries were extremely powerful, and almost impossible to ignore. They became, in practice or potentially, the cornerstone of feature films. In addition, strong, postwar cultural messages penetrated into feature films. Although these messages were covert, their stamp is obvious in films made after World War II, which tended to avoid implications or deep treatment of the physical and sexual abuse of the women inmates, choosing instead to blend the issue into the general mistreatment of all camp prisoners.

Between 1945 and the 1960s, approximately 120 feature films were made worldwide with the Holocaust as a central theme. However, they were never blockbusters, and they had very little relative impact on how history was recorded.[9] These were the years of minimal means, of *arte povera* and Hollywood's almost complete avoidance of the Holocaust as subject. In contrast, in European countries, several films were made that reflected what went on within their borders during the Nazi occupation. Surprisingly, the subject of these films was not historiographic but anecdotal. Numerous scholars have classified the films into two categories:

1. Films that refer to Nazism as a phenomenon, a colossal social disturbance expressed primarily in the association between Nazism/Fascism and sexual domination. See, for example, these films by Italian directors: *Kapò* (Dir. Pontecorvo, 1959), *The Night Porter* (Dir. Cavani, 1974), *Seven Beauties* (Dir. Wertmüller, 1975), *The Damned* (Dir. Visconti, 1969) and *Salò* (Dir. Pasolini, 1975).

2. American-made Holocaust films featuring heroism, such as *Exodus* (Dir. Preminger, 1960) and *The Pawnbroker* (Dir. Lumet, 1964). *Exodus* includes a controversial scene in which a survivor describes his work in the *Sonderkommando* (gas chamber and crematoria crew), and mentions the "work" of the women serving the Germans. *The Pawnbroker* has an explicit scene in which Professor Nazerman is forced to watch his wife being raped by Germans as part of the "special handling" meted out to him. In both

films, the victims experience physical and mental rape simultaneously. Both women and men were sexually abused in one way or another during their incarceration in the camps.

While these categories are useful, a deeper look at the film industry in the West during these years shows that both types of films share a common narrative: woman as a vehicle for conveying the Nazi/Fascist message, for carrying out their sex crimes, sexual exploitation, and pimping, and as a means through which pure evil works itself out in all its ugliness. Despite all this, women are missing from the films' central discourse, as the real "heroes" are men.

Kapò, The Night Porter, and Witness from Hell

The central plot of the film Kapò is the story of Nicole, a young Jewish woman who takes the identity of a non-Jewish political prisoner, and her status as one of the Prominenten (important prisoners) after she is lured into providing sexual services to the men. The potentially life-saving "choiceless choice" of this young woman to be a sex slave to the Nazis stands out in the conversation between her and a friend who attempts to dissuade her. Their conversation ends with Nicole's challenge, her consent to barter sex for food, which means life, in contrast to her friend who represents sublime human values. The German soldier's "conquest" of the fifteen-year-old girl is mentioned in a scene in which she is led to his room, as he jokes with his friend that he likes them young and thin. Nicole's body therefore represents a model of male fantasy, especially that of a pedophile, who believes that the young girls really desire him. The film problematizes the essential choice that Nicole makes. This is why the importance of Nicole's narrative disappears and she will pay for it with her life. From the filmmaker's viewpoint, she is not a "heroine" who can become part of the pantheon of "heroes of the Holocaust." The opposite is true: it is obvious that the director is embarrassed by the "job" that the protagonist has "chosen." Thus the film abandons Nicole and presents instead the figure of the brave Soviet soldier, who enters the plot in the last third of the film as the central figure through whom the deeds of the Nazis and their collaborators will be condemned.

The Night Porter, an extremely controversial film from 1974, has been studied a great deal and classified as a film on the border of power relations and sex. I would like to disagree with this classification, which usually originates in the male gaze that interprets the sexual discourse between man and woman as simply what is on the surface.[10] However, this film can be seen from a viewpoint that has never before been treated in full: this is the stance of the child-woman who learns the "secrets of love" from a much older man.[11] He beats her and rewards her with the head of a prisoner who had tormented her. He tortures her physically and mentally, uses her for sadistic experiments, and explains to her that therein lies the root of his love. Her absolute love for him is a love conditional on her humiliation. Her reflex reaction to him, even many years later, is as automatic as her behavior as a battered woman who returns to the "scene of the crime" again and again out of love and blind faith in her beloved. Patterns of love associated with survival were, in her case from a very young age, patterns that were violent, humiliating, and painful—and patterns that were imprinted upon her. Any other analysis of the film misses the point. The power plays and domination between the child-woman and the man, which others tend to focus on, are misconstructions. They come from the position of the viewer who wishes to see sex between the two characters as pornography and does not look more closely at the psychological layers of the relationship that bring about the tragic death of the heroine who cannot behave otherwise.

The film *Witness Out of Hell* (*Zeugin aus der Hölle*, Dir. Artur Brauner, 1965), made about a decade earlier, is similar and aroused a no less sensational reaction. What is obvious in this film is the heroine's struggle to cope with narratives from the tortuous labyrinths of the past that flooded her in the present. Leah Weiss, a survivor of Auschwitz, is summoned to testify against Nazi officers who had abused her as a sex slave in the "Moulin Rouge" camp brothel as well as used her for horrific "medical" experiments. The ghosts of the past (a lobby of Nazi officers and their relatives who survived the war) pursue Weiss in an attempt to prevent her from testifying. And, indeed, her testimony does not receive the screen time one expects. Instead, the viewer accompanies Weiss's memories through flashbacks.[12]

The film's covert message is that Leah Weiss's humiliation and survival are her illusion. She herself is represented as an unstable woman due to the traumas she underwent, while preserving morality and justice in court are the film's overt messages. This ploy is the sterile means through which the viewer is supposed to be impressed by the plot. The testimony of *Witness from Hell* treads a very narrow path of silence and repression,[13] although the covert message bubbles up and penetrates through the bones the more one looks deeply into the film. Leah Weiss becomes twice a victim: first, of the past, and second, of a present in which she must bear witness and then defend herself for lack of corroborating evidence. Before she can testify and let the world hear her truth, Leah Weiss dies.

Sadistic Torture in Feature Films

Spielberg's box-office hit *Schindler's List* (1993) hints unambiguously in the scene in the cellar that Helene, the Jewish housekeeper/servant of the sadistic camp commandant Amon Goeth, is beaten by him and probably serves him in bed as well. Goeth not only beats her but also humiliates and exploits her, similar to Lucia's story in *The Night Porter*. In return, each time he grants her life for another day.

In all of the films discussed here, the figure of the heroic woman remains absent from the screen. The tortures that were done to women have been presented under the guise of medical experiments, such as in the "sexploitation" film *Ilsa, She-Wolf of the* SS (Dir. Don Edmonds, USA, 1975) in which pornographic depictions of the female body are shown for a great deal of time, featuring full nudity and torture with objects such as electrical vibrators. However, there are no close-ups of the experiments historically made on the vaginas of torture victims, which would demonstrate the ability to tolerate pain.

Another type of hint at an unexpected kind of rape is seen in the Chinese production *Red Cherry* (*Hong Ying Tao*, Dir. Daying Ye, 1995). This film narrates the true story of an elementary school student from China, brought by her parents for ideological reasons to Soviet Russia to attend a boarding school. When the Nazis occupy the area, they imprison her in a castle fortress under the command of an army doctor whose favorite hobby is tattooing his victims. The women prisoners have tattoos on their upper and lower limbs, as well as on intimate areas of their bodies. After torturing and threatening the protagonist, the Germans undress her, and her back becomes the "canvas" for the doctor's masterpiece: the Nazi eagle in full color. She is unable to hide the tattoo because it is so big. In great mental distress, she attempts to burn it off with a torch and kill herself. However, the Russian liberating forces save her. The trauma remains with her for her entire life as she lives by herself, never marries, but carries her suffering and shame alone.

Tim Blake Nelson, director of *The Grey Zone* (USA, 2001), boldly depicts two scenes of sexual abuse and sadism, which were never screened in full. One scene represents in detail the sadistic and vicious torture of the young women in Auschwitz who had assisted in the *Sonderkommando's* revolt, as a way of forcing them to give up their accomplices. Against the backdrop of hellish tortures filmed explicitly, the viewer has time and opportunity to understand the motives of the young women, their heroism, and their choice of death over a life of humiliation and deathly tortures. It is doubtful that any other films devote enough screen time to the participation of the young women in the dynamiting of the crematoria at Auschwitz. The director is to be commended for his decision to integrate their part in the plot and give them considerable footage, including the vicious collective punishment meted out to the women in their block. However, gender-specific experiences do recede into the background of the cinematic portrayal of the insurrection by the *Sonderkommando* in which crematoria I and III were destroyed with the smuggled explosives.

According to writer and cultural critic Susan Sontag, the United States chose to address the horrors of the Holocaust rather than America's own past history of genocide and human rights abuse.[14] Europe, in contrast, is ashamed of its past and prefers to expose well-known events through intellectual Holocaust literature that attempts to explore the recesses of the human soul. Authors who reflect this are Jean Améry, Jorge Semprun, Imre Kertész, and Primo Levi. Precisely because of this European dedication to intellectual approaches, films such as *Seven Beauties* by Lina Wertmüller and *The Night Porter* by Liliana Cavani were considered perverted, scandalous films. Directed by women, both films had as their subject women and femininity in the camps, women crushed under the male boot, or women who were victims of themselves.

Israeli Feature Films on the Holocaust

Israeli cinema has treated the subject of the Holocaust in a different manner than has the rest of the world.[15] The theme is not really part of the repertoire of the Israeli film industry, which offers very few films on the subject. The few that do mention the Holocaust summon the ghosts of postwar survivors, their arrival in the Homeland and the chilly reception from the *sabras* (native-born Israelis). I have found a clear and consistent narrative line common to all of the Israeli filmmakers in relation to the Holocaust: male and some women survivors are insane, and women survivors, especially, were the Germans' whores or worked for them (hence, their survival). The concepts of rape, coercion, and abuse did not exist except in the frame of insanity. The survivors were haunted by their past, which had no concrete details, and bear the scars of their past in their outward appearance.

The number tattooed on the forearm of a young Jewish woman survivor from Salonika, the heroine of *Newland* (*Eretz Hadasha*, Dir. Orna Ben-Dor Niv, Israel, 1994), was considered by the *sabras* in the *ma'abara* (transit camp) as solid evidence that she was a whore in Auschwitz. Otherwise she would not have survived. In *Henrik's Sister* (Dir. Ruti Peres, Israel, 1997), survivors arrive in Palestine before the Germans can murder them, but the behavioral patterns of

the Diaspora Jews—"these women," according to the director—follow them to
their new homeland. The protagonist willingly becomes the whore of another
conqueror, the British. In *Tel Aviv-Berlin* (Dir. Tsipi Trope, Israel, 1987) three
young German-Jewish women whom the Berlin-born hero meets are represented as German field-whores, which is supposed to explain their survival.

None of these films depict or explain the actual act of rape. Nor is there any
narrative depth enabling viewers to understand these women, identify with
them, and have compassion for them. On the contrary: the explanation is
concealed according to the taste of the filmmaker, who decided in advance
to point a finger of blame at the survivors. The viewer is imprisoned in this
view as if by historical truth. It is interesting to note that all three of the above
films were directed by women. However, in contrast to Wertmüller and Cavani, who depicted rape and coercion within the context of the immediate need
for survival and had psychoanalytic views of human behavior, these Israeli
women directors show no understanding for the women victims, but only
offer selected slogans to advance the plot.

Love as Abnormality

The film *Death in Love* (USA) premiered in 2008, directed by Israeli filmmakers
Boaz Yakin and Alma Harel, both of whom live in the United States. The film
is exceptionally crude in its view of the relationship between survivors and
what has come to be called "the second generation of the Holocaust." A seemingly normal American family copes with the shadows of the Jewish mother's
past, which impact unbearably upon her husband, her children, and herself.
She had been a prisoner in the infamous block 11 in Auschwitz-Birkenau,
where terrible medical experiments were perpetrated upon the women. Most
of the experiments were of a brutal sexual nature, accompanied by crude rape
of the young women, amputation of limbs, and destruction of the women's
bodies in horrific ways. In the film, all this is a prelude to a surrealistic "love
affair" taking place between a sadistic doctor and one of the prisoners, initiated by the woman to save her life. She receives preferential treatment, such
as food and warm shelter, in exchange for frequent sexual relations with the
doctor. When the war ends, the doctor promises to search for her when the
time comes. Many years later, he seeks her out. By then, she is unhappily married and the mother of two. One child has a self-destructive bent, and the
second, who lacks life skills, is codependent upon the mother and an irritable
complainer.

When the Nazi doctor and survivor meet after so many years, there are no sadomasochistic relations as in *Night Porter*. Instead, we view relations that border on mental illness. As an act of foreplay, the doctor murders two of the survivor's acquaintances, an act meant to demonstrate his love for her and desire to be with her again, whether she likes it or not. When they finally rendezvous in a luxury hotel, despite their advanced age they replay their first meeting in the camp and make love. The camera exposes the sex act between the elderly partners, a former victim and perpetrator.

Unlike previous films on the subject, *Death in Love* attempts to discuss several aspects associated with sex, sexual abuse, and the Holocaust. First, the sexual relations between the Nazi and the Jewish prisoner take on a loaded meaning because of the power construct of their relationship and the emotional tie that develops beyond the relations coerced by authority. Second, everything that the young woman experiences in the camp through her repeated meetings with the Nazi has direct implications on her life after liberation and on that of her children, the so-called second generation. She suffers from an eating disorder, is extremely neurotic and frigid with her husband, and engages in repeated infidelities with his friends. In addition, she displays compulsive behavior toward her codependent sons, who are erotically bound to her in a love-hate relationship.

Alma Harel's screenplay is structured as a chapter hanging in the middle of this family's lives. There is no consolation for the survivors, whose past will continue to haunt them and the subsequent generation that has not personally experienced the Holocaust. There is no making peace with the past, but only emptiness and failure when facing the future. The memory that the mother (played by Jacqueline Bisset) thought she had, which had sustained her for all those years, contains nothing but emotional and spiritual death and lust that has not abated at an advanced age. The film is extremely critical, with an obvious, strong desire to shatter accepted conventions in collective memory referring to the survivors' righteousness and the Nazis' evildoing.

Rape and Its Cinematic Representations

In the arena of rape, as Ariella Azoulay has stated, only the victim and hangman exist, and whatever happens, it is his word against hers.[16] Violence directed against the woman under these circumstances, hidden from view, creates a closed space very difficult to describe in words. The imagined representation, in contrast, or its demonstration by actors, can often transmit the reality better than words can.

Why, then, we may ask, has the issue of abuse of women not been raised more explicitly in cinema about the Holocaust (except in pornographic films not included in this category)? After all, we use the power of photographs to determine our relationship to reality,[17] and the image of a woman being raped could be useful when the goal is to show the horrific situation of the lives of the women in the camps, in hiding, and in secret, and the specific act taking place between aggressor and victim. Filmmakers might have desired to preserve the dignity of the survivors, not to injure or damage the memory of those who were murdered and of those who survived and live among us. In addition, we need to consider the extent of the filmmaker's sense of responsibility and desire to expose human ugliness without creating antagonism in the viewer. To that end, the director treads a tightrope and navigates between terror and curiosity, between the viewer eager for knowledge and the viewer who comes to the movies to be entertained.

Susan Sontag notes that in the modern age, the viewer prefers the photograph to the thing itself, the copy over the original, the representation over reality, the appearance above the experience.[18] The casual viewer who looks at photographs is likely to adopt them as reality itself and to appropriate the contents as the real thing. This phenomenon is so obvious that often some subject seems "better" in a photograph, or at least creates the impression that it is preferable to the "real" event. And indeed, as Sontag states, one of the functions of photography is to improve the look of things (because of this, we feel disappointed when we see a photograph that is unflattering).[19]

In the case of films such as those about the Holocaust, any attempt to beautify what is ugly and horrific will be considered unreal, grotesque, or lacking sensitivity.[20] Furthermore, to arouse the viewer's active response, the director must shock the viewer. From a practical viewpoint, if he or she does so, the shock of seeing sexual abuse, which offers no enjoyment but only pain and humiliation,[21] is likely to do fundamental damage to the sensitive narrative of young women who were exploited. Filming for shock effect can transform a scene from a war crime to a kind of commercial pornography that may injure not only the image of survivor women but also that of the actresses themselves.

Furthermore, a director filming to shock may dilute the crime by equating it to pornography by virtue of his choice of actress. An outstanding expression of this problem is the American "star" system: the representation of a woman raped can miss the point if a "soft core" porn star such as Sylvia Kristel plays the heroine. In addition, the representation of the raped woman is problematic if portrayed by cultural figures well known to viewers from other films, such as Meryl Streep in the film *Sophie's Choice*. The audience identifies with Streep as a strong, independent woman, so it is difficult for them to imagine her as a victim. Likewise, much of the controversy surrounding the film *The Accused* (Dir. Jonathan Kaplan, USA, 1988) was due to the part of the raped woman being played by a star, Jodie Foster.

Conclusions

Despite all we know about sexual violence, coercion, and rape, and despite photographic records of the horrors that simultaneously reinforce and confirm facts, we still perceive rape in terms of shame and respond to it by silencing it. Thus the difficulty in cinematically depicting the explicit violent sexual act and its implications still exists, and many filmmakers prefer, out of shame or respect for survivors, not to directly show the act. Yet if we, as viewers, witness no example of this act in a film in which rape figures, we may consider the abuse exaggerated. The absence of rape in film can be contrasted with the representation of death. Here the most horrific form of death can be depicted but not felt, because the visual aspect of the dead person, no matter how violent the death, is peaceful and looks asleep. Death in war is universal and constitutes an axiomatic consensus. Rape and sexual injury, however, are not included in this consensus. Death in war is easier to stage on film and speaks for itself. In contrast, rape, with all its ramifications, involves physical and emotional injury that cannot be seen.

Films engaged in the depiction of war in all forms have created and structured cinematic consensus according to which the mood and spirit of the time are expressed, as well as the tone of social and cultural events associated with wars. Rape and sexual abuse do not appear as conventions of war.[22] The narrative of the Holocaust, although a unique event related to World War II, is in this context considered a sub-category of the genre of war movies. The conventions of war in cinema apply to this sub-genre as well.

Furthermore, because publications based on historical research do not provide enough evidence that rape and sexual exploitation were part of the bureaucratic directives for managing the death camps, some have stated that these events took place sporadically and were not institutionalized.[23] It is possible that filmmakers working with Holocaust materials have not seen fit to depict sexual violence because they lacked images that clearly proved it existed. But it is more likely that, with a covert or overt hint, the filmmakers have had one purpose: to advance the plot and have the viewer enter the hellish atmosphere in which the women prisoners and men prisoners were incarcerated together, and no more.

On one hand, some films have succeeded in taking rape and abuse out of its sexual context and restructured it as an act of violence. On the other hand, cinema represented the heroine's stance to the viewer so that the viewer could identify with the protagonist as injured party and someone with legitimate grounds for complaint. Several Italian and American films of the 1970s attempted to attribute an additional, broader interpretation to sexual abuse. Perhaps their sin was writing the screenplay and focusing the camera with inappropriate emphasis, with resulting derivative interpretation.[24] However, European cinema seems to have fallen silent in the 1980s, when the United States came to the forefront. In the American films of the 1990s, filmmakers created a "balance of terror" between all of the horrors and humiliations perpetrated on all the female and male prisoners. Most Israeli cinema did not do so, but instead seems to have treated the women survivors scornfully, selecting less flattering, backhanded ways to delineate the complexity of women's character.

It may seem that by the beginning of the twenty-first century the bounds of cinematic representation of sex would have broadened and that the representation of sex and sexual abuse of women during the Holocaust would have broken through previous boundary lines. However, I found that the discourse on sexual abuse is still private and represented only in suggestive ways.

Notes

1. Alan L. Mintz, *Popular Culture and the Shaping of Holocaust Memory in America* (Seattle: University of Washington Press, 2001), 36–84. Mintz proposes two models for the study of Holocaust culture and its cinematic representation, the exceptionalist and the constructionist approaches.

2. Catherine Russell, *Narrative Mortality: Death, Closure and New Wave Cinemas* (Minneapolis: University of Minnesota Press, 1995), 1–30.

3. "Women" in this article refers to girls, adolescents, and women of all ages, religions, and nationalities.

4. Christopher Browning, *Ordinary Men: Reserve Police Battalion 101 and the Final Solution in Poland*, Hebrew ed. (Tel Aviv: Yediot Ahronot, 2004), 186–198 (first published in English, New York: HarperCollins, 1992).

5. *The Nazi Concentration Camps*, directed by George Stevens (1945: Department of Defense, European Command, Office of Military Government for Germany (U.S.), Office

of the Chief Counsel for War Crimes). Produced and presented as evidence at the war crimes trial of Hermann Göring and twenty other Nazi leaders held at Nuremberg.

6. Lawrence Douglas, *The Memory of Judgment: Making Law and History in the Trials of the Holocaust* (New Haven: Yale University Press, 2001), 11–38.

7. Liat Ben-Haviv, director, Yad Vashem Visual Center, interview with the author, August 2008. Between 1994 and the end of 2008, 52,000 testimonies were filmed by the Shoah Foundation. They joined 15,000 testimonies, some of which were collected on videotape (since 1987) and others on audio tape (since 1953) in the Yad Vashem Archives. See http://college.usc.edu/vhi/testimoniesaroundtheworld/location.php for more information on where the collection is housed (Accessed March 24, 2010).

8. Yvonne Kozlovsky-Golan, "The Shaping of the Holocaust Visual Image by the Nuremberg Trials: The Impact of the Movie *Nazi Concentration Camps*," in *Search and Research*, vol. 9, *Lectures and Papers* (Jerusalem: Yad Vashem, 2006): 6–50.

9. Lawrence Baron, "Representations in Film and Television," in *The Oxford Handbook of Holocaust Studies*, ed. Peter Hayes and John K. Roth (Oxford: Oxford University Press, forthcoming 2010). Also see Lawrence Baron, *Projecting the Holocaust into the Present: The Changing Focus of Contemporary Holocaust Cinema* (Rowman & Littlefield: New York, 2005), 10: "the American film industry accounted for 40 percent of movies about the Holocaust produced between 1945 and the 1960s."

10. It is important to note that this is one of the few films directed by a woman; its messages may be understood as opposite of what they seem. The male critic must, therefore, view the film from the director's viewpoint, and even read it differently. See Marcia Landy, "They Were Sisters: Common Sense, World War II, and the Woman's Film," in *Film, Politics, and Gramsci* (Minneapolis: University of Minnesota Press, 1994), 99–120.

11. Dana Renga, "Staging Memory and Trauma in French and Italian Holocaust Films," *Romanic Review* 97 (May–November 2006): 461–483.

12. "Lihi Nagler, *"Passenger* and *Witness Out of Hell*: Can Women's Traumas Return as Film?" in *Gendered Memories: Transgressions in German and Israeli Film and Theater*, ed. Julia Köhne and Vera Apfelthaler (Vienna: Turia and Kant, 2007), 27–42.

13. Marianne Hirsch, *Family Frames: Photography, Narrative and Postmemory* (Cambridge: Harvard University Press, 1999), 9, 24.

14. Susan Sontag, *Regarding the Pain of Others* (New York: Farrar, Straus and Giroux, 2003), 87–88.

15. Yvonne Kozlovsky-Golan, "The 81st Blow: Representation of the Holocaust Survivor in Israeli Cinema in the Last Decades of the 20th Century," in *"Beyond Camps and Forced Labour," Proceedings of the Current International Research on Survivors of Nazi Persecution* —60 Years On (London: Second Multidisciplinary Conference at the Imperial War Museum, 2006), 771–785.

16. Ariella Azoulay, "The Civil Contract of Photography," *Fetish: An Israeli Series for Cultural Studies* (Tel Aviv: Resling, 2006). See also, Ariella Azoulay, *The Civil Contract of Photography* (New York: Zone Books, 2008).

17. Susan Sontag, *On Photography* (New York: Farrar, Straus and Giroux, 1977), 158.

18. Ibid., 153.

19. Susan Sontag, *Regarding the Pain of Others*, 81.

20. Roland Barthes, *Camera Lucida: Reflections on Photography* (New York: Hill and Wang, 1981), 4–6.

21. In contrast, for example, to a pornographic film containing pain and humiliation designed for viewers' "enjoyment."

22. In June 2008, the United Nations defined rape as "a means of warfare." The language formulated stated that sexual violence was a "military tactic designed to humiliate, control, frighten, and deport civilians of certain ethnic communities or ethnic origins." Violence is likely to worsen the state of armed conflicts and prevent peacemaking and security measures (see Shai Roth, *Ha'aretz*, June 27, 2008, 9).

23. Because of regulations against mingling with "non-Aryans," direct sexual contact was prohibited between Nazis and Jewish women, but contact under the guise of medical experimentation opened the narrow door to bend the prohibition "for the benefit of science."

24. Some critics consider this genre a sign characterizing male filmmakers who describe women unwittingly from a male viewpoint or ignore the feminine narrative. In my opinion, Wertmüller's and Cavani's films were analyzed with tools foreign to the directors' feminine viewpoint. In time, the analysis pattern became an inseparable part of their films and caused their reputation to suffer.

THE
Violated Self

15

Sexual Abuse of Jewish Women during and after the Holocaust

A Psychological Perspective

EVA FOGELMAN

I can never forget the story of the young, beautiful, pregnant Greek Holocaust survivor in Orna Ben-Dor Niv's film *Eretz Hadasha* (Newland) who went for a medical examination in the *ma'abara* (transit camp) in Israel. As the woman exited the office, she heard the doctor telling the nurse in Hebrew, "Her child is an offspring of an SS officer she slept with. That's how all pretty women survived the concentration camps."[1] Though her Hebrew was limited, the young Holocaust survivor understood what the doctor said. She returned to her tent, took an iron and attempted to burn off the numeric tattoo on her arm. She had lost her husband and daughter in Auschwitz. When it was all over, she had met a man who had lost his wife and son, and together they were bringing new life into the world.

The assumptions of the Israeli doctor in this film mirrored the real-life contempt for the Holocaust survivors who arrived in Palestine after the war. They were universally disrespected and treated as less than human—for being sheep that were led to the slaughter, for being psychologically damaged merely by the fact of survival. It was generally assumed that beautiful women who survived had traded their bodies for life; had they not, they would have been dead. In the postwar era, this contempt was not just generated by non-survivors. It hurt more to know it also came from fellow survivors. When members of a community suspected that a female survivor had been raped, they labeled her as "tainted goods," thereby unfit for marriage.

Because people often like to blame victims instead of perpetrators, there is a long history of silence about sexual abuse during the Holocaust and the post-liberation period. This silence has been compounded by researchers, who, like the survivors, resist broaching the topic. Ilana Rosen, an interviewer of female Holocaust survivors from Hungary, wrote in *Sister in Sorrow* that "delving too deeply in their intimate and sexual affairs is a kind of betrayal of their trust—expressed by their agreement to tell me their life histories as fully and sincerely as they can—and a superfluous repetition of the initial assault on their privacy and lives."[2]

First Attempts to Address Sexual Abuse

When Joan Ringelheim and Esther Katz organized the watershed conference on "Women Surviving the Holocaust" in 1983, they publicly addressed for the first time the topic of women as sex objects during the Holocaust.[3] The conclusions, however, were not definitive. Historian Sybil Milton argued there that because of the Nazi prohibition on *Rassenschande* (race defilement), which barred sexual relations between "Aryans" and "non-Aryans," SS men and German soldiers rarely raped Jewish women. On the other hand, Vera Laska, a survivor and resistance leader in Czechoslovakia and Hungary, maintained that the "purity of race" prohibition did not always protect Jewish women from sexual violence by Germans. There were also encounters with other men in German-occupied lands—for example, Polish, Ukrainian, and Latvian partisans—who had no compunction about becoming rapists. Laska, a non-Jewish resistance fighter, was incarcerated in three concentration camps as a political prisoner. Although they did not agree about the extent of sexual violation, these two scholars' viewpoints opened the discussion on this issue for participants.[4]

At the 1983 conference, one female survivor, on condition of anonymity, told the press she had been raped. Women panelists who had survived concentration camps were confronted by one group in the audience who demanded that the women "admit" that they had been sexual objects of the SS. The survivors explained that soon after their arrival in these camps they no longer had any sexual appeal. They felt the audience didn't accept the fact that in camps they were bald, filthy, smelly, and they looked like skeletons under their baggy, shapeless uniforms. Those survivors who felt they were being assaulted discussed the humiliations they had been subjected to as their hair was shaved off. They said that they had to parade in the nude and had to deal with their menstrual periods before starvation caused amenorrhea.

Testimonies about Sexual Abuse

The myth that beautiful women survived by serving as sexual prey for their guards is just that, a myth that applies to an unknown number of Jewish women.[5] For the most part, women chosen to serve as sexual objects were taken early on in their incarceration and were then murdered. The longer the period of imprisonment, the less appealing a woman became.

Of the 52,000 interviews conducted by the University of Southern California Shoah Foundation Institute of Visual History and Education (USC Shoah Foundation), 1,040 testimonies, mostly from women, refer to fear of rape and sexual molestation.[6] This figure includes 609 general references. Most of the rapes were perpetrated by liberators—508 incidents. In the camps there were 262 reported incidents, and in the ghettos, 272. There were 108 interviews that mentioned the camp brothels. References to fear of sexual violence in other situations were fewer: sexual violence perpetrated by aid givers, 39; in hiding, 33 (it is not clear whether this includes hiding with partisans); in prisons, 24; during deportation, 21; on forced marches, 12; during transfers and refugee camps, 7; in forced labor battalions, 1.

In the Fortunoff Video Archives at Yale University, just 10 survivor testimonies out of several thousand recount sexual assault perpetrated on the women being interviewed or women known to them. One reason for the smaller number of candid testimonies about sexual assault may be that these tapes were mainly designed to be shared with family members and school children. There is shame in knowing that a son or daughter or grandchild might hear about a parent or grandparent being raped or sexually abused by a German, a fellow partisan fighter, or a liberator. Another possible reason for the dearth of information may be that the subject was not broached at the time that the interviews housed at Yale were taped, ten to twenty years before the USC Shoah Foundation interviews were conducted. With a changing cultural climate and growing knowledge of how the Jews were victimized in the Holocaust, some Holocaust survivors may have decided in the later interviews for the USC Shoah Foundation to be more candid in order to validate their experiences.

The pattern of how women talk about sexual abuse during or after the Holocaust is similar to the general pattern survivors use to discuss their ordeal of surviving years of persecution under the Third Reich. Most share bits and pieces, without much detail. The exceptions are those who are totally silent and those who talk incessantly. Women who talk in generalities speak of the humiliation of showering naked in front of German guards. Many women share their fears of the Russian liberators, who were known for raping the women they liberated. We learn that women tried to stick together as a group to be less vulnerable. If women do not want to expose their own fears of sexual assault or experiences of sexual abuse, they tell stories about other women. In some cases, women dissemble and openly deny that they were victims of sexual abuse. What is more surprising is that there are some instances of women who have testified that their years of persecution consisted of one sexually abusive episode after another.

The Strange Testimony of Doris Roe

One of the most graphic narratives of endless sexual abuse in the collection of the USC Shoah Foundation is told by Doris Roe. She is known as Doris R. in the testimonies archive and gives her permission there for her name to be used. She has also written a self-published seventy-three-page account.[7] Doris's testimony is unlike any other I have seen by a sexually abused Holocaust survivor. In general, while parts of her testimony are legitimately her life story, she may have taken some of her narrative from a random collection of information and misinformation that she gathered. In short, she seems to be mixing fantasy with reality, and we will never know precisely which is which. Doris's distorted perception of reality may well be the result of abuse, including sexual abuse. She claims that she was born Doris Barbet Betty von Lindorf in Vilkaviskis, Lithuania, on June 4, 1925. Her mother was Johanna Goldberg, and her father's first name was Adolf, she said. According to her testimony, soon after her birth, her parents abandoned her to her Aunt Jenny Rubin (her mother's sister) and then left for the United States, never to be heard from again. She lived with this wealthy aunt in East Prussia and had quite a miserable, lonely, and unloved childhood.[8]

In July 1938, Aunt Jenny brought Doris to Grodno and left her there to live with some distant cousins. Doris tells a garbled story about a Captain Franco, who crashed his plane while taking a radio to the underground. She twice insists that she was arrested by the Nazis in Grodno on May 1, 1939. This, of course, is impossible, as there were no Nazis in Grodno then. Nevertheless, Doris insists that on that date the Nazi occupiers discovered a radio used to make reports about German troop movements, and Doris was picked up by a German soldier and put on the back of an army truck with other arrested Jews.[9] After a grueling four-day trip in a cattle car, she claims, she arrived at the Pillau detention camp. She was taken from there to a nearby prison, where she was interrogated by three people speaking at the same time, and she suspected this approach was taken on purpose to confuse her. As in the cases of some other small work camps, no available records have been found for a work camp in Pillau.[10]

Doris recalls in her USC Shoah Foundation testimony that the Nazis wanted her to tell them names. She said there was a hatchet, and they threatened to cut off her head and put it in a basket. She asked if she could pray first, for herself as well as for them. During a subsequent interrogation, a Gestapo man asked her, "I hear you prayed for us, did you really mean it? Why did you do it?" Doris responded, "My aunt Jenny told me if someone hurts you, pray for them." He gave her a piece of chocolate. A day later she was given a meal of sauerkraut, stewed potatoes, and meat in the prison.

In her testimony, Doris remembers a very nice woman coming into the barrack in Pillau at night before she was allowed to go to sleep, and this woman was also in the prison. Doris says she had noticed the blonde beautiful woman, who reminded her of her aunt, when she first came into the camp, and she remembered thinking she would become the woman's "pet." The woman, whom Doris describes as a Gestapo officer and commandant of the Pillau camp, gave her a sugar cube with some brown liquid, telling her that she would go right to sleep and sleep comfortably.[11] After three days of interrogation in the prison, Doris was sent back to the camp.

On the seventh day, a guard came and told her that someone wanted to see her. Doris relates that she was excited to see the beautiful blonde woman again because she felt she was getting closer to her. The woman took Doris into her room, where there was a single bed behind the closed door, and then sat in a chair. The bed was covered with nice sheets, and Doris remembers looking at the woman and admiring her beauty. Then the female "Gestapo camp commandant" told Doris to take off her clothes. As she did so, Doris says, the setting reminded her of her doctor's office at home and she thought she was about to be examined by a doctor. She was handed a comb and told to take her braids down. The Gestapo woman combed the back of her hair and told her to lie down on the bed.

Doris recounts that there were straps on the bed, but that she hadn't noticed them. At this point her account becomes graphic. The Gestapo woman, with a whistle on a cord around her neck, tied Doris's arms behind her to the sides of the bed, and her legs to the top. She then blew the whistle, the door opened, and three nude SS men entered.[12] It is not clear how Doris could be sure that these naked young men were actually members of the SS, nor why SS men would listen to the instructions of a female camp guard, most likely subordinate to them. Furthermore, rapists rarely parade around nude before the act. Doris says that up to this point in her life she had never seen a nude male body, not even a baby's. For a minute, she thought they were also going to see the doctor.

"She told them to rape me," Doris testified. "The first one didn't want to do it, so she told him to come a little closer, and she played with his private parts. He was twenty-one, twenty-two, twenty-three years old."[13] Doris says that when the rapes began she started yelling, and the Gestapo woman said: "I want to see more blood." Doris thought she would soon be dead. She says that she continued to be raped by three other groups of three men on that occasion. One soldier put his "private parts" in her mouth and she bit down hard and was severely beaten. As punishment, the commandant subjected Doris to six weeks of oral sex. Such punishment is highly unlikely and perhaps did not happen. Here Doris seems to be fantasizing.

This shocking scenario could illustrate an element of perversion in some instances of sexual abuse in the camps, but it just does not fit in with most other testimony by sexually abused Holocaust survivors.[14] It is most likely at least partially a fantasy that Doris created after the war. Regarding the perversion of sexual abusers such as those described by Doris, psychoanalyst Louise J. Kaplan explains that "every perversion is an effort to give some expression to, while yet controlling, the full strength of potentially murderous impulses to chew up, tear apart, explode, hack to pieces, burn to ashes, rip through to create one hole out of mouth, belly, anus, and vagina." Kaplan goes on to explain, "By violating every boundary between one body part and another, the pervert totally eliminates the distinction between the sexes and with it all distinctions between child and adult generations."[15]

Doris says that after her ordeal she did not get much comfort from her inmates, except for a cup of water that she poured on her crotch because the blood was turning brown. She says:

> "I screamed and I cried, and a girl named Tania said: 'We cannot talk to you, it is nine or ten o'clock and people have to go to work.' So I bit my arm, so as to not yell out loud. I was hoping to get more water. I heard them say, 'I got to get to work.' I didn't know how I would get to work. A nurse had a silky paper with a shiny powder in it. She said: 'This will help the pain.'"

Doris says she hoped it would kill her. The next morning she asked the nurse whether she could have more of the powder, and the nurse gave her some and told her she didn't have to go to work that day. A few days later, she was taken by a guard to a room across from that of the beautiful sadist whose name, she learned, was Elsa. Probably not by coincidence, Elsa and a derivative of this name, Ilsa, are often used in Nazi exploitation or "Nazisploitation" films.

Prior to her gang-rape, Doris says, the women in the barrack had not informed her about what to expect. Now, they felt she was one of them and let her know that Elsa was known as the "Black Widow," and the place where she had been raped was called the "Room of Blood." Luckily, Doris says, the Black Widow was transferred and a Major Holz arrived.[16]

Doris says she was asked to work on Major Holz's farm, caring for his two children. He told her that if she married a German she would not have to go back to the camp. One wonders what happened to *Rassenschande*. Germans didn't always fear the law against sexual relations with Jews, but there would have been no way for a marriage to take place between a Nazi and a woman claiming to be Jewish. According to her testimony, the young soldier who first raped Doris proposed to her, supposedly by sending her a love letter. Doris replied, via Major Holz, "I wouldn't marry any German. I hope you have nightmares the rest of your life, and that you never sleep again." It is, of course, highly unlikely that Doris would have written such a letter. In fact, as she elsewhere testifies, she did not know how to write, and it is beyond imagination that she would have dictated these words to a Nazi officer or his wife.

Doris was next sent away to Wehlau, a forced labor camp whose location is also difficult to pinpoint or confirm. After working on the farm for one year, she looked healthy again, and she says that a Greek laborer raped her along with other prisoners working in the field. A week later he brought a German soldier with him, and the soldier raped her. Doris says she became pregnant and was not sure which one of these men was the father.[17]

In Wehlau, Doris was aware that survival depended on pleasing the camp commandant and in not showing any sign of sickness. Once again, she was chosen to work for the camp commander and here worked on an assembly line alongside Gypsy prisoners making parts for hand grenades. One of the Gypsies, an experienced nurse, helped her deliver her baby girl. Doris says she could not breastfeed her baby because German soldiers had bitten and destroyed her nipples. A Nazi female guard discovered her baby when she was twenty-two days old and killed the baby by smashing her head against the bunk bed.

Doris claims to have witnessed other rape scenes when she was moved to Angerburg forced-labor camp, another place that is hard to trace. Assigned to cleaning cabins in a tourist area close to the camp, she opened a door to a cabin and saw a pistol and wedding band on a night stand. An SS officer was in the middle of the room with a young Russian girl. But, we may ask, why would the SS man allow Doris to witness this? Why didn't she knock on the door before entering? Doris says the officer ordered the girl to take her clothes off and lie on the bed, and the girl cried that she was saving herself for a Jewish man and that she was ready to die. The SS officer knocked her on the floor, reached for his fancy umbrella, spread her legs, and shoved the umbrella up into her private parts, ramming it further into her body. The girl died, and Doris was knocked down with the sharp edge of the umbrella and told to go about her business as if nothing had happened. If Doris had been a witness to such an event, it is more likely that she would have been murdered.

Doris says she eventually ended up in Auschwitz-Birkenau. During one of the roll calls, an SS officer had all the prisoners stand in line nude.[18] He rode a motorcycle up and down the line, and when a woman appealed to him he squeezed her breasts while balancing himself on the motorcycle. Doris was subjected to one of his squeezes, and when she didn't fall on her knees from the pain, he hit her with his rifle. Again, she may be fantasizing, although such an event could have occurred.

The trajectory of Doris's time in various camps is not clear, and the list that she gave to the USC Shoah Foundation does not make sense. It even places her in Theresienstadt, an unusual destination for a Lithuanian shtetl Jew or a non-Jewish forced laborer. She gives a detailed description of people being branded with tattoos as they entered Theresienstadt, but this event never happened. Her excuse for her own lack of such a tattoo is that she was under eighteen years of age.

Doris claims to have met Nazi high officials such as Heinrich Himmler and Wilhelm Keitel during the war and says she was working at a Siemens plant in Berlin at war's end. She says she made her way to the American zone of Germany after the war, soon married an American army mechanic, and gave birth to five children. First, she says, she underwent surgery to repair damage from multiple rapes. In 1957, she was diagnosed with multiple sclerosis, and she also survived two operations for cancer of the uterus and ovaries. Even her postwar testimony seems fragmented and confused. Toward the end of her testimony, she states that Hitler was both a Communist and a Nazi.

Doris says that the abuse and abandonment she had suffered continued in her marital relationships. Her first husband abandoned her and took four of her younger children with him. She was told they were killed in a car accident. Fifteen years later she learned they were alive. Then she discovered that her second husband was already married to two other women. Her third husband was an alcoholic, physically abusive, and forced violent sex on her. On his death bed he confessed to her that he was bisexual. Only her fourth and last husband was good to her. All of her children were involved with drugs. She said that she supported herself by working as a crop-picker and waitress, by knitting and crocheting, and at different times owning a thrift shop and café.[19]

Doris's early abandonment caused damaged self-esteem, with undeveloped ego strength. Her identity formation could not mature and was arrested at an earlier level of emotional development. This was a precursor to an unsolidified identity, fluid at its core. As an adolescent Doris assumed an identity that was astute at knowing what other people wanted, both verbally and nonverbally. She learned to comply, taking on the identity that was expected of her. This coping behavior was a result of her earlier trauma of abandonment, which continued as she sought to survive during World War II. She said that she had noticed a blonde SS woman upon her arrival at her first work camp and wanted to be her "pet." Having survived a rape that she described in graphic sadomasochistic detail, she used that incident as the lens through which she encountered the remaining years of maltreatment. She knew that if she complied, she could survive sexual abuse.

In Doris's post-Holocaust life we again observe parallels. She finds someone to marry soon after liberation, attesting to her ability to know how to acquiesce to other people's desires and get what she needs. In the situation after the war, some women wanted to marry to be safe from the rape of the Russian liberators. Given Doris's earlier history, she is a prime victim to again be abused and abandoned. Ultimately, she claims, she found a real savior and had a happy life.

Doris's bizarre testimony as a "Lithuanian Jewish survivor" who was sexually abused beyond belief may be plausible if understood in the full context of what seems to have been a traumatic childhood and the personality structure that she developed. There have been cases of false survivor testimony. While such may not be exactly Doris's case, we will never know how much of her testimony actually occurred. The USC Shoah Foundation interview took place more than fifty years after liberation, in Gridley, California, in November 1996.[20] She died on May 26, 2006, and is buried in California, so we will never be able to question her further. That Doris does not exhibit the usual feelings of shame that are associated with being raped and that she provides graphic testimony, when most other sexually abused women have kept silent, are telling pieces of Doris's personality. She took pride in having mastered survival.

In narrating her story to school children and others, Doris may have embellished the truth to fend off feelings of inadequacy. She also knew how to satisfy her audience and get positive attention and adulation for having survived. The more gruesome the details, the more she was probably praised for her survival. She also received ego gratification by teaching a new generation of young boys not to rape women.

In rare instances when survivors tell their story over and over again, the story begins to take on exaggerated components that will appeal to an audience and move the story out of the realm of the ordinary. Doris was interviewed by the USC Shoah Foundation after she had told her story numerous times. It may be that the more her audiences were drawn to sexual details, the more her narrative moved away from reality and took on a life of its own. In such cases, a narrator begins to live in her imagination in order to tell the story. In Doris's case, she seems to have lost the historical verity along the way.

The Testimony of Celia K. and Her Daughter's Doubts

The theme of sexual imagery seeping into the minds of the second generation of Holocaust survivors is common, one that is depicted in Orna Ben-Dor Niv's 1994 film. In therapy groups and "rap" groups, members of the second generation have had the opportunity to share their fantasies about their mothers, aunts, and sisters having been taken advantage of sexually during the Holocaust. However, with exceptions such as Doris Roe, most survivors themselves seem not to have indulged in fantasies at all. In the years following liberation, women who had been sexually abused during the German occupation of European countries did not benefit from rape counseling. Rather, they experienced the fate of most rape victims—they were blamed for what happened to them.

The psychological, physical, emotional, and social consequences of sexual assault are overpowering, whether or not the survivor talks about her ordeals. Sometimes she is in denial about some aspects of the horrific past, but her child suspects that her mother was sexually abused. This pattern is not uncommon and is well demonstrated by the case of Celia K.[21] Celia's daughter Cindy (pseudonym) never fully knew what happened to her mother, who in turn never wanted to talk about her experiences. Cindy had a general idea that her mother was in a ghetto in Poland, and after the liquidation of the ghetto, at age seventeen, she ended up hidden by farmers in a small hole under their barn. Cindy knew only the following scant details: The farmers had been business associates of Celia's family. After about half a year, Celia had been joined in the hole by her sister, who had escaped from the ghetto where their mother and older sisters had been killed. Celia ended up fighting with the partisans in the nearby woods, along with her two brothers. After liberation, she and her younger sister and two older brothers were together. Celia was in a displaced persons (DP) camp for a while, where she was deathly ill. After she recovered, she married, had a daughter, and came to the northeastern part of the United States, where she had two more children.

This was the extent of Cindy's knowledge about her mother's past. However, when she was an adult with children of her own, Cindy met people who had known her mother when she was with the partisans. They told her what had really happened to Celia. Cindy learned that when her mother was seventeen or eighteen years old and living in a ghetto, she was assigned to work in a German command building. One day one of the Germans made sexual advances, and she slapped him in the face. A German official had her whipped and put a pistol to her head. When he shot into the air, he permanently damaged her hearing, and he then tossed her into the ghetto latrine. Cindy later confirmed this story with documents at Yad Vashem.

When there was a roundup in the ghetto, Cindy discovered, Celia tried to escape into the woods. She then returned to the ghetto to be with her family. At this time, a male Polish high-school classmate who was in love with Celia arrived in a horse-drawn wagon and demanded that she leave with him. Celia resisted, but her mother encouraged her to leave, saying: "I don't want to see you again." Celia was taken five miles out of town to a farm where she was hidden in the barn when the Germans came to inspect. When the ghetto was liquidated, her sister joined her in the barn. After being denounced by a neighbor, the sisters escaped to the partisans.

Cindy obtained the name of her mother's rescuer from her mother's fellow partisans and traveled to see him in Belarus.[22] She said, "I am Celia's daughter." The first question she was asked was the date of her birth. Celia's rescuer's daughter then told Cindy that her father had been in love with Celia. According to the rescuer's wife, people had told her, "He always loved a Jewish girl. Don't marry him."

When Cindy returned to the United States and told her mother she had seen the man who had saved her life, Celia was in shock. She said: "I did what I had to do to save my sister."[23] Cindy feels that her mother had sexual relations with this non-Jew, and it isn't possible to ascertain whether she considered it sexual abuse or not. In 1998, Cindy had Yad Vashem certify the man who had saved her mother's life as one of the Righteous Among the Nations. He had initiated the rescue of Celia K. and later also saved her sister at great risk to himself and his family.

A deeper story emerges from the two interviews that Celia K. gave to the Fortunoff Video Archive for Holocaust Testimonies at Yale University. While

Cindy has a copy of these interviews, it is pertinent that she has never watched them. Growing up, Cindy lived with the nonverbal pain of her mother's suffering, and she went through her own struggles. Cindy did not hear any details about what had happened to her mother in a ghetto, in hiding, or with the partisans. Today Cindy is a successful, professional, happily married woman with several children of her own, but the pain that her mother endured is never far from the surface.

Celia K. was one of the first interviewees for the Fortunoff project in 1980, and she was interviewed again in 1987. Her name does not come up as one of those who spoke of sexual abuse or rape. Celia is pretty, composed, intelligent, articulate, and looks upper-middle-class. She has an intelligent and appealing smile. She became upset toward the end of the second Fortunoff interview, when she talked about her experiences in the United States. The only time she cried was when, at the end of this interview, she talked about not having been in love and having been stuck in a marriage of convenience. Celia's husband had died seven months before the second interview, and she speaks about the frustrations and regrets related to their marriage.

Two leading psychoanalysts who are Holocaust survivors also interviewed Celia K. in the United States. One of them was Hillel Klein, director of Eitanim Hospital and president of the Israeli Psychoanalytic Association, with whom I worked in Israel in 1978. Klein did not ask about Celia's sexual encounters, but he was the first to alert me to the fact that I should be asking survivors about sex and that I had been leaving this topic out of my interviews. Clearly, even psychoanalysts who are accustomed to delving into the sexual lives of their patients have natural reservations about broaching the topic with survivors of the Holocaust.

The main theme in Celia's two testimonies with the Fortunoff archive is that she was not raped. This topic recurs in her testimony many times. Celia relates:

One incident I would like to tell about took place in the ghetto. It was very unique. Only one girl went through it. The war started with the Soviets walking in. It was very bad for us because we were considered bourgeoisie. There was a Polish captain who wanted to have a restaurant way back in Poland. In small towns, there was only one permit [granted] for [selling] liquor since World War I. He wanted a permit and my family wouldn't give him theirs. He said, "Some day I'll take revenge."

When the ghetto was formed, he became the commandant. Every night they arrested two wealthy persons. They would torture them. Jews would buy out these people—each day another person, another pail of gold. One night two police-men came for me.

"Me? I'm seventeen years old?"

"Yes, you, we have orders to arrest you." They brought me to the comman-dant. I said, "Why am I being arrested, I'm only a child?"

He said: "I want you to be my mistress."

I said to him, "You want me to be your mistress?" I knew that they didn't have to ask permission. If [they] wanted to rape a girl, they just did it. The girls were too terrified to resist.

He said, "Yes, I want you to openly move in with and live with me as my mistress."

I said, "No, I won't."

He said, "I'll kill you."

I said, "I know you will, but I won't."

Now I have a lot of people from my town who know it's the truth.

He said, "Well, you'll change your mind by tomorrow."[24]

Afterward, Celia said, they put her in an interrogation room with "maybe fifty policemen lined up," and they beat her with a rubber hose. The beating contin-ued throughout the night, and she lost consciousness. "I don't remember one thing," she said. "I just remember at dawn, I woke up and this commander was standing over me. It was very cold, the floor—they put water and it froze, and I was on this ice and stuck to it from the blood." When the commandant asked if she had changed her mind, she replied in the negative. He told her she would be shot. Celia continued her narrative:

I didn't know that during the night everyone was alerted to send gold to buy me out. And there were pails of gold and valuables because I was liked in the ghetto. I was a young girl and it [had] never happened to a young girl before. I was the first one. And everyone, whatever they had, they offered to buy me out and they were running to the commandant, and he said, "No, it's not going to help you, she's going to die." This was his revenge [for her family's refusal to grant him their liquor license] because my two older sisters were married. And I was next in line at seventeen.

In [villages in] Poland, there's a big square. At one side of the square were our properties; at the other side was the *Kommandantur* (headquarters). The cemetery was beyond the ghetto. Four policemen were leading me past the ghetto. Everyone was hanging on the fences: children, women, men, adults, old people—everyone. Everyone was screaming my name, reaching out with their hands to touch me. But they couldn't. The policemen were guarding me too closely; I was in the middle of the four. And they took me to the cemetery. And the commandant told them that: "She's a very stubborn . . ." and he called me a nice name. "And when she'll get scared and says she'll be my mistress, shoot her. If she'll say no, let her go," the commandant said.

At the cemetery, Celia again refused to be the commandant's mistress. After that, all she remembered was hearing shooting, and then she woke up back in the ghetto. There she told her mother, "He didn't do it, he didn't do it," and her mother responded, "It's fine, it's fine, don't worry." Celia said it took her weeks to recuperate from her fright. "I was completely insane for months and months," she said. "And the whole ghetto saw it." She said that she couldn't relate to her family, nor to anyone around her. Yet she insisted that she had not been raped or abused. She continued:

> How I made it I don't know. Why he didn't shoot me, I don't know. How he didn't shoot me. He did not rape me; not one of the policemen raped me. No one touched me. This is a mystery to me, up until today. I don't understand. I really don't. Their cruelty was such that I don't know why he didn't shoot me, he could have. Why didn't he rape me, I don't know. But he let me go. And I returned to the ghetto. And then the ghetto was exterminated anyway a few months later.

Celia was next given the job of working in the *Kommandantur*. She said she was chosen because she was clean and pretty and well-mannered, and she worked as a waitress, serving three meals a day there. She was not mistreated and was given soap and cosmetics. Because she could read German well, she was able to spy and help people escape from the ghetto. But, again, people suspected that she had been raped. She repeated, "Never, no one ever raped me," and then explained the importance of not being raped.

> Well, being a Polish girl you know what virginity meant. If a girl was not a virgin it was the end of the world. And my mother, when they took me away to be shot, and the whole ghetto saw how seven policemen with rifles took me to the cemetery and heard shots. Everybody thought that the whole police department had me. No one touched me. I can't believe that this happened that no one touched me; I was beaten with rubber hoses all night long. The dress was in my body; it was bloody. They had to soak me, literally—they didn't have bathtubs—to get the dress out of my body. Yet no one raped me.

Celia insists that she was never raped during the entire war. In contrast to herself, she mentions a friend who succumbed to the German's sexual demands. She says, "A girlfriend worked with me in the police department—a beautiful girl, a sixteen-year-old with brown hair and blue eyes. She slept with every policeman out of fear. She was the first one to be shot. I said, 'Don't do it.' She said, 'I'll stay [alive] longer maybe.' She slept with every one of them— thirty a night maybe." While this may be an exaggeration, Celia uses such a high number to compare her friend's "transgressions" with her own "purity." Celia even explained why she was not raped by all the policemen, although her reason is not necessarily plausible: "No one touched me, because he [the commandant] kept me for himself." She continues to be plagued by the fact that no one believes her. "I have twenty people who can testify to this," she said—obviously an impossibility. "Nobody believes me anyway. My mother didn't believe me, even. Mother said—nobody even now—people say if you were down there all night with [commandant's name] and his policemen, they say sure you were touched. They don't believe me."

When Celia is asked if she is angry that people don't believe her about not being raped she says: "I don't care. My children believe me. That's what's important." However, it is not at all clear that her daughter indeed believes her. Celia describes not being raped during the night of her arrest as "some kind of miracle," especially since she described herself as "an attractive girl, seventeen years old."

Stating that not every German was bad, Celia again insisted, "Frankly speaking, I was never raped by a German. Not one German ever laid a finger on me." She said that they liked her looks, but treated her like a Fräulein, giving her food and milk for her children. (However, she was only seventeen and didn't have any children.) She also said the Germans she worked for gave her a pass so she would not be searched and told her to put string around the knees of her pantaloons and place the food there so that no one would see it in the ghetto. By contrast with her praise of the Germans, she said: "What I do hate is Ukrainians and Poles. I shiver when I see them in the streets now. I literally get the shakes physically when [I] see [a] Ukrainian in the street."

Celia then spoke of the young man who rescued her from the ghetto, saying he had liked her when she was a small child. "I think he loved me. I didn't know what love was. I didn't know," she said. She spoke of him and his family as "primitive" and probably not literate. She said she had no feelings for the young man: "I never had feelings; I was like a stone. No love, no hate, some semblance of gratefulness." Celia left the family who had hidden her and joined the partisans.

Celia has fond memories of being with the partisans but said the fear of rape didn't leave her. "It was beautiful fighting with the partisans," she said. After the war she and her brothers and sister set up housekeeping together.

"We tried to resume life, but it was extremely difficult," she said. "No money, no skills. I never learned to do anything because I was pampered, in school, we had maids. I didn't know what to do. So first thing I did, I got married. I saw a man who wanted me, and I got married. I didn't know how to do anything for myself. The only way for me to survive was to get married. So I was looking for a husband." She married after knowing her future husband for only three weeks, and one of her reasons for the rush was that "everyone was out raping girls." They left Poland for Czechoslovakia and then immigrated to the United States. "There was no romance, no compatibility," she said. "A lot of marriages got made like this in 1944, 1945."

"It was very hard to start a life after the war was over, and I was pretty suicidal," Celia said. "I gave birth to a child. The child had a very hard time for many years. The child is fine. I was sick. I had no business giving birth to a child in the state I was in. I can see it now. All my children really suffered for it." Celia said that she knew she had "wounds that needed to be healed," and she sought help. However, she complained both about her therapy group, which "weighed her down," and her husband, who did not understand her or "cater to her needs." She said she and her husband "did not have any communication," but she "never had any other man" and didn't know what it would be like.

Celia implies that she had no sexual relations with the young man who saved her and her sister and that she regrets her marriage. "When I married I did not know my husband," she said. "Missing all the fun a teenager should have. I never loved; I never dated; I was never kissed by a boy. Literally, never did. I mean it. I was an innocent, pampered little girl and found myself in bed with a man I did not know." Celia insists that she never kissed a boy before meeting her husband after the war. And yet, when Cindy went to see the farmer in Poland, the first thing he wanted to know was her age, possibly trying to find out if she was his child. This led Cindy to believe that her mother had a sexual relationship with the man who saved her.

Most women survivors did not seek out professionals for psychological problems, and when they did, they were not understood. Celia K. confirms this sentiment, "I don't think any therapist understood me. Intellectually, I was on their level. I understood more of what was happening between us than they did. They thought I'm some kind of a lunatic, coming out of the war missing a few screws. I did not miss any screws." The therapeutic community failed the women survivors in general, and particularly those who were raped. For the most part, women who had been violated sexually during the war or by the liberators married for better or worse, had families, and suffered silently with their secrets. Committing to a man helped women who were raped during the Holocaust to feel safe from the possibility of rape in the future. Love was not as crucial as establishing boundaries of safety.

Post-Holocaust Abuse: The Testimony of "Hanna"

Even more taboo than the subject of rape during the Holocaust is that of child survivors who were taken in by Jewish families after the war and then sexually abused by their supposed protectors. After surviving the Holocaust, losing parents and siblings, these vulnerable children had to yet experience persecution at the hands of Jews in what was supposed to be their new safe haven. Hanna (pseudonym), who survived the war in hiding in Western Europe, is one such case.[25] Her parents were deported to concentration camps, and her father was murdered. Although her mother survived, she was hospitalized after the war and was too ill to care for her daughter. As a result, Hanna, then eight years old, was taken in by a Satmar Hasidic family in the Williamsburg section of Brooklyn, New York.[26] The foster care was arranged by a Jewish organization and the family was paid. More than sixty years after liberation, Hanna still vividly envisions the sofa bed in the living room in which she slept. One day she was sick, and she liked the attention the man in the house was giving her. She then became very uncomfortable because he started to fondle her body and also tried to manually penetrate her, although she says that he did not succeed. She doesn't recall how she reacted at the moment, except that she didn't like it and tried to avoid him and go to the home of one of his relatives after school. Hanna thinks that she may have run to the relative after the incident.

Hanna, who was separated from her own father at age four, had trouble connecting with men. She was afraid of them and, as an adult, afraid to engage in consensual sex. While she engaged in petting as a teenager, she was late in having intercourse. Hanna always delayed having sex as long as possible, until she was very comfortable with the man. She had a period of time when she was very angry with men. It still takes her a long time to trust them, and even then she says, "trust is relative."

For a good part of her life she was terrified of sex. She has been in therapy for most of her life. It was not until she had the support of other children who, like her, had been hidden during the Holocaust, that she understood her particular emotional conflicts. Hanna rebelled against religion. She thinks it is a sham and hypocritical. When Hanna was hidden she was raised as a devout Catholic, and to this day she considers herself spiritual but not religious.

When a Jew was sexually violated by another Jew, the abuse was more diffi-cult to overcome than was abuse by the Germans, Poles, Ukrainians, or the Russian liberators. From the persecutors, one came to expect the worst. From one's fellow Jews, one came to expect refuge, safety, and compassion. I em-phasize compassion, because it has become clear that empathy was rarely to be found.

Conclusions

Survivors find solace when they are with other survivors who had similar expe-riences. Child survivors have their own organizations, and their own memo-ries, of the traumas of sexual abuse as children during the Holocaust. One of the Holocaust child-survivor organizations used to hold informal support groups at their annual meetings. Unlike other sessions at the conference, this meeting was not listed in the program, and participants who had been sexually abused as children were extremely secretive about attending. One issue they had was the fear of exposing the fact that rescuers of children sometimes took advantage of the situation and molested the child in hiding. At one of the an-nual meetings, around 2001, one of the hidden children said: "We are coming out of hiding, why not come out about sexual abuse?"

Women and girls were the most vulnerable to experiencing sexual assault during the Holocaust and its aftermath. This fact does not negate the reality that men and boys were also subject to such violation. The psychological im-pact of their abuse is as taboo a subject as that of the women's. Validating the experiences of rape, molestation, sadomasochistic sexual abuse, and sodomy gives victims permission to speak and write of these atrocities, thereby allow-ing the full measure of their experiences under the Nazis and their collabora-tors to be told. Doing so will not only help to ease the pain of the surviving victims of these acts, but will also broaden and deepen historical and psycho-logical studies, as well as, hopefully, helping to prevent future recurrences.

Notes
Thank you to Jeanette Friedman of The Wordsmithy and www.whyshouldicareonthe web.com, and to Hannah Meyers of Yale University for archival work.

1. *Eretz Hadasha*, film, directed by Orna Ben-Dor Niv (1994); released in the United States as *Newland*.

2. Ilana Rosen, *Sister in Sorrow: Life Histories of Female Survivors from Hungary* (Detroit: Wayne State University Press, 2008), 41.

3. See Esther Katz and Joan Ringelheim, eds., *Proceedings of the Conference of Women Surviving the Holocaust* (New York: The Institute for Research in History, 1983).

4. Milton, who died in 2000, was a leading scholar on Nazi Germany and a senior historian at the United States Holocaust Memorial Museum; Laska, who died in 2006, wrote about women in the Resistance and was a professor of history at Regis College in Massachusetts.

5. For further discussion about the construct of beauty in concentration camps, see chapter 5 by Monika Flashka in this volume.

6. Special thanks to Crispin Brooks of the University of Southern California Shoah Foundation Institute for Visual History and Education (USC Shoah Foundation).

7. Doris Roe, interview 23687, USC Shoah Foundation testimony, November 27, 1996, Gridley, CA, by interviewer Sue Steinberg; Doris Roe, *Child Prisoner 29418 Doris Barbet Betty von Lindorf* (Pine Bluff, AR: D. Roe, 2002), available in the United States Holocaust Memorial Museum library.

8. When asked by the USC Shoah Foundation interviewer about her mother's name change from Bartheleit to Goldberg, and the family's name change from Rubinstein to Rubin, Doris waved her hand and said, "All the people changed their names."

9. There were no Nazis in Grodno on May 1, 1939. A Gestapo outstation was first established there in September 1941, and Jews were ghettoized on November 1, 1941. Deportations began on November 2, 1942, when the ghetto was sealed.

10. Pillau (now Baltiysk) is on a peninsula near Kaliningrad, formerly called Königsberg. It was a place of strategic importance, with a U-boat garrison. If Doris was taken there, she may have been classified as a German refugee or forced laborer rather than a prisoner. The Germans used Königsberg as a major center to evacuate their citizens from the advancing Red Jewish Army. For more information on Pillau, see Isaak Kobylyanskiy, *From Stalingrad to Pillau: A Red Army Artillery Officer Remembers the Great Patriotic War* (Lawrence: University of Kansas Press, 2008).

11. Doris Roe, USC Shoah Foundation testimony, part 3. There were no female Gestapo officers or camp commandants, although a small number of labor sub-camps had women in charge of them.

12. Doris Roe, USC Shoah Foundation testimony, part 3.

13. Ibid.

14. For another explicit description of sexual abuse, see the testimony by Sara M. (interview 29016, USC Shoah Foundation testimony) in chapter 7 by Helene Sinnreich in this volume.

15. Louise J. Kaplan, *Female Perversions: The Temptations of Emma Bovary* (New York: Doubleday, 1991), 127.

16. Doris Roe, USC Shoah Foundation testimony, part 3.

17. This episode is in the self-published manuscript but not in the USC Shoah Foundation testimony.

18. Doris Roe, USC Shoah Foundation testimony, part 6.

19. Doris Roe, *Child Prisoner 29418*, 71–72.

20. Doris Roe was living there at the time, but also had connections to Pine Bluff, Arkansas.

21. Celia K. Holocaust testimony, T-36, is used with permission of the Fortunoff Video Archive for Holocaust Testimonies, Yale University Library (FVA). Celia K. was interviewed in 1980 and 1987. Her daughter "Cindy" (pseudonym) was interviewed by author Eva Fogelman in May 2009 and gave her permission to use the interview.

22. Cindy, interview with the author, May 2009.

23. Ibid. Cindy reported her mother's reaction verbatim.

24. Celia K., FVA interviews, 1980 and 1987.

25. Hanna (pseudonym), interview with the author, 1991 and June 2009, used with interviewee's permission.

26. Satmar Hasidism is a movement of Hasidic (ultra-Orthodox) Jews, mostly from Hungary and Romania, who survived the Holocaust. It was founded by Hungarian-born Rabbi Yoel Teitelbaum. Its two largest communities are in Williamsburg and Kiryas Joel, New York.

CHAPTER

16

The Shame Is Always There

ESTHER DROR AND RUTH LINN

While Holocaust survivors rarely speak about sexual abuse, especially from first-person experience, our interviews with Israeli survivors included several who commented about this usually taboo subject. In this chapter we present the insights of "Leah," "Roza," and "Reuven," all of whom shared with us memories that involve various forms of sexual abuse. These three interviewees were among twenty-eight participants (twenty-four women and four men) in a study that took place in Israel between 2006 and 2009.[1] Without being told the study's purpose, the female participants were asked to share their wartime experiences as women, and men were asked what they knew about women's experiences. Leah, Roza, and Reuven were interviewed by co-author Dror, and Reuven's son was interviewed by co-author Linn. Due to the sensitivity of the topic, we have protected our interviewees by changing their names and not revealing their places of birth.

Although *Rassenschande* (race defilement), prohibited by the Nuremberg Laws of 1935, may have reduced the number of rapes in the ghettos and camps, it did not prevent them entirely. As these three survivors testify, sexual humiliation, rape, and forced prostitution of women victims all occurred. Even on their way to extermination, "[t]here were also instances of SS men of all ranks pushing their fingers into the sexual organs of pretty young women," according to one survivor.[2] In addition, there were cases of the use of sexuality as a recourse for survival—sex in exchange for food and basic necessities—and "romantic" connections.

Even if they survived physically and mentally, the women victims almost never told this chapter in their Holocaust narratives. In Israel the national narrative, the historians, and the educators preferred to focus on the sphere of heroism—the *Läuferin* (female messenger) in ghettos or women who helped the partisans to kill Germans or save helpless Jews. Except for rumors and guesses, sexual abuse never had a place of its own in the Israeli Holocaust narrative—even sexual abuse and exploitation as modes for rescuing oneself or others are still not used in constructing categories of bravery.[3] On rare occasions, fictitious stories were told by men.[4] When told by women survivors they ranged from examples of forced choice between death and survival to prostitution to vague statements such as "they chose whom they wanted," without indicating the purpose of the choice.[5]

Unlike these women's testimonies, Italian diplomat and journalist Curzio Malaparte describes a brothel established in 1941 in the city of Soroca, Romania, by the medical service of the 11th German Military Division. This brothel for soldiers "employed" a group of young Jewish women as slave laborers, about a ten at a time, from the city and its environs. According to Malaparte, "Every twenty days the Germans provided a change of girls. Those who left the brothel were shoved into a truck and taken down to the river. Later Schenk [the Nazi *Sonderführer*] told me that it was not worth while [*sic*] to feel sorry for them. They were not fit for anything any more. They were reduced to rags, and besides, they were Jews."[6]

What is an appropriate story of a female Holocaust survivor in the face of potential sexual abuse? Is it a narrative of survival? Of sexual violation? Of women's place in a society at war? More than sixty-five years after the Holocaust, this chapter attempts to locate women's narratives of victimization and survival.

"Leah"—One Can Always Choose

"Leah" was an adolescent when Germany occupied Poland in September 1939. She arrived at Auschwitz-Birkenau in August 1944, after a long period of edicts, persecution, and suffering in her city and then in a ghetto. After a few weeks in Auschwitz-Birkenau, she and her companions were sent to Bergen-Belsen, where they stayed until December. They managed to survive under the harshest conditions of hunger and disease, before being transferred to a German armament factory in a forced labor camp. In April 1945 Leah and her friends were liberated by the U.S. Army and transferred to a displaced persons camp set up in a magnificent building in the area.

Upon returning to her native city, Leah did not find anyone from her family. She joined a group of people intending to immigrate to pre-Israel Palestine, who first settled in a model preparatory kibbutz in Italy. There she met "Avraham," whom she later married. Now a popular lecturer in Israel, Leah speaks before students and Israel Defense Force soldiers and has published a book about her experiences during the Holocaust, in which she writes specifically about sexual abuse. Data for Leah's narrative was based on her published book and on three taped and written conversations with co-author Dror. These interviews lasted about two hours each, and took place between January and March 2007.

In interviews, Leah recalled various episodes connected to sex as a survival resource. For example, she spoke about a friend in the ghetto, orphaned, poor, and suffering from tuberculosis, who was taken in by a wealthy man. He took care of her, and she, in return, had sexual relations with him and his son. By contrast, Leah said she refused a similar proposal made by the manager of the factory where she worked, and through her own resources found an alternative way of obtaining medicine for her ill mother.

In Birkenau, Leah resisted the temptation of accepting a spoon from a Polish prisoner, a maintenance man in Camp C, when she understood that in return for the gift she would have to have sexual relations with him. She made this choice despite the fact that a spoon was literally a lifesaver in the camps. Without it one had to drink soup from the same vessel as everyone else, risking exposure to contagious diseases such as tuberculosis.

In her book, Leah wrote that in Bergen-Belsen one of her friends became the German camp commander's mistress. In return, he appointed her in charge of all the tents, a role that she used to good advantage to mitigate the conditions of her fellow inmates as much as possible. Leah further related that after liberation by the Americans, when the women had regained their health and their bodies had filled out, American soldiers began arriving in search of companionship and sex. Some of the women responded to their advances in return for gifts such as chocolate and silk stockings. Despite providing this information, Leah's initial reaction to the idea of doing research on sexual abuse during the Holocaust was: "On that topic . . . I have zero knowledge. I know nothing." Immediately afterward, she spoke about the traumatic meeting with the Polish maintenance man who offered her a spoon in exchange for sex. She said:

> I open—a spoon. I say: "I'm so grateful to you." . . . Then he asks me: "When will we meet?" I then comprehend what it is about and I throw the spoon at him and run off. I was afraid he'd chase me, because he was really angry. But right away he found someone else who agreed. In Auschwitz, too, I heard there was a song to a popular Polish tune: "For kisses . . . she will get a pat of margarine. Margarine. Godina Margarine." It was a kind of song. That's what I heard. Anything more about sex—I haven't a clue.

Despite the fact that among her friends from the ghetto, in the camp, and even after liberation, there were those who bartered sex for survival, and even though she herself had received and refused a proposition, Leah says: "I know nothing" and "I haven't a clue." Why is her story told from a viewpoint of denial? It seems that more than once Leah found herself rejecting rumors in which she herself was a victim of sexual abuse. For example, in meeting with her surviving sisters, she discovered that they had been told that she had been taken for prostitution. Leah said she responded by saying: "What are you talking about? You know what we looked like—shaved heads, rags. I looked like a nine-year-old girl." She also had to defend herself from rumors and accusations when she was about to be married. She recalled that her future husband's cousins said, "Avraham, she was in a concentration camp. She most probably slept with all the Germans." Leah said her husband then came to her and asked: "What is this I hear?" And she told him: "Listen . . . there's one thing I know—that we will marry and then you will know if I am a virgin or not. That's all I know."

On various occasions Leah asserts that those who used sex as a means of survival cannot be judged. But where she herself is concerned—as a young, innocent woman who had received a strict upbringing in a religious home— the option does not even arise. Despite her assertion that "those who did it" in such dire circumstances are not to be judged, she claims that sexual abuse of all types depends on conscious acquiescence on the part of the victim: "I want to say that even there, in that same 'graveyard,' one had free choice. . . . the ability to be bad, the ability to be good, the ability to be wanton, and the ability . . . to keep your honor, to preserve your body. No one raped, no one forced." Unfortunately, various other women's testimonies negate this statement.

Perhaps in order to cope with the accusations against her, Leah alludes to witnesses who can testify that she did nothing of which to be ashamed. She said: "Because I have girlfriends from the same city who were with me, and they know my book like the back of my hand, and I couldn't bluff in the book . . . so they can testify. . . . We were always in a correct and good way. So that . . . I'm not the right address, not on matters of sex."

Why does Leah repeatedly claim that she knows nothing about sexual abuse during the Holocaust, despite having described, both in her book and in interviews with us, situations in which young women bartered sex for survival and benefits, and despite the fact that she, herself, was similarly propositioned? Is it possible that, within the research framework, the very fact of being approached to speak about this topic is perceived as an accusation, as if to know means to be part of it? Her attitude regarding the issues of sexual abuse and bartered sex is twofold: "not to judge" on one hand, and "no one was raped, always the possibility to choose" on the other. The subtext that can be read in her words supports the stereotype in which the victim of rape is to blame (typical of patriarchal attitudes towards victims of rape),[7] as well as the widespread tendency in Israeli society to blame the victims and survivors of the Holocaust for what happened to them.[8] Is it possible that today, more than sixty-five years after these events, she is still defending herself against the same rumors and accusations and feels that she must "bear the burden of proof"?

Two authors of early memoirs wrote that, like Leah, they resisted temptation and protected their honor at all costs.[9] Gisella Perl related how she gave up a string, vital for keeping her oversized shoes on her feet, when she understood that the "seller" was asking for sex in exchange. Olga Lengyl stated that she preferred to starve to death rather than to succumb to the Polish prisoner who proposed extra food in exchange for sex. In a lecture in Beit Terezin, survivor Ruth Bondy spoke of her choice not to accept the tempting proposal of a Polish plumber who offered her two slices of bread for sex: "[I refused] because I had received a Puritan upbringing from a home in which words such as sex, menstruation, and pregnancy were never mentioned," she said.[10]

Contemporary research exploring various aspects of sexual abuse and sex as a resource for survival during the Holocaust also demonstrates that survivors of both genders rarely speak about subjective sexual experiences. Women often mention that they knew of, and even were witness to, the bartering of sex for food, but almost never relate this as a personal experience.[11] Men, on the other hand, tend to talk about the revulsion they felt when they witnessed or were propositioned for homosexual acts.[12]

This type of omission can also be observed during times of peace. Researchers and mental health clinicians report that rape victims or survivors of sexual abuse are laden with shame and guilt and have difficulty verbally articulating their experiences.[13] These events often become "forgotten" and turn into dark secrets that can hardly be located. Gabriele Rosenthal claims that in most cases stories of rape or sex bartering can only be understood between the lines, and that Holocaust survivors who experienced these things do not tell them to their children or grandchildren. For example, Rosenthal's interviewees "Sarah" and "Irena" testified that they, themselves, avoided capitulation to the sexual demands of prisoners who gave them "presents," but they hinted that their younger sister, "Tamara," improved their living conditions for a time through prostitution. Tamara testified that other women sold their bodies, but denied that she, herself, did the same.[14] Is it possible that survivors tend to tell the story as if it happened to someone else, and not to them, themselves? And if so, why?

It cannot be known whether Leah experienced and repressed events during the Holocaust. However, avoiding thoughts or feelings connected to traumatic events and activities or situations that are reminiscent of sexual abuse is a common strategy among trauma victims, including Holocaust survivors, and engaging these realms is an inevitable part of the rehabilitation process. Many Holocaust survivors were unable to see themselves actually related to the atrocities they experienced and found it difficult to believe the plausibility of their stories. The disgrace associated with experiences of a sexual nature tended to create a heightened experience of shame and guilt,[15] as well as trigger forgetting as a dissociative defense.[16]

Another reason that survivors of sexually related trauma during the Holocaust refrain from telling their stories is that their respective families cannot understand and cope with such memories. The sons and daughters often cannot bring themselves to question their mothers on this subject and sometimes find it difficult to hear the memories that a mother does want to share with them.[17] Not only family members find it difficult to hear about sexual abuse or sexual bartering. Joan Ringelheim writes about her own speechlessness when, at the start of her research in the field, an interviewee told her that she had been raped in Auschwitz. Only years later, on a return visit, did the researcher pluck up the courage to ask the interviewee what had actually happened to her.[18] This kind of difficulty is described not only by Ringelheim but also by psychotherapists working with Holocaust survivors. Within a therapeutic framework, they sometimes connect with survivors' traumas in ways that can leave them speechless or unable to listen to their patients.[19] As the daughter of a camp survivor, co-author Dror has psychological involvement with the subject that creates personal sensitivity. This factor was particularly apparent during interviews with Leah, when Dror felt embarrassed and ashamed even to present the subject of the research.

"Roza"—It's the Silent Thing

"Roza," another participant, was born in 1914 in Hungary, the daughter of a wealthy family. Data for her narrative are based on six hours of taped and written conversations with her at her home between August and September 2006. At her exalted age, she expressed herself clearly and sharply. In a mixture of faulty Hebrew, English, and German, she told fascinating stories about her life, often seasoning her narrative with humor.

Roza was a newlywed in a city far from her birthplace when she was betrayed by an informant and apprehended by the Germans. She almost died during torture to extract information about her family's assets. Roza was highly regarded by the group of Jews rounded up with her to be sent to Auschwitz, despite the fact that she was in a poor physical state after the torture. As she was fluent in German she became an interpreter and mediator between the Nazis and the Jews. Whenever the train stopped during the journey to Auschwitz, she translated to her companions what she overheard the Germans saying, and she continued to translate after arrival. Her dominant personality, sharp intelligence, and knowledge of languages turned Roza into a leader throughout her ordeal—from Auschwitz through the death marches to the German work camps. In Auschwitz-Birkenau she was appointed a *blockova* (prisoner in charge of a block), and after liberation, she worked with the U.S. Army as a Nazi hunter.

Roza had much to say about sexual abuse and enforced prostitution, and, in particular, about those with positions such as hers who had sexual relations with German guards. When the subject of this research was presented to her, she responded without hesitation. Friends who arrived with her in the transport to Auschwitz had advised her to join them to be sent away on a special transport, she recalled. They said, "Today there's a group they want to send somewhere, and they want young women with good bodies and good faces and everything. Come with us— you have a good body." She was suspicious of the proposal. Roza remembered her response:

> I said, "Look, if they want a good body for work, I don't like it . . . Don't go! . . . There's no easy work" . . . They didn't listen to me and they went. And afterward, when we were already there, we heard rumors from the army . . . whores. They made them into prostitutes for the soldiers. If they fell pregnant when they were in . . . they were killed. Many girls from the city where I married went with the group. . . . To this day it pains me.

After she was sent from Auschwitz to work camps in Germany, Roza organized social activities, including a theater group, for her companions. The lead actress was pretty and talented. She was a Hungarian whose mother had married a Jew, and she considered herself non-Jewish. She had decided to tie her fate to that of her mother and stepfather and go with them to the camps. This same actress, according to Roza, did not hesitate to have sexual relations with men if, in exchange, she could receive more food, a warm garment, or necessities.

Roza understood the motives of the women who sold sex to survive. She is less forgiving of the women who engaged in sexual relations with the Germans and were given supervisory functions, as she had been given, and who used that status to beat the other prisoners. One of those women was from Roza's city, and Roza's generous parents had been of great help to her parents. This young woman arrived in Auschwitz on the same transport as Roza's sister, and she was cruel not only to the daughter of her parents' benefactors but also to other prisoners in the block. Roza knows another woman who, according to third-party information, was a *blockova* during the war. Not only was she notorious for being particularly cruel, but she also slept with German guards. The same woman later became religious, now lives in an ultra-Orthodox neighborhood in Jerusalem, and is involved in charity work on behalf of good causes. She never talks about what happened during the war. Roza is of the opinion that whoever was a victim of sexual abuse or used sex to survive does not talk about it—not to others, and not even to herself. Roza explains:

> It's the thing of silence . . . no speaking. No speaking to themselves, either. You understand? As if it happened with . . . the fifth neighbor. . . . And we know that there were, in . . . that a piece of bread—she slept with and afterward the Germans gave. And she is in Jerusalem and we know who she is. We don't talk. It didn't happen. Only, she has some sort of conscience that she needs . . . but not because she did those things, the fifth neighbor did those things . . . a far away row . . . from another city. But inside something tells her that she has to make things, what happened, good. But not with her, with the far neighbor. Those things are not talked about, don't know. Even if I heard that she did. She, too, doesn't talk. Not with herself and not with anyone.

Roza repeatedly emphasizes that she personally was not sexually abused and did not barter for sex: "It's interesting that no one . . . from me, thank God, that all the time I had the [supervisory] position . . . I can talk about that . . . that they came to me and I didn't do it." Moreover, she says that even as someone who held a supervisory position she has nothing to be ashamed of: "There's no one that I've met from Auschwitz, at work, that can say a bad thing. That I know and about that . . . I have a clear conscience." In Roza's words, the thought of the future, and the fact that she would have to live with her choices, whatever they were, always accompanied her. She did everything in her power to take care not only of the physical well-being of the women for whom she was responsible, but also their human dignity. As a case in point, she said that she noticed that one of the women was particularly thin. When she discovered that this woman's daughter had been eating her mother's portion, she intervened. "In the event that we stay alive, could you live with the fact that you had killed your mother?" Roza says she asked the daughter. "You would never be happy in your life."

This moral behavior, as Roza remembers and relates it, is remarkable, considering the reported behavior of other women who held similar supervisory positions. For example, "Bracha," who was interviewed for our research during the summer of 2006, related that the *blokova* of her block in Auschwitz enjoyed material comforts because a German guard took care of her. In her book *From Ashes to Life*, Lucille Eichengreen writes about a chance meeting many years after the war with the *Kapo* (supervising prisoner) Maja. After the writer confronted her about her past, the *Kapo* confessed to having had a relationship with someone in the SS: "A nameless faceless SS man came every night. I feared for my life and thought it would ensure my survival in Auschwitz. . . . he kept me out of the gas chamber. He gave me food. I did not think about the future then. I lived one day at a time. Whatever I did was my way of surviving."[20]

In a situation in which most of the camp prisoners aspired, like Maja, just to survive another day, Roza's testimony stands out for its description of her resilience, integrity, and unusual self-control. However, her narrative also includes a traumatic element that accompanies her until today—the fear of being raped by the SS-auxiliary *Aufseherinnen* (female guards), who, according to her, were all lesbians. Roza was well built and went around Auschwitz practically naked, wrapped in a blanket as she didn't receive any clothing after her arrival. In this vulnerable situation she was worried that one of these female guards would harass her. With a look of disgust on her face, Roza says that until this day she recoils from fresh flowers and cannot bear them near her. They evoke the memory of the lesbian *Aufseherinnen* meeting and kissing each others' hands, each with a flower in her lapel. The fear that one of them will see her repeatedly overwhelms her. "And I'm afraid that one will single me out. That's why I can't see live flowers," she said.

Why is Roza's trauma so deep in sharp contrast to her articulated life? Was she, herself, a victim of rape or attempted rape? In keeping with her own remarkable insight about herself, if such things did occur, they happened to someone else—someone not from the same city.

"Reuven"—"Mother was a magnetic force, like a rock in the sea"

"Reuven" was a first grade pupil in Slovakia when the war broke out at the end of 1941. His narrative here is based on his testimony to Yad Vashem during the winter of 2008, as well as two hours of conversation with co-author Dror in July 2008. After a period of hostility from non-Jewish neighbors and restrictions on Jewish students, the Germans, abetted by informers, rounded up Jews and sent many of them to the Nováky forced labor camp. Reuven, age seven, and his friends were caught while at school and taken to the camp in a truck. Their worried parents arrived later to be reunited and interned with their children. The family—including his mother, his father, Reuven himself, and his younger brother, Michael—was interned in Nováky for three years. His sister Tzipi was born in the camp in 1943. In an atmosphere of anxiety and despondency, the family suffered from hunger and hard labor. The shadow of frequent transports to Auschwitz, which slowly reduced the camp's population, also tormented them. While the parents worked, the children remained alone and neglected, resorting to risking their lives by sneaking outside the camp fence to forage for food. Those who were caught were beaten or killed.

After the Slovakian uprising at the end of 1944, the family fled to the mountains, under the fire of German airplanes that killed many escapees. The father, who apparently straggled behind, disappeared. Then nine-year-old Reuven helped his mother carry his young siblings up the mountainside, where they met Russian partisans who agreed to protect them. However, the partisans required the children to go down into the villages at the foot of the snowy mountains to bring back food, as well as to fire guns at executions of informers. Meanwhile, the women cooked and, Reuven said, served the sexual needs of the men.

After liberation Reuven's mother and her children returned to her parents' home, where she gave birth to Yehuda. According to Reuven, Yehuda was the son of his father, conceived in Nováky. As his father told him many years later, "Life went on." Reuven, at the age of ten, was his mother's midwife. The family later returned to their city of origin and were reunited with Reuven's father, who had been with another group of partisans. Reuven was sent to Israel in 1948 under the auspices of Youth Aliyah and taken into a kibbutz. In 1951 he joined his family, who had settled in the north of Israel. Reuven's brother Michael was killed in 1969 by a mine that exploded while he was working in a field near Israel's border.

Reuven talks about the sexual abuse of Jewish women in the Nováky forced labor camp. What he saw through the eyes of a young boy became apparent to him as he thought about it as an adult. In his interview with co-author Dror he said:

> Afterward I remember other things: that the soldiers were actually the local collaborators and the commander was German. They gave orders. And then, many times they would make a feast and take the women, the prisoners. They would "live it up" with them. We, the children, when I was older, when I started to remember, I understood what had happened. At the time we didn't exactly understand. What we did see was that many times they were so drunk that after everything they did . . . they would beat the women. There were a few times that they even took bayonets and stabbed the women and tore them . . . All these things, she . . . you understand, so much dizzying, so much . . . that I couldn't do much, at that age, I was about seven to ten years old, so that I didn't absorb the things so much. Only when I was older, when I was older, I began to . . . to translate all the things by myself.

According to Reuven, the family survived thanks to the strength and resourcefulness of his mother, Sarah, whom he describes as "a magnetic force, like a rock in the sea." He also credits his little brother Michael, who looked "Aryan." Every day in the afternoon his mother would take Michael to the office of the camp's commanding officer, explaining to Reuven that the commander liked playing with the little boy, who reminded him of his children in Germany. In exchange, the family received food and, more important, evaded the transport to Auschwitz.

Reuven described his brother Michael as "an 'Aryan' child, blond and . . . a very, very beautiful boy." He said in his testimony to Yad Vashem:

> One day, when my mother was outside with [Michael], a German commander standing nearby saw him and ordered her to come to him. She didn't want to. She tried to flee, but she was caught and brought to him. Suddenly he began to play with my brother. And since then every day in the afternoon she had to bring him to the commander's office. He would play with him for half an hour, and that was it. In retrospect, again, I think he was reminded of his children at home. Possibly because he was a real "Aryan" child. . . . We survived, we withstood it like everyone, and we were never put in the transport . . . and today as I look at that I understand that it just could be there is a connection. There must be some kind of connection.[21]

Michael, with his "Aryan" appearance, was the "winning card" in the family's struggle for survival. But at the same time the mother became a suspect. In our research interview, Reuven said, "He was really 'Aryan,' the boy was

'Aryan.' Blond, with blue eyes. You would've gone crazy. I don't know from whom he was, I don't know from where he was born. And then [the commander] really fell in love with him. [My mother] had to come to him every day. And he would play with him."

We questioned Reuven about what he meant when he said he didn't know "from where he was born." We asked, "Do you think that perhaps your father was not his father?" Reuven answered:

That . . . was an added story, drop it, that's by the way . . . that's a family story, that's . . . I don't know. . . . [My father] accused my mother all the time. He accused my mother that he was not his child. But that's not part of the story. He also didn't resemble . . . he didn't resemble our family. [He shows a photo of a young, large-framed, light-skinned, curly-haired, good-looking man riding a bicycle.] Look, look at him and look at me. Is there a resemblance? My brother [Yehuda] looks like me, like two drops of water. Two drops of water, my brother. And this, is there a resemblance? At all, right? Look at his height, look at his figure. But that's not relevant to the issue.

"So father accused and mother denied?" Reuven was asked. "Mother didn't deny, mother didn't talk about it at all," he said. "Because . . . mother was smart enough. Where is the truth, I don't know. And I don't care. My mother is my mother, nothing to be done about it."

The Russian partisans sexually abused the women whom they accepted into their groups. Reuven talked about this both in his testimony to Yad Vashem and in the interview with us. In our interview with him, he asked: "When we were with the partisans, what did the partisans do, the Russians?" Then he answered himself:

Drink, right? And when they drink what do they want? What do they want, to "screw." Whom? They had women. My mother held me every night between her legs. I didn't understand why. Between her legs closed like this. I sat here like this and that's how I sat with her all the night. And in addition to all that . . . then at night when we would go [to bring food back from the villages], when I came, yes. But until this [when we returned], they also succeeded.

Since he clearly seemed to be indicating that his mother had been raped by the partisans, we asked him: "Succeeded in raping her?"

"It's not called 'to rape,'" he responded. "It's not. It's to satisfy their needs. It's the needs of a man."

Again we pressed Reuven to come to terms with what had happened to his mother: "It's not called 'to rape'?" we asked.

"No, I don't think that that's 'to rape'—that's war. . . . In war everything is allowed. . . . it was the norm," he responded.

What was "normative" and considered legitimate in the reality of war—for survival during the war—became, with the changing times, a source of shame. The strong woman, with the incredible power and resourcefulness, "a force to be reckoned with," as described by her son, faded away in Israel, particularly after her son, Michael, was killed. "Like a candle. She melted down until she was finished. At the age of sixty-five," he said to us. As her son and a man, Reuven attributes the struggle for survival that included aspects of sexual violence as the central factor of her demise. "From my mother's perspective it was shameful," Reuven said. He continued:

> It was shameful. She told me. . . . in Israel, we would often talk about it. . . . when she reached the age of sixty she, apparently as a result of the war, went crazy. She was treated . . . and when I spoke with the doctors then they told me that the pressure expresses itself after many years. Everything is inside, inside, until it explodes. And . . . she told me many times. She said: "I was ashamed, but I knew it was part of life. If you want to live, because, otherwise, he could have put a bullet through your head and it would all be over." She was also alone. No husband, no one.

Reuven's story about his mother demonstrates the enormous difficulty in the transition between two conflicting worlds. There is the world of war, in which the willingness to do anything in order to survive one more day is an adaptive quality. And there is the free and comfortable world, which tests survival according to the criteria of values, culture, and self-respect (preserving human dignity). Reuven's mother was a fearless heroine who fought with every means at her disposal in order to survive and to save her family. However, in a free and comfortable, well-fed world, she could only feel ashamed and remain silent.

The Testimonies of "Leah," " Roza," and "Reuven"

The personal stories of the three Holocaust survivors documented in this chapter—"Leah," "Roza," and "Reuven" (telling his mother's tale)—range from sexual humiliation and oppression to accepting sexual abuse as a resource for survival. In extreme conditions of deprivation and depravity, femininity and sexuality were sources of both vulnerability and survival. Physical and sexual humiliation were part of the camp absorption process. There were also incidents of rape in the ghettos, forests, and hiding places, and Jewish and other women imprisoned in the camps were sometimes chosen and taken away to serve as prostitutes for soldiers. Providing sex to individual camp guards in exchange for food and basic necessities was sometimes a survival tactic. Likewise, "romances" between women dependent on SS guards or male prisoners for existential goods or protection were part of the reality.

From the testimonies of Leah, Roza, and Reuven, we see that being sexually abused and providing sex in order to survive are both connected with women's suffering and resistance during the Holocaust—in the ghettos and the camps, in hiding and in the forests, and even after liberation. The abuse was experienced as sexual humiliation, sexual assault, and forced prostitution. Sexuality as agency could be expressed through "romances" with prisoners or with Germans. Whether they were victims of sexual assault or provided sex in the service of survival, women who had these experiences tended to refrain from speaking about them. In published diaries and in interviews with us, survivors related how they personally managed to avoid rape and how someone else was raped instead. They also spoke of other women or teenage girls, not themselves, paying for food or survival with sex.

When women survivors speak of sex as a means of survival, their stories are usually that they themselves withstood the temptation and avoided it because they were very young, with strict upbringing and values. Concerning other teenage girls and women who used sex as a resource to survive, there are two perspectives: a) a type of agent evocative of the biblical Queen Esther, an adolescent or woman who had sexual relations with a German officer and thereby saved her friends; b) an evil person, a *Kapo* who beat her companions and had sexual relations with the Germans.

The literature reveals that to survive in extreme conditions people will do everything—will use all possible resources—without thinking of a future point in time when they will have to deal with the consequences. Part of the reality during war is that sexual availability becomes currency, providing another possibility for survival. Furthermore, in patriarchal societies the power of women as agents is often connected to their ability to use their sexuality as a resource. Even in Jewish history, female agents such as Yehudit, Esther, Yael, and Delilah were possessed with the ability to direct their sexuality in the service of a particular goal.

Men and women alike knew that sex was one of the accepted means of payment during the Holocaust. In addition to using sex to barter, romantic connections were made between Jewish women prisoners and male prisoners, particularly Poles,[22] and between young women who served as *Kapos* and German guards.[23] After liberation, many Jewish women accepted the sexual or romantic advances of American soldiers in return for chocolate, silk stockings, and other goods. A woman's chances for remaining alive seemed to be greater if a man took care of her, whether the connection between them was romantic or in exchange for sex.

In the words of Anna Pawelczynska, "erotic availability" became an invaluable currency, in exchange for which it was possible to obtain the opportunity to survive.[24] Diaries written during the Holocaust and contemporaneous first-hand research such as that of journalist Cecilia Slepak, murdered in Treblinka, document active bargaining as a means of survival in the ghetto or Auschwitz, particularly in the latrines.[25] Later, however, such behavior was condemned, and women who experienced sexual abuse found it hard to live with these memories.[26]

We saw how Leah actively and continually preserves her integrity with the aid of "proof" that she did not engage in prostitution. Roza emphasizes that she, herself, was not a victim of sexual assault and that her conscience is clear. What she says she did at that time is admirable by today's standards, as well. Perhaps her distaste for live flowers originated in the sexual trauma that was not hers, but rather that of the "fifth neighbor, far from here." In contrast to Leah and Roza, whose narratives do not include their own sexual trauma or systemic disintegration, Reuven's mother was unsuccessful in disconnecting herself from the past.[27] What she experienced as a survival strategy during the Holocaust became a source of shame. Even losing her son—the child whose "Aryan" looks saved the family and who died while working to better the Jewish homeland of Israel—could not diminish her feelings of disgrace.

Notes

1. This study about the sexual aspect of women's Holocaust experience was conducted by co-author Esther Dror for her doctoral dissertation, under the guidance of co-author Ruth Linn.

2. Bernard Mark, *The Scrolls of Auschwitz* (Tel Aviv: Am Oved, 1985), 209.

3. Sandra Brand, *I Dared to Live* (Rockville, MD: Shengold Books, 2000).

4. See, for example, Yitzhak Sadeh, "My Sister on the Beach." For the full poem in English translation, see Ronit Lentin, *Israel and the Daughters of the Shoah: Reoccupying the Territories of Silence* (New York: Berghahn Books, 2000), 207. The original Hebrew, "Achoti al hachof," is in *Sefer ha-Palmach*, A [The book of the Palmach, vol. 1], ed. Zerubavel Gilad (Tel Aviv: HaKibbutz Hameuhad, 1953), 724. Also see Idith Zertal, *Israel's Holocaust and Politics of Nationhood* (Cambridge: Cambridge University Press, 2005), 170.

5. Marlene Heinemann, *Gender and Destiny: Women Writers and the Holocaust* (New York: Greenwood Press, 1986), 18; Maria Nooke and Christina Miller, "The Kubiak/Grinwald

Family Dialogue: Blocking out the Theme of Migration from Israel to East Germany," in *The Holocaust in Three Generations*, ed. Gabriele Rosenthal (London: Cassel, 1998), 118–142.

6. Curzio Malaparte, *Kaputt*, trans. Cesare Foligno (New York: New York Review of Books, 2005), 312. Readers should note that Dan Hofstadter, who wrote the afterword to the Malaparte book, stated that the author's treatment of the sex slaves of Soroca may be a blend of fact and fiction, 436.

7. Linda M. Alcoff and Laura Gray, "Survivor Discourse: Transgression or Recuperation?" *Signs* 18 (1993): 260–291.

8. Hanna Yablonka, *Achim Zarim* [Alien brethren] (Hebrew) (Jerusalem: Yad Yitzhak Ben Zvi, 1994), 67–68 ; Ruth Bondy, *Shevarim Shlemim* [Whole fractions] (Hebrew) (Tel Aviv : Gvanim, 1997), 68; Ruth Linn and Ilan Gur-Zeev, "Holocaust as Metaphor: Arab and Israeli Use of the Same Symbol," *Metaphor and Symbol* 11, no. 3 (September 1996): 195–206.

9. Gisella Perl, *I Was a Doctor in Auschwitz* (New York: Ayer Co., 1948), 58; Olga Lengyel, *Five Chimneys* (Chicago: Academy Chicago Publishers, 1995, first published 1947), 59–63. For an additional discussion of Perl and Lengyel on sex for survival, see S. Lillian Kremer, chapter 11 in this volume.

10. Ruth Bondy, "Men Without Women—Women Without Men," (paper presented at the Third International Conference, Women and the Holocaust—Gender Issues in Holocaust Research, Givat Haim, Beit Terezin, Israel, September 4–6, 2005).

11. Gabriele Rosenthal, "Surviving Together and Living Apart in Israel and West Germany: The Genzor Family," in *The Holocaust in Three Generations*, 32–50.

12. Thomas Geve, *Neurim B'kvalim* [Youth in chains] (Jerusalem: Yad Vashem, 2003) 76–77, 84–85. Published in English as *Guns and Barbed Wire: A Child Survives the Holocaust* (Chicago: Academy Chicago Publications, 1987).

13. Janice A Gasker, "Freud's Therapeutic Mistake with Jung's Disclosure of Childhood Sexual Abuse: Narrative Lessons in the Do's and Don'ts of Validation," in *Journal of Poetry Therapy* 13 (1999): 81–95.

14. Gabriele Rosenthal, "Surviving Together and Living Apart," 35–36.

15. Rachel Lev-Wiesel and Marianne Amir, "Post-traumatic Stress Disorder Symptoms, Psychological Distress, Personal Resources, and Quality of Life in Four Groups of Holocaust Child Survivors," in *Family Process* 39 (2000): 445–459.

16. Bessel A. van der Kolk et al., "Dissociation, Somatization, and Affect Dysregulation: The Complexity of Adaptation of Trauma," in *American Journal of Psychiatry* 153, (July 1996): 83–93.

17. See, for example, Dina Wardi, *Memorial Candles: Children of the Holocaust* (London: Tavistock/Routledge, 1992); Esther Fuchs, "Exile, Daughterhood, Writing: Representing the Shoah as Personal Memory," in *Representing the Shoah for the 21st Century*, ed. Ronit Lentin (Oxford: Berghahn Books, 2004), 252–268.

18. Joan Ringelheim, "The Split between Gender and the Holocaust," in *Women in the Holocaust*, ed. Dalia Ofer and Lenore J. Weitzman (New Haven: Yale University, 1998), 341–344.

19. Yael Danieli, "Counter-Transference in the Treatment and Study of Nazi Holocaust Survivors and their Children," *Victimology* 5 (1980): 355–367; Henry Greenspan, *On Listening to Holocaust Survivors: Recounting and Life History* (Westport, CT: Praeger, 1998); and Dori Laub, "Truth and Testimony: The Process and the Struggle," in *Trauma: Explorations in Memory*, ed. Cathi Caruth (Baltimore: The Johns Hopkins University Press, 1995), 61–75.

20. Lucille Eichengreen, *From Ashes to Life* (San Francisco: Mercury, 1994), 190.

21. Reuven, testimony to Yad Vashem, 2008 (identifying details protected by the co-authors).

22. Raya Kagan, *Nashim be-lishkath ha-Gehinom* [Hell's office women] (Hebrew) (Merhavia: Sifriat HaPo'alim, 1947).

23. Lucille Eichengreen, *From Ashes to Life*, 190.

24. Anna Pawelczynska, *Values and Violence in Auschwitz* (Berkeley: University of California Press, 1979), 99.

25. Dalia Ofer, "Her View through My Lens: Cecilia Slepak Studies Women in Warsaw," in *Gender, Place and Memory in Modern Jewish Experience*, ed. Judy Tydor Baumel and Tova Cohen, (London: Vallentine Mitchell, 2003): 29–50.

26. Lucille Eichengreen, *From Ashes to Life*, 190.

27. For a personal account of life with the partisans, including sexual abuse, see Jack and Rochelle Sutin, *Jack and Rochelle: A Holocaust Story of Love and Resistance*, ed. Lawrence Sutin (Saint Paul, MN: Graywolf Press, 1995).

Contributors

DR. HELGA AMESBERGER, a senior researcher at the Institute of Conflict Research in Vienna, is a social scientist focusing on Nation Socialist persecution of women and oral history. She is the co-author of *Sexualisierte Gewalt in NS-Konzentrationslagern* (Sexualized violence in National Socialist concentration camps).

DR. ELLEN BEN-SEFER is a senior lecturer at Schoenborn Academic College of Nursing in Tel Aviv, dividing her research time between nursing research and such Holocaust-related issues as children, women, and transit camps. She has also developed a model program in Australia and Israel for teaching nursing students about relevant Holocaust issues.

KIRSTY CHATWOOD, an independent researcher who studies questions of gender, sexuality, rape, and "resistance" in the context of genocide, has degrees from University of Alberta and University of Lethbridge in Canada. She is currently conducting research that includes studying the connections between sexual vulnerability and sex for survival in concentration camps.

ESTHER DROR is a doctoral candidate in the Faculty of Education at the University of Haifa, Israel. Her writings include "Unraveling the Curtain of Silence: Leading to Redefinition of the Survival of Women during the Holocaust," presented at the fourth Women and the Holocaust International Conference in Israel in 2007.

DR. MONIKA J. FLASCHKA has a doctorate in Modern European History from Kent State University. Her dissertation, "Race, Rape and Gender in Nazi-Occupied Territories," analyzes the intersection of gender and racial ideology in court-martial cases of rape, attempted rape, and child abuse committed by German soldiers and non-German men in the occupied territories.

DR. EVA FOGELMAN, a psychologist in private practice in New York City, is co-director of Psychotherapy with Generations of the Holocaust and Related Traumas and Child Development Research, Training Institute for Mental Health. The author of *Conscience and Courage: Rescuers of Jews During the Holocaust*, she wrote and co-produced *Breaking the Silence*.

DR. BRIGITTE HALBMAYR, a social scientist and senior researcher at the Institute of Conflict Research in Vienna, focuses on racism, National Socialism, the Holocaust, and gender. She co-authored *Das Privileg der Unsichtbarkeit. Rassismus unter dem Blickwinkel von Weißsein und Dominanzkultur* (The privilege of invisibility. Racism from the viewpoint of being white and of the dominant culture).

DR. SONJA M. HEDGEPETH is a full professor in the Department of Foreign Languages and Literatures at Middle Tennessee State University. In addition to German, she has taught extensively about the Holocaust, women's issues, and world literature. She has published a book on Else Lasker-Schüler, as well as co-edited a book on this famous German-Jewish writer.

DR. YVONNE KOZLOVSKY-GOLAN teaches history and cinema at the University of Haifa's Department of Cinema and Television, as well as at Sapir College of the Negev and Kibbutzim College in Israel. She researches the cinema's influence on viewers' knowledge of history. She is the author of *"Until You Are Dead": The Death Penalty in the USA: History, Law, and Cinema.*

DR. S. LILLIAN KREMER, university distinguished professor, emerita, Kansas State University, is the author of *Witness Through the Imagination: The Holocaust in Jewish American Literature* and *Women's Holocaust Writing: Memory and Imagination*, the editor of *Holocaust Literature: An Encyclopedia of Writers and Their Work*, and the author of many critical essays.

NOMI LEVENKRON, an Israeli attorney, headed the anti-trafficking department at the Hotline for Migrant Workers in Israel. She is currently the professional director of "Matters"—The Law and Society Clinical Center, College of Management, Academic Studies, and director of the Human Rights Clinic. She also teaches courses about prostitution and trafficking at Tel Aviv University.

DR. RUTH LINN, a former dean of the Faculty of Education at the University of Haifa, Israel, studies moral psychology and focuses on issues associated with resistance to authority. Among her four books is one about the suppressed story of Auschwitz escapees. She has been a visiting scholar at Harvard University, University of Maryland, and University of British Columbia.

DR. ANATOLY PODOLSKY, a historian, is the director of the Ukrainian Center for Holocaust Studies in Kiev, Ukraine, and a senior researcher at the Institute of Political and Ethnic Studies of the National Academy of Sciences of Ukraine. He is the author of "A Reluctant Look Back: Jewry and the Holocaust in Ukraine," as well as many other published articles.

DR. ROCHELLE G. SAIDEL, a political scientist, is director of Remember the Women Institute in New York City and a senior researcher at the Center for the Study of Women and Gender, University of São Paulo, Brazil. She is the author of *The Jewish Women of Ravensbrück Concentration Camp* and editor of *Fiorello's Sister: Gemma La Guardia Gluck's Story.*

DR. HELENE SINNREICH is the director of the Center for Judaic and Holocaust Studies and associate professor of history at Youngstown State University. She is editor-in-chief of the *Journal of Jewish Identities* and executive director of the Ohio Council for Holocaust Education. Her research focuses on victim experience during the Holocaust.

DR. MIRYAM SIVAN, originally from New York City, teaches at the University of Haifa and at the Emek Yizrael College, Israel. Her book *Belonging Too Well: Portraits of Identity in Cynthia Ozick's Fiction*, was published in 2009. Her novella, *City of Refuge*, was adapted for the stage at a theater conference in London in 2007. She has recently completed a novel, *Make It Concrete*.

DR. ROBERT SOMMER received his doctorate from the Institute of Cultural Studies at Humboldt University in Berlin in 2009. In 2007, he organized an international conference, "Forced Prostitution and War in the 20th and the Beginning of the 21st Century," at the Ravensbrück Memorial, and also served as scientific project supervisor there for an exhibit on camp brothels.

DR. ZOË WAXMAN is a research fellow in history at Royal Holloway, University of London. She is the author of *Writing the Holocaust: Identity, Testimony, Representation* and articles on the Holocaust and women's Holocaust experiences.

Index

abortions: elective due to dire circumstances, 159, 162–63, 167, 168, 172n29, 182–83; forced, 37–38, 42n34, 43n37, 159, 167–69; as part of genocide strategy, 157; shame factor, 169–70

acculturation of women and ability to pass for "Aryan," 125–26

The Accused (Kaplan) (film), 248

Adelsberger, Lucie, 162–63

Adorno, Theodor, 203–4

Afro-Germans, persecution of, 159

agency, 61–73

Alison, Miranda, 31, 32

amenorrhea in concentration camps, 34, 81, 181

Améry, Jean, 132

Amir, Marianne, 200

And the Rat Laughed (Semel), 217–31

anti-Semitism, gendered perspective, 3

Anya (Schaeffer), 180

Appelman-Jurman, Alicia, 127–28

Armenian genocide, 110

Artzi, Itzhak, 221–22

Artzi, Margalit, 218

"Aryan" master race concept and reproductive control, 9n6, 37, 151–52, 157, 159

"asocial" category for Nazi regime's "undesirables," 38, 48, 52, 55, 158–59

Astor, Olga, 84–85

attractiveness narrative for rape stories, 6, 68, 77–89, 92n31, 121n38, 269

Auschwitz-Birkenau: abortions at, 162–63, 182; agency in, 61–73; brothel at, 51, 53, 54; fears of sexual violence at, 186; humiliations at, 34, 81–82, 177–80; prisoner physicians' dilemmas, 162–63; prostitutes from, 48; rape at, 18, 26n20, 77, 111, 280; sex for survival at, 187–88, 192, 283; sterilizations at, 37, 160–61; trauma of motherhood in, 146

Auschwitz-Monowitz labor camp, 46

Auschwitz: True Tales from a Grotesque Land (Nomberg-Przytyk), 66, 178

aus der Fünten, Ferdinand Hugo, 165, 166

Axer, Oliver, 236–37

Azoulay, Ariella, 246

Babi Yar, mass murders at, 98

Baer, Elizabeth, 3

Barber, Jacques, 223

Barry, Kathleen, 209, 210

Bartelsman, Mirjam, 165, 166, 172–73n39

Bartenschlager, Fritz, 115

bartering sex for survival. *See* sex for survival strategy

Bartov, Omer, 210

beauty and targeting for rape, 6, 68, 77–89, 92n31, 121n38, 269

Be'er, Haim, 202–3

Beevor, Anthony, 18

Beinfeld, Solon, 168

Belzec extermination camp, 97, 101

Benedict, Susan, 164

Ben-Mayor, Tor, 239

Benze, Susana, 236–37

Bergen, Doris, 116
Bergen-Belsen concentration camp, 143, 162
Bergman, Anka, 141–43, 150, 153n9
Bershad ghetto, 103
Betts, Erica, 82
Biebow, Hans, 112–14
Birnbaum, Suzanne, 68
birth and motherhood. *See* mothers
blaming the victim in sexual assault, 13, 192–93, 241, 244–45. *See also* social ostracism of survivors
Bloch, Gottfried, 86
Blood from the Sky (Rawicz), 125
Bodenstab, Johanna, 148
Boder, David P., 140
body searches and sexual assault/ humiliation, 18, 22, 30, 34
Bogner, Nahum, 225, 228
Bondy, Ruth, 15–16, 279
Borowski, Takeusz, 187–89
Brack, Viktor, 160, 161
Breedonk camp, 237
Breuer, Elsa, 86
brothels: in concentration camps, 19, 25n4, 45–55, 59n44, 92n42, 115–17; evidence concerning Jewish women's involvement in, 53, 59–60nn 52, 55, 92n42, 115–17; in ghettos, 19; living conditions in, 49–51; male prisoner's perspective, 188–90; Romanian, 276
Browning, Christopher, 109, 113
Brownmiller, Susan, 200
Buchenwald concentration camp, 46, 49

Cahill, Ann, 78
Campagna, Norbert, 54
Carmel, Marco, 239–40
Cavani, Liliana, 244
center-periphery relations under Nazis, 109
Chang, Iris, 110

children: concentration camp conditions and mother's dilemmas, 144–48; and death narratives, 147, 148–49; in hiding, sexual abuse of, 221–31; infanticide, 38, 144, 152, 153n9, 162–63, 164, 182–83; legacy of trauma passed from mother, 150–51; moral dilemma of, 145; postwar birth rates, 150; reconciliation with mothers, ambivalences around, 149; relationship to those born after liberation, 150–51; second generation, 223–24, 245–46, 264; as sexual slaves, 202–13; sterilization of, 159, 162; survivor support groups for sexually abused, 272; traumas of, 149–51, 228. *See also* abortions
Choko, Isabelle, 81
cinema, sexual violence depiction in, 234–49
Clauberg, Carl, 160–61
Cohen, Judy, Weiszenberg, 7–8
Cohen, Lya, 84
concentration camps: amenorrhea in, 34, 81, 181; brothels in, 19, 25n4, 45–55, 59n44, 92n42, 115–17; consequences of sexualized violence in, 39–40; constant personal boundary violation, 34–35; vs. extermination camps, 41n13; forced abortions, 37–38, 162–64; forced nakedness, 9n7, 22, 33–34, 98, 178, 186; forced sterilization, 37, 160–62; gender identity and rape in, 77–89; physical examinations, 18, 22, 30, 34; pregnancy as death sentence in, 140–41, 143, 168, 169, 182; racism's role in victimization, 33, 36–38, 39–40; rape in, 18, 35–36, 77–89, 111–12, 114–15; resistance in, 61–73; sex for survival in, 35, 187–88, 192, 283. *See also* humiliations; *individual camp names*

Copelon, Rhonda, 117
Cymerman, Ana, 84
Czelny, K. T., 63–64
Czernikow, Adam, 19

Dachau concentration camp, 82
Dajches, Mussia, 18
Danzinger, Etti, 212
Dasberg, Haim, 229
Davidovski, Anton, 97
death and dying: film depiction vs. rape,
    248; and mother/child death
    narratives, 147, 148–49
Death in Love (Yakin and Harel) (film),
    245–46
death sentence for pregnancy and birth,
    140–41, 143, 168, 169, 182
dehumanization. See humiliations
delousing, 179
Derderian, Katharine, 110
Dering, Wladislaw, 161
Desbois, Fr. Patrick, 96, 104
Diaspora and Israelis on sexual violence,
    201
Different Voices: Women and the Holocaust
    (Rittner and Roth), 3
Dinur, Yehiel (Ka-Tzetnik), 201–13,
    214n14, 216n65
documentary film evidence of sexual
    abuse, 235–36, 237–38, 239–40
Douglas, Lawrence, 237
Dragon, Shlomo, 63
Dror, Zvi, 205, 280
Druijf, Hartog, 166
Dwork, Debórah, 21, 228
Dworkin, Andrea, 2–3
Dychkant, Anna, 96–97

Edelman, Marek, 206
Eder, Harriet, 235–36
Edmunds, Don, 243
Eichengreen, Lucille, 283
Eichmann, Adolf, 158

Eisenschmidt, Otto, 114–15
elective abortion due to dire circum-
    stances, 159, 162–63, 167, 168,
    172n29, 182–83
Emmerich, Wilhelm, 61
Epelfeld, Naum, 99
Eschebach, Insa, 29
ethnic cleansing, rape and gender
    identity, 78
Ettinger, Elzbieta, 183–84
eugenics, 42–43nn34, 37
euthanasia by Nazi regime, 157, 158, 160
Experience and Expression: Women, Nazis,
    and the Holocaust (Baer and Golden-
    berg), 4

false survivor testimony, 263
families, loss of, 147, 149
feature film treatment of sexual abuse in
    Holocaust, 240–48
Felman, Shoshana, 211
Female Sexual Slavery (Barry), 209
femininity and rape, 78, 89, 90n11
Fénelon, Fania, 69–72, 179, 181, 186,
    191–93
Ferst, Gucia, 85
fictionalized accounts, 180, 183–84,
    187–89, 193–94, 217–31
Figenberg, Moshe, 169
film, sexual violence depiction in,
    234–49
Final Solution, 5, 108–9, 170n10
Fink, Ida, 183, 184
Five Chimneys (Lengyel), 177–78
food, bartering sex for, 20–22
forced abortion. See abortions
forced divorce for mixed-"race" couples,
    158
forced nakedness, 9n7, 22, 33–34, 98,
    178, 186
forced pregnancies in wartime setting,
    40n5
forced sterilization. See sterilization

Fortunoff Video Archive for Holocaust Testimonies, 265–66
foster mothers, postwar adjustments, 149–50
France, Jewish women in Nazi brothels, 116
Frank, Anne, 124
Freiberg camp, 141–42, 153n12
Freiermuth, Else, 162
Frick, Wilhelm, 157
From Ashes to Life (Eichengreen), 283

Gabori, Eve, 84
Galicia District, Ukraine, 100–101, 106n12
Galtung, Johan, 30
Gelissen, Rena Kornreich, 126, 127
Gemmeker, Albert Konrad, 165, 167
gendered discourse: on anti-Semitism, 3; and depictions of sexuality, 193–94; and heroism, 241, 243–44; on Holocaust experience, 177; and motherhood, 139–40; and sex for survival strategy, 69; sexism as component of persecution, 32, 139, 152, 180; and split memory about Holocaust, 156
gender identities: definitional issues, 79; forced sterilization/abortion as attack on, 157; hair, importance for feminine identity, 36–37, 77, 81, 82, 83, 84, 179; importance of sociocultural context, 92n31; and rape in concentration camps, 77–89
gender research, lack of, 2–4, 15, 131
genocide, sexual violence as endemic to, 14, 31, 78, 157
Germany, open hiding experiences in, 126–27. See also Nazi regime
Gesetz zur Verhütung erbkranken Nachwuchses (Law for the Prevention of Genetically Diseased Offspring), 158
Getz, Ellen, 18

ghettos: birth prohibitions in, 167–69; brothels in, 19; recruitment of Jewish women for brothels, 116; sexual violence in, 100–103, 110–11, 112–14
Glöwen camp, 112
Goldenberg, Myrna, 3
Goldman, Paul, 220–21
Gone to Soldiers (Piercy), 180–81
Gormans, Ruth, 167
Gottesmann, Pearl, 77, 81–82
Gottsfeld Heller, Fanya, 129
Grese, Irma, 26n20, 187
The Grey Zone (Nelson) (film), 243–44
Grodzisk Mazowiecki, Poland, 110
guards: brothel services for, 45, 49–50, 52, 59n44; sexual harassment as reminder of feminine identity, 81, 84–85; as sexual violators, 9n6, 18, 34, 53, 92n47, 111–12, 180, 186–87, 219–20
Gypsies, 33, 37, 38, 159, 161, 162

Hada, Yossi, 223–24
hair, importance for gender identity, 36–37, 77, 81, 82, 83, 84, 179
Hájková, Anna, 51
Harel, Alma, 245–46
Hart-Moxon, Kitty, 64
"A Hat of Glass" (Semel), 217–19
Hausner, Gideon, 162
Hautval, Adelaide, 161
health care workers, prisoner. See Lengyel, Olga; Perl, Gisella
Heberer, Patricia, 158
Heftman, Yosef, 202
Heilman, Anna, 81
Heineman, Elizabeth, 207
Hereditary Health Courts, 158
heroism: complexities of adopting, 131–32; film's use of, 235, 240–41, 243–44; of French prostitutes, 71; Israeli focus on, 275–76

Hertzberger, Ellis, 167
Herzberger, Magda, 67–68
Heydrich, Reinhard, 158
hiding: children, abuse of in, 221–31; isolation of, 128–29, 228; Jewish women and sexual abuse, 21, 27n38, 124–33, 183–84, 221–31; men's difficulties in, 225–26
Himmler, Heinrich, 37, 45–46, 47, 158
Hitler, Adolf, 45, 116
Hitler's Hit Parade (Axer and Benze) (film), 236–37
Hofinger, Aloisa, 147
homosexuality, 86–88, 93n56
hope and heroism in early Holocaust films, 235
Horowitz, Sara R., 6, 139
hospital conditions for pregnant women, 142
Hössler, Franz, 48
House of Dolls (Ka-Tzetnik), 201–13
humiliations: body searches, 18, 22, 30, 34; during camp induction, 36–37, 178–81; forced nakedness, 9n7, 22, 33–34, 98, 178, 186; hair removal, 36–37, 77, 81, 82, 83, 84, 179; relieving/toileting exposed to male gaze, 34, 35; summary of, 177–78
Hyman, Paula, 125

ideology of sexualized violence, complexities of, 32
IG Farben, 46
Ilsa, She-Wolf of the SS (Edmonds) (film), 243
Incendies (Mouawad), 30
Incidents in the Life of a Slave Girl (Jacobs), 207
infanticide: by fellow prisoners to save mothers' lives, 162–63, 182–83; by Nazis, 38, 144, 152, 153n9, 162; by prisoner nurses, 164
intergenerational narrative, breaking of, 222–25

International Military Court in Nuremberg, 22
International Tracing Service, 1
Isaacson, Judith Magyar, 124, 179, 183, 186
isolation: of hiding, open or not, 128–29, 228; of rape victim, 132–33
Israeli views of sexual violence in Holocaust, 201–2, 244–46, 255, 279

Jacobs, Benjamin, 64–65
Jacobs, Harriet, 207
Jankowski, Stanislaw, 62–63
Jewish men: sexual abuse/exploitation by, 18, 21, 35–36, 113, 120n27, 132, 187–89, 271–72
Jewish women: evidence for camp brothel presence, 53, 59–60n55, 59n52, 92n42, 115–17; in hiding, 21, 27n38, 124–33, 183–84, 221–31; low position in prison hierarchy, 33; as sex slaves, 220–21
Jones, Adam, 80
juvenile delinquency, sterilization for, 158

Kagan, Raya, 18, 21
Kammler, Hans, 45
Kaplan, Jonathan, 248
Kaplan, Louise J., 260
Kaplan, Marion, 126, 159
Kapò (film), 241
Kapos (supervisory prisoners): compromise vs. principle, 280–83; male-on-male sexual violence by, 86–87, 92n47; as rescuers, 218–19; sexual exploitation by, 71, 187–88; social judgment against, 71–72
Kappeler, Susanne, 194
Karay, Felicja, 115
Katz, Esther, 3, 256
Ka-Tzetnik (Yehiel Dinur), 201–13, 214n14, 216n65

Kenrick, D. A., 194
Khassin, Arkady, 103
Kielar, Wieslaw, 64
Kindergarten (Ettinger), 183–84
Klein, Hillel, 266
Klein Schönau, 218, 231–32n3
Klüger, Ruth, 159
Koegel, Max, 49
Kolischer, Herbert, 87
Koltun, Harry, 85
Kos, Marta, 36
Kovitska, Anna, 145–46
Kovno ghetto, 167–68
Kraków ghetto, 110–11
Krall, Hanna, 206
Krause, Johanna Lindner, 158–59
Krause, Kurt, 114
Kremer, Elizabeth, 103–4
Kufus, Thomas, 235–36
Kuperman, Alexander, 103
Kuritskaya, Sima, 104

labor, slave. See slave labor
Langer, Lawrence, 127, 132–33, 148
Laska, Vera, 256
Lau, Meir Israel, 204–5
Law for the Prevention of Genetically
    Diseased Offspring (Gesetz zur
    Verhütung erbkranken Nachwuchses), 158
Lebensborn program, 158
Leitner, Isabella, 82
Lengyel, Olga, 177–78, 181–82, 183, 191,
    279
lesbian sex slavery, 219–20, 283
Levi, Primo, 113
Lev-Wiesel, Rachel, 200
Lewkowicz, Anna Langsam, 35–36
liberators, rape by, 256, 258, 272. See also
    Russians
Libya, destruction of Jews in, 239–40
Lichtenstein, S., 166
Liebman, Irena, 36

Lindorf, Doris Barbet Betty von (Doris
    Roe), 258–64
Linz, Daniel, 209
Lipschutz, Eugene, 86
literature, sexual violence depiction in:
    abortion and infanticide, 182–83;
    brothels in camps, 188–90; Dinur/
    Ka-Tzetnik and sexual slavery,
    202–13; eroticization of sexual
    violence by male writers, 193–96;
    guards and Kapos as instigators of
    violence, 186; humiliation during
    camp induction, 178–81; introduction
    to memoir and fiction, 177–78; Israeli
    views on sexual violence in Holocaust,
    201–2; medical experimentation,
    181–82; rape, 183–86, 222–23; And the
    Rat Laughed, 217–31; sex for survival
    experiences, 190–93
Lithuania, 111, 167–69
looting of Jewish homes, 110
Love in Auschwitz (Ben-Mayor) (film), 239
Lovely Green Eyes (Lustig), 189
Lower, Wendy, 109
Lustig, Arnošt, 189, 206
Lvov ghetto, 100–102, 116
Łódź (Litzmannstadt) ghetto, 112–14

Malamuth, Neil, 209
male-on-male sexual violence, 79–80,
    86–88, 92n47
Mann, Franceska, 63, 73–74n9
Marcus, Sharon, 78
martyrology, national call to, 23
masculinity: and homosexuality, 93n56;
    and rape, 78, 80, 90n11
mass murder of Jews in Ukraine, 94–104
A Matter of Time (Carmel), 239–40
Mauthausen concentration camp, 36, 45,
    142
medical experimentation: as excuse for
    violating racial mixing rules, 251n23;

prisoner physician participation in, 162, 238–39; sterilization methods as, 160, 161, 181–82; types of procedures, 188–89. *See also* sterilization

memoirs, 177–79, 181–82, 186–87, 190–92, 206

memory, reconciliation of, 222–23, 229–31

Mengele, Josef, 182, 186

menstruation, loss of, 34, 81, 181

Metz, Gilbert, 86, 87

Micheels, Louis J., 69

Michman, Dan, 211

Mielnicki, Michel, 66

Milch-Sheriff, Ella, 230

Miller, Arthur, 192–93

Milton, Sybil, 256

Mirchuk, Petro, 63

Mischlinge (half-Jewish persons), 158, 159, 161

Mittelbau-Dora camp, 50, 53

mixed-"race" couples, sterilization of Jewish partner, 158, 165–67, 173n39

modesty: and humiliation of camp induction process, 179; and social ostracism of victims, 14, 24

Molotov-Ribbentrop Pact, 100

moral judgment: by Israelis of women survivors, 244–45, 255, 279; against sex for survival strategy, 69–72, 192–93, 241. *See also* shame factor; social ostracism of survivors

mothers: after-effects of trauma, 149–51; avoiding stereotypes, 139–40; Nazi expectations of "Aryan," 37, 151–52; pregnancy and birth stories, 140–44, 148, 168, 169, 182; summary, 151–52. *See also* abortions; children; infanticide; sterilization

Mouawad, Wajdi, 30

Mühlhäuser, Regina, 29, 32

Müller, Filip, 65

Musik, Erna, 149

My Private War (Eder and Kufus) (film), 235–36

"My Sister on the Beach" (Sadeh), 201

Nachtmanová, Libuše, 37

nakedness, forced, 9n7, 22, 33–34, 98, 178, 186

national identity/nationalist discourse: call to martyrology, 23; and rape as masculinity reinforcer, 78; rape as violation of, 200; and sex for survival story, 70–71; women as symbolic of, 31. *See also* war

Nazi Policy, Jewish Workers, German Killers (Browning), 109

Nazi regime (National Socialists): "asocial" category for "undesirables," 38, 48, 52, 55, 158–59; and attitudes leading to sexual abuse, 235–37; and brothel policy in concentration camps, 45, 115–16; children as useless for labor, 144–45; conflicted attitudes toward Jewish women, 15; euthanasia by, 157, 158, 160; literary depictions vs. reality, 212; Nuremberg Racial Laws (1935), 158, 170n10; purposeful extermination of Ukrainian Jews, 97–98; racism as dominant ideology of, 33; *Rassenschande* (race defilement), 9n6, 36, 108, 116, 118, 256; sexuality and population policies, 37, 139, 141, 151–52, 157–59; unevenness in carrying out Final Solution at local level, 108–9

Nelson, Blake, 243–44

Netherlands occupation, forced sterilization and abortion during, 164–67

Night (Wiesel), 203, 205, 206–7

The Night Porter (Cavani) (film), 241–42
Nir, Zipora, 37
Nomberg-Przytyk, Sara, 66, 178–79
Nováky camp, 284
Nuremberg Racial Laws (1935), 158, 170n10
nurses, prisoner, infanticide by, 164

Ofer, Dalia, 3
open hiding and threat of sexual violence, 124–33, 183–85
Operation T4, 157, 158
Ottosen, Kristian, 164
Ozick, Cynthia, 183, 213n5

Pamiętnik z getta łódzkiego (Diary from the Łódź ghetto) (Poznanski), 113
partisans, sexual assault by, 22, 134n26, 184, 284
passing as "Aryan," and threat of sexual violence, 124–33
patriarchy: and attitudes about motherhood, 145, 151–52; and acceptance of sexualized violence, 32, 40; and sexual manipulation as form of agency for women, 288
Paul, Christa, 49
Paulsson, Gunnar S., 131
Pawelczynska, Anna, 289
pedophilic rape, 201–13, 221–31
Peretz, Aharon, 167–68
Perl, Gisella, 83, 154n22, 163, 182, 187, 190–91, 279
"physical examinations" in concentration camps, 18, 22, 30, 34
piecework wage system, 46
Piepel (Ka-Tzetnik), 201–12
piepel, defined, 213n7
Piercy, Marge, 180–81
Pister, Hermann, 49
Playing for Time (Fénelon), 69, 179
Pohl, Oswald, 45
Poland, 110–11, 125, 126, 127. *See also individual concentration camps*

Popkin, Jeremy, 204, 211
Porat, Dina, 203, 209
pornography, sexual abuse Holocaust literature criticized as, 207–9
power relations: as core of sexualized violence, 30, 32, 200; and feminization of victims, 78, 80; and male dominance of females during camp induction, 180; and Nazi killing of children in camps, 148; and pornography definitions, 208. *See also* patriarchy; rape
Poznanski, Jakub, 113
Prämien-Vorschrift (bonus order), 46–47
pregnancy and birth experiences, 140–44, 148, 168, 169, 182
Preiss, Leah, 168–69
Presser, Jacob, 164–65
Price, Lisa S., 78
Primozic, Slava, 35
prisoners: as clients of brothels, 19; as collaborators in women's humiliation, 179; health worker dilemmas, 162–63, 164, 238–39. *See also Kapos* (supervisory prisoners)
Pronicheva, Dina, 98–99, 194
prostitution, 20, 53–54, 71–72, 85. *See also* sexual slavery
psychological perspective: and assaults on motherhood, 145–47; child-related traumas, 149–51; children's traumas, 228; cost of sex for survival strategy, 16, 190, 265, 277–89; costs of suffering in silence, 128–31; emotional separation from experience, 180–81; initial attempts to address sexual abuse, 256; introduction, 255–56; legacy of trauma, 39–40, 150–51, 242, 271–72; perceived mental illness as result of Holocaust experience, 244–46; projection and denial, 277–80, 282, 283, 284–87; splitting and substituting other women for one's own

experience, 268–69, 277–80, 282, 283, 288; survivors' difficulties with psychotherapy, 270, 280. *See also* shame factor; suppression of sexual violence stories

Quakernack, Walter, 65, 74n14

racial purity laws, 36, 108, 116, 118, 157–59, 256
racist ideology: concentration camps, 33, 36–38, 39–40; definitional issues, 41–42n15; and forced sterilization/abortion, 157; and pregnancy and childbirth, 151–52; and prohibition on racial mixing in brothels, 53–54, 251n23; role in sexual victimization, 116
Rahe, Thomas, 143
Rapaport, Lynn, 212
rape: attractiveness narrative for, 6, 68, 77–89, 92n31, 121n38, 269; of children, 201–13, 221–31; in concentration camps, 18, 35–36, 77–89, 90n11, 111–12, 114–15; as conscious tool of psychological warfare, 31, 200, 251n22; definitional issues, 10n22, 15, 79; dilemma of film depiction, 246–48; Doris Roe's testimony, 258–64; in ghettos, 100–103, 110–11, 112–14; judicial treatment of in war crimes tribunals, 22–23; lesbian, 283; by liberators, 14, 18, 134n26, 256, 258, 263, 272, 286; literary depictions, 183–86, 222–23; male-on-male, 79–80, 86–88, 92n47; as national helplessness, 78, 200; suppression of stories on, 108; testimonial strength about, 256; threat of in hiding, 21, 27n38, 124–33, 183–84, 221–31; in Ukraine, 94–104; in violation of racial purity laws, 9n6, 108–9, 117–18. *See also* sexual slavery
Rape of Nanking, 110

Rassenschande (race defilement), 36, 108, 116, 118, 256
Ravensbrück concentration camp: abortion decrease to enhance slave labor survival, 38; childbirth at, 142, 144; and children's care, 148; overview of population, 57n20; rape at, 112; as recruitment source for brothels, 48–49; secret abortions in, 163–64; sterilizations at, 160–61
Rawicz, Piotr, 125
Reading, Anna, 224
recruitment of women for camp brothels, 48–49
Red Cherry (Ye) (film), 243
Reibmayer, Ilse, 142
Reichskommissariat Ukraine, 98–100
relieving/toileting exposed to male gaze, 34, 35
reproduction: amenorrhea in concentration camps, 34, 81, 181; Nazi control methods, 140–41, 151–52, 158, 170n10. *See also* mothers
Resilience and Courage (Tec), 108
resistance: agency as, 62; Kovitska's, 146; and open hiding, 131–32, 183–84; Schillinger's death at hands of female prisoner, 61–67; sex for survival as, 67–68, 72–73; sexuality as, 65–66
Resistance movement, 71, 238. *See also* partisans, sexual assault by
Ringelbaum, Emmanuel, 17, 19, 20
Ringelheim, Joan, 3, 128, 256, 280
Rittner, Carol, 3
Roe, Doris (Doris Barbet Betty von Lindorf), 258–64
Romania, 102–3, 276
Roma people (Gypsies), 33, 37, 38, 159, 161, 162
Romney, Claude, 162
Rosen, Ilana, 256
Rosen, Norma, 177
Rosenblum, Bella, 21
Rosenthal, Gabriele, 279

Roth, John K., 3, 5
Rozansi, Jan, 110
Rubenstein, Marc, 87
Rubinstein, Erna, 81
Rumkowska, Regina, 113
Rumkowski, Mordechai, 113
Russell, Diana E. H., 208–9
Russians, rape by, 14, 18, 134n26, 258, 263, 286
Ruzkensky, A. A., 116

Sadeh, Yitzhak, 201
sadistic torture in feature films, 243–44
Safszycka, Eva, 127
Saidel, Rochelle, 164
Salamandra (Ka-Tzetnik), 202
Salzberg, Jack I., 87
Scarry, Elaine, 132
Schaeffer, Susan Fromberg, 180
Schillinger, Josef, 61–67, 72
Schindler's List (Spielberg) (film), 243
Schoenfeld, Gabriel, 9n16
Schumann, Horst, 161
Schwadron, Ursula, 85
A Scrap of Time (Fink), 184–85
second generation, 223–24, 245–46, 264
secret abortions to save mothers, 159, 162–63, 167, 168, 172n29, 182–83
Seed of Sarah: Memoirs of a Survivor (Isaacson), 179
Seifert, Ruth, 117
Semel, Nava, 217–31
Serra, Edith, 143–44
Sessler, Debora, 84
sex for survival strategy: and agency, 61; brothel work as, 54; in concentration camps, 35, 187–88, 192, 283; and deals with partisans, 134n26; film depictions, 239, 245–46; gendered discourse's complications for, 69; moral judgment against, 69–72, 192–93; and national identity, 70–71; overview, 20–22; and perceived loss

of dignity, 70–72; psychological toll of, 16, 190, 265, 277–89; as resistance, 67–68, 72–73; and sex as currency, 289; and suppression of stories, 132, 282
sexism as component of persecution, 32, 139, 152, 180
sexuality as resistance, 65–66
sexual/sexualized violence: definitional issues, 29–30; dissociative defensiveness about, 277–80; documentation challenges, 1–2; as endemic to genocide, 14, 31, 78, 157; as form of warfare, 31, 200, 251n22; frequency of, 1; ideology of, 32; introduction, 1–8; locally authorized culture of, 110, 111, 112–15, 118; nature of testimony/storytelling about, 257–58; and Nazi control over motherhood, 151–52; power relations as core of, 30, 32, 200; research issues, 1–5, 15–17, 118, 139–40, 156; and resistance/agency, 61–73; UN denouncement of, 29; universality of, 30–32
sexual slavery: in concentration camps, 38; fictionalized treatments, 201–13, 218–19; film depictions, 241; and forced abortions, 38; Jewish women in, 115–17; overview, 19–20. See also brothels
shame factor: and child protection dilemmas, 284–87; distancing strategies in storytelling, 276–83; and humiliation of camp experience, 179; for Jewish men who could not protect women, 129; over death of child, 147; and postwar consequences of abuse, 130–33; and sterilization/abortion stories, 169–70; suicide response, 18; and suppression of stories, 16, 257, 275–76. See also social ostracism of survivors
shaving as humiliation, 36–37, 77, 81, 82, 83, 84, 179

Shavli ghetto, 169

"The Shawl" (Ozick), 183, 213n5

Shiver, Helene, 82

Shoah Foundation Institute for Visual History and Education, 1, 96, 115, 239

Shorer, Haim, 212–13

silence, the. See suppression of sexual violence stories

Sinti people (Gypsies), 33, 37, 38, 159, 161, 162

Sister in Sorrow (Rosen), 256

Skarżysko-Kamienna camp, 114–15

slave labor: abortion decrease to enhance survival of, 38; and brothel services to increase productivity, 45–47; children as useless for, 144–45; importance of sterilization for, 160

Slavic women, forced service in brothels, 116

social ostracism of survivors: and desire for denial, 210–12; by fellow survivors, 255; of mothers who did not sacrifice self for child, 145; as national entity protection strategy, 23–25; overview, 14–15; psychological consequences of, 32, 39, 264; research imperative, 15–17; of sex for survival strategists, 69–72; of Ukrainian rape victims, 103–4; of women who worked in brothels, 55. See also suppression of sexual violence stories

Sofsky, Wolfgang, 32

Sonderbauten. See brothels

Sontag, Susan, 207–8, 244, 247

Sophie's Choice (film), 248

Soviet Union: censoring of historiography, 95; ostracism of Jewish survivors in Ukraine, 103–4; rape by soldiers of, 14, 18, 134n26, 258, 263, 286

Spanier, Fritz, 165–66

split memory over gendered discourse about Holocaust, 156

SS. See Nazi regime

Starachowice camp, 109

Star Eternal (Ka-Tzetnik), 206

starvation and loss of feminine identity, 69, 80–81, 256

Starvation Camp near Jaslo (Szymborska), 16

sterilization: at concentration camps, 37, 160–62; as consequence of sexual violence, 117; and eugenics, 42–43n34; fears of, 181; of Jewish partner in mixed-"race" couples, 158, 165–67, 173n39; as medical experimentation, 160, 161, 181–82; and Nazi racist ideology, 37; during Netherlands occupation, 164–67; overview, 157–59; shame factor in, 169–70

Stiffel, Frank, 206

The Subtenant (Krall), 206

suffering, aesthetic vs. realistic description of, 205–6

suicide as response to shame of rape, 18

supervisory prisoners (Kapos). See Kapos (supervisory prisoners)

suppression of sexual violence stories: in film, 238–39, 242; and intergenerational narrative losses, 222–25; and isolation of hiding, 128; lack of film attention, 235; psychological costs of, 128–31; research challenges of, 15–16, 108; and sex for survival strategy, 132, 282; and shame factor, 16, 257, 275–76; and social ostracism/taboos, 32, 39, 108, 128–33; and split memory concept, 156–57; sterilization/abortion stories, 169–70

survival strategies. See hiding; sex for survival strategy

Szeintuch, Yechiel, 212

Szymborska, Wislawa, 16

talk and silence, conflict between, 222–25. See also suppression of sexual violence stories

Tec, Nechama, 108, 134n26
Telsia (Telz), Lithuania, 111
Theresienstadt concentration camp, 141, 162
This Way for the Gas, Ladies and Gentlemen (Borowski), 187–89
Thomas, D. M., 193–96
Tillion, Germaine, 164
To Outwit God (Edelman), 206
torture, rape as, 117, 132–33, 226
Transnistria, 102–3
Tschenstochau-Pelzery camp, 112
Tulchin ghetto, 102–3

Ukraine: and challenges of hiding, 130; Galicia District, 100–101, 106n12; Jewish women's fate under Nazi occupation, 94–104; Lvov ghetto, 100–102, 116
Ukrainian collaborators, sexual violence by, 17–18, 26n18, 49, 57n26, 98
United States Holocaust Memorial Museum, 1
The Unloved: From the Diary of Perla S. (Lustig), 206
Uris, Leon, 161

Valent, Paul, 226
Vanas, Aadrianus, 166
van den Berg van Cleef, Jeanne, 167
van der Hoevern, J., 166
Varon, Laura, 111
venereal diseases, 18, 24, 102, 116
verbal degradation, 35
Vilna ghetto, abortions in, 168–69
voyeurism: during camp induction process, 180; forcing Jewish men into sexual relations with women, 17; and sadism of SS, 186–87; various forms in concentration camps, 34, 35, 37. *See also* humiliations

Wagner, Rosa, 101–2
walking dead and loss of will to live, 146
Wannsee Conference (1942), 158, 170n10
war: group pride damaged by enemy rape, 23; rape of women as form of warfare, 31, 200, 251n22; ubiquity of sexual assault during, 13–14, 31, 109, 117, 236; UN denouncement of sexual violence, 29
Wardi, Dina, 147
Warsaw, Poland, 110, 125
Wasserman, Golda, 102–3
Weinstein, Paula, 21
Weitzman, Lenore, 3, 125–26, 131–32
Westerbork transit camp, 164–67
The White Hotel (Thomas), 193–96
Wiesel, Elie, 203, 205, 206–7, 212
Wijnberg, Rosalie, 166
Williams, Linda, 208
Wirths, Edward, 161
Wirtschafts- und Verwaltungshauptamt (WVHA), 45
Wiseman, Hadas, 223
Witness from Hell (Brauner) (film), 242
Włocławek, Poland, 110
A Woman in Berlin, 18
Women in the Holocaust (Ofer and Weitzman), 3–4

x-ray sterilization method, 160, 181–82

Yad Vashem, 1, 2, 115
Yakin, Boaz, 245–46
Yanov camp, Ukraine, 100–101
Ye Daying, 243
Young, James, 66
Yugoslavia, former, 78, 109–10
Yukovski, Naama, 18–19
Yuter, Alan J., 212

Zywulska, Krystyna, 48